0521 558 298

Although Weber's path-breaking work on *The Protestant Ethic and the Spirit of Capitalism* has received much attention ever since it first appeared in 1904–5, recent research has uncovered important new aspects. This volume is the result of an international, interdisciplinary effort. It throws new light on the intellectual and cultural background of Weber's work, debates recent criticism of Weber's thesis, and confronts new historical insights on the seventeenth century with Weber's interpretation. Revisiting Weber's thesis serves to deepen our understanding of Weber as much as it will stimulate further research.

PUBLICATIONS OF THE GERMAN HISTORICAL INSTITUTE
WASHINGTON, D.C.

Edited by Detlef Junker
with the assistance of Daniel S. Mattern

# *Weber's* Protestant Ethic: *Origins, Evidence, Contexts*

# THE GERMAN HISTORICAL INSTITUTE, WASHINGTON, D.C.

The German Historical Institute is a center for advanced study and research whose purpose is to provide a permanent basis for scholarly cooperation between historians from Germany and the United States. The Institute conducts, promotes, and supports research into both American and German political, social, economic, and cultural history, into transatlantic migration, especially in the nineteenth and twentieth centuries, and into the history of international relations, with special emphasis on the roles played by the United States and Germany.

*Other books in the series*

# Weber's Protestant Ethic

ORIGINS, EVIDENCE, CONTEXTS

Edited by
HARTMUT LEHMANN
and
GUENTHER ROTH

GERMAN HISTORICAL INSTITUTE
*Washington, D.C.*

CAMBRIDGE
UNIVERSITY PRESS

Published by the Press Syndicate of the University of Cambridge
The Pitt Building, Trumpington Street, Cambridge CB2 1RP
40 West 20th Street, New York, NY 10011-4211, USA
10 Stamford Road, Oakleigh, Melbourne 3166, Australia

First published 1987
First paperback edition 1995

Printed in the United States of America

Library of Congress Cataloging-in-Publication Data is available.

A catalogue record for this book is available from the British Library.

ISBN 0-521-44062-9 hardback
ISBN 0-521-55829-8 paperback

# Contents

v

## PART II
## RECEPTION AND RESPONSE

# *Preface*

Both in German and in American historiography and intellectual life, in the humanities as well as in the social sciences, certain scholarly works have had – and in some cases still have – a particular impact that deserves the attention of those who are interested in the transfer of ideas from the Old World to the New and from the New World to the Old. Jakob Burckhardt's *The Culture of the Renaissance in Italy* is such a work of transatlantic significance; others are Erwin Panofsky's *Studies in Iconology* and *Early Netherlandish Paintings,* Ernst Kantorowicz's *Laudes Regiae* and *The King's Two Bodies,* and Erik H. Erikson's *Young Man Luther.* There is no work, however, that has been and is still the subject of such lively discussion on both sides of the Atlantic, and that has attracted and continues to attract the attention of so many scholars from so many different disciplines, as Max Weber's famous essay *The Protestant Ethic and the Spirit of Capitalism,* first published in 1904–1905.

In the past decades, research on this work has developed in three distinct directions. Historians of seventeenth-century history, and especially those involved in the history of countries in which Calvinism had taken root, used Weber's thesis in order to clarify whether, and if so how, ascetic Protestantism had indeed initiated and advanced the growth of capitalism. Although some of them found proof that supported Weber's thesis, others claimed that they could refute it. At the same time, Weber's essay, published in 1920 in expanded form, was taken as a milestone in Weber's intellectual development that seemed to reveal how he had gained a new level of scholarly competence while recovering from the illness that had forced him to give up lecturing at the University of Heidelberg before the turn of the century. Moreover, for biographers of Weber, his essay served to exemplify his theoretical remarks on the use of ideal

vii

types in writing history. Sociologists of religion, finally, used Weber's thesis on the relationship of ascetic Protestantism and the spirit of capitalism in order to gain arguments for constructing universally applicable laws of development that, in turn, could be used to strengthen the work ethic, and thus capitalism, in developing countries.

Although the members of these three groups used the same text as a point of departure, in the past decades the way they interpreted the text, and some of their conclusions, drifted further and further apart. Moreover, for American scholars compared to European students of Weber, as a result of the different history of Weber scholarship since 1920, his essay played a different role when they discussed its meaning and importance. Considering this, it seemed appropriate to assemble those Weber scholars who had occupied themselves particularly with the *Protestant Ethic* in recent years in order to confront conflicting interpretations and probe the possibility of gaining common ground. With Guenther Roth (from Columbia University) and myself acting as conveners, a group of historians, sociologists, and historians of religion assembled in the German Historical Institute in Washington, D.C., from May 3 to 5, 1990, for an exchange of ideas that was very lively, very intense and instructive, and sometimes controversial. The authors have attempted to incorporate whatever they had learned from the discussions into their papers, which are presented here in a revised form with the necessary notes.

Of the various results of our scholarly enterprise, several deserve to be noted. Most speakers agreed that Weber's insights and his conceptualization of the historical meaning of the influence of the *Protestant Ethic,* as well as his terminology, were very much determined by the level of scholarship of his own time. In this sense, Weber's thesis is clearly dated, and two generations after his death is only of relative importance. At the same time, many participants of the conference pointed out that Weber had articulated his thesis in a way that had stimulated research on the rise of capitalism in a most remarkable way and continued to do so, and that no one since him has had an influence on research that equaled his. Although the conclusions drawn by historians and sociologists from reading this text of Weber may be different, the conference served to underline the lasting importance of his work.

It is a most pleasant duty to thank all those who have supported this venture through the various stages of development. Without the help of Guenther Roth, without his expertise and guidance, we would not have succeeded. The Fritz Thyssen Foundation did not hesitate to give us generous financial assistance. Although the Institute had moved into new premises shortly before the conference, its staff labored hard to help provide a setting equally suited to doing hard work and getting some relaxation. Those who had contributed to the conference were quick and thorough in preparing their papers for publication. Dr. Kenneth Ledford helped us with much diligence in editing the volume. Guenther Roth and I trust that this volume is an expression of the commitment of all those who have supported us and to whom we are deeply indebted, and a fitting sign of gratitude to them.

April 1991
Washington, D.C.                                         Hartmut Lehmann

# Contributors

PHILIP BENEDICT is Professor of History at Brown University.

HARVEY S. GOLDMAN is Associate Professor of Sociology at the University of California, San Diego.

FRIEDRICH WILHELM GRAF is Professor at the Institute for Evangelical Theology at the University of Augsburg.

KASPAR VON GREYERZ teaches history at the University of Kiel.

JAMES A. HENRETTA is Professor of History at the University of Maryland, College Park.

HARTMUT LEHMANN is the Director of the German Historical Institute, Washington, D.C.

KLAUS LICHTBLAU teaches social sciences at the University of Kassel.

HARRY LIEBERSOHN is Associate Professor of History at the University of Illinois.

MALCOLM H. MACKINNON is Professor of Sociology at the Erindale Campus of the University of Toronto.

PAUL MÜNCH is University Professor of History at the University of Essen.

The late THOMAS NIPPERDEY was Professor of Modern History at the University of Munich.

GUY OAKES is Kvernland Professor in the School of Business at Monmouth College, New Jersey.

GIANFRANCO POGGI is Professor of Sociology at the University of Virginia.

HANS ROLLMANN is Associate Professor of Religious Studies at the Memorial University of Newfoundland.

GUENTHER ROTH is Professor of Sociology at Columbia University.

HELWIG SCHMIDT-GLINTZER is Professor at the Institute for East Asian Studies, Sinology, of the University of Munich.

HUBERT TREIBER is Professor of Administrative Science in the Faculty of Law of the Technical University of Hannover.

DAVID ZARET is Professor of Sociology at Indiana University.

# Introduction

GUENTHER ROTH

## I

When Bismarck created Imperial Germany in 1871, the United States was not yet a world power, but the two states were rising Protestant empires with rapidly growing, religiously heterogeneous populations. In the age of imperialism the three Protestant empires, the third being Great Britain, were bound to compete with one another, France, and Russia, yet the form of the conflict, peaceful or military, and the kind of coalition were historically open. After the Spanish-American War of 1898 – an ascending Protestant power defeating a moribund Catholic power – Imperial Germany launched not only a naval armament program against Great Britain, but also a cultural offensive toward the United States aimed at containing the dominant Anglo-Saxon influence. At a time when German emigration had tapered off, academic travel to America became fashionable for German professors, exchange professorships were established – and many illusions were nourished. The St. Louis World Congress of 1904, attended by Max and Marianne Weber, Ernst Troeltsch, and many other German academics, was a high point in this cultural endeavor. Part of this story is told by Hans Rollmann in this volume.[1] Few contemporaries would have believed that it would take

---

[1] See also my chapter, "Deutsche Ambivalenzen gegenüber den Vereinigten Staaten," ch. 6 of *Politische Herrschaft und persönliche Freiheit* (Frankfurt: Suhrkamp, 1987), esp. 175–200. It is indicative of Max Weber's strong interest in the United States that he planned to attend the 1893 Chicago World's Fair with his friend Paul Göhre. See the letters of Nov. 26, 1892, and Jan 7, 1893, to his sister Clara in *Jugendbriefe* (Tübingen: Mohr, 1936), 353 and 357. Weber's quick engagement to Marianne Schnitger in March 1893 prevented the plan. A catalyst of his youthful interest seems to have been the liberal Reichstag deputy Friedrich Kapp (1824–1884), a close family friend, who had lived in the United States from 1849 to 1870 and had been a major figure in New York Republican politics. See the, for Weber, extraordinarily warm appreciation at Kapp's death (letter to Hermann Baumgarten, Nov. 8, 1884, *Jugendbriefe*, 139ff.).

1

until 1987 before an institution like the German Historical Institute in Washington, D.C., would be established. Unavoidably, the intellectual transactions became entangled with the political ups and downs in the relations between the two countries that confronted one another in two world wars. The first war, fought by most German academics under the banner of *Kultur contra Zivilisation,* damaged the international prestige of German culture significantly. The second completely destroyed the claims once advanced by Max Weber's generation on behalf of Germany's global *Kulturmission.*

Paradoxically, the very fact that Nazism drove so many scholars, scientists, and writers into exile in the United States in the 1930s and 1940s helped preserve a modicum of German influence. Weber's reception in the United States, and to a lesser extent in England, is testimony to this paradox. Many different interests and motives had to intersect, however, in Weber's mind and among generations of readers to make the oeuvre internationally significant. Ironies abound. How could the writings of a committed German nationalist who cared passionately about his country's standing as a world power become, long after his death, so successful in the Anglo-Saxon world? On the most general level, of course, the answers involve the international entanglements of the United States after World War II and the parallel turn of American social science to one or another form of modernization theory. But why is *The Protestant Ethic and the Spirit of Capitalism,* first published in 1904–1905, its thesis reaffirmed in 1920, the only German historical study from the years before World War I that is still alive and controversial in the English-speaking world? (Only a tiny number of American specialists now read German historians from that period.) Clearly, Weber's general standing in twentieth-century social science has helped keep the thesis alive. Moreover, from the very beginning, the study has been understood as an effective argument against historical materialism and for the importance, if not autonomy, of ideal as against material factors. It certainly served this purpose in the United States during the decades of the Cold War. But there are other reasons for the essay's long-range success in America.

One important ideological reason has to do with Weber's attitudes toward England and America. In the superheated nationalist atmosphere of his time, Weber proved to be one of the last liberal Anglophiles. He admired the Puritan and sectarian legacy, the democratic institutions, and the English and American roles in world politics. On this score he found ready resonance among an Anglo-American public that took the linkage of Protestantism, political liberty, and world power for granted. Weber embraced the exalted self-image English Whig historians had fashioned about the "Puritan Revolution" and its liberal consequences. He exaggerated the world-historical role of Calvinism and Puritanism to dramatize his cultural and political critique of Imperial Germany. In the 1920s a young American congregationalist and exchange student, Talcott Parsons, accidentally encountered *The Protestant Ethic* in Heidelberg. Its linking of Puritanism and capitalism fascinated him so much that he translated the work.[2] In due course Parsons made his Weber reading part and parcel of his structural-functionalist theory of normative system integration. Since he came to view the professions as crucial to the functioning of bureaucratic capitalism, Weber's stated aim – to analyze "Protestant asceticism as the foundation of modern vocational civilization (*Berufskultur*) – a sort of 'spiritualist' construction of the modern economy" – fitted his mature paradigm very well. If Weber had not written *The Protestant Ethic,* the young Parsons might not have absorbed his later writings so eagerly, just as, without the prestige of American sociology, especially Parsonianism, Weber might not have been revived so successfully in Germany. (The young Wolfgang J. Mommsen's famous 1959 dissertation on *Max Weber and German Politics. 1890–1920* could have contributed to burying Weber rather than being part of the resurrection.) As it was, the original Whig interpretation, adapted by Weber for polemical reasons, was reimported by Parsons and others into the Anglo-American realm and helped reinforce the American orthodox understanding of an inherent connection between Protestantism and liberal democracy.[3] The exportation and reimportation of Protestant self-interpretation, if not self-congratulation, appears to me an important element in accounting for the American receptivity to the Weber thesis. If the thesis was, for the German side, a kind of negative foundation myth – the "birth defects" of Imperial Germany – it embellished the myth of America. In William McNeill's term, it was a powerful instance of "mythistory."[4] Thus, Weber's theory joined two other great myths of his generation: Frederick Jackson Turner's 1893 frontier thesis and

---

2 See Talcott Parsons, "The Circumstances of My Encounter with Max Weber," in Robert Merton and M. W. Riley, eds., *Sociological Traditions from Generation to Generation* (Norwood, N.J.: Ablex, 1980), 39. Citations to *The Protestant Ethic* (hereafter abbreviated "PE") are to Talcott Parson's translation (New York: Charles Scribner's Sons, 1958).
3 Only recently has this orthodox understanding been subjected to critical scrutiny within American sociology. See David Zaret, "Religion and the Rise of Liberal-Democratic Ideology in Seventeenth-Century England," *American Sociological Review,* 54 (1989): 163–179.
4 See William H. McNeill, *Mythistory and Other Essays* (Chicago: University of Chicago Press, 1986).

Charles Beard's 1913 economic interpretation of the Constitution. By definition, mythistory is controversial, producing plenty of ideological heat and political hostility. There is always more involved than just a challenging historical proposition that stimulates further inquiry by adherents and critics.

It is customary to revisit major scholars and works in order to take stock of our knowledge and to search for novel insight. Sometimes a half-forgotten work continues to slide into oblivion in spite of much effort – through complete or critical editions, for instance; sometimes it is successfully revived for the benefit of another generation. In either case, "revisited" indicates some distance in time and perspective. In a sense, the Weber thesis needs no revisiting because it has refused to die in spite of many often exasperated efforts to be done with it once and for all. In the eyes of quite a few scholars it has become counterproductive; its very longevity appears a nuisance. It is true that for a specific historical thesis rather than a broad sociological theory it is by now rather old, having survived the half century Weber envisaged as a maximum for the life of a scholarly work. Inevitably, however, the passage of time removes the work more and more from our immediate grasp. Our very interest in the political, social, and cultural issues out of which Weber's preoccupations emerged demonstrates a shift to a larger context. The same is true for issues of reception in relation to recent interpretations of the seventeenth century.

Over the last decade there has been increasing interest in the background and origins of Weber's thought. In Germany this trend has been connected with a political need to reconsider the German past, especially the role of the bourgeoisie (*Bürgertum*) and of liberalism, although the debates on the German *Sonderweg* and the *Historikerstreit* have been overshadowed by the sheer fact of German unification, which is bound to change the parameters of historical discourse. In the United States and England, "ideas in context" (witness the Cambridge University Press series of that title) have found renewed interest. In social theory, in particular, there has been a spirited debate on the relative virtues of historicist readings as against presentist exploitations of classical authors.

For several years, then, some German writers have probed the philosophical antecedents and sources of Weber's work. In part this has to do with the decline of German social science and its presentist and activist concerns since the 1970s and the recovery of history, in a conservative period, both as subject matter and as a discipline. Moreover, some German political theorists and literary scholars have been busy bringing Weber home from America, in particular, wresting him away from American social science and its Americanized German counterpart. Mainly in France and the United States, poststructuralist and deconstructionist forces have attacked the "metanarratives" of the West, of which Weber's theory of rationalization and especially of Protestant inner-worldly asceticism is an important part. As an editorial enterprise, our volume does not follow either tendency – neither the "repossession" nor the "postmodernization" of Weber – although individual contributors may see themselves closer to one or the other. The volume remains in the orbit of intellectual and cultural history. All authors stay within that broad realm, despite the appearance, in formal affiliation, of an even division between historians and sociologists. The contributors are evenly divided between Americans and Europeans, with some transplanted scholars standing in between. The Germans were selected more for the first purpose of the volume – origins and setting – the Americans more for the second – the viability and longevity of the Weber thesis in some areas, but also its ineffectiveness in others.

## II

There are three biographical aspects to *The Protestant Ethic and the Spirit of Capitalism*. First, Weber reached maturity at the end of decades of bitter conflict between Catholicism and Protestantism, at a time when there still were some unhappy memories of the enforced union of Lutheranism and Reformism (Calvinism). Second, in his formative years Weber witnessed close up the defeat of political and economic liberalism and the triumph of authoritarianism in state and industry. Third, he grew up with and eventually involved himself in the *Methodenstreit,* the protracted struggle between natural and cultural science, positivism and hermeneutics, theory and history, a struggle complicated by crisscrossing lines of contestation.

The essays devoted to Weber's origins and context explore these three aspects in varying combinations. The first four contributions share as an underlying theme the importance of religious conflict, not only for Weber but for historiography and social science in general. Besides being a conflict among Catholic church, Protestant monarchy, and liberal bourgeoisie, the *Kulturkampf* involved the whole

meaning of modern society and modern scholarship. Graf shows that
Weber was the German economic historian most deeply steeped in
theological discourse. He demonstrates the significance of Weber's
main theological source, Matthias Schneckenburger, for the stark
juxtaposition of Lutheranism and Calvinism, and examines the political context of the theological debates before and after the unification
of the Protestant churches and of the nation. Influenced by Ernst
Troeltsch – an influence Graf judges to have been much greater than
was acknowledged by Weber himself and many others – Weber opposed Albrecht Ritschl, the leading Lutheran theologian of the time.
Both Ritschl and Weber fought the orthodox and conservative establishment in the state church, but the former saw a historical continuity between outmoded Catholicism and the varieties of ascetic
Protestantism, whereas to the latter, Lutheranism was closer to Catholicism. For Ritschl a National-Liberal *Kulturprotestantismus* was the
Empire's proper ideological buttress; for Weber the absence of an
ascetic tradition was a heavy political liability because Lutheranism
had produced a mentality of authoritarian subordination. By taking
the theological context of the time as his major point of reference,
Graf can conclude that the question of the historical adequacy of
Weber's analysis becomes relatively secondary.

Behind Weber's study lies, however, not only a debate within Protestantism but also a long history of mutual stereotyping and prejudice on the part of both Catholics and Protestants. Using popular
literature, from religious tracts to travelogues, Münch presents an
archaeology of the Weber thesis. He agrees with Graf that for a long
time the denominations did not differ greatly in their traditionalist
understanding of economic ethics – a point insufficiently recognized
by Weber. Of course, the secularization of church lands and the
closing of monasteries had a great impact, and to contemporaries the
abolition of saint worship and saints' days made Protestantism appear
a cheaper religion and Catholics less productive. Whereas the early
modern state had a mercantilist interest in tolerating religious minorities, including Catholic ones, the Enlightenment diminished in both
Catholic and Protestant eyes the perceived cultural importance of
religious differences. The first third of the nineteenth century can
even be seen as a period of relative religious accommodation, when
Catholic and Jewish dignitaries sometimes participated in Reformation feasts. These were the decades when the dissolution of the ecclesiastic territories in the Napoleonic period turned out to have greatly

weakened the institutional supports of German Catholic culture. From the 1830s on, a new era of conflict began and revived the militant rhetoric of bygone days. In a Germany dominated by triumphalist Protestant nationalism, Catholics were increasingly marginalized and denigrated as an alien element, until the anti-Catholic propaganda reached its high point a decade before Weber wrote his study. Thus, to Münch, Weber appears at best as a giant standing on the shoulders of dwarfs – the manufacturers of anti-Catholic stereotypes and prejudices.

In the wake of the *Kulturkampf,* which was formally settled in the 1880s, Catholics vigorously pressed for equal treatment, especially in the civil service, but to liberals and Jews their demands appeared often enough not as universalist, but as a particularist interest in patronage. As Nipperdey shows, it is here that "moral statistics" achieved importance, not only as a new means of research but also of political discourse. Since it turned out that Catholics were also underrepresented in the free professions and the universities, even Catholic spokesmen such as Georg von Hertling, who became Chancellor in 1917, helped popularize the notion of a Catholic educational deficit. In general, however, statistical researchers paid little attention to religion as a factor in accounting for confessional differences. For that matter, the rise of nationalism changed the terms of the older debates and made French historians, for example, downplay the role of the Reformation in creating the modern world. In a secular climate that looked at religion increasingly as an irrational phenomenon, Weber insisted, however, on its causal importance. Nipperdey concludes that Weber's study should be seen both as a contribution to German economic and social history and as part of the general debate on the nature of modernity.

Weber's essay moves indeed from the social differences between German Catholics and Protestants to the fate of modern vocational culture, but his political and cultural critique holds up an Anglo-Saxon past as a mirror to the German present. Throughout much of the nineteenth century, many German liberals looked at England as a constitutional model. My own contribution tries to show that Weber stands at the very end of this tradition, to which he was linked through family ties. But since Imperial Germany had become a great power militarily and industrially, Great Britain appeared in Weber's program of *Weltpolitik* not only as a constitutional and imperial model, but also as the main competitor. In his study Weber drew on his Westphalian family history to illustrate the spirit of capitalism, but curiously, he omitted any reference to his extensive English family connections. On his maternal side he was descended from a wealthy Huguenot family clan that was as much at home in Manchester and London as in Frankfurt and Milan, and that embodied economic adventurism much more than his spirit of capitalism, not to mention any Protestant ethic. Weber's relatives were cosmopolitan Europeans and were not yet affected by the intense nationalism of his own lifetime. Some of his own political ambivalence may be traced to his ambiguous combination of Anglophilia and German nationalism.

Significantly, Weber's concept of national identity – Liebersohn's topic – contrasts strongly with the linguistic, ethnic, and racial theories so popular at the time. *The Protestant Ethic* discounts national character as an explanatory factor and insists on the autonomy of religious beliefs and on the believer's ability to make linguistic innovations. In other contexts, Weber emphasized the role of a shared political fate in forming a sense of nationhood. Thus, he did not anchor his notion of national identity ontologically but purely historically. For this reason, he also found descriptive ethnography useful while remaining highly skeptical of racial theories. It is true that he employed the Social Darwinist rhetoric of his time, but his preoccupation with the ethically integrated personality in all spheres of life made him hostile to scientific monism, of which eugenics was a part. It is here that Weber's relation to Nietzsche warrants clarification.

Treiber approaches the relationship between Nietzsche and Weber in terms of elective affinity rather than any causal connection, between the former's idea of a "monastery for freer spirits" and the latter's ideal type of the Puritan sect. Treiber demonstrates how the two men shared an intense interest in ascetic personality formation but differed radically in their understanding of science and politics. Nietzsche encountered the educational uses of asceticism in the famous Protestant boarding school of Schulpforta, which continued some of the traditions of its Cistercian past, and he also harked back to the friendship cult of the Romantic era. Given the crisis of Christianity, the goal of ascetic self-education among friends aimed at total intellectual liberation from the idols of the time and at the creation of a strictly empirical moral science, which was patterned after the most advanced notions of natural science. Treiber recounts the project of a monastery for freer spirits, which was tried out in Basel in the early 1870s but mostly dreamed about and idealized in later years, and the role of the men and one woman – Louise von Salomé – whose names are still somewhat famous. Moreover, he recalls the mostly forgotten contributions of the preceding generation of scholars and scientists that attracted Nietzsche and his friends. This amounts to drawing up the "intellectual inventory" of the age by reconstructing the friends' "monastic library" (including the books borrowed from the University of Basel). The comparative study of language, they believed, had become a strict science that could help create the "ethics of the future." Weber, however, broke radically with a notion of monistic science that made the logic of geology or chemistry relevant for ethical reconstruction. Instead, he replaced laws with ideal types and turned to historical causality, the genesis of the Protestant ethic. Although Weber's ideal type of the ascetic personality retained an elective affinity with Nietzsche's ethical ideal, he sought the practical solution not among a circle of friends or in a new monastic or sectarian experiment, but on the level of the national community. In that regard, he remained closer to Treitschke's patriotic state religion.

Drawing on Foucault's "practices" of the self, Goldman analyzes the relation between Weber's notions of self-mastery and world mastery in the face of rationalization and bureaucratization. The older bourgeois ideal of *Bildung* appeared no longer viable to Weber. Only ascetic specialization could save the individual's autonomy and ability to cope creatively with the dangers of institutional ossification. Goldman recognizes a misunderstanding by Foucault: Weber was concerned not with the ascetic price of reason, but with the ways in which the "empowered self" can master rationalization itself. Just as the Puritan self had destroyed the fetters of tradition, so the modern secular self should control and guide rationalization. But in Imperial Germany the possibilities for an ascetic socialization of the self were undermined by the whole weight of economic, cultural, and social development that favored the dominance of a bureaucratic mentality. However, Weber's political reform program, Goldman concludes, was marred by his very inability to conceive of an autonomous self that was not structurally identical to the Puritan's self and to reconcile his ascetic ideal with the realities of modern mass democracy.

Given his powerful attraction to inner-worldly asceticism, it was inevitable that Weber would not only fight the conformist "law and order" types (*Ordnungsmenschen*) but react even more viscerally against the "new ethic" of sexual liberation, with its amalgam of neo-Romantic, anarchist, eugenic, and hedonist elements. Each component was unacceptable in itself; the combination was anathema to him. The men and women who embraced "disorder" in their radical critique of the family, bourgeois society, and authoritarian state appeared to him as incapable as the "men of order" of coping with the motivational and institutional imperatives of modernity. Lichtblau shows that Weber's concern with asceticism was closely related to the interest of men like Simmel and Freud in repression and instinctual sacrifice as conditions of cultural achievement and economic exchange. But ultimately Weber did not remain consistent, and his own inner conflicts came to reflect some of the general tensions brought about by the new currents. Moreover, his own illness can be explained in terms of such prominent diseases of the age as hysteria and neurasthenia. Fears of personal and collective decadence became mixed up with one another. Max and Marianne Weber had to face the new eroticism and the demand for free love in their immediate circle at a time when they actively defended an ascetic ideal of ethically buttressed monogamy. In depicting the rejection of sensual culture and the elevation of positive science by the Puritans, Weber's study portrayed his personal ethos, but in the following years his evolving theory of separate and conflicting value spheres explicitly recognized the autonomy (*Eigenwert*) of erotic and aesthetic values. This made Weber aware of the great break between the aesthetic and hedonistic rationales of modernism and the continued ascetic requirements of institutional modernity. Thus, Lichtblau can rank Weber paradoxically among the "antimodernist modernists" of his time.

Next to the concept of autonomy (*Eigengesetzlichkeit*) of value and institutional spheres, Weber employed the notion of elective affinity in order to relate heterogeneous phenomena such as the Protestant ethic and the spirit of capitalism. In contrast to his many careful definitions, however, he never defined elective affinity and thus allowed it to retain the connotations it acquired in Goethe's novel. The term stems from alchemy and "the science of divorce" (*Scheidekunst,* an old name for chemistry) and denotes the "magical" dissolution and recombination of elements in terms of their "attractiveness." Lichtblau reminds us that Weber harked back to the terminology of a way of thinking that Werner Sombart had set aside in his explanation of the awakening of the spirit of capitalism. After a period of intensified gold digging, treasure hunting, and alchemistic experiments, some people finally discovered that wealth could be accumulated through normal economic activities.

Lehmann treats the ambivalent relationship of Sombart and Weber. As self-conscious outsiders they were comrades in arms, fellow editors of the *Archiv für Sozialwissenschaft;* they were also eager rivals in their ultimately successful effort to shape the academic agenda. There is no doubt that Sombart's big study, *Modern Capitalism* (1902), stimulated and challenged Weber. Sombart considered the economic impact of Protestant groups such as Calvinists and Quakers too well known to require concrete historical demonstration. Yet, impressed by Jellinek's study of the religious origins of the enacted rights of man, Weber decided to look closely at the unintended economic effects of certain religious beliefs and anxieties.

The essays concerned with the viability and impact of Weber's thesis respond in part to a 1988 critique by MacKinnon, who here restates this argument but also blames three generations of critics for the longevity of Weber's thesis. The critics, according to MacKinnon, did not recognize Weber's theological misreading, especially his mistaken perception of a crisis of proof with its unintended consequences for worldly action, or they charged Weber with monism or idealism, when it was easy for him to demonstrate his causal pluralism. By and large, the critics merely repeated their mistakes from Rachfahl's early critique through Sombart and Brentano to Robertson, Tawney, Trevor-Roper, and more recent writers. MacKinnon's basic argument is that Calvinism did not give religious legitimation to secular callings because the covenant theology underlying the Westminster Confession of Faith obliterated Calvin's predestinarianism and works remained in effect spiritual. If there was no dogmatic crisis of proof, Weber's theory of salvation anxiety and of psychological premiums collapses. As it was, Weber succeeded in keeping his critics at bay insofar as they did not engage his theological premises.

It is true that Weber tended to turn his fellow economists and historians into dilettantes by declaring the theological experts (*Fachleute*) his primary reference group. In his anticritique he expressed great satisfaction that some theologians had shown interest in his problem: "That was my hope, and I now await fruitful and informative criticism from the theological side, but not from dilettantish, bungling polemicists such as Rachfahl."[5] An effective critique of Weber's thesis indeed requires close study of the seventeenth-century

---

5 Weber, "Anticritical Last Word on the Spirit of Capitalism," *American Journal of Sociology,* 83 (1978): 1127; see also Weber's first footnote in the 1920 revision, PE 187.

sources, and this is undertaken by Zaret and von Greyerz. Zaret also pays particular attention to methodological issues. In the face of MacKinnon's insistence on the theological consistency of Calvin and the Puritans, he proceeds from the general proposition that ideological virtuosi use the ultimately irreconcilable mixture of deterministic and voluntaristic elements in their doctrines to respond selectively to challenges from various sides – the issue of contextual selectivity. This strategy increases the danger of exegetical selectivity on the part of the historian or sociologist. Thus, it makes a difference whether Calvin responded to Pelagian or Antinomian views. Similarly, covenant theologians emphasized voluntarism in some respects but stressed determination by grace in opposing, for instance, radical lay initiatives. Zaret restores to Calvin's doctrine a modest degree of voluntarism and to Puritan covenant theology a large dose of determinism, in fact making it often more Calvinist than Calvin himself. By drawing on additional primary evidence and more broadly on secondary accounts, Zaret can conclude that Puritanism was indeed an anxiety-inducing creed and can uphold key points of Weber's thesis, including the lifelong search for evidence of grace and the spiritualization of secular vocation.

Greyerz joins Zaret's argument that study of the theological texts must be supplemented by biographies, diaries, letters, and similar documents. Weber and Troeltsch tended to rely largely on the pastoral literature for their inferences about the laity. In line with more recent interests in social history, Greyerz advocates looking from the grass roots up, not just from the top down. A reading of a large number of the extant autobiographies and diaries reveals to him that the great majority of the religiously inspired writers were concerned not primarily with predestination or covenant but with the special providence of a close, personal God who promised the universality of grace. Given the high mortality rate of the age, awareness of the precariousness of life was shared by Puritans and non-Puritans alike. The resulting encouragement of inner-worldly asceticism was not necessarily connected with the doctrine of predestination. In the second half of the seventeenth century this doctrine declined at the same time that the spiritual elite increased, if anything, the systematic character of its self-observation. Spiritual bookkeeping was a widely deployed means for pursuing a methodical way of life and using time systematically. The personal sources also demonstrate that providentialism encompassed not only individual fate but also collective and natural events from wars to earthquakes. Contrary to Weber's view of the consequences of disenchantment, providentialism made God more accessible, if not calculable, yet this did not mitigate asceticism. In fact, it appears that personal and collective sanctification as continuous conduct became more important than a preoccupation with the event and timing of (one's own) conversion. Thus, providentialism seems to have been able to counteract for some time the mechanistic world view that loomed larger and larger over the believer's horizon.

In contrast to Zaret and Greyerz, who address the adequacy of Weber's thesis on the basis of a larger range of sources than Weber employed, Oakes raises the possibility of a methodological paradox. He calls attention to the fact that in *The Protestant Sects and the Spirit of Capitalism,* which Weber wrote immediately after *The Protestant Ethic,* predestination is replaced as an explanatory premise by sect organization and discipline. The viability of Weber's arguments, Oakes suggests, may rest not necessarily on a correct reading of theological sources – the level of MacKinnon's critique – but on identifying the ethos of the "consumers" of religious ideas. Paradoxically, Weber may be right about a connection between the Protestant ethic and the spirit of capitalism in spite of or even because of his possible misreading of theological doctrines. Applying Weber's own view of the paradoxical relationship between intention and consequence, Oakes concludes that *The Protestant Ethic* may "qualify as an instance of the type of phenomenon it analyzes." Ironically, how an author understands the premises of his explanation may differ from the conditions on which its validity rests.

For sociologists, moreover, the question of whether the Weber thesis is historically tenable is secondary to its generalizable significance. Poggi takes off from a observation by Barrington Moore that it remains unsettled whether *The Protestant Ethic* was an important breakthrough or a blind alley. He considers this alternative too radical in view of the internal and external reasons that make a resolution so difficult. On internal grounds, what appears to be a straightforward thesis proves hard to verify because of the heterogeneity of the elements connected by it. On external grounds, it has turned out to be a daunting enterprise to relate causally facts of economic history to the religious structure of meaning – a relationship presupposed by Weber and his contemporaries. Social theorists can afford to keep their distance from these complexities as long as *The Protestant Ethic* seems to illustrate, in an exemplary manner, generic insights about the interdependence of action and structure.

Poggi is not content, however, to move from the level of historical specificity to the higher reaches of sociological theorizing about modernity. Since *The Protestant Ethic* has recently been linked to Weber's general agenda of moral education, Poggi expresses his personal objections to the Weberian moral aristocracy as it appears in Goldman's presentation. But where Goldman is critical from the viewpoint of American democratic theory, Poggi, akin to Münch, pits his own brand of humane, secular *Kulturkatholizismus* against Weber's Protestant moralism and heroism.

When Weber appealed to theological expertise as the proper ground for critique, he was aware, of course, that most theologians would not be interested in his tangential economic problem. Indeed, as Benedict shows, historians of Continental Calvinism have largely rejected the Weber thesis, in good measure because of their own theological concerns. It is true that confessional rivalries gradually declined, but this did not change the relative indifference or hostility to what was believed to be, often quite inaccurately, Weber's theory. Examining general histories of Calvinism, Benedict finds that Weber's study exercised remarkably little influence on research. The reasons lay not only in theological preoccupations but in national, if not nationalist, articulations of research agendas. Moreover, substantive advances in our knowledge about inner-worldly asceticism weakened the relevance of Weber's theory when it turned out that there were greater behavioral similarities between Protestantism and post-Tridentine Catholicism than Weber realized. For that matter, the old arguments, dismissed by Weber, about the importance of religious minority status and of diaspora networks look stronger today. Finally, Benedict shows how Weber fared much better in England and the United States, given the trends in English social history and the American fascination with the legacies of Puritanism on both sides of the Atlantic.

It is easy to demonstrate that there was a broad connection between the Protestant ethic and diligence in one's calling among Puritan and Quaker virtuosi in mid-seventeenth-century New England. Yet there was, Henretta explains, a tension between religious individualism and collectivism and a social and economic split between the interests of merchants and investors as against those of farmers and artisans. When John Winthrop's communitarian ethic prevailed over Anne Hutchinson's mystical ethic, authoritarian Calvinism and (free grace) sectarianism parted ways. The communitarian ethic defended debtors against creditors and enforced the "just price," but within a social hierarchy that privileged the "visible saints" economically. In this situation, enterprising merchants faced severe handicaps until, in the second and third generations, internal and external factors combined to relax religious and social control in the commercial towns. The countryside, however, remained backward and communitarian until the revolutionary period. Its Puritan and sectarian religiosity promoted a traditionalist way of life (in Weber's sense) much more than modernization through a capitalist spirit. As the merchants became more Arminian and Latitudinarian, the countryside turned out to be more receptive to the great revivals. This dissolved the affinities postulated by the Weber thesis. Instead, by the first half of the eighteenth century, population pressures required more intensive and systematic labor, and capitalist development was further promoted by the expansion of a rational legal system that replaced juries using communitarian standards with judges ruling on written debt instruments. The vaunted American system of "a government of laws and not of men" ushered in the capitalist age with a vengeance.

Although Weber defended his thesis intransigently, he did not continue his studies either by looking more probingly into English Protestant casuistry or by comparing the impact of Protestantism in other European countries. Schmidt-Glintzer wants to qualify both Wilhelm Hennis's view that Weber did not change his basic position in later years and Benjamin Nelson's that *The Protestant Ethic* was only a tentative first step in the direction of the great comparative sociology. Schmidt-Glintzer points to Weber's closeness to the *religionsgeschichtliche Schule,* with its comparative emphasis, and to his increasing interest in a historical sociology of rationalism. By studying comparatively the relations between world views and social structures on a world-historical scale, Weber could concretely continue his critique of laws of historical development, whether unilinear or cyclical, as well as of reductionist explanations in terms of national character or race. Schmidt-Glintzer concludes that the systematic requirements of *Economy and Society* also structured the parallel studies on *The Economic Ethics of the World Religions.* Both works provided a universal (*universalgeschichtliche*) context for *The Protestant Ethic*, which changed not the content but the larger significance of the thesis.[6]

## III

This volume omits two important topics that it would have been desirable to treat: Weber's reading of Benjamin Franklin as representing the spirit of capitalism and the relation of *The Protestant Ethic* to Georg Jellinek's *The Declaration of the Rights of Man and of Citizens* (1895). In lieu of an independent treatment of Franklin, it may be useful for the reader to recall Lujo Brentano's 1916 critique and that of Weber's nephew, Eduard Baumgarten (1898–1982), who in 1936 published in German *Benjamin Franklin. The Teacher of the American Revolution*.[7]

In a famous passage Weber illustrated his spirit of capitalism, if only "provisionally" (PE 48), with some quotations from Benjamin Franklin's "Advice to a Young Tradesman" (1748) and "Necessary Hints to Those That Would Be Rich" (1736) in order to provide an example of "classic purity." In a 1920 addition he underlined that Franklin's formulations indicated not "mere business astuteness" but

6 The strengths and weaknesses of "The Economic Ethics of the World Religions" in the light of present-day knowledge are treated in the six volumes edited by Wolfgang Schluchter, *Max Webers Studie über das antike Judentum* (1981), *Max Webers Studie über Konfuzianismus und Taoismus* (1983), *Max Webers Studie über Hinduismus und Buddhismus* (1984), *Max Webers Sicht des antiken Christentums* (1985), *Max Webers Sicht des Islams* (1987), and *Max Webers Sicht des okzidentalen Christentums* (1988) (Frankfurt: Suhrkamp). Schluchter's introductions have been reprinted in Vol. 2 of his *Religion und Lebensführung* (Frankfurt: Suhrkamp, 1988). An English version of the introductions to the first four volumes is found in Schluchter, *Rationalism, Religion, and Domination. A Weberian Perspective*, Neil Solomon, trans. (Berkeley: University of California Press, 1989), 85–248.

7 See Georg Jellinek, *Die Erklärung der Menschen- und Bürgerrechte* (Leipzig: Duncker & Humblot, 1895); second enlarged ed., 1904. The authorized English translation by Max Farrand appeared as *The Declaration of the Rights of Man and of Citizens* (New York: Holt, 1901). Lujo Brentano, *Die Anfänge des modernen Kapitalismus* (Munich: Akademie der Wissenschaften, 1916). Eduard Baumgarten, *Benjamin Franklin. Der Lehrmeister der amerikanischen Revolution* (Frankfurt: Klostermann, 1936), Vol. 1 of *Die geistigen Grundlagen des amerikanischen Gemeinwesens*. (Vol. 2, *Der Pragmatismus: R. W. Emerson, W. James, J. Dewey*, 1938.) Baumgarten first presented his interpretation in a Göttingen lecture in November 1932, "Benjamin Franklin und die Psychologie des amerikanischen Alltags," published in 1933 and reprinted in Baumgarten, *Gewissen und Macht*, ed. Michael Sukale (Meisenheim: Hain, 1971), 65–86; on Weber, esp. 68 and 76.

   In the Weber literature, Baumgarten's book has been just as much neglected as the empirically rich study by Johann Baptist Kraus, *Scholastik, Puritanismus und Kapitalismus. Eine vergleichende dogmengeschichtliche Uebergangsstudie* (Munich: Duncker & Humblot, 1930). As a student of R. H. Tawney, Kraus was thoroughly familiar with seventeenth-century English sources. As a German, he was conversant with the German scholarly literature, taking a position close to Brentano's. A Jesuit professor in Tokyo, he showed little Catholic bias.

"an ethos. This is the quality which interests us" (PE 51). Brentano perceived here a *petitio principii* in Weber's definition: By excluding money making for the sake of enjoyment (*Genuss*), prestige, and power and even for its own sake, nothing remained but "an ethically colored maxim."[8] Brentano suggested that Weber had "allowed himself to be goaded by Ferdinand Kürnberger's malicious characterization of American culture into mistreating Franklin rather badly."[9] Kürnberger had quoted some of the same passages in his best-selling novel *The Man Tired of America* (1855, 1889) and concluded about Franklin's apparent philosophy of avarice: "They make tallow out of cattle and money out of men" – an allusion to father Franklin the tallow chandler. Against this American maxim he set the "German word": "We make spirit out of men, not money!"[10] It was characteristic of Weber's Anglophilia and his rejection of German perceptions of American cant that he saw spirit where Kürnberger saw money: Franklin expressed an ethos, not a spiritless materialism.[11]

8 Brentano, 131.    9 Ibid., 148.

10 Ferdinand Kürnberger, *Der Amerikamüde, Amerikanisches Kulturbild* (Leipzig: Reclam, 1889), 32. The novel was based on the American disappointments of the Austrian poet Nikolaus Lenau (1802–1850). First published in 1855, it was written during the exodus of the 1848ers to America at the height of the reactionary period. Ironically, Kürnberger appears more utilitarian than Franklin when he argues that the only ground on which one might forgive his exploitativeness was his invention of the lightning rod. The 1889 introduction by the Viennese writer V. K. Schembera portrays Kürnberger as a cross between "steely" Puritan and soulless machine: "The basic feature of his character was steely (*stahlharte*) reliability. . . . His mental apparatus worked with the precision of a machine set to be accurate to the thousandth of a millimeter. . . . He hated sentimentality as much as anything untrue and unclear" (p. 5). Schembera helps us see that Weber's famous metaphor about the *stahlharte Gehäuse* (usually translated as "iron cage") and the *stahlharte* Puritan merchants reflects contemporary phraseology borrowed from technological advances.

11 It appears to me that Weber's defense of Franklin reflects Friedrich Kapp's exuberant apologia:

> Franklin's industry and conscientiousness differ radically from the despicable chase after the almighty dollar, although in Germany he has at times been contemptuously called its herald. Instead of making such a senseless charge, we Germans would be better advised to learn from his example, after we finally left dreamland for the firm ground of plain reality. Franklin's example can teach us something about the preconditions of social effectiveness and the securing of political freedom. We lag behind the materially more developed peoples, especially the Americans, in appreciating the proper role of money-making and material means in achieving spiritual and moral purposes.

Kapp recommended Franklin "to aspiring young people as a shining example of conscientious work, faithful execution of duty and gladly rendered public service. May every German father put Franklin's autobiography into his son's hands as a textbook." See Friedrich Kapp, "Benjamin Franklin," in *Aus und über Amerika. Tatsachen und Erlebnisse* (Berlin: Springer, 1876), 46 and 89. In view of Kapp's personal interest in the young Weber, I assume that Max knew his Franklin interpretation. As early as 1879, he had read up on the history of the United States. See the letter of October 1 to his cousin Fritz Baumgarten, *Jugendbriefe*, 28 f. At age sixteen, Weber visited on his own Kapp's estate in Silesia. See the letter to his father of July 15, 1880, *Jugendbriefe*, 33.

But where Weber saw in Franklin's popular writings a new spirit that "would both in ancient times and in the Middle Ages have been proscribed as the lowest sort of avarice" (PE 56), Brentano viewed the Puritan ethic as a continuation of the traditionalistic ethic of petty-bourgeois strata and Franklin's own position as resembling Aristotle's Nicomachean ethic. Where Weber understood Franklin's reference to his father's advice – Solomon's saying: "Seest thou a man diligent in his business? He shall stand before kings" (Prv. 22. 29) – as a defense of money making as a vocation, Brentano read it as the customary pride of artisans. Parents of every denomination, he argued, have tried to instill in their children an achievement drive by pointing to the honorable status to be gained from their work.[12]

Eduard Baumgarten too singled out the example of Solomon's saying and claimed that in this "very dramatic passage of his construction Weber missed the political goal of Franklin's money ethic by a hair's breadth."[13] If he had paid more attention to the context, he should have seen that for Franklin money and industry were not ends in themselves, but means for the pursuit of happiness. After living in the United States from 1924 to 1929, Baumgarten was aware that Weber had not only failed to read Franklin carefully but also had not understood sufficiently his style and irony. Weber had been motivated to master the English language from early on, but he did not have the advantage of Brentano, who had lived in England as a teenager. Weber certainly did not lack confidence in handling eighteenth- and seventeenth-century authors, but some linguistic subtleties, historical allusions, and some of the literary context were bound to escape him.

In his rejoinder to Brentano, Weber had already insisted, taking up his critic's formulation, that at issue was indeed a "rationalization of life in the form of irrational conduct" (PE 194). Given his understanding of Calvinist rational self-discipline vis-à-vis an inscrutable and irrational God, Baumgarten argued, Weber was misled to formulate the auxiliary hypothesis that as a secularized Puritan, Franklin too would subscribe to an ultimately irrational vocational ethic. In a third volume (never published) Baumgarten wanted to demonstrate, in connection with Jonathan Edwards, that Weber's notion of an

---

12 In the meantime, Herbert Lüthy has called attention to the Catholic writer Jacques Savary, whose widely read "The Perfect Tradesman" offered advice to Catholics and Protestants alike a hundred years before Franklin. See Lüthy, *From Calvin to Rousseau* (New York: Basic Books, 1970), 11.
13 Baumgarten, *Franklin,* 99.

irrational rationalism (in the sense of a principled hostility to the pursuit of happiness) was not even tenable in the case of religious Puritanism in America.[14] Baumgarten rejected Weber's assertion that Franklin represented the spirit of capitalism "in almost classic purity" (PE 48) also on the ground that Franklin's social ideal was the independent farmer who would never "dig more than ploughdeep," which means, would never turn into a prospector and speculator.

Weber had more than linguistic difficulties with Franklin. He did not grasp the extent of Franklin's sense of humor and roguishness. Weber, explains Baumgarten, did not get the jokes! When Franklin advises his young tradesman that "he that murders a crown, destroys all that it might have produced, even scores of pounds" (PE 49), Weber believes that "the ethical quality of the sermon . . . is impossible to mistake, and that is the characteristic thing. A lack of care in the handling of money means to him that one, so to speak, murders capital embryos and hence it is an ethical defect" (PE 196). Weber seems to have been ignorant of what American readers understood at the time: This funny formulation reminded them of Franklin's famous Polly Baker Speech, published a year earlier (1747).[15] In this fictitious speech a young woman, standing trial for the fifth time for having borne an illegitimate child, accused one of the judges, who had been her original seducer, of having murdered scores of potential embryos by remaining a bachelor. Baumgarten knew his uncle as a "man of great humor" and therefore was struck all the more that "nations are curiously incapable of understanding each other's sense of humor and wit."[16] This failure also affected the German audience. Misunderstanding Franklin's humor, Weber "carefully constructed an elaborate theory of Franklin's ascetic economic ethos as one of the essential foundations of modern capitalism, a construction that up until today [1936] is repeated uncritically from all kinds of pulpits – economic, theological, literary, philosophical – with learned mien and a pronounced shyness to consult the sources."[17] For that matter, added Baumgarten, in thirty years of scholarly debate nobody saw fit to compare Weber's theory of the ascetic Franklin with Franklin's own theory of asceticism.[18]

Baumgarten answered a possible rejoinder that Franklin undeniably

14 See now Edmund Leites, *The Puritan Conscience and Modern Sexuality* (New Haven, Conn.: Yale University Press, 1986).
15 See "The Speech of Miss Polly Baker" in Benjamin Franklin, *Writings* (New York: Library of America, 1987), 305–308.
16 Baumgarten, *Franklin,* 112.    17 Ibid.    18 Ibid., 119.

offered an extreme, quantitatively oriented advice to his tradesman
with the argument that Franklin's humor was serious in its very
instrumentality – Franklin being a master of distance and indirection
(*Vermittlung*). In contrasting Lutheran religiosity – man as the vessel of
divine grace – and Anglo-Saxon Calvinism and Puritanism – man as
God's tool – Weber had prematurely identified a harsh asceticism in
the latter instead of considering the possibility that such instrumentality was truly a means for serenity and playfulness. Finally, although
Weber wanted to counter the German prejudice about Anglo-Saxon
virtues being hypocritical, he did not sufficiently grasp Franklin's
notion of the appearance of modesty and its relation to his humor.
Resorting to his deus ex machina, Weber recognized asceticism behind
the facade of utilitarianism and thus missed, says Baumgarten, the core
of Franklin's thinking. If Weber had scrutinized certain passages more
closely – in this case the story of the founding of a library – he would
have seen that Franklin addressed "the impropriety of presenting one's
self as the proposer of any useful project that might be supposed to
raise one's reputation in the small degree above that of one's neighbors,
when one has need of their assistance to accomplish that project."[19]
The appearance of modesty was not a matter of deception, as Weber
tended to read it, or a vicarious virtue, but a practical virtue allowing
effective cooperation with one's fellow citizens. Thus, Baumgarten
derived the American tradition of humorous self-deprecation, which
public speakers must practice to this day, from Franklin's spirit of
humane instrumentalism.

If Weber was provoked by Kürnberger to misread some of Franklin's writings, he wrote *The Protestant Ethic* also under the sway of
Georg Jellinek's *The Declaration of the Rights of Man and of Citizens*. In
the first edition he declared not only that Jellinek's essay was "basic
for the history of the origin and political significance of freedom of
conscience," but also that he "owed directly to this essay the incentive to study Puritanism again."[20] In this passage the political context
of Weber's interest is more visible than in the 1920 revision. He added
a long footnote on the major historical representatives of toleration
because in a Reichstag speech, Adolf Gröber, one of the leading
figures in the Catholic Center Party, had "once more asserted the
historical priority of toleration in Maryland over Rhode Island. Yet

19 Franklin, cited in ibid., 139.    20 *Archiv für Sozialwissenschaft,* vol. 21 (1905): 43.

toleration for opportunistic reasons and toleration as a religious principle are two very different things. . . . As with toleration, so it is with the modern 'liberal' idea: The religious repudiation of all human authority as idolatry of the flesh . . . as it appears most strongly among the Quakers and in mitigated form in all ascetic sects, this hostility to all constituted authority from positive religious motives was the historically decisive psychological basis of freedom in the Puritan countries. No matter how high one may want to rank the historical significance of the Enlightenment, its ideals of liberty were not anchored in such positive motives, which alone could secure their persistence. Only such motives, incidentally, gave Gladstone's politics their 'constructive' character."[21]

Weber was impressed by two sweeping claims advanced by Jellinek. The first declared "the idea of legally establishing inalienable, inherent and sacred rights of the individual not of political but religious origin. What has been held to be a work of the Revolution

---

21 Ibid., Weber referred here to the national debate in the wake of the Catholic Center Party's draft bill on religious toleration. In November 1900 the Center Party submitted the "Draft of an Imperial Law on Freedom of Religion." Its primary motivation was the removal of restrictions on the activities of the Jesuits. The Center Party appealed to the liberal legacy of basic rights in the Frankfurt imperial constitution of 1848 and the Prussian constitutions of 1848 and 1850. Adolf Gröber (1854–1919), the draft's main author, propagated it in the Catholic press under the slogan *Toleranzantrag* (Draft on Religious Toleration) in a tactical move to force the hand of the liberals. When Weber remarked that "the Catholic church cannot accept [toleration as a religious principle] because as God's instrument it has the duty to save people from damnation, the inevitable result of heresy" (p. 43), this may be read in connection with contemporary Protestant arguments that the Papal Syllabus of 1864 demanded rights for Catholics in Protestant countries that Catholic principles denied to Protestants. Indeed, in December 1900 the Catholic deputy Ernst Lieber agreed that in demanding "civil tolerance" he did not advocate "dogmatic tolerance," which appeared to him inherently impossible. Although restrictions on the Jesuits were eventually removed, the bill never passed, but it continued to be debated during and after the time Weber wrote his essay. See Karl Bachem, *Das Zentrum in Berlin in den Jahren 1898 bis 1906,* Vol. 6 of *Vorgeschichte, Geschichte und Politik der deutschen Zentrumspartei* (Cologne: Bachem, 1929), 101–23, 228–235.

Several years later, Weber referred to the *Kulturkampf* illustratively in his contrast between church and sect (in *Economy and Society*): "The Catholic's 'freedom of conscience,' [Hermann von] Mallinckrodt said in the Reichstag, 'consists in being free to obey the pope,' that means, in following his own conscience. However, if they are strong enough, neither the Catholic nor the (old) Lutheran church, and, all the more so, the Calvinist and Baptist old church recognizes freedom of conscience for others. . . . [Only] the consistent sect gives rise to an inalienable personal right of the governed against any power, whether political, hierocratic or patriarchal. Such freedom of conscience may be the oldest Right of Man, as Jellinek has argued convincingly; at any rate, it is the most basic Right of Man because it comprises all ethically conditioned action and guarantees freedom from compulsion, especially from the power of the state." Max Weber, *Economy and Society,* Guenther Roth and Claus Wittich, eds. (Totowa: Bedminster Press, 1968), 1209; cf. 563, 576 (hereafter cited as "ES").

was in reality a fruit of the Reformation and its struggles. Its first apostle was not Lafayette but Roger Williams." The second claim asserted "with irrefutable certainty" that "the principles of 1789 are in reality the principles of 1776."[22] Jellinek attributed the failure of the French Revolution and the German revolution of 1848 in good measure to the fact that the rights proclaimed preceded the institutions necessary to sustain them, whereas in America freedom of conscience originated in religious struggles that led Roger Williams to insist on its inclusion in the patent and charter of Rhode Island, a step that was gradually followed by other colonies. As Jellinek clarified after an exchange with the French scholar Emil Boutmy, he had not claimed that the demand for religious liberty was the source of all human rights, but that their enactment went back to this demand. Given the antagonism to France in Imperial Germany and the increasing hostility to the legacies of the Enlightenment in German culture, it is not surprising that Jellinek and Weber, partly in conformity with and partly in reaction to these trends, shifted the origins of human rights back to the religious seventeenth century and the Anglo-American realm. This was not only in line with liberal Anglophilia, but also was an argument that might make basic rights more palatable to conservatives. In criticizing Ritschl for his opposition to any notion of Christian natural rights, Weber added that "after all we owe to this notion everything that today even the most reactionary person considers a minimum of individual freedom" (PE 245).

At about the same time that Baumgarten pointed to the persistence of Weber's Franklin interpretation, Otto Vossler, one of the few German historians competent to judge the matter, wrote that Jellinek's thesis had remained dominant in Germany in spite of its untenability. Vossler's critique dealt in part with the extreme spiritualism and dualism of Roger Williams, which made it inappropriate to celebrate him as "the apostle of the rights of man," and in part with the history of the bill of rights in Virginia, which led him to the conclusion that Jellinek's thesis "can neither explain the origin of the idea of human rights nor its positive enactment."[23] Baumgarten's and Vossler's cri-

---

22 Jellinek, 77 and 89.
23 See Otto Vossler, "Studien zur Erklärung der Menschenrechte" (1930), in *Geist und Geschichte. Gesammelte Aufsätze* (Munich: Piper, 1964), 111; see also my discussion of Vossler and Perry Miller in "Geist des Kapitalismus und kapitalistische Weltwirtschaft," *Kölner Zeitschrift für Soziologie,* 33 (1981): 736ff.

tiques are more than half a century old and warrant an update. In the case of Jellinek's thesis, our present state of knowledge of colonial history is represented, for instance, by Rhys Isaac's 1982 study on *The Transformation of Virginia 1740–1790*.[24] Basing his study on much primary evidence, Isaac demonstrates the complex pattern of conflict and cooperation between Anglican gentry, separate Baptists and other sects, and Enlightenment secularists such as James Madison and Thomas Jefferson. The passage of the latter's Bill for Establishing Religious Freedom in 1786 – an act "utterly without precedent in the Atlantic world, declaring the unqualified separation of church from state"[25] – was the result of an "unholy alliance" of sectarians and Deists, with the gentry trying to contain the potential political threat from the lower ranks of society by abandoning its support of established religion. The sectarians saw their opportunity to get rid of established religion and the burden of being taxed for it in the new state that arose out of a revolution against traditionalist authority. But whereas Weber postulated that logically sects must demand freedom of conscience out of conviction, my reading of the evidence leads me to suspect that the Virginia sectarians, no less than the gentry, were guided largely by opportunist considerations. It was the rationalist republicans who believed in toleration as an ideological principle.

In his insistence that mere literary doctrines are unable to change the world – at least in part a reflection of his own sense of powerlessness – Weber agreed with Jellinek's position that "literature alone never produces anything, unless it finds in the historical and social conditions ground ready for its working. When one shows the literary origin of an idea, one has by no means therewith discovered the records of its practical significance."[26] Weber's *Protestant Ethic* was an effort to demonstrate the practical significance of religious convictions and conduct, and he freely acknowledged that Jellinek's "proof of religious traces in the genesis of the Rights of Man . . . gave me a crucial stimulus . . . to investigate the impact of religion in areas where one might not look at first."[27] The search for practical signifi-

---

24 Rhys Isaac, *The Transformation of Virginia 1740–1790* (Chapel Hill: University of North Carolina Press, 1982).
25 Ibid., 284.  26 Jellinek, 57.
27 From the memorial address on Jellinek in Marianne Weber, *Max Weber: A Biography*, tr. Harry Zohn, with a new introduction by myself on "Marianne Weber and Her Circle" (New Brunswick, N.J.: Transaction Books, 1988), 476.

cance justified their joint program of turning *Geisteswissenschaft* into *Sozialwissenschaft*.[28] But in their concrete efforts they pressed the historical evidence too hard, thus challenging later generations to reconsider the record with endlessly varying emphasis.

28 Hubert Treiber called my attention to the fact that Jellinek welcomed the turn from *Geisteswissenschaft* to *Sozialwissenschaft* as early as 1874. See Jellinek, "Moralstatistik und Todesstrafe," repr. in *Ausgewählte Schriften und Reden* (Aalen: Scientia, 1970), Vol. 1, 69–75.

# PART I

*Background and Context*

# 1

# The German Theological Sources and Protestant Church Politics

FRIEDRICH WILHELM GRAF

In the dispute surrounding *The Protestant Ethic* in 1907, Max Weber explained that an "objective, fruitful critique" of his investigation of the genetic connection between Protestant asceticism and the spirit of capitalism "is only possible – in this field of endlessly intertwined causal relations – through a mastery of the source material."[1] "Although it may seem to some as an outdated attitude, I expect a critique from the theological sphere to be the most competent."[2] In later years, Weber repeatedly emphasized that for him the most important participants in the debate over *The Protestant Ethic* were the "experts" in religious matters, the theologians. From them alone he expected a "fruitful and instructive critique."[3]

How can we explain Weber's obvious esteem for academic theology? There is, first of all, a biographical reason. From the beginning of his university studies, Max Weber cultivated strong contacts with Protestant theologians. He spent his first semester in a close living and working relationship with his cousin Otto Baumgarten, a Protestant theologian, who was six years older than Weber.[4] From 1894 on, Baumgarten taught as a professor of practical theology in Kiel, maintaining a very close relationship with his cousin in Heidelberg and also with Marianne Weber. Through his connection with Baumgarten, Weber met numerous religious liberals and Protestant theologians who were critical of the church, and after 1890,

---

1 Max Weber, "Kritische Beiträge zu den vorstehenden 'Kritischen Beiträgen,'" in Johannes Winckelmann, ed., *Die protestantische Ethik II,* 5th ed. (Gütersloh, 1987), 27–37, 31 (hereafter cited as *PE*).
2 Ibid., 36.
3 Max Weber, "Antikritisches Schlusswort zum 'Geist des Kapitalismus,'" in Winckelmann, *PE,* 283–345, 345.
4 For further information about Otto Baumgarten, see Hasko von Bassi, *Otto Baumgarten. Ein "moderner Theologe" im Kaiserreich und in der Weimarer Republik* (Frankfurt, 1988), and Wolfgang Steck, ed., *Otto Baumgarten. Studien zu Leben und Werk* (Kiel, 1986).

27

together with his "favorite cousin," he was involved with the Protestant Social Congress. His work with the Protestant Social Congress
intensified his involvement with liberal Protestantism. When Weber
moved from Freiburg to Heidelberg in 1896, a theologian in the
circle of young Heidelberg professors, Ernst Troeltsch, became his
closest friend. Moreover, Weber established contact with other professors in the faculty of Protestant theology at the University of
Heidelberg: in particular, the Old Testament scholar Adalbert Merx
and the New Testament scholar Adolf Deissmann.

Weber said of himself that he was *unmusikalisch* in religious matters.[5] Otto Baumgarten, however, pointed out in 1926 how complex
his cousin's relations with traditional Christianity had been. Even
when Weber could not attain "that religious certainty" that is the
decisive feature of a religious character, he was "a man of the strongest reaction regarding all experiences of an irrational, mysterious
otherworld. Certainly one can call Weber neither irreligious nor non-
Christian, rather his sensitivity to religious values and his emotional
penetration of religious experiences forms an essential component of
his scientific and personal vocation."[6] Indeed, as difficult as it has
always been to answer the question about Weber's personal religious
attitude, his heroic agnosticism was closely bound up with a great
practical interest in contemporary German Protestantism and concrete engagement in church politics. It is true that after the turn of the
century, Weber no longer actively participated in the Protestant Social Congress.[7] But even into World War I, he supported church-
political activities initiated by liberal Protestant university theologians. In 1894, he signed appeals for liturgical and cultural reform
in the Prussian church. In 1902, in collaboration with Ernst
Troeltsch, he fought against measures taken by the government of
Baden, under pressure from the Catholic Center Party, to reverse the
ban against men's orders that originated during the *Kulturkampf*. In
1911, he signed two declarations of protest against the Prussian High
Consistory that appeared in Christian publications. With these declarations, liberal theologians spoke out against the Prussian church

5 Letter to Ferdinand Tönnies from 1908 in Eduard Baumgarten, ed., *Max Weber. Werk und
  Person* (Tübingen, 1964), 398 f. and 670, note 1.
6 Otto Baumgarten, "Das Dennoch des Glaubens. Ein Briefwechsel," *Schleswig-
  Holsteinisches Kirchenblatt* 22 (1926): 225–228.
7 Rita Aldenhoff, "Max Weber and the Evangelical-Social-Congress," in Wolfgang J. Mommsen and Jürgen Osterhammel, eds., *Max Weber and His Contemporaries* (London, 1987), 193–
  202.

leadership's efforts to subject the liberal Cologne pastor Carl Jatho to disciplinary procedures.[8] In 1906, Weber published the essay "Kirchen und Sekten" in *Die Christliche Welt*, in which he had already published in the 1890s. Edited by the theologian Martin Rade, this magazine was the most important theological organ of the liberal *Kulturprotestanten*. Weber's essay originally carried the subtitle "A Sketch of Church and Social Politics."[9] This subtitle reveals that the essay not only pertained to religious sociology, but was also a contribution to religious debates in Germany.

What does Weber's close connection to a liberal Protestant intellectual milieu mean for the interpretation of *The Protestant Ethic*? In his 1988 book *Fate and Utopia in German Sociology 1870–1923*, Harry Liebersohn suggested that *The Protestant Ethic* should be interpreted not only as a historical study or as a cultural analysis of the genesis of modern capitalism, but also as symptomatic of the times, an "allegory about Germany in [Weber's] own day."[10] The way Weber described the difference between Calvinism and Lutheranism was strongly marked by his critique of the political indecisiveness of the German bourgeoisie and by his despair over the authoritarian political culture of the Wilhelmine Empire. He regarded the spirit of Lutheranism as essentially responsible for this political passivity. A politically motivated, radical critique of Lutheranism was fundamental to Weber's analysis of "pseudo-constitutionality" in the political system of the Wilhelmine Empire and to his polemic against the political impotence of the National Liberal bourgeoisie.[11] Therefore I would like to take up Harry Liebersohn's interpretative suggestion

8  See Friedrich Wilhelm Graf, "Max Weber e la teologia protestante des suo tempo," in Marita Losito and Pierangelo Schiera, eds., *Max Weber e le scienze sociali del suo tempo* (Bologna, 1988), 279–320.

9  Max Weber, " 'Kirchen' und 'Sekten' in Nordamerika. Eine kirchen- und sozialpolitische Skizze", *Die christliche Welt. Evangelisches Gemeindeblatt für Gebildete aller Stände* 20 (1906): 558–562, 577–583.

10  Harry Liebersohn, *Fate and Utopia in German Sociology, 1870–1923* (Cambridge, Mass., 1988).

11  A striking example is found in Weber's letter of February 5, 1906, to Adolf von Harnack: Luther towers above all others, but Lutheranism is – I don't deny it – in its historical articulation the most frightening of terrors for me. Even in the ideal form in which it appears in your hopes for the future, it lacks, I fear, in its impact on us Germans, sufficient transformative power to shape life. It is a difficult and tragic situation: None of us could be a sectarian, a Quaker, a Baptist, etc. Everybody must recognize the superiority of the institutional church in non-ethical and non-religious [i.e., cultural] respects. The time of the sects, or of something equivalent to them, is definitely over. But the fact that our nation never went through the school of hard asceticism, in no form whatsoever, is the source of everything that I hate about it (and about myself). I can't help it, but in religious terms the average American sect member surpasses our

and demonstrate how forcefully certain ideals of liberal Protestantism are reflected in the historical interpretation of *The Protestant Ethic.* To that end, I turn my attention primarily to the original text of
1904–1905. Here Weber explained that his "sketch, as far as it is
concerned with the purely dogmatic sphere, depends entirely on the
secondary literature in church history and dogmatics, [and] inasmuch
[it] makes absolutely no claims to originality."[12]

More than 40 percent of the modern literature that Weber used in
*The Protestant Ethic* derived from German theologians of the nineteenth and early twentieth centuries. With impressive expertise,
Weber incorporated the works of the leading church historians. Even
with regard to the specialized literature on Lutheran ethics of vocation and on Methodism, Weber fully mastered contemporary research.[13]

Weber included not only historical material from theological literature. His question about the potential social consequences of a religious value system was distinctly informed by the dogmatic-
historical debate in German-speaking universities at the time. This
debate was by no means purely an academic discourse, involving
only historians and focused on the past. In the discussions about the
relationship between Protestantism and modern culture, the fundamental legitimacy of the German Empire was always an underlying
theme. This not only indicates the prominent role that theological
discourse played in the educated public before 1914, it also reveals the
political implications of the theological controversies over Protestantism's effect on politics and culture in modern German history. The
self-understanding of leading Protestant dogmatic and church historians of the time reflects these political implications. With few excep-

institutional Christians as much as Luther excels, as a religious personality, Calvin,
Fox, et tutti quanti.

Max Weber, *Briefe 1906–1908, Max Weber Gesamtausgabe,* Abteilung II, Vol. 5 (Tübingen,
1990), 32–33. See also Wolfgang J. Mommsen, *Max Weber and German Politics 1890–1920,*
trans. by M. Steinberg (Chicago, 1984), 94.

12 Max Weber, "Die protestantische Ethik und der Geist des Kapitalismus II: Die Berufsidee
des asketischen Protestantismus," *Archiv für Sozialwissenschaften und Sozialpolitik* 21 (1905):
1–110, 3 (hereafter cited as PE II).

13 In the first part of the essay, which appeared in 1905, Vol. 20 in the *Archiv* (1–54), including
the following sections: 1. Confession and social stratification, 2. The "spirit" of capitalism,
and 3. Luther's concept of vocation. Problems of investigation, approximately one-quarter
of the recent literature cited (excluding, therefore, source material, such as Luther's writings) comes from Protestant theologians of the nineteenth and early twentieth centuries.
The contribution of theologians of the aforementioned epoch in the methodologically more
important second part of the essay, Vol. 21 of the *Archiv,* including sections 1. The religious
foundations of innerworldly asceticism and 2. Asceticism and capitalism, is double that
amount; almost half of the literature cited comes from theologians of that period.

tions, they understood their discipline as a "cultural science" that not only provided insight into the origins of the present, but concurrently should establish normative principles for the development of politics, culture, and certain cultural values.[14] Therefore, it was not interest in religious ideas or dogmatic systems as such, but the search for a connection between religious thought and cultural models that motivated the dogmatic and church historian.

In *The Protestant Ethic,* Weber thematized "the relationship between logically and psychologically mediated consequences of certain religious ideas for the practical behavior" of the individual.[15] Weber proceeded from a concept of religious consciousness as it was embraced by contemporary Protestant theology and classically defined by Friedrich Daniel Ernst Schleiermacher. Religious consciousness was not merely a function of other value systems or spheres of interest, but also represented an autonomous realm, "a separate province of the mind." Only on this basis could one then also consider its potential cultural consequences, its meaning for individual conduct (*Lebensführung*) or for the actions of certain social groups. German-speaking Protestant theologians of the nineteenth century mostly followed a psychological classification that allowed not only for the independence of religion, but also for the instructive power of religious ideas. Weber shared these psychological orientations.[16] He primarily consulted dogmatic-historical literature in which Protestant theology and religion were structured according to certain psychological ideal types. This heavy dependence on the theological discussion also indicates that more value judgments, and specifically denominational ideology, are present in *The Protestant Ethic* than Weber himself realized or present interpreters are aware.

I

In spite of the vast literature on *The Protestant Ethic,* we still do not know enough about the academic and historical background of

---

14 Friedrich Wilhelm Graf, "Rettung der Persönlichkeit. Protestantische Theologie als Kulturwissenschaft des Christentums," in Rüdiger vom Bruch, Friedrich Wilhelm Graf, and G. Hübinger, eds., *Kultur und Kulturwissenschaft um 1900. Krise der Moderne und Glaube an die Wissenschaft* (Stuttgart, 1989), 103–131.

15 PE II, 25.

16 Compare also Troeltsch's characterization of Weber's endeavors concerning the concept of asceticism: "Weber explained the transformation of the term in its particular Calvinist manifestation from a rigorous other-worldly way of thinking into an economic-capitalist activity in religious and psychological terms," Ernst Troeltsch, "Die Kulturbedeutung des Kalvinismus," in Winckelmann, *PE,* 188–215, 197.

Weber's work, his sources, and the intellectual climate in which he formed his position. It is known, however, that the relationship between Protestantism and the rise of modern bourgeois society in various European societies had been discussed since the end of the eighteenth century.[17] A liberal *Kulturkampf* mentality informed this discussion, an anti–Catholic invocation of the achievements of economic modernization by Protestants, especially Calvinists. It is further known that Weber's search for the religious roots of an attitude that promoted economic modernization was influenced by Georg Jellinek's *The Declaration of the Rights of Man and of Citizens*.[18] Recent authors have also noted that engagement with Werner Sombart's book *Die Genesis des Kapitalismus* was probably more important for Weber than he admitted in the explanations of *The Protestant Ethic*.[19] Less well known is the great extent to which Ernst Troeltsch influenced *The Protestant Ethic*. During the years that Weber worked on it, Troeltsch wrote a major book on a closely related theme, *Protestantisches Christentum und Kirche in der Neuzeit*, which appeared in 1906.[20] Troeltsch presented a lecture in April 1906 at the Ninth German Historians Conference in Stuttgart on "Die Bedeutung des Protestantismus für die Entstehung der modernen Welt"[21] instead of Weber, who for unknown reasons declined the invitation. Troeltsch's lecture stimulated a widespread debate among German historians on the role of Lutheranism in German history.

In this debate, there was much discussion about the "Troeltsch–Weber thesis." Reviews of the published edition of Troeltsch's Stuttgart lecture and critics of his major publication, *Protestantisches Christentum und Kirche in der Neuzeit,* consistently maintained that the two Heidelberg scholars developed their view of ascetic Protestantism in

17  Cf. Gianfranco Poggi, *Calvinism and the Capitalist Spirit. Max Weber's Protestant Ethic* (London, 1983); Gordon Marshall, *In Search of the Spirit of Capitalism. An Essay on Max Weber's Protestant Ethic Thesis* (London, 1982), 19ff.

18  Georg Jellinek, *The Declaration of the Rights of Man and of Citizens,* trans. by Max Farrand (New York: Holt, 1901). The first German edition appeared in 1895: *Die Erklärung der Menschen- und Bürgerrechte* (Leipzig). See also Reinhard Bendix and Guenther Roth, *Scholarship and Partisanship. Essays on Max Weber* (Berkeley, 1971), 308–310. See the essay by Roth in this volume.

19  Sombart, *Der moderne Kapitalismus,* Vol. 1 (Leipzig, 1902). See Hartmut Lehmann, "Asketischer Protestantismus und ökonomischer Rationalismus: Die Weber-These nach zwei Generationen," in Wolfgang Schluchter, ed., *Max Webers Sicht des okzidentalen Christentums. Interpretation und Kritik* (Frankfurt, 1988), 529–553.

20  Ernst Troeltsch, "Protestantisches Christentum und Kirche in der Neuzeit," in Paul Hinneberg, ed., *Die Kultur der Gegenwart. Ihre Entwicklung und ihre Ziele.* Teil I, Abt. IV/I: Geschichte der christlichen Religion (Berlin, 1906), 253–458.

21  First edition 1906; a substantially expanded edition appeared in 1911 as Vol. 24 in the *Historische Bibliothek* of the *Historische Zeitschrift,* published by Oldenbourg in Munich and Berlin.

mutual conversations. In his discussion with the Kiel historian Felix Rachfahl, Weber vigorously stressed that "absolutely no collaboration whatsoever, not even of a latent nature, has taken place."[22] Barely two months after the appearance of the second part of *The Protestant Ethic,* in August 1905, Weber wrote to the historian Georg von Below, "Troeltsch's excellent contribution may be traced in many respects to the stimulus of our conversations and my essays (perhaps even more than he knows) – but he is the theological expert."[23] On the other hand, Troeltsch repeatedly emphasized his independence from Weber and pointed out that he had developed the essential features of his program of a cultural history of late Protestantism even before the appearance of *The Protestant Ethic.* Indeed, as difficult as it is to judge the problematic academic relationship between the two friends,[24] their exchange over questions that preoccupied them both was probably much closer than Weber was willing to admit in the controversy over *The Protestant Ethic.* In any case, Weber's selections of theological literature and his opinions of certain theological authors reveal strong similarities between *The Protestant Ethic* and works published earlier by Ernst Troeltsch.

Moreover, Weber explicitly took into consideration his friend's imminent publication plans, explaining that he would treat certain themes "only suggestively, because I hope E. Troeltsch will consider these issues with which he has dealt for many years (*lex naturae,* etc. . . .), and as an expert will naturally handle them better than I could, despite my best intentions."[25] At the end of the essay, Weber quoted Troeltsch's text, written no later than 1902 but published in 1903, on Reformed Protestantism in England, which presented a striking similarity to the theme and conception of *The Protestant Ethic.* Here the Heidelberg theologian maintained that the doctrine of predestination was central for Reformed religious devotion. He also saw the doctrine of predestination as a strong mercantile impulse, since "moral achievement . . . reveals election, . . . the most vital energy" is revealed "by the doctrine of predestination."[26] For all its

---

22 Max Weber, "Antikritisches Schlusswort zum 'Geist' des Kapitalismus," in Winckelmann, *PE,* 149–187, 150.

23 Cit. see Wilhelm Hennis, *Max Webers Fragestellung. Studien zur Biographie des Werks* (Tübingen, 1987), 118, note 5.

24 See Friedrich Wilhelm Graf, "Friendship Between Experts: Notes on Weber and Troeltsch," in Mommsen and Osterhammel, eds., *Max Weber and His Contemporaries,* 215–233.

25 PE II, 4.

26 Ernst Troeltsch, "Art. 'Moralisten, Englische,'" in *Realencyclopädie für protestantische Theologie und Kirche,* 3rd ed., Vol. 13, 436–461. A slightly expanded version appeared in Ernst

similarity to Weber, there was also, however, a difference: In "Calvinist countries . . . there prevails . . . a more liberal attitude toward economic activity and the capital that promotes it. In contrast to the patriarchalism and economic conservatism of the Lutherans, the Calvinists subscribe to the doctrine of political and economic utilitarianism, and this utilitarianism is supported by the Christian demands for temperance, legality, and industriousness, in which the Gospel proves to be conducive also to material prosperity. Thus the Calvinist countries become the supporters of a capital-economy, trade and industry, and a utilitarianism moderated by Christianity, which has significantly influenced their . . . actual economic development. Next to modern political development, economic development has been mightily promoted by Christian utilitarianism. Whoever is so absolutely sure – through predestination – of his earthly goal and his salvation hereafter, can apply his natural energies all the more freely to the acquisition of wealth as a natural goal and need not fear an excessive love of earthly possessions."[27] Here Troeltsch's argument was the complete opposite of Weber's; he deduced the disposition of Calvinistic asceticism toward the development of the spirit of capitalism directly from the certainty of salvation. In contrast, Weber stressed, much more convincingly, the uncertainty of the state of grace, a result of the doctrine of election. Troeltsch later concurred with Weber's opinion. Nevertheless, he insisted at the same time that Weber's concept of "ascetic Protestantism" had already been "prepared" in the nineteenth-century Protestant history of dogma.[28]

## II

The most important theological source for *The Protestant Ethic* comes from the Bern theologian Matthias Schneckenburger, *Vergleichende Darstellung des lutherischen und reformierten Lehrbegriffs,* a series of posthumously published lectures, edited in 1855 by Eduard Güder from his mentor's papers.[29] Weber proclaimed the book to be a reliable historical source, because Schneckenburger had analyzed the dif-

---

Troeltsch, *Aufsätze zur Geistesgeschichte und Religionssoziologie,* ed. by Hans Baron (Tübingen, 1925), 374–429, 391 (hereafter cited as GS IV).

27 Ibid., 393.

28 Ernst Troeltsch, *Die Soziallehren der christlichen Kirchen und Gruppen* (Tübingen, 1912), 950 f., note 510.

29 Matthias Schneckenburger, *Vergleichende Darstellung des lutherischen und reformirten Lehrbegriffs.* Aus dem handschriftlichen Nachlass zusammengestellt und hrsg. von Eduard Güder (Stuttgart, 1855).

ference between Lutheran and Calvinist religiosity "to the exclusion of all value judgments."[30] Weber firmly rejected the criticism directed at Schneckenburger by other Protestant theologians, arguing that the criticism itself was not historically "objective" and was only the expression of dogmatic prejudice. He strongly disagreed with the most influential German-speaking Protestant theologian of the late nineteenth century, Albrecht Ritschl, professor of systematic theology and dogmatic history at Göttingen. Much evidence supports the assumption that Troeltsch influenced Weber in his preference for Schneckenburger over Ritschl. Additionally, there is a noteworthy "affinity" between Schneckenburger's approach to church history and Weber's own historiographic conception. In his treatment of historical material, Schneckenburger focused on certain religious-psychological ideal types. In his presentation of the differences between Calvinism and Lutheranism, Schneckenburger wanted "to give an exhaustive account of the differences that lie in the original construction of religious meaning in both denominations, to reduce these differences to psychological laws and to understand them as such."[31] This "reductive mechanism," the selection of historical material according to certain psychological ideal types, may have made Schneckenburger's dogmatic history the most important theological source for *The Protestant Ethic*.

Schneckenburger came out of Württemberg Lutheranism. He had no academic background, and his ancestors were farmers, merchants, and manufacturers. He studied and taught theology first at the Tübinger Stift and then in Berlin. After holding a position as Repeater at the Tübinger Stift and a clerical office in the Württemberg church, at the age of thirty he was appointed full professor of theology at the university in Reformed Bern.[32] Thus, as a born Lutheran, he had to teach dogmatics "for the training of future pastors in the Calvinist church."[33] This led him to develop a strong

---

30 PE II, 21.
31 Matthias Schneckenburger, "Die neueren Verhandlungen betreffend das Princip des reformierten Lehrbegriffs," in *Baur's und Zellers Theol. Jahrbuch* 1848; cit.: Karl Bernhard Hundeshagen, *Beiträge zur Kirchenverfassungsgeschichte und Kirchenpolitik insbesondere des Protestantismus.* Erster Band (Wiesbaden, 1864; Frankfurt, 1963); Weber cites this work of Hundeshagen in PE II, 17.
32 For Schneckenburger's biography, see E. T. Gelpke, *Gedächtnisrede auf den Doktor und Professor der Theologie Matthias Schneckenburger, gehalten bei seiner Leichenfeier in der Aula der Hochschule zu Bern den 16. Juni 1848. Nebst der Grabrede von C. Wyss* (Bern, 1848). Karl Bernhard Hundeshagen, Art. "Schneckenburger," in *Realencyclopädie für protestantischen Theologie und Kirche*, 2d ed., Vol. 13 (Leipzig 1884), 602–608 (hereafter cited as RE2).
33 Ibid., 605.

interest in doctrinal differences between Swiss Reformed Protestantism and German Lutheranism. Explicating the difference between
Lutheranism and Calvinism was virtually forced upon him as a life
task, but he sought to promote the union between the Protestant
denominations as it had been introduced in several German Protestant territories during the second and third decades of the nineteenth
century. This union met with substantial resistance from groups of
Lutheran theologians and laity, who rejected the leveling of the difference in teachings between the Protestant creeds as bogus enlightenment, bureaucratic egalitarianism, and the destruction of the
central truths of the Lutheran tradition. In the late eighteenth and
early nineteenth centuries, a denominational New Lutheranism arose
in opposition to the union. It emphasized the old differences in teachings between Lutherans and the Calvinists in a new way. This New
Lutheranism sought to validate a specifically Lutheran identity, not
only in the realm of theological teachings, but also on the level of
religious practice. Despite the fact that Schneckenburger remained
closer to the Lutheran tradition,[34] even as a professor in Bern of
"comparative dogmatics," he wanted to combat denominational
Lutheranism and prepare the way for a new and stronger union. His
central thesis can be formulated as follows: The denominational critique of the union had found broad support because, until then, the
union had been insufficiently justified in theological terms, and the
leading union theologians, above all Schleiermacher, had underestimated the importance of the conventional differences in the teachings. Only one who could grasp the depth of the difference between
the Protestant creeds could also adequately justify a theological reconciliation. Thus, Weber's most important theological source served
the church's political program by understanding the contrasts as
clearly as possible, precisely because only that understanding could
achieve a genuine union. Schneckenburger wrote history with a practical intent, and his analysis of the differences between Old Calvinism and Old Lutheranism of the sixteenth and seventeenth centuries, at first sight purely historical, was largely informed by an
internal polemic between Protestant denominations as it first developed in the union debate of the nineteenth century.[35] Schneckenburger developed a sharply delineated view of Protestant denomina-

34 K. B. Hundeshagen speaks of a "certain preference for the Lutheran type." RE2, 606.
35 On the topic of Schneckenburger and union, see Eduard Güder, "Vorwort des Heraus-
   gebers" in Schneckenburger, *Vergleichende Darstellung*, III–XLIII, VIIIff.

tional differences. Calvinism and Lutheranism were contrasted antithetically, a product of a nineteenth-century perspective. Schneckenburger projected his own denominational and political interests into the past. Inasmuch as Weber followed him, he accepted a notion of denominational and political differences within Protestantism in which the complex historical reality of the sixteenth and seventeenth centuries – as it appears to us today – was simplified to fit the definitional models of nineteenth-century dogmatics. New research into the denominational problems in German territories in the early modern period has shown that in the sixteenth century, there was no sharp distinction between denominations. Rather, the confessional milieus originated first during the lengthy formation of denominational identity, or in other words, through gradual "denominationalism." Especially in the realms of religious practice and devotion, the differences were much less stark between Catholicism, Lutheranism, and Calvinism than Weber suggested in line with nineteenth-century literature.

## III

How did Schneckenburger define the contrast between Calvinism and Lutheranism? He sought to find a definite relation between theological teachings and religious life. Weber also assumed an affinity between dogma and devotion. For Schneckenburger, the differences between Calvinism and Lutheranism were by no means purely doctrinal. They resulted from – in terminology borrowed from Schleiermacher – "a difference in a religious state of mind, and indeed a profound dissimilarity in the most personal sphere of devotion."[36] Christianity is not primarily doctrine, but a way of life. Theological dogma is only a secondary abstraction of Christian life or of pious self-consciousness. Thus Schneckenburger recognized a "religious psychology" behind theological doctrine that reflected the religious states of mind. From the dogmatic texts, he wanted to identify underlying states of religious consciousness. He asked how teachings reflected religious life and, conversely, what teachings meant for actual religious practice. Therefore he concentrated particularly on those doctrines that concerned the Christian subject directly, primarily the doctrines of conversion, sanctification, and salvation.[37] Methodologically, this meant that Schneckenburger understood the

36 Ibid., 52.    37 See ibid., V.

dogmatic differences between the denominations as indicators of the differences in religious ways of life. In addition to dogmatic publications by university theologians, his presentation of history was based on confessional literature, catechisms and books for religious instruction, sermons, and religious tracts.[38] There remained, of course, a persistently dogmatic perspective, the interpretation of religious practice as determined by theological doctrine.

The thesis that the Reformation secured the pious individual's rights against the institution of the church belongs to the basic models of theological self-interpretation in nineteenth-century German liberal Protestantism. Schneckenburger too claimed that the religious subjectivity of the individual, the "immediate self-consciousness,"[39] was central to Protestantism. Hence, one must reconstruct the differences between the Protestant denominations as divergent theories of subjectivity: "It seems in each case to have to do with a different original concept of self-consciousness applied to the notion of salvation."[40] On the basis of Schleiermacher's idealistic psychology, Schneckenburger distinguished three elements in the concept of subjectivity: intellect, volition, and soul. Within it, he also distinguished self-consciousness (*Selbstbewusstsein*) from the self's action (*Selbsttätigkeit*). These psychological categories distinguished between Lutheran and Calvinist religiousness in the following way: The Calvinist subject knew himself essentially as intellect and volition, whereas the Lutheran subject operated with a deeper unity of these two elements in the realm of the soul. In the language of the idealistic theories of subjectivity influenced by Schleiermacher, this association of the Lutheran spirit and "depth of soul" reads as follows: The "Lutheran teachings" appeared "to be that doctrinal body of Christianity which emerges from the standpoint of predominant self-consciousness; the Calvinist is that which emerges from the standpoint of self-activity."[41] In the Calvinist religion "the active states prevail over the passive ones,"[42] whereas in the Lutheran religion

---

38 In the *Realencyclopädie,* 606, K. B. Hundeshagen explains the following: "With tireless diligence, Schneckenburger studies the representatives of orthodox Calvinist theology and its various schools, and since he has become convinced that the spirit of the Calvinist faith comes more from the catechism, catechistic commentaries, sermon and prayer books, and other didactic books than from the creeds, he also dedicates himself, in spite of their dryness, to these readings, discovered in used bookstores far and wide with a perseverance known only to him."

39 Schneckenburger, *Vergleichende Darstellung,* 159.      40 Ibid.

41 Ibid., XXXVI.      42 Ibid., 158.

"the quiescent consciousness" dominates. By considering the way of life of religious subjects, Schneckenburger differentiated Lutheranism and Calvinism according to the scheme of activity and receptivity, production and reception.

Many of Schneckenburger's contemporaries admired the intellectual skill with which he pursued this differentiation, especially the subtleties of the particular theological doctrines and his bold attempt to draw conclusions from the dogmatic differences. Even for a highly abstract theological construct, such as the doctrine of the Three Offices of Jesus Christ, he tried to establish that existing profound differences between Lutheranism and Calvinism are the results of opposing religious psychologies. Thus it was critical that in the passages in his lectures regarding material dogma, he granted the doctrine of predestination a central position. The "variation of religious states of mind is causally linked with predestination as the effect of doctrine."[43] Predestination by no means stood in opposition to the specifically Calvinist design to master the world. It had decisively promoted and influenced the latter. The Calvinist doctrine of double election brought about an uncertainty about the state of grace. This uncertainty of salvation could only be transformed into certainty of salvation through a "proof of activity," through ethical activity.[44]

Other nineteenth-century Protestant theologians, however, challenged Schneckenburger's thesis. Karl Bernhard Hundeshagen, a Bern colleague and friend of Schneckenburger, another mediator who also taught in Switzerland, as well as numerous other Calvinist dogmatists, declared that there were no intrinsic connections between conceptions of predestination and the moral conduct of devout Calvinists, because predestination was such a highly abstract theological doctrine. The Calvinist doctrine of election was only the dogmatic construct of scholars and did not influence the piety of the people whatsoever. Weber knew of the criticism of Schneckenburger's religious-psychological interpretation of the predestination doctrine. Nevertheless, he followed this conception and adopted Schneckenburger's thesis that a distinguishing feature of Reformed religiosity, in opposition to Lutheranism, was a desire to achieve a knowledge of grace through ethical activity. To this extent, Ernst Troeltsch's contention that what was crucial to Weber's analysis of

43 Ibid.   44 Ibid., 159.

ascetic Protestantism as already set forth by Schneckenburger was correct.[45]

The very construction of *The Protestant Ethic* is characterized by a fundamental distinction between Lutheranism and Calvinism. Although Lutheranism had upgraded temporal activity, Lutheran religiosity remained traditional. It was a quietistic "submission of self" to given authorities.[46] Thus it did not contribute to the emergence of Protestant asceticism, which indirectly promoted economic modernization by furthering modern rational capitalism. In this image of traditional Lutheranism and of modernizing Calvinism, Weber follows the psychological antithesis of activity/passivity that was fundamental to Schneckenburger's construction. His interpretation of Methodism exhibited this especially clearly, for despite a broad consideration of historical material offered by other dogmatic historians, it was most decisively determined by Schneckenburger's categories. In an explicit connection with Schneckenburger's argumentation, Weber referred to the potential ambiguity of the Calvinist attempt to overcome uncertainty about the state of grace.[47] Schneckenburger emphasized that the Reformed sense of vocation did not lead exclusively to an active quest for sanctification. Methodism[48] illustrated that the "earnestness of the struggle for sanctification" could also deteriorate into "antinomian reveling in confidence or, in some character types, an insolence of spiritual arrogance."[49] Although Weber referred to the "inferior development of the sense of sin" in Meth-

---

45 "Without Weber, I certainly would not have thought of the term 'ascetic Protestantism' in such clear terms, as it was set forth by Schneckenburger and Ritschl. Incidentally, one needs only to study carefully the works of the two exceptionally astute and knowledgeable scholars to come across this notion." Ernst Troeltsch, *Soziallehren,* 950 f., note 510. See note 27.

46 For Weber's assessment of Lutheranism, especially in regard to its political consequences, see PE II, 36 f, note 74.

47 In PE II, 60, Weber writes: "The emotional character of [Methodist] religiosity does not lead therefore to an emotionalized Christianity in the manner of German Pietism. That this . . . has to do with the inferior development of the sense of sin, Schneckenburger has already demonstrated, and this has remained a persistent point in the critique of Methodism." See ibid., note 120a; there Weber says, that the "often markedly pathological character of Methodist emotion, in contrast to the relatively mild emotionalism of Pietism may . . . *perhaps* also [have to do with] a stronger ascetic penetration of life in the regions in which Methodism spread."

48 For Weber's conception of Methodism, see PE II, 57 ff. See PE II, 60 f. and ibid., note 120a.

49 Matthias Schneckenburger, *Vorlesungen über die Lehrbegriffe der kleineren protestantischen Kirchenparteien,* ed. by K. B. Hundeshagen (Frankfurt, 1863), chap. IV: Methodism, 103–151, 144. In *The Protestant Ethic,* Schneckenburger's name is incorrectly cited as J. Schneckenburger (see PE II, 59, note 115). It is, however, correctly given as M. Schneckenburger when his *Vergleichende Darstellung* is mentioned.

odists,[50] he made Schneckenburger's theological critique of Methodist piety expressly his own and used it parallel to his critique of Lutheranism. The culturally determined meaning of the "struggle for sanctification" in the theologically legitimized form of Reformed piety, above all Puritanism, became much clearer against the double background of quietistic Lutheranism and the theological perversion of Reformed piety in Methodism. From the perspective of a present-day observer, Weber's adoption of Schneckenburger's theological value judgments certainly has a problematic consequence. From the beginning, the key terms of religious psychology with which Schneckenburger described the differences between Lutheran and Calvinist piety excluded the possibility of recognizing the former's potential for modernization. Given his starting point, Weber remained fixed on a rigid antithesis, which prevented him from appreciating the potentially productive participation of the Lutheran tradition in the formation of a modern bourgeois society. His polemic against Ritschl's interpretation of Lutheranism illustrated this especially well. In explicit opposition to Schneckenburger, Ritschl interpreted Lutheran religiosity primarily in terms of the concept of vocational loyalty. Not quietism and passive submission to given rules, but ethical activism and a religious release of moral energy were, according to Ritschl, characteristic of the Lutheran tradition. Along with Schneckenburger's religious-psychological ideal types, Weber accepted particular value judgments and thus could not perceive the possible merits of Ritschl's interpretation of Luther.

## IV

Weber's inability to recognize the potential Lutheran contribution to the modern economy was illustrated especially well in his dispute with the interpretation of Lutheranism by Albrecht Ritschl, the most influential German-speaking Protestant theologian of the late nineteenth century. Weber fiercely challenged Ritschl's publications, as well as individual dogmatic histories by various Ritschl students. He based his assessment on Ritschl's major work, *Die christliche Lehre von Rechtfertigung und Versöhnung,* which first appeared in three volumes between 1870 and 1874. Weber used the partially revised third edition, published in 1889. He also was familiar with the rich three-

50 PE II, 60.

volume *Geschichte des Pietismus*,[51] the "standard work"[52] at the time, and a collection of essays by the Göttingen theologian.[53] Weber clearly appreciated "the magnificent intellectual sharpness" of the "great scholar"[54] and followed Ritschl's history of Pietism in many of its historical particulars.

Ultimately, however, Weber represented a view contrary to Ritschl's, especially with regard to the difference between Calvinist and Lutheran piety, as well as in his evaluation of the cultural implications of ascetic Protestantism. To exaggerate a bit, *The Protestant Ethic* can be considered a counterthesis to Ritschl's definition of the relationship between Lutheranism and modern society in Germany. In the notes, *The Protestant Ethic* criticizes no other author as frequently or contentiously as Ritschl.[55]

Central to this critique is the view that Ritschl's historical presentation "suffers from value judgments connected with his church politics."[56] This was especially true of Ritschl's view of Lutheranism, as Weber explained: "From the great diversity of religious thoughts and sentiments, what were valid as 'Lutheran' teachings, even for Luther himself, is determined by Ritschl's value judgments – characterized by what is perpetually valuable in Lutheranism: Lutheranism as it should have been (according to Ritschl), not always as it was."[57] Weber criticized even more sharply Ritschl's interpretation of the Anabaptists of the sixteenth century and the Pietistic reform movements of the seventeenth and eighteenth centuries. Ritschl measured Pietism and Baptism according to a theological standard that from the outset excluded an unbiased view of historical phenomena in favor of an idealized image of Luther's Reformation. For Weber, Ritschl was a philistine who was sensitive neither to the apocalyptic beliefs of the Baptists nor to the ascetic strictness of Pietism. Ritschl's critique of the Baptist movement smacked theologically of a "bourgeois point of view."[58]

51  Albrecht Ritschl, *Geschichte des Pietismus,* 3 vols. (Bonn, 1880–1886; reprint ed., Berlin, 1960).
52  PE II, 49, note 92.
53  *Gesammelte Aufsätze von Albrecht Ritschl,* ed. by. Otto Ritschl (Freiburg im Br., 1893).
54  PE II, 5, and 40, note 76.
55  See PE II, 5, 9, 21, 31, 40, 46, 47, 49, 50, 52, 61, 62, 63, 89, 91. To what extent Weber was also here influenced by Ernst Troeltsch is not apparent in Weber's text. Since the early 1890s, Troeltsch, who studied with Ritschl from 1886 until 1888, increasingly cast his critical views of the history of German Lutheranism in the form of a critique of his Göttingen professor. In its basic form, there is much agreement between Troeltsch's and Weber's critiques of Ritschl.
56  PE II, 5 and 40.     57  PE II, 6.     58  PE II, 62, note 123.

Ritschl comprehended his historical research as an integral part of his systematic program. At the same time, he developed his dogmatic position primarily in the form of an historical presentation of the central teachings of Protestantism, the doctrines of justification and expiation. Thus, in his work, the borders between the historical and the systematic dissolved. Ritschl sketched a picture of the history of Protestantism that was strongly informed by normative theological assumptions and also by political interests. He wanted to support the *Kulturkampf*,[59] the struggle against the Roman Catholic minority led by German liberals and especially the Prussian government under Bismarck, as well as the fight against the "atheistic" Social Democrats. This double political stance against Catholicism and the Social Democrats also marked his construction of history. In the conflict of world views, the writing of history had for him the function of legitimization; it was meant to assert the superiority of National-Liberal Protestantism over Catholicism and Social Democracy.

The new nation-state, the *Kaiserreich,* that emerged from the war against Catholic France in 1870–1871 could endure only on the basis of Protestant values. Catholicism and the Social Democrats were internationally oriented and represented cultural values that weakened the nation-state. Moreover, both represented forms of Christianity that had been definitively overtaken since the Reformation. In its essence, Catholicism was traditional and backward; it represented a medieval form of Christianity in which a universal church attempted to control state and culture and tried to suppress all independent civic life. Social Democracy similarly preached a world view that had also been historically overcome since the Reformation. The Socialist hope for revolution and the creation of a new world represented only a secularized late form of the utopian belief in an immanent Kingdom of God that the Anabaptists had preached in the sixteenth century.

In contrast, Protestantism was for Ritschl the principle of cultural progress. The Reformers, Martin Luther above all, developed a new meaning of Christian freedom. They provided new validity to the New Testament viewpoint that in God's universal will to mercy, man is in principle absolved as a sinner without having to produce religious or ethical achievements. Under the conditions of sin, a human

---

59 For the political dimension of Ritschl's work, see Manuel Zelger, "Nationalliberale Theologie: Albrecht Ritschl," in Friedrich Wilhelm Graf, ed., *Profile des neuzeitlichen Protestantismus*, Vol. 2 (Gütersloh, 1991).

being is not free, but is bound to his animal state and to the natural world. As one who is absolved, one knows oneself to be capable of spiritual mastery over the temporal world. Catholicism teaches a freedom from the world. In its ethics, which is hostile to the temporal world, mysticism, asceticism, and contemplation are the central values, so that turning toward God is synonymous with an escape from concrete, earthly responsibility. In contrast, Protestantism sees freedom as moral mastery of the world. It releases the state, science, art, business, and everyday civil life from the power claims of the church and teaches that temporal work is to be understood as a form of worship. For Luther, piety is realized not in a turning away from the world, but in temporal worship, respectively, in the "vocation." The monk, who tries to draw closer to God through asceticism and retreats from the everyday world, is not the ideal Christian. Genuine Christians recognize their worldly tasks as a duty inspired by God and fulfill them with religious dedication in a moral loyalty to vocation. For Ritschl, then, Protestantism was precisely the religion of progress, because he attributed a religious dignity to working in secular institutions toward ever higher levels of culture. This interpretation of freedom as an ethical mastery of the world – a legacy of the Reformation – served to justify the claim that the state was a Protestant *Kulturstaat* and that National-Liberal Protestantism had to become the dominant cultural force in the *Kaiserreich*.

In Ritschl's image of Protestantism, the confessional difference between Calvinists and Lutherans counted for much less than the shared Protestant opposition to Catholicism. Like Schneckenburger, Ritschl wanted to promote the union between Lutherans and Calvinists and to fortify the sense of unity among Protestants. At the center of his historical dogmatics lay an "essence" or "principle" of Protestantism that unified Calvinists and Lutherans and transcended all formal doctrinal differences. Even in the method of presentation, all differences were relativized in favor of the general idea of Protestantism. In individual doctrines, there existed, to be sure, significant differences between Calvinists and Lutherans. Incomparably more important, however, was a fundamental agreement central to piety and religious ethics. With regard to absolution and a new consciousness of redemption, Calvin and Zwingli followed Luther. Differences in the dogmatic educational concept were, in contrast, secondary. For Ritschl, Luther was a true modernizer whose "ethics of vocation" Calvin and Zwingli assumed.

Ritschl's interpretation of Lutheran piety was diametrically opposed to Weber's image of Lutheranism. Indeed, Weber followed Ritschl insofar as he granted Luther's conception of vocation a great historical value, and he explained the high regard for a worldly career as a central ethical contribution of all Protestant creeds. He also shared the stereotypes of the Protestant critique of Catholicism as Ritschl theologically legitimized them. For Ritschl as well as for Weber, Catholics were traditionalist, hostile to progress, and culturally "inferior." But Weber followed Schneckenburger's basic psychological dichotomy of activity/passivity in stressing a practical continuity between Catholicism and Lutheranism. Lutheranism represented a deficient form of Protestant religiosity, closer to the level of traditionalist Catholic conduct than to the ethical activity of the Calvinists. Because of his pronounced anti-Catholicism, Ritschl was, in contrast, interested in emphasizing the break between late medieval Catholicism and Luther's Reformation. He deduced from Luther's plea for a worldly vocation the claim that Lutheranism, properly understood as the original Protestantism of Luther, offered a religiosity that released high moral energies. In Ritschl's view, it was not quietism and passive self-submission that were characteristic of Lutheranism, but an ethical mastery of the world and thus the religiously motivated promotion of secular culture.

With his high regard for the cultural potential of Lutheranism, Ritschl combined a sharp critique of all Protestant movements whose piety was determined by mystical introspection and rejection of the temporal world. That Ritschl made Pietism a central focus in his historical research followed from his theological program. The historical description served as a fundamental theological critique of a Pietistic religiosity. At the same time, he pursued a political interest: As a National-Liberal, Ritschl wanted to deny Protestant legitimacy to Lutheran orthodoxy and the old, politically conservative elite. He wanted to demonstrate that the Lutheran conservatives in government and church had betrayed the spirit of the Reformation and had cultivated a religious sensibility that was basically Catholic. Ritschl saw a continuity between Pietism and Lutheran conservatism above all in the early-nineteenth-century revival movement.

Ritschl suspected the Pietism of the seventeenth and eighteenth centuries of having promoted a re-Catholicization. The Pietists had indeed understood themselves to be the legitimate heirs of Luther's Reformation and had demanded the renewal of the Protestant church

in the spirit of the Reformation. In its sweeping receptivity to mystical traditions and the new regard for asceticism, however, Pietism
presented a perversion of the Reformation's worldly religiosity. The
establishment of conventicles and small religious groups, in which
the most pious dissociated themselves from the mass of believers,
destroyed the notion of the Reformed church and of the general
priesthood of all believers. Contemplation, emotional bliss, and
mystical devotion led to a new notion of good works, to the illusion
that absolution could be attained through religious deeds and asceticism. The tendency to shut oneself off from the world in small
religious groups, conventicles, and, in effect, in the community of
the few truly pious, contradicted the Reformation's concept of vocation. Thus, Pietism was at its core a regression to Catholicism. This
was especially true of reformed Pietism. In the Pietistic reform
movement, Ritschl saw no bearers of historical progress – rather,
only the powers of persistence. Thus, the diametric opposition between Ritschl's and Weber's interpretations of Lutheranism is paral-
leled by a sharp contrast in the cultural meaning of ascetic Protestantism. Ritschl constructed a continuity between Catholicism and
ascetic Protestantism. Conversely, Weber saw Lutheranism as determined by continuity with Catholic traditionalism. For him, ascetic
Protestantism presented the single consistent Protestant antithesis to
Catholic religiosity. This contrast in historical interpretation also expressed a deep political difference. Ritschl wanted to overcome the
integration crisis of German society by an internal renewal of
Lutheranism. He proclaimed a patriotic Lutheran bourgeoisie, oriented to the original principle of Luther's Reformation, to be the
most important force of cultural advancement. Conversely, Weber
saw the Lutheran tradition as the power that prevented the political
emancipation of the German bourgeoisie and perpetuated the bias
toward traditionalism and authoritarianism. For him, political modernization and social progress exist only in opposition to Lutheranism.

Since the time of Troeltsch and Weber, the limits of Ritschl's image
of history have been recognized in Pietism research. His sweeping
critique of Pietistic religiosity, the thesis of regression to Catholicism, serves as a dogmatic construct that does no justice to the com-
plexity of historical reality. To this extent, Weber was right in his
critique of Ritschl's "religious-political value judgments." This does
not, however, mean that Weber himself gave a purely objective his-

torical account, free from his own value judgments. The intensity of his polemic against Ritschl reveals the great extent to which his concept of Protestantism was guided by certain value judgments. In fact, in one decisive respect, Ritschl's concept of history corresponded more to historical reality than Weber's view.

Ritschl continually emphasized that a close communal relationship was fundamental to all Christian religiosity. There can be certainty of grace for the individual only if it is mediated through the community of believers. Therefore, his history is strongly oriented to community and church. This emphasis on the whole community explains his sharp rejection of Protestant sects and small religious groups in Pietism.

By contrast, on the basis of his psychological categories and the central place of religious subjectivity, Schneckenburger defined the consciousness of redemption independent of any reference to community. It is true that Schneckenburger was fascinated by the social ethic of the Calvinists. What impressed him about Bern was precisely the tight interwovenness of church life and political life, as well as the system of social welfare for the elderly and the sick that originated in the application of the spirit of brotherly love. But according to the conceptual structure of his argumentation, Schneckenburger represented a religious individualism. He differentiated Lutheran and Calvinist religiosity exactly according to how the respective relationship of the individual to God was determined. The community ranked far below the pious individuals. Ritschl rejected Schneckenburger's position precisely because of this orientation to the religious individual. It seems likely that Weber incorporated Schneckenburger because of his affirmation of individualism and rejected Ritschl because of his orientation to community. But is Schneckenburger's and Weber's image of the individual worshipper, isolated and drawn into himself before the hidden God of the dogma of predestination, historically plausible?[60]Do not communal worship or the individual's ties with the religious community or the worshippers' companionship play any role in gaining a consciousness of redemption? Is not the religious life in Protestant sects characterized by a high level of communal pressure? Is not the vaunted individualism that characterizes Schneckenburger's and Weber's conception of the worshipper more likely a specific product of the nineteenth century?

---

60 See Lehmann, "Asketischer Protestantismus."

Such questions carry special weight against the background of the controversies over Ritschl's communitarian theology as they were conducted in Weber's time. Above all, the theologians of the *religionsgeschichtliche Schule,* and here especially Ernst Troeltsch, moved the relationship between the individual and the community of believers to the center of their critique of Ritschl. They argued for the right to religious individualism. Is the image that Weber draws of the pious only a construct of the liberal Protestantism that shaped him even in his agnostic distance from the beliefs of the institutional Lutheran church? Is his high regard for the heroic individual the "religious-political value judgment" that gives definition to his image of history?

## V

In the past few years, the debate over *The Protestant Ethic* in English literature has turned mainly on the question of the validity of Weber's historical judgments. A number of writers have pointed out how questionable many of Weber's conclusions are in light of recent findings. Conversely, some Weber apologists have appeared on the scene and undertaken the task of defending his every historical deduction.

If one takes the outlined historical context as one's major point of reference, then this conflict appears less productive. If, in interpreting *The Protestant Ethic,* one focuses on the German theological literature used by Weber, then the question of how correct Weber's individual historical interpretations are becomes relatively uninteresting. Instead, the methodological problems of his analysis come to the fore. M. Rainer Lepsius has called attention to the strong degree to which Weber's sociological analysis depended upon the incorporation of specialized knowledge from different cultural fields;[61] the sociologist of culture remains "dependent on the experts for their cultural inventories, and yet must be able to reformulate their results in such a way that they are useful for his kind of questions. In the process, Weber himself acquired a wealth of knowledge about these fields."

*The Protestant Ethic* demonstrates that Weber became involved in

---

61 M. Rainer Lepsius, "Interessen und Ideen. Die Zurechnungsproblematik bei Max Weber," in Friedhelm Neidhardt, M. Rainer Lepsius, and Johannes Weiss, eds., *Kultur und Gesellschaft,* Sonderheft 27, *Kölner Zeitschrift für Soziologie und Sozialpsychologie* (1986), 20–31. Reprinted in Lepsius, *Interessen, Ideen und Institutionen* (Opladen, 1990), 34.

theological discourse more than any other sociologist of the century. Can one then understand the program of *The Protestant Ethic* at all without becoming involved in this specialized discourse? Being aware of the theological discourse that informed Weber's research allows us at least to dedramatize the debate over the historical adequacy of his analysis. The question of the hermeneutic power of disclosure in Weber's main categories is probably more productive than are the controversies about specific historical claims. Taking the specialized disciplinary context seriously protects Weber and his interpreters from ahistorical critiques. How can a level of knowledge about the theology and religiosity of ascetic Pietism be expected from Weber that even the experts, the German theologians, did not possess?

# 2

# The Thesis before Weber:
# an Archaeology

PAUL MÜNCH

The thesis of a relation between Protestant ethics and the spirit of capitalism has never gone out of fashion since Max Weber wrote his fascinating articles in the years 1904–1905.[1] The discussion, since the first reviews and Weber's rejoinders,[2] offers a highly contradictory picture, as does the entire debate, which now shows signs of reviving.[3] The whole discourse seems to go around in a circle, despite all progress in detail.

This persistent fascination results, above all, from the fact that the interdisciplinary discussion never really went far enough. From the beginning, the party of convinced Weberians, mainly recruited from among sociologists, faced irreconcilable opposition from a party· of professed Weber critics who came from different historical camps.[4] The numbing discussion shows some of the traits of that fruitless casuistry popularly called "scholasticism." The struggle sometimes amounts almost to a war between "believers" and "infidels." Some sociologists, who see their subject as a social science without any

Because of space limitations, this essay is only a first step into a neglected field of research. We intend to remind scholars of a discourse lost in the present discussion of Weber. Not all the nuances of this discourse can be shown, only its rough contours. A detailed study of Germany is in preparation. I would like to thank Hamide Azis (Tübingen) and especially my colleague, Dr. Rainer Walz (Siegen), for much assistance in translating the manuscript.

1 First published in *Archiv für Sozialwissenschaft und Sozialpolitik* 20/21 (1905); reprinted in Max Weber, *Die protestantische Ethik I. Eine Aufsatzsammlung*, 3rd ed., ed. by Johannes Winckelmann (Munich, 1973).
2 See Max Weber, *Die protestantische Ethik II. Kritiken und Antikritiken*, 2d ed., ed. by Johannes Winckelmann (Munich, 1972).
3 See *Telos* 1988, 1989; *British Journal of Sociology* 1988; *Sociology* 1989.
4 See Ephraim Fischoff, "Die protestantische Ethik und der Geist des Kapitalismus. Die Geschichte einer Kontroverse," in Weber, *Die protestantische Ethik II*, 346–379; see also Paul Münch, "Welcher Zusammenhang besteht zwischen Konfession und ökonomischem Verhalten? Max Webers These im Lichte der historischen Forschung," in Hans-Georg Wehling, ed., *Konfession – eine Nebensache? Politische, soziale und kulturelle Ausprägungen religiöser Unterschiede in Deutschland* (Stuttgart, 1984), 58–74.

historical background, evidently know little about the cultural, social, and economic history of early modern times, unlike Weber and
his contemporaries. For these ahistorical sociologists, capitalism is
the inseparable reverse of the Calvinist coin. Some of these opponents do not argue from the historically variegated Calvinism, but
only from Weber's ideal type. Starting from this ideal type, they
come to regard Calvinism as the breeding ground not only of economic but also of political and scientific progress – a conclusion for
which Weber is only indirectly responsible. In contrast, many historians have partially or completely rejected Weber's thesis, above all
because they consider his method of the ideal type, with its attractive
possibility of universalizing generalization, to be a sociological idol.[5]
German historians of early modern times have adopted Weber's
methodology and his sociology of domination in the realm of constitutional history, but they have neglected his sociology of religion.[6]

The situation seems confused. On the one hand, several disciplines
pursue a highly ramified discourse that can hardly be popularized.
On the other hand, we can observe a naive popular reception of the
Weber thesis that is not at all influenced by the scholarly discourse.
This popular reception misunderstands the relation between cap-
italism and Protestantism as an automatic causal nexus.

At present, the debate also is burdened by additional political implications. Against the background of the dramatic decay of the states
of "real socialism" in Eastern Europe, Max Weber's thesis can gain
new meaning outside the realm of social science. In the United
States, Weber has always been claimed as the prophet of Western
values *against Marxism*. I fear that the canonization of Weber as a
classic of sociology and a "sociological giant" (Robert K. Merton)
could gain an additional hagiographical dimension through the present political constellation. This process might even be furthered by
the German complete edition of Weber's works (*Max Weber Gesamtausgabe*). Such a process could restrict the sensitivity that is required
for the reception of Weber's highly nuanced Protestantism-capitalism

5  "The attraction of the universalizing generalization has, as so often, proved too much for the
   skeptical spirit which alone saves the historian from falling into the pitfalls dug by his own,
   very necessary, imagination. In the face of the long and ramifying controversy, sadness is the
   only proper feeling: sadness at so much misguided effort, and sadness at the willingness of
   historians to worship the graven images set up by the sociologist." (Geoffrey Elton, *Reformation Europe, 1517–1559* (New York, 1963), 318.
6  See, however, Hartmut Lehmann, *Das Zeitalter des Absolutismus. Gottesgnadentum und
   Kriegsnot* (Stuttgart, 1980), esp. 144–52; Hartmut Lehmann, "Pietismus und Wirtschaft in
   Calw am Anfang des 18. Jahrhunderts," *Zeitschrift für württembergische Landesgeschichte* 31
   (1972): 249–277.

thesis and make his invention look even more like a patented and proprietary device than has been true so far.

In this situation, it is useful to recall the context of the traditions in which Weber developed his thesis. Analysis would stop short if it examined only the contemporary roots of the thesis. If the editors of his writings on the sociology of religion indeed succeed in tracking down Weber's contemporary sources – that is, the influences and borrowing that can be found in his work and in the "Ego documents" – they will still be able to identify only those tracks that the giant clearly left behind. We will never know whether there were traces that he wanted to cover for reasons only he knew. We know even less about the unconscious influences and deep-seated ideas of his time that Weber could not evade. Whoever wants to grasp the deeper dimensions of Weber's thesis must look at traditions now buried. These traditions advanced theories about the relation between religion and economy since the religious confessionalization of the sixteenth century. The focus of this essay, then, is upon the Weber thesis before Weber; upon the archaeology of the discourse on religion and economy, on economic progress, and Protestantism from the sixteenth to the nineteenth centuries. Max Weber by no means stood at the starting point of this discussion. At most, he reinforced an historical thread of argumentation with new and original ideas. Weber's isolation of the religious factor led to vexations that disappear only if we consider his restricted intentions: He wanted to show only one causal nexus; later additions should follow and unravel other influences and reciprocal effects. Those additions were never realized.[7]

As a dwarf "on the shoulders of the giant,"[8] I seek to show some of the buried traditions that perceived a relation between religion and economy long before Weber. There was a widely ramifying discourse on confession and economy whose extent has not yet been clarified. Hardly anyone has tried to relate the features of this discussion to the Weber thesis so as to reconstruct the prehistory of *The Protestant Ethic and the Spirit of Capitalism.*[9]

7 See Münch, "Welcher Zusammenhang," 67.
8 See Robert K. Merton, *On the Shoulders of Giants – Auf den Schultern von Riesen* (Frankfurt, 1980).
9 Some hints appear in Wilhelm Schwer, "Der Kapitalismus und das wirtschaftliche Schicksal der deutschen Katholiken," in Wilhelm Schwer and Franz Müller, eds., *Des deutsche Katholizismus im Zeitalter des Kapitalismus* (Augsburg, 1932), 7–74 and 209–215; Reinhard Bendix, "The Protestant Ethic – Revisited," in idem and Guenther Roth, eds., *Scholarship and Partisanship* (Berkeley, 1971), 299–307. See also *Religious Thought and Economic Society. Four*

From the onset of the debate, ecclesiastical and theological thinkers participated in this discourse. In the age of mercantilism and cameralism, economic writers eagerly took it up in the interest of their states. Then, during the Enlightenment, it became connected with the intellectual discussion about the social function of religion. In the nineteenth century in Germany the discourse hardened into the stereotypes of the German industrious Protestant and the lazy, ultramontanist, politically unreliable Catholic. Though the factors and arguments of this discourse intermingle in a complex way, I try to separate the tracks of the discussion and describe them individually. First of all, the church – that is, the theologians – have their say, then the representatives of state and economy. After that, I trace the evolution of confessional stereotypes in the context of the new public discussions since the late eighteenth century. Finally, I summarize the specific achievements of the whole early modern discourse on religion and economy.

As we know today, the Christian denominations that have come into existence since the sixteenth century stood for a traditionalist economic ethic. Lutheran, Reformed, and Catholic theologians differed very little on the question of the permissibility of taking interest, the doctrine of calling, or criticism of the accumulation of wealth, and they agreed that a human being is only in a very limited sense capable of independent action. Humanistic anthropology, assuming the special "dignity of man," emphatically stressed the autonomous power of human creativity, in sharp distinction to the rest of nature.[10] The Christian theologians, by contrast, generally attributed a reduced influence to human agency. The idea that human toil can be profitable only with God's blessing stood in diametric opposition to the humanistic motto *"Labor vincit omnia"* ("Work conquers all"). All denominations believed that it was God rather than humankind who in the last instance was always responsible for success.[11] Just as

---

*Chapters of an Unfinished Work by Jacob Viner,* ed. Jaques Melitz and Donald Winch (Durham, N.C., 1978), chapter four ("Protestantism and the Rise of Capitalism"), esp. 159ff. ("Explanations Prior to Weber of Protestant Economic Superiority").

10 As an excellent example, see Pico della Mirandola, *On the Dignity of Man* (Indianapolis, 1982).

11 See, for example, "Aber doch also/das keiner so nerrisch sey/der darumb dencken wollte/ das yhn seine geschigligkeit/vleis vnd arbeit neere ond reich mache/Denn solches gar ein Heidnischer/glaubloser/ia gantz vnd gar ein gotloser vnd abgöttischer yrthum ist. Denn gleich wie Gott gepeut/das man arbeiten/vnd durch arbeit narung suchen sol/also verpeut er auch/das auff seine arbeit niemand vertrawen/noch sich darauff verlassen/auch davon nichts rhümen sol/als were es seine hand/die yhn ernerete/Sondern sol wissen/wie das Evangelion sagt/es sey Gottes benedeyung vnd segen vom hymel herab/davon wir

Christian belief made almost everything dependent on the blessing of God, by turning this maxim completely around, it was presumed that those who stood outside the accepted confessions must logically have gained their economic success with the aid of God's antithesis, the devil. The accusation that intolerance toward confessional outsiders damaged business was countered by two pastors from the Netherlands using the question "Must now Satan instead of God provide us with the profit?"[12]

Despite a common Christian belief in the fundamental dependence of economic success or failure upon transcendent contexts, from the beginning the confessional reforms had direct and indirect practical economic results. Protestant theologians permitted the secularization of church property and rejected holy orders, which had been founded upon the *consilia evangelica* and were now branded as unproductive. The secularization of monasteries and the abolition of celibacy were measures that deeply affected social and economic life, even if the arguments of the reformers were based on eternal salvation and not on worldly profit. The reduction of the number of holy days, which resulted from the rejection of the veneration of saints and was carried out most successfully by the Reformed churches, assumed particular significance.[13] As early as 1597, in his "Treatise of the Vocations or Callings of Men," the Puritan English clergyman William Perkins put not only monks and mendicant friars but also Catholics ("Papists in general") in the category of rogues, beggars, and vagabonds because they added fifty-two further saints' days to the fifty-two sabbaths appointed to God, thus spending "more than a quarter of a year in rest and idleness."[14] Perkins deduced economic

erneret werden / wie Christus vnser herr leret Matthei. 6." Justus Menius, *An die hochgeborne Fürstin / fraw Sibille Hertzogin zu Sachsen / Oeconomia Christiana / das ist / von Christlicher haushaltung. Mit einer schönen Vorrede D. Martini Luther* (1529), quoted by Paul Münch, ed., *Ordnung, Fleiss und Sparsamkeit. Texte und Dokumente zur Entstehung der "bürgerlichen Tugenden"* (Munich, 1984), 48.

12 "Moet nu de Satan ons in plaets van Godt gewin toesturen?" In *Een schoon tractaet, des godtgeleerden Theodori Bezae, van de straffe, welcke de wereltlycke Overichkeyt over de ketters behoort te oeffenen . . . overgheset . . . door de Dienaers des G. Woorts binnen Sneeck* (Franeker, 1601), quoted by Erich Hassinger, "Wirtschaftliche Motive und Argumente für religiöse Duldsamkeit im 16. und 17. Jahrhundert," in Ernst Walter Zeeden, ed., *Gegenreformation* (Darmstadt, 1973), 333; see also Wiebe Bergsma, "Calvinismus in Friesland um 1600 am Beispiel der Stadt Sneek," *Archiv für Reformationsgeschichte* 80 (1989): 275–276.

13 See the article "Feste und Feiertage," in *Theologische Realenzyklopädie* (Berlin and New York, 1983), 11, esp. 124–132; see also Paul Münch, "Volkskultur und Calvinismus. Zu Theorie und Praxis der 'reformatio vitae' während der 'Zweiten Reformation,'" in Heinz Schilling, ed., *Die reformierte Konfessionalisierung in Deutschland. Das Problem der "Zweiten Reformation"* (Gütersloh, 1986), 291–307.

14 Quoted by Christopher Hill, *Puritanism and Revolution. Studies in Interpretation of the English Revolution of the 17th Century* (London, 1965), 226.

loss clearly and directly from deviating religious practice. From then on, confessional enemies no longer appeared only as adversaries in the creed but also experienced a basic social stigmatization as a pack of unproductive outcasts. Adherents of the old church, who had been blamed for the partial misuse of money by sending it to Rome, had to bear the verdict of inefficiency. Critical comments about lazy monks developed into the negative stereotype of the lazy Catholic. "The fact that Protestantism was a cheaper religion than Catholicism became a seventeenth-century commonplace."[15]

As a result of ecclesiastical reforms and in reaction to the Protestant prescription, the Roman Catholic Church reduced its opulent calendar of holy days in the centuries that followed. It adopted the idea that economic success depended upon a certain practice of piety. In 1642, Pope Urban VIII limited the number of feasts to thirty-four, including regionally or locally celebrated feasts of patron saints. Even more drastic were the reductions within the framework of the Catholic Enlightenment during the eighteenth century, which sought a general and rigid limitation of traditional forms of piety.[16] These reductions led to bitter controversies within the Roman Catholic Church. Ultimately the Catholic states abolished a whole series of traditional feasts, reduced others in length, and combined still others. State governments directed this process, for it supported their cameralistic interest. As a result, the Lutheran feast calendar also saw reductions. The economic argument dominated the struggle among the confessions, as well as the church–state struggle for power. Enlightened theologians in all camps criticized the superstitious remnants of traditional practices of piety, practices that were certainly far more prevalent within Catholicism. Thus these theologians found themselves directly or indirectly in accord with the state's position, which viewed the traditional practice of religion as a useless waste of time that unduly limited the modern, rationally organized economic process.[17] Influenced by teachings of the Enlightenment, theologians from all camps defined the social role of the "Christian in the world" in a very similar manner, despite their dogmatic differences in indi-

15  Ibid., 43.
16  See A. Brittinger, *Die bayerische Verwaltung und das volksfromme Brauchtum im Zeitalter der Aufklärung* (Munich, 1938); Barbara Goy, *Aufklärung und Volksfrömmigkeit in den Bistümern Würzburg und Bamberg* (Würzburg, 1969); Christoph Dipper, "Volksreligiosität und Obrigkeit im 18. Jahrhundert," in Wolfgang Schieder, ed., *Volksreligiosität in der modernen Sozialgeschichte* (Göttingen, 1986), 73–96.
17  See the following discussion on pp. 63ff.

vidual points. The decent, orderly, industrious, and content citizen, who quietly and steadily went about his other business, represented the ideal of the good Christian for all the confessions.

On this basis, in the early nineteenth century the atmosphere among the confessions remained, for the time being, tolerant, relaxed, indeed marked by mutual respect. In many places the Lutheran and Reformed churches formed Protestant unions, and Catholics frequently participated, with floral decorations and bell ringing, in the Reformation feasts of their Protestant fellow Christians. "This active civil tolerance regarded the confessional churches as competing religious associations that also invited non-members in the respective town to their founder's day feasts" (Johannes Burkhardt).[18]

But parallel to this apparent tolerance, since the end of the eighteenth century confessional prejudices began to build, which would develop in an even more complex way in the nineteenth century.[19] The journalism of the Enlightenment drew a dark picture of the Catholic parts of the German Empire, above all in the ecclesiastical territories.[20] The polemical stereotypes of the Reformation period experienced a renaissance in which confessional borders were not of only minor importance. The front lines were primarily determined by the perceived progress of enlightenment in a given country. For the Reformed theologian Johann Ludwig Ewald, writing in 1790, the degree of education was the standard according to which he ranked the European states into a hierarchy in which England, Prussia, and

18  "Diese aktive bürgerliche Toleranz verstand die Konfessionen als konkurrierende Religionsvereine, denen auch die Nichtmitglieder in der jeweiligen Stadt zu ihren Stiftungsfesten die Ehre gaben." Johannes Burkhardt, "Reformations- und Lutherfeiern. Die Verbürgerlichung der reformatorischen Jubiläumskultur," in Dieter Düding, Peter Friedemann, and Paul Münch, eds., *Öffentliche Festkultur. Politische Feste in Deutschland von der Aufklärung bis zum Ersten Weltkrieg* (Reinbek, 1988), 221–222. See also ibid., 222: "Den Höhepunkt aufgeklärter Urbanität bezeichnet der nach der Volksbewegung nachgeholte Leipziger Festzug zum Konfessionsjubiläum von 1830: 'Der feierliche Zug durch die Stadt wurde eröffnet durch den Rabbiner mit der Thore, dem die Patres der katholischen und der Archimandrit der griechischen Kirche folgten; danach schritten die Geistlichen der lutherischen Kirche und die Pastoren der reformierten Kirche, und aus dem Auge so mancher Guten floss eine Thräne der himmlischen Freude, als die würidigen Diener des Vaters im Himmel so vereint, als von gleichen Gesinnungen beseelt, dahin walleten'."

19  See the following discussion on pp. 69ff.

20  See the contemporary writings, above all Friedrich Karl Freiherr von Moser, *Uber die Regierung der geistlichen Staaten in Deutschland* (Frankfurt and Leipzig, 1787); Joseph Edler von Sartori, "Gekrönte statistische Abhandlungen über die Mängel in der Regierungsverfassung der geistlichen Wahlstaaten, und von den Mitteln, solchen abzuhelfen," in *Journal von und für Deutschland* 4 (1787), 2. u. 4. Stück and 6. u. 7. Stück; for further contemporary writings see Schwer, "Der Kapitalismus," 209; see also footnote 54, this essay.

the Netherlands received first, second, and fourth place, and the Catholic states of Tuscany, Spain, Portugal, and the Papal State took the last ranks. That France had second place shows that for Ewald education was clearly more important than confession, even if the confessional focus never disappeared.[21]

There is still some dispute as to which side first revived the confessional controversy in the nineteenth century. Protestant historians impute this revival to the Catholics or, more exactly, to the ultramontanist changes of the church and its new forms of popular piety after the 1840s. They regard the *Syllabus of Errors* in the appendix to then encyclical *Quanta cura* of Pope Pius IX in 1864 as a furious challenge to the modern world.[22] The Roman Catholic side, however, blames the large-scale dissolution of the ecclesiastic territories at the beginning of the nineteenth century for the cultural inferiority of the Catholic areas in Germany and for the aggravation of the confessional climate.[23] Catholic scholars still advance this explanation today. The national question became the pivot of confessional dissent. Ever since the three-hundredth anniversary of Luther's theses in 1817, Martin Luther has been celebrated as a German patriot.[24] During the *Kulturkampf,* Protestants claimed the word *deutsch* (German) for Luther, the "most German of Germans," and for his Reformation.[25] The Protestant usurpation of the positive characteristics of diligence and sense of duty associated with the German national character excluded Catholics from the German stereotyped self-image and placed them on the national sidelines: *Catholic* became synonymous with un-German, ultramontane, uncivilized, and lazy.[26] The *Kulturkampf* thus latched on to the typology that had originated in the eighteenth century, but beyond that reactivated in

21 Johann Ludwig Ewald, *Über Volksaufklärung; ihre Gränzen und Vortheile* [. . .] (Berlin, 1790) and the diagram in Münch, *Ordnung, Fleiss und Sparsamkeit,* 282–283.

22 For example, Thomas Nipperdey, *Deutsche Geschichte 1800–1866. Bürgerwelt und starker Staat* (Munich, 1983), 410–413, quotations 411 and 413.

23 See, for example, Heribert Raab, "Auswirkungen der Säkularisation auf Bildungswesen, Geistesleben und Kunst im katholischen Deutschland," in idem., *Reich und Kirche in der frühen Neuzeit* (Freiburg and Schweiz, 1989), 401–433; see also idem., "Geistige Entwicklungen und historische Ereignisse im Vorfeld der Säkularisierung," in ibid., 367–399.

24 See Lutz Winkler, *Martin Luther als Bürger und Patriot. Das Reformationsjubiläum von 1817 und der politische Protestantismus des Wartburgfestes* (Lübeck and Hamburg, 1969).

25 See Burkhardt, "Reformations- und Lutherfeiern," 225; see also Hartmut Lehmann, "Martin Luther als deutscher Nationalheld," *Luther* 55 (1984): 53–65.

26 See Heribert Raab, "Kirchengeschichte im Schlagwort," in idem., *Reich und Kirche,* 459–529; most important is Christel Köhle-Herzinger, *Evangelisch-katholisch. Untersuchungen zu konfessionellem Vorurteil und Konflikt im 19. und 20. Jahrhundert vornehmlich am Beispiel Württembergs* (Tübingen, 1976).

almost all areas the excessive interconfessional polemics of the Reformation, and thus also the political and economic dynamite that had lain dormant. When a Thuringian Protestant clergyman in 1883, on the occasion of the Reformation feast, called upon the assembled crowd to sing the *Wacht am Rhein "gegen Rom,"*[27] this meant a direct renaissance of early reformist sentiments against curial fiscalism and the drain of German funds to Rome, which had been deplored throughout the *Gravamina der deutschen Nation.* In this aggressive climate, militant *Streitschriften* such as the *Flugschriften des evangelischen Bundes* (since 1886) and its Catholic, no less intolerant, analog, flourished. The defamatory writings of the Jesuits, Ludwig von Hammerstein and Franz Xaver Brors, and of their Protestant opponents, Paul Tschackert, Friedrich Hummel, and many others, exemplified the loss of enlightened tolerance as well as the intellectual lethargy of the economic argument.[28]

During the early modern period, the restrictive economic ethics of the different denominations lost ground to the increasingly autonomous state and the economic sector. In the early period, theologians had attempted, certainly not always successfully, to subordinate "life in the world" to their teachings. Since the Enlightenment, both state and economy had emancipated themselves from the transcendent relations and established themselves as autonomous exponents of a new, confessionally neutral discourse. This process fundamentally redefined the connection between religion and economy. The social role of the Christian confessions now seemed mostly bound to the interest of the states.

At the end of the Middle Ages, the German Empire, the territorial states, and the towns tried to solve economic problems with religious restrictions. Even before the Reformation, they began to regulate the pressing problem of poverty in order to control its most detrimental

---

27 Burkhardt, "Reformations- und Lutherfeiern," 226.
28 See especially Paul Tschackert, *Evangelische Polemik gegen die römische Kirche* (Gotha, 1885); Ludwig von Hammerstein, *Konfession und Sittlichkeit. Replik auf die Broschüre: "Konfessionelle Bilanz oder: wie urtheilt der Jesuitenpater von Hammerstein über die Unsittlichkeit (Selbstmord, uneheliche Geburten, Prostitution) unter den Konfessionen. Von einem Deutschen"* (Trier, 1893); [Anonymous], *Die Protestanten – doch unsittlicher!? Vom Verfasser der Konfessionellen Bilanz. Resultat einer Kontroverse mit Jesuitenpater v. Hammerstein* (Marburg, 1893); Ludwig von Hammerstein, *Katholizismus und Protestantismus* (Trier, 1894); Franz Xaver Brors, *Moderne A.B.C. fuer Katholiken aller Stände. Kurze Antworten auf die modernen Angriffe gegen die Katholische Kirche* (Kevelaer, 1902), especially the entries on *Amerikanismus, Arbeit, Armut, Ascese, Bettelorden, Fortschritt, Inferiorität, Katholizismus, Mönche* in J. Burg, *Kontrovers-Lexikon. Die konfessionellen Streitfragen zwischen Katholiken und Protestanten. Eine Antwort auf protestantische Angriffe* (Essen, 1904).

social consequences. By a flood of legal restrictions, the secular authorities tried to exclude all beggars capable of work from poor relief.[29] The measures of Catholic and Protestant towns differed only slightly.[30] In the end, able-bodied beggars were put into houses of correction and workhouses, in Protestant towns since the sixteenth century, in Catholic states since the eighteenth century at the latest.[31] The quick appropriation of ecclesiastical property by Protestant princes showed to what degree they were prepared to use the economic resources of the church in the state's interest. Reforming princes and Protestant authorities agreed completely in their eagerness to halt the flow of money to Rome and to free property from mortmain. This agreement even survived disputes about the details of how to use the money. The problem of tolerating religious minorities[32] became the touchstone of orthodox confessional principles, in particular the principle of territorial confessional conformity.[33] Opinions differed on whether confessional dissidents were to be tolerated according to their usefulness to the economy.[34] As a rule, state authorities carried out their settlement programs, regardless of whatever stance the theologians took. As early as the mid-sixteenth century, Mennonites from the Netherlands found a new home in the Weichsel Valley because of their special expertise in hydraulic technology and, it seems, even with the approval of the Catholic episcopate. Count Ernst II of Schaumburg settled Reformed church members, Mennonites, Catholics, and Jews in Altona – against the protests of the Lutheran clergy. With the founding of the towns of

29  Hans Maier, *Die ältere deutsche Staats- und Verwaltungslehre. Ein Beitrag zur politischen Wissenschaft in Deutschland*, 2d ed. (Munich, 1980); Peter Preu, *Polizeibegriff und Staatszwecklehre. Die Entwicklung des Polizeibegriffs durch die Rechts- und Staatswissenschaft des 18. Jahrhunderts* (Göttingen, 1983).
30  See Thomas Fischer, *Städtische Armut und Armenfürsorge im 15. und 16. Jahrhundert. Sozialgeschichtliche Untersuchungen am Beispiel der Städte Basel, Freiburg i.Br. und Strassburg* (Göttingen, 1979).
31  See Christophe Sachsse and Florian Tennstedt, *Geschichte der Armenfürsorge in Deutschland. Vom Spätmittelalter bis zum 1. Weltkrieg* (Stuttgart, 1980), 113–125, 342–346; Adalbert Nagel, *Armut im Barock* (Weingarten, 1986); Bernhard Stier, *Fürsorge und Disziplinierung im Zeitalter des Absolutismus* (Sigmaringen, 1988).
32  See Joseph Lecler, *Histoire de la tolérance au siècle de la Réforme* (Paris, 1955); Henry Kamen, *The Rise of Toleration* (London, 1967); Heinrich Lutz, ed., *Zur Geschichte der Toleranz und Religionsfreiheit* (Darmstadt, 1977); Hans R. Guggisberg, *Religiöse Toleranz. Dokumente zur Geschichte einer Forderung* (Stuttgart, 1987).
33  See Klaus Schreiner, "Rechtgläubigkeit als 'Band der Gesellschaft' und 'Grundlage des Staates,'" in Martin Brecht and Reinhard Schwarz, eds., *Bekenntnis und Einheit der Kirche. Studien zum Konkordienbuch,* (Stuttgart, 1980), 351–379.
34  For the following, see Hassinger, "Wirtschaftliche Motive."

Hanau (1597),[35] Glückstadt on the Lower Elbe (1617), and Friedrichstadt on the Eider (1621), there arose in the seventeenth century additional sanctuaries for members of religious minorities. Flemings and Dutch were even able to found a Catholic parsonage on the island of Nordstrand because of their special dike-building capability. The Würzburg prince-bishop Philipp von Schönborn granted to the Lutherans of Kitzingen the right to exercise their religion in public, above all for economic reasons.[36] A series of states (England; the Netherlands; Switzerland; in the Reich, above all, Brandenburg, Saxony, Württemberg, and Hesse-Kassel) profited from the handicraft, trade, and manufacturing knowledge of the French Huguenots who fled Louis XIV in 1685.[37] Their contemporaries were convinced that the new subjects increased the wealth of German electors and princes.[38]

The principle of territorial confessional unity was broken again and again after the sixteenth century, not only for reasons of state but also for reasons of economic utilitarianism. Economic motives led to

35  Heinrich Bott, *Gründung und Anfänge der Neustadt Hanau 1596–1620* (Marburg, 1970).
36  See Ernst Walter Zeeden, "Ein landesherrliches Toleranzedikt aus dem 17. Jahrhundert. Der Gnadenbrief Philipps von Schönborn für die Stadt Kitzingen (1650)," *Historisches Jahrbuch* 103 (1983): 158–159; see also Walter Grossmann, "Städtisches Wachstum und religiöse Toleranzpolitik am Beispiel Neuwied," *Archiv für Kulturgeschichte* 62–63 (1980–1981): 207–232.
37  See Heinz Duchhardt, ed., *Der Exodus der Hugenotten. Die Aufhebung des Edikts von Nantes 1685 als europäisches Ereignis* (Cologne and Vienna, 1985); Rudolf von Thadden, ed., *Die Hugenotten: 1685–1985* (Munich, 1985); *300 Jahre Hugenotten in Hessen. Herkunft und Flucht, Aufnahme und Assimilation, Wirkung und Ausstrahlung* (Kassel, 1985); Willi Stubenvoll, *Die deutschen Hugenottenstädte* (Frankfurt, 1990).
38  The Duchess Elizabeth Charlotte of Orléans wrote to her aunt Sophie of Hannover on the Huguenots on September 23, 1699: "Mons. Colbert soll gesagt haben, dass viel untertanen der Könige und fürsten reichtum seye, wollte deswegen, daß alles sich heuraten sollte und kinder kriegen: also werden diese neue untertanen der teutschen Kurfürsten und fürsten reichtum werden." *Briefe der Lieselotte von der Pfalz*, ed. and introduced by Helmuth Kiesel (Frankfurt, 1981), 127; see also Guggisberg, *Religiöse Toleranz*, 194, note 2. In 1801 the enlightened writer Garlieb Merkel described the advantages Hamburg had gained from the reception of religious refugees from the Netherlands, Spain, and Portugal since the sixteenth century. About the Huguenots he wrote: "Als Ludwig XIV. die reformierten Protestanten aus Frankreich vertrieb, zogen sie in grossen Scharen nach Hamburg und erboten sich, den damals wüsten Platz, den jetzt die Georgsvorstadt einnimmt, zu bebauen, wenn man ihnen erlauben wolle, ein Bethaus zu besitzen. Die Prediger erhoben sich keifend dagegen, und bei den damaligen inneren Unruhen der Stadt war der Magistrat ausserstande, seine weislich mildere Gesinnung geltend zu machen. Die Fremdlinge erhielten eine abschlägige Antwort und zogen hin, Brandenburg zu bereichern. Hätten sie außer ihrer Industrie auch bare Schätze mitgebracht, so würden sie wahrscheinlich die geistlichen Hutdrachen besiegt haben." Briefe über einige der merkwürdigsten Städte im nördlichen Deutschland," in *Freimütiges aus den Schriften Garlieb Mekels,* ed. Horst Adameck (East Berlin, 1959), 270–271.

the acceptance of members of all religious beliefs; the reputation of special economic powers of achievement was by no means limited to Reformed Christians. This was apparent in the Netherlands, where the argument that confessional intolerance was associated with economic loss was also used against the local Reformed authorities by non-Reformed groups who carried economic weight.[39] Orthodox Calvinist clergymen strictly rejected toleration for economic reasons. Wealth gained by the toleration of heretics was regarded as a devil's gift.[40] We know of rearguard battles between adherents of the same confession even in the second half of the seventeenth century. When the Leiden Calvinist Pieter de la Court passionately pleaded in 1662 for the grant of free religious worship to resident and immigrating adherents of other confessions, in order to achieve economic advantages for Holland, his essay "Interest of Holland" aroused the enraged opposition of Calvinist zealots.[41]

In the eighteenth century, the principle of toleration won out on all levels.[42] The confessional argument had lost its impetus. Bernard Mandeville offers an extreme case. For him, women's love of luxury was more the motor of economic progress than religion.[43] An en-

---

39 Hassinger, "Wirtschaftliche Motive," 337, 344–345; see also Guggisberg, "Wandel der Argumente für religiöse Toleranz und Religionsfreiheit im 16. und 17. Jahrhundert," in Lutz, *Zur Geschichte,* 469–470.

40 Hassinger, "Wirtschaftliche Motive," 345, 349; see also the quotation in footnote 12, this essay.

41 *Interest van Holland ofte Gronden van Hollands-Welwaren, angewezen door V.D.H.* (? 1662); see Hassinger, "Wirtschaftliche Motive," 346–352.

42 See Helmuth Kiesel, "Problem und Begründung der Toleranz im 18. Jahrhundert," in Horst Rabe, Hansgeorg Molitor, and Hans-Christoph Rublack, eds., *Festgabe für Ernst Walter Zeeden* (Münster and Westfalen, 1976), 370–385; Joachim Whaley, "Pouvoir sauver les apparences: The Theory and Practices of Tolerance in Eighteenth Century Germany," in Heimo Reinitzer and Walter Sparn, eds., *Verspätete Orthodoxie. Über D. Johann Melchior Goeze (1717–1786)* (Wolfenbüttel, 1989), 9–26.

43 "I protest against Popery as much as ever Luther and Calvin did, or Queen Elizabeth herself, but I believe from my Heart, that the Reformation has scarce been more Instrumental in rendering the Kingdoms and States that have embraced it, flourishing beyond other Nations, than the silly and capricious Invention of Hoop'd and Quilted Petticoats. But if this should be denied me by the Enemies of Priestly Power, at least I am sure that, bar the great Men who have fought for and against that Lay-Main's Blessing, it has from its first beginning to this Day not employ'd so many Hands, honest industrious labouring Hands, as the abominable improvement on Female Luxury I named has done in few Years. Religion is one thing and Trade is another. He that gives most Trouble to thousands of his Neighbors, and invents the most operose Manufacturers is, right or wrong, the greatest Friend to the Society." *The Fable of the Bees, or, Private Vices, Publick Benefits,* first volume (London, 1957), 356; without any doubt, Mandeville is one of the first authors to suggest the idea that capitalism started from the female economy of luxury. Later on, this thesis was developed by Werner Sombart [see Werner Sombart, *Luxus und Kapitalismus,* 1913, reprinted as *Liebe, Luxus und Kapitalismus. Über die Entstehung der modernen Welt aus dem Geist der Verschwendung* (Berlin, 1983)].

lightened agnostic such as Frederick II of Prussia saw no problem in granting freedom of belief, out of utilitarian-economic considerations, even to non-Christian denominations. In 1740, he stated indifferently: "All religions are equal and good if only those people who practice them are honest people. If Turks and heathens were to come and settle on the land we would build mosques and churches for them."[44]

This absolutist interest on the part of the ruler, which here unscrupulously brushed aside confessional objections, was part of a new theory of state and economy that sought to instrumentalize religion for political aims. Although as a rule the dogmatic and ceremonial concerns of a religion were left to the *ius in sacra* of the ecclesiastical authorities, the rulers, with their right of *ius circa sacra*, turned the outward form of religious practice into a state matter.[45] As part of the mercantile-cameralistic scheme, the denominations in the country became subordinated to religious and ecclesiastical policy and supervision of the state.[46] The moral condition of the subjects seemed best guaranteed if civil, moral, and religious virtues were in accord.[47] Here religion was awarded first place. But it was no longer necessary for the maintenance of civil order.[48] Religion only functioned as guiding reins (*Leitriemen*)[49] or leading strings (*Gängelband*),[50] with the help of which the people could most easily be led to virtue or could be bridled. Insofar as the Christian denominations fulfilled this function, the absolutist state judged them generally equal in worth as a matter of *raison d'etat*. This outcome had already been made clear in the seventeenth century.

In the age of enlightened despotism, these positions were developed into a closed theory that fully subordinated the religious com-

44 "Alle Religionen seindt gleich und guth, wan nuhr die leute, so sie profesieren, Ehrlige leute seindt, und wen Türken und Heiden kämen und wollten das Land pöplieren, so wollen wir sie Mosqueen und Kirchen bauen." *Aus den Randbemerkungen,* ed. G. Borchardt (Potsdam, n.d.), Bd. 1: 70–71.

45 See Johannes Heckel, *Cura religionis. Ius in sacra. Ius circa sacra,* 2d ed. (Darmstadt, 1962).

46 See, for example, Johann Heinrich Gottlob von Justi, *Die Grundfeste zu der Macht und Glückseligkeit der Staaten* [. . .], Bd. 2 (Königsberg and Leipzig, 1761), 27ff. ("Von der Religions-Policy"); *Policy- und Cameral-Magazin* [. . .], Bd. 5, ed. Johann Heinrich Ludwig Bergius (Frankfurt a.M., 1770), Art. ("Kirchenpolizei"), 283ff.; see also Dipper, "Volksreligiosität und Obrigkeit," 76ff.

47 See Justi, *Die Grundfest,* 7.

48 Ibid., 20.

49 Joseph von Sonnenfels, *Grundzüge der Polizey-Handlung- und Finanzwissenschaft* (Vienna, 1970), d: 118.

50 Johann Kaspar Riesbeck, *Briefe eines reisenden Franzosen über Deutschland,* ed. Jochen Golz (Berlin, 1976), 236.

munities in a region to the common good as the ultimate aim of every republic. Johann Heinrich Gottlob von Justi, who most clearly articulated this church policy, considered religions fundamentally important to the welfare of the state. But the role of the church that Justi recommended to his regents consisted of keeping a watch on religious opinions, insofar as they could stir up unrest, keeping an eye on the clergy, and finally, putting the public side of religion to the state's use.[51] To this Justi added the regulation and determination of holy days as a central point. The authorities should not permit too many of these, as they greatly affected the diligence of the people and the level of sustenance. In 1761, Justi calculated that a single holy day in a nation of 8 to 10 million inhabitants caused a monetary loss of over 1 million florins, and if the usual additional expenses were included, the total came to two million.[52] Philipp Peter Gordon arrived at similar figures in 1768.[53] In 1772 an anonymous author, possibly the Catholic Johann Adam Freiherr von Ickstadt, added to the calculation of the economic loss incurred by a Catholic region through so many holy days the waste of money and time on church services, pilgrimages, and other pious acts in order to show the enormous economic damage caused by incorrect forms of pious practice.[54] In the opinion of the Lutheran parson Johann Friedrich Mayer of Kupferzell in Hohenlohe, the difference between wealthy Protestants and poor Catholics resulted solely from the difference in the number of holy days celebrated. Because Catholics had 120 per year and Protestants only 60, the latter were thus able to record a profit from the extra 60 work days.[55] The cameralist Johann Friedrich Pfeiffer at-

---

51  See Johann Heinrich Gottlob von Justi, *Grundsätze der Policeywissenschaft* [. . .], 3rd ed. (Göttingen, 1782), 235ff.

52  Justi, *Die Grundfeste*, 37.

53  *Polizey der Industrie, oder Abhandlung von den Mitteln, den Fleiss der Einwohner zu ermuntern* [. . .] (Braunschweig, 1768), 170; partly reprinted in Münch, ed., *Ordnung, Fleiss und Sparsamkeit*, 167–177; see also Münch, "Fêtes pour le peuple, rien par le peuple. 'Öffentliche' Feste im Programm der Aufklärung," in Dieter Düding, Peter Friedemann, and Paul Münch, eds., *Öffentliche Festkultur. Politische Feste in Deutschland von der Aufklärung bis zum Ersten Weltkrieg* (Reinbeck, 1988), 30.

54  *Christian Friedrich Menschenfreunds Untersuchung der Frage: Warum ist der Wohlstand der protestantischen Länder so gar viel grösser als der katholischen* (Salzburg and Freisingen, 1772); reprinted by K. Walcker in the "Flugschriften des evangelischen Bundes," No. 181–183 (Leipzig, 1900), under the title *Des Reichsfreiherrn Wirkl. Geh. Rats Prof. Dr. jur. J. A. v. Ickstatt katholische Lobschrift auf den Protestantismus;* partly reprinted in Münch, *Ordnung, Fleiss und Sparsamkeit,* 178–182. Jacob Viner mistakenly regarded Adam Müller as the author; see *Religious Thought and Economic Society,* 161, note 24.

55  J. F. Mayer, *Lehrbuch für die Land- und Hausswirthe in der pragmatischen Geschichte der gesamten Land- und Hausswirtschaft des Hohenlohe Schillingsfürstlichen Amtes Kupferzell* (Nuremberg, 1773) (reprinted ed., Schwäbisch Hall, 1980), 267.

tempted a comparison on the international level: England, which had fifty fewer holy days than France, could draw a yearly profit of 12 million pounds sterling: France in fact lost 30 million pounds sterling. If only it abolished forty holy days, Russia would be in a position to raise its annual gross national product by 80 million rubles.[56]

Such calculations were quite popular at the end of the eighteenth century.[57] They reflect an attempt, using the rationalistic approach of the epoch, to provide a pragmatic explanation for the varying relationship between confession and economy. To the supporters of the Enlightenment, a quantitative approach to a visible reality seemed best calculated to explain economic success by means of the various religious practices. Some observers, however, were not content with this; they attempted to discuss the relationship in terms of a given mentality. Bad economic conditions in a country, in Justi's opinion, were also connected with a lack of "genius" and "diligence on the part of the nation." By the term "genius," Justi meant the "desire and ability to distinguish oneself by means of skill, industry, and diligence." Where this genius was missing, everything was in a state of drowsiness and inertia. One contented oneself with existing sorts of foods and forms of food processing, dictated by habit, however bad they might be and however meager and miserable. No one bothered to invent new manufacturing processes or to attain a higher level of skill. And Justi concluded that this was the situation in Spain, Portugal, Poland, and a few other northern states; it was exactly this reason that prevented most of the Catholic states in Germany from achieving a flourishing level.[58] Justi's definition of the terms "genius" and "diligence" were fully contained in the concept of "industry,"

---

56 [Joh. Friedrich von Pfeiffer], *Natürliche aus dem Endzweck der Gesellschaft entstehnde Allgemeine Policeiwissenschaft*, 1. Teil (Frankfurt a.M., 1779), 412–413.

57 See Münch, "Fêtes pour le peuple," 29ff.

58 "In allen Ländern, wo der Nahrungsstand eine schlechte Beschaffenheit hat, wird man auch gar bald gewahr werden, dass es vornämlich an diesem Genie und Arbeitsamkeit des Volkes ermangelt. Es fehlet dem Volke an derjenigen Begierde und Fähigkeit, sich durch Geschicklichkeit, Fleiss und Arbeitsamkeit untereinander hervorzutun, als welches eigentlich dasjenige ist, was man unter dem unbestimmten Worte des Genies verstehen muss. Alles befindet sich in einer gewissen Schläfrigkeit und Trägheit. Man begnüget sich mit denen, durch die Gewohnheit einmal eingeführten, Nahrungs-und Bearbeitungsarten; so schlecht dieselben auch beschaffen seyn mögen, und so kümmerlich und elend man auch dadurch seinen Unterhalt gewinnet. Niemand klügelt, neue und vorzügliche Bearbeitungsarten zu erfinden; und niemand geibt sich Mühe, vorzügliche Geschicklichkeiten zu erwerben. Das ist der Zustand in Spanien, Portugall, Pohlen, und einigen anderen Nordischen Staaten; und eben dieses ist die Ursache, welche die meisten catholischen Staaten in Deutschland hintert, zu einem blühenden Nahrungsstande zu gelangen." Justi, *Die Grundfeste*, 1:687–688.

which appeared more graspable to contemporaries and rapidly took over. It stemmed from the French and was popularized by Philipp Peter Guden in his prize-winning essay *Polizey der Industrie, oder Abhandlungen von den Mitteln, den Fleiss der Einwohner zu ermuntern* (*Policy of Industry or Treatises on the Means of Encouraging the Diligence of the Population*), published in 1768.[59] The *Krünitz*, the most important reference work of the epoch, defined "industry" as creative diligence, meaning the "skill of drawing the best possible advantage from all the favorable circumstances at hand."[60] Upon examining these contemporary writings, it becomes clear that the backwardness of Catholic states was often attributed to confessional factors or to the specific lack of this spirit of industry, but this was not exclusively the case.[61] The innovative spirit that inspires the "industrious" citizen was only one of many possible explanatory factors for the Protestant countries' lead in production.

During the eighteenth century, the discourse on the relation between economy and religion left the close circle of scholarly economic and theological discussions. Before then, confessional differences had been seen almost exclusively in dogmatic and ceremonial questions. The discussions of toleration as a problem of state policy or of economic prosperity touched upon the possible economic differences of confessions, but it suggested no resolution. When the

---

59 See footnote 33, this essay.

60 "Industrie, aus dem Lat. Industria, und Franz. Industrie. In der gemeinen Sprache übersetzt man dieses Wort bald durch Geschicklichkeit, bald durch Arbeitsamkeit, Arbeitsbetrieb, Betriebsamkeit, Emsigkeit, Gewerbsamkeit, Kunstfleiss, u. d.gl. In der Finanzsprache aber erschöpft keines dieser deutschen Wörter völlig den Begriff, den der Franzose mit dem Worte Industrie verbindet, nämlich den Begriff eines erfinderischen Fleisses, wobey man alle Vortheile seiner Kunst oder seines freyen Gewerbes zu der Absicht anwendet, sich vermittelst seiner Arbeit ein solches Aequivalent zu verschaffen, wodurch sich alle Bedürfnisse befriedigen lassen. Man behält daher, wenn vom Finanzwesen und der Staatswirthschaft die Rede ist, gemeiniglich auch im Deutschen das kräftigere Wort Industrie bey, und versteht darunter den betriebsamen Fleiss der freyen Arbeiter und der Kaufleute, nebst dem so genannten savoir-faire, oder der Geschicklickeit, aus allen sich darbiethenden günstigen Umständen den möglichsten Vortheil zu ziehen." Münch, *Ordnung, Fleiss und Sparsamkeit,* 284–285. For this problem see also Focko Eulen, *Vom Gewerbefleiss zur Industrie. Ein Beitrag zur Wirtschaftsgeschichte des 18. Jahrhunderts* (Berlin, 1967); Johannes Burkhardt, "Das Verhaltensleitbild 'Produktivität' und seine historisch-anthropologische Voraussetzung," in *Speculum* 21 (1974): 277–289; Hubert Treiber and Heinz Steinert, *Die Fabrikation des zuverlässigen Menschen. Über die "Wahlverwandtschaft" von Kloster- und Fabrikdisziplin* (Munich, 1980); Wolfgang Dressen, *Die pädagogische Maschine. Zur Geschichte des industrialisierten Bewusstseins in Preussen/Deutschland* (Frankfurt, 1982); Rudolf Schenda, "Fleissige Deutsche, fleissige Schweizer. Bemerkungen zur Produktion eines Tugendsyndroms seit der Aufklärung," in Hans-Jürg Braun, ed., *Ethische Perspektiven: "Wandel der Tugenden"* (Zurich, 1989), 189–209.

61 See also Justi, who speaks only of "most Catholic states" and also sees a lack of genius in the northern (i.e., Protestant) countries (footnote 58, this essay).

interest in economic questions increased in the context of mercantilist and cameralist theories from the late seventeenth century on, the economic factor began to dominate general discourse. The eighteenth century saw the incipient development of national and confessional stereotypes. These stereotypes ascribed to Protestantism an active and productive role in the economy, to Catholicism a retarding influence. Contact with foreign countries and societies during the European expansion sharpened the eye for cultural differences among peoples. Simultaneously, the historiography of the epoch drew attention to the examples in history that one could employ fruitfully for one's own discourse. Many individual pieces of information consolidated in the end to form fixed national stereotypes that defined the "nature of the people"[62] in completely varying ways and at the same time served to clarify one's own cultural identity. In this discourse, the ancient Egyptians and the Spartans, as well as contemporary China, appeared as models worthy of imitation, models, that is, of a rigid organization of labor regulated by laws. Along with the Lapplanders and the North American Indians, the inhabitants of the tropical zones in particular served as negative examples.[63] Up to now, there has been too little notice of the fact that alongside the flattering image of the "noble savage," its negative counterimage, the myth of the lazy native, was also created.[64]

The bourgeois public that was in the making and that considered labor and production essential to human existence[65] also defined its own social role in the context of the confessional and national stereotypes that were taking shape. The economic argument moved more and more into the foreground, and even more important, economic differences were more and more attributed to confessional differences. At the end of the eighteenth century, travel reports in particular came to influence the bourgeois self-image.[66] They formed the reservoir into which the whole of the early modern theological, economic, and political discourse flowed and began to coalesce into easily assimilated stereotypes. A new version of history that departed

62 Johann Heinrich Zedler, "Naturell der Völcker," in *Grosses Vollständiges Universal-Lexikon*, Bd. 25 (Leipzig and Halle, 1740), Sp. 1246–1251.
63 There are many examples in the cameralistic writings.
64 See Syed Hussein Alatas, *The Myth of the Lazy Native. A Study of the Image of the Malays, Filipinos and Javanese from the 16th to the 20th Century and Its Function in the Ideology of Colonial Capitalism* (London, 1977).
65 See generally Münch, *Ordnung, Fleiss und Sparsamkeit*.
66 See the bibliography in Peter J. Brenner, ed., *Der Reisebericht. Die Entwicklung einer Gattung in der deutschen Literatur* (Frankfurt, 1989), 524–531.

from the paradigm of chronology and of loyalty to dynasty and aimed at the integration of material and cultural phenomena[67] created a new forum for the subject of confession and economy. There was scarcely a travel report of the era that did not deal with this theme in detail.

The authors of such writings belonged to various confessions. The spirit of the Enlightenment, which inspired most of them, certainly mitigated the perceived disparity of religion and led to a far-reaching consensus on the question of the relation between confession and economy. Therefore one should not mistakenly suppose that these documents, in which the scrutiny of very divergent geographical, political, economic, social, and cultural conditions provoked a comparison among states and regions, already contained an elaborate structure of prejudice. In this literature, Protestant countries did not everywhere hold the leading position in economic progress, and Catholic states did not necessarily rank at the bottom of the scale.

The Protestant Swabian Wilhelm Ludwig Wekhrlin, for example, believed that the obvious difference between Catholic Upper Swabia and Protestant Lower Swabia was caused not by the form of government or by religion, but by the far more powerful influence of the cultural "horizon."[68] In 1784, the "traveling Frenchman," Johann Kaspar Riesbeck, also used the confessional argument with a certain reserve. This did not prevent him, as a keen Catholic advocate of the Enlightenment, from pouring insults and mockery upon the Bavarians because this region, according to him, suffered substantial economic loss as a result of its 5,000 monks fattening up in its 200 monasteries. He called for the extirpation of monasteries and monks. Yet for him, no regularity was without an exception. Whoever sang the praises of the Protestants on account of their enlightenment, industry, and good breeding and reproached the Catholics for their stupidity, indolence, and slovenliness should, so said Riesbeck, remember the Lutheran Danes in order to understand the obvious ineffectiveness of religion in the betterment of humankind. In his opinion, the Danes were similar to the Bavarians and the Portuguese in terms of mental dimness, clumsiness, indolence, slovenliness, and bigotry. In France, the Austrian Netherlands, and some Italian states,

---

67 See Jörn Garber, "Von der Menschheitsgeschichte zur Kulturgeschichte. Zum geschichtstheoretischen Kulturbegriff der deutschen Spätaufklärung," in *Kultur zwischen Bürgertum und Volk* (Berlin, 1983), 76–97.
68 Anselmus Rabiosus, *Reise durch Ober-Deutschland* (Salzburg and Leipzig, 1778), 93; see also footnote 21, this essay (Ewald).

industry and enlightenment, for example, coexisted with a strong dose of Catholic superstition and "monkishness." By contrast, the German Catholic was far less disposed to industry. Religion was here not so much the active but rather more the incidental cause. The local circumstances were of greater significance. The fact that in Alsace and in Lower Swabia more of a "spirit of industry" was to be found among Protestants than among Catholics was only partly because of the religion. Pedagogy, social condition, and mentality had also to be taken into consideration. Riesbeck's ambivalent attitude was most clearly seen in his portrayal of the Rhineland between Cologne and the Netherlands. Although the effect of false religious principles could be studied extensively in the case of Cologne – to him in every respect Germany's most disgusting city – in the confessionally mixed region of Westphalia and the lower Rhine, religion had little influence on the civil condition of the people. Diligence of the inhabitants, natural fertility of the land, an excellent government, blurred confessional differences – these were for Riesbeck the reasons for its economic prosperity.[69]

In the most important travelogue of the end of the eighteenth century, Friedrich Nicolai's *Description of a Journey through Germany and Switzerland in the Year 1781,* the 5,000 pages of which appeared between 1783 and 1796,[70] this nuanced view seemed to have been abandoned. Nicolai wrote as a Protestant, a supporter of the Enlightenment, and a representative of the rising middle class.[71] This orientation led him to grant an almost exclusive priority to the role the denominations play in the economy. Here, clearly, the confessional stereotypes of the nineteenth century were in the making. The Catholic part of the Reich fell under the harsh verdict of the author on account of its faulty religious principles. In contrast to Catholic idleness, negligence, and addiction to pleasure, the Protestant German seemed a treasure trove of civil diligence, moderation, and innovative spirit.

This Protestant view experienced a considerable renaissance during the *Kulturkampf.* But now it was mixed with the usual national prejudices in the fields of ethics, religion, politics, intellectual ac-

---

69 *Briefe eines reisenden Franzosen,* 13ff., 61ff., 414f., 517, 539–543.

70 Friedrich Nicolai, *Beschreibung einer Reise durch Deutschland und die Schweiz im Jahre 1781, nebst Bemerkungen über Gelehrsamkeit, Industrie, Religion und Sitten,* 12 vols. (Berlin and Stettin, 1783–1796).

71 See Wolfgang Martens, "Ein Bürger auf Reisen," in Bernhard Fabian, ed., *Friedrich Nicolai 1733–1811. Essays zum 250. Geburtstag* (Berlin, 1983), 99–123.

tivity, and social dynamics.[72] Protestantism[73] conveyed to a country a higher culture, that is, greater vitality and dynamic progress. This was missing in the Catholic states.[74] In general, Roman Catholicism appeared as the "religion of the stationary, relatively non-advancing races and nations."[75] One factor sufficed to make this difference plausible. Nonreligious causes like nature, climate, or race could "never sufficiently explain the inner, characteristic certainty of a development." "At its most basic," it was a matter "of the life, of the spirit, and also, the history of a confession and its respective people" was "only the history of the effects of the spirit living within that confession."[76] Ten years after these statements[77] were made, Max Weber published his study on the relation between Protestantism and the spirit of capitalism.

Since the sixteenth century there has been a voluminous literature on the relation between religion and economy. The rejection of monasticism, the secularization of church property, and the alterations in

72 See the writings quoted in footnotes 28 and 54 of this essay.
73 See Friedrich Hummel, *Was gibt der evangelische Protestantismus den ihm zugehörigen Völkern bis heute vor den römisch-katholischen Völkern voraus? Vortrag, gehalten bei der VII. General-Versammlung des Evangelischen Bundes zur Wahrung der deutsch-protestantischen Interessen in Bochum. 9. August 1894* (Leipzig, 1895).
74 "Wir sehen in der Entwicklung der Völker das wirklich bestätigt, dass der römische Katholizismus ungünstig für dieselbe wirkt. Der Katholizismus hat über die ihm zugehörigen Gebiete so geherrscht, dass ihnen die protestantischen Völker an den Gütern äusserlicher und innerlicher Kultur, am Reichtum sittlich-religiöser Wahrheit, an Kraft freier Geistesbildung, an Wohlstand und Wohlfahrt thatsächlich weit vorauskamen. Und heute noch giebt der Protestantismus seinen Völkern an Lebenskraft und an lebendigen Fortschritt in sittlich-religiöser, intellektueller, politischer und gesellschaftlicher Beziehung so viel voraus, dass die höhere Kultur offenkundig auf dieser Seite liegt, dass auch das Höhensteigen der Menschheitsentwicklung und die Lösung der grossen Aufgaben, welche uns gestellt sind, nur in evangelischem Sinn und Geist möglich erscheint." Ibid., 12.
75 In this, Hummel follows James Johnston, *A Century of Christian Progress and Its Lessons* (London, 1888), quoted by Hummel, *Was gibt der evangelische Protestantismus,* 3.
76 "Wir brauchen die nationalökonomische Vergleichung nicht weiter auszudehnen, als wir schon seither gethan haben: Sie spricht deutlich zu gunsten des Protestantismus. Sie bestätigt von sich aus die Wahrheit, dass Rasse und Klima die innere, eigentümliche Bestimmtheit einer Entwicklung nie ausreichend erklären können. Das muss ja überhaupt für alle, die auf dem Boden der Offenbarungsreligion stehen, von vornherein ausgemacht sein. Denn es handelt sich im tiefsten Grund um das Leben des Geistes, und auch die Geschichte einer Konfession oder Kirche, bezw. des ihr zugehörigen Volkes, ist nur die Geschichte der Auswirkung des in ihr lebenden Geistes. Derjenige müsste doch wohl eigentlich noch gefunden werden, welcher die ungleiche höhere geistige und materielle Kultur der evangelisch-protestantischen Völker bloss aus Rasse und Klima wissenschaftlich erklären könne." Hummel, *Was gibt der Protestantismus,* 18–19.
77 Hummel already designs a kind of consistent Protestant ethics, which starts from the free and responsible personality and the fulfilling of vocational duties (see ibid., 74–75). But he set it clearly off against the modern materialist enthusiasm for nature and culture (76; see also 113–114), and he does not yet base it on any doctrine of predestination.

the calendar of the saints by the Protestants had created the first confessional differences relevant to economy. The settlement of denominational minorities because of pragmatic economic considerations had led in many communities to the acceptance of the principle of practical tolerance. We cannot see that Protestants were preferred on account of the work ethos ascribed to them. Since the late seventeenth century, the political interest displayed here had led to a basic instrumentalization of religion for the purposes of the state. Cameralistic policies toward the confessions trimmed them to the state's needs. Enlightened absolutistic doctrines made the argument of economic utility the only yardstick of modernizing measures. Furthermore, since the mid-eighteenth century, the discourse on religion and economy had been connected with the debate over whether the individual confessions were useful or harmful for the rise of civil society.

Insofar as there was any subtlety to the arguments of the epoch, religion was only one of many possible factors explaining economic productivity. But there was no consensus on its effect and influence. Some, for instance Bernard Mandeville, denied the economic significance of religion, whereas the majority saw a connection between confessional molding and economic situation. The lead in productivity of the Protestant states over the Catholic countries was, of course, not always seen as solely dependent on the confessional factor. If the marked quantifiable differences, such as the greater number of working days in Protestant countries, were stressed, further explanatory factors that played down the confessional argument were anthropology, education, social organization, political constitution, mentality, and local, provincial, or national character.

Only during the *Kulturkampf* was the confessional dispute, forgotten since the Enlightenment, fully resumed. Now it became the most important argument, nationalistically charged at that, for ascribing positions in Wilhelmine society. The essentially materialistic approach of the late eighteenth century was gradually replaced by an *idealistic* standpoint that could find a satisfactory explanation in the "working of the spirit." Without a doubt, Max Weber stands in this tradition as a German, a Protestant, and a representative of the educated middle classes – at best as "a giant on the shoulders of dwarfs."

# 3

## Max Weber, Protestantism, and the Context of the Debate around 1900

### THOMAS NIPPERDEY

Weber began his essay on *The Protestant Ethic and the Spirit of Capitalism* with the assurance that it was the conventional opinion of his contemporaries that there was a close connection between religion and society. They especially believed that the differences between Protestants and Catholics had a strong impact on social structure and social status; in a society composed of mixed religions, the higher strata, the more advanced and more modern elements, were definitely more Protestant than Catholic: scholars, business leaders, white-collar employees, even skilled workers. The burden of proof was not with those who held this assumption but with those who would deny it.

The modern reader normally will skim over these paragraphs in Weber's essay, but Weber himself did not pretend that his selection of this problem was in any respect an original one. He quoted some literature of rather varying character and quality – Bendix went through some of this stuff – and relied heavily upon a doctoral dissertation of one of his students, Martin Offenbacher, on the state of Baden, religious affiliation, and social stratification; in fact Weber chose this as the title of his own first chapter.

I leave aside the British authors, such as Henry Thomas Buckle, Matthew Arnold, and various economists, who pointed to the connection between the beliefs of the Puritans, their habits, their asceticism and spiritual discipline, and their work ethics, especially because these authors often were making observations, as the English like to do, about the Scots. I concentrate my comments on the German discussion, and I pick up four points.

The German discussion begins with politics. Weber did not mention this root, but all his readers knew this context. The Catholics – 45 percent of the population in the Reich – were the ones who were

73

complaining about discrimination. Given the political and social conditions of the time, this complaint was primarily directed against the confessional composition of the higher civil service; it was about parity and disparity. This had become a major issue since the 1880s in public and parliamentary debates and campaigns. Given the style of argument at that time, one had to come up with statistics, to count heads. What was needed as a weapon in this conflict were scholarly, objective social surveys. The claim of Catholics at this point was a claim for quotas. This, however, had a divisive effect on its potential allies against discrimination, namely, liberals and Jews. The Catholic drumbeat for parity was not regarded as a universalistic civil rights movement, but as a partisan campaign to establish a system of patronage and spoils, an attack on the idealized neutrality of the civil service and the principle of achievement. Jews had fundamental objections against quotas and the statistics used for this purpose, which were frequently and easily exploited by anti-Semites. There is a farce by Ludwig Thoma, one of the most famous radical satirical writers of the time, in which a Jewish widow, Sarah Eichenlaub, dedicates to the state a home for babies of all religious creeds. This leads to a political crisis; the minister in charge has to persuade Sarah to adopt a quota system: 17 Catholic babies, 2 Protestant, 0.33 Jewish, and only when the housekeeper finally switches denomination is the crisis resolved. This story reveals the atmosphere in which Weber wrote.

Now of course, there was massive discrimination against Catholics and great suspicion of their loyalty. Prussia was historically a Protestant state, and all the hidden and built-in mechanisms favored Protestants. But even in Bavaria, the Catholic majority, more than 70 percent, complained about the Protestant character of the bureaucracy. The Berlin government normally denied any intention of discrimination and argued that there had been fewer Catholic candidates for government service, and the Catholics counterargued that exactly this was one of the major consequences of discrimination.

The statistical approach, however, had, as everyone knows, its own logic and dynamic: One had to differentiate, to split global figures, to compare with other groups. We might consider two examples. In the hard core of the authoritarian state's personnel, in the administrative sector, Catholics made up 16.9 percent less than their proportion in the population at large, Protestants 14.91 percent more. Even Jews, religious Jews, were overrepresented by 1.86 percent. In the somewhat more liberal justice service (judges, prosecutors, and other civil servants), the numbers were −12.59 percent, +8.28 percent, and +4.86 percent, respectively. And in the liberal free profession of lawyers, where there was no state discrimination, the figures were still −11.78 percent for Catholics and +16.8 percent for Jews. A similar result appeared in another hotly contested terrain of discrimination, the Protestant-dominated universities. In 1901, a devoted Catholic, a professor of chemistry, showed that the ratio of untenured academic teachers to tenured ones was 86.9 percent for Protestants, 36.7 percent for Catholics, and 358.8 percent for Jews. There were very few differences between disciplines with strong discrimination (like public law or the humanities) and those with weak or no discrimination (like medicine). So the disparity issue apparently involved factors other than discrimination. What were these factors?

The Catholics themselves developed a sophisticated self-criticism. In 1896, several research-based articles appeared in newspapers about the disproportionally weak enrollment of Catholics in high schools and universities. A prominent spokesman for Catholic laymen, Count Hertling (a philosopher and deputy in the Reichstag, in 1917 chancellor of the Reich), took up the issue in addressing Catholic gatherings and conventions; he coined the term of the "deficit" of higher education among Catholics. Behind such a statement was a growing uneasiness and concern among Catholic academics about the anti-intellectualism of clerics, popular organizations, and Catholic popular (and populist) culture in general. In 1897 a professor of Catholic "apologetic" theology, Hermann Schell, coined another famous term, the "inferiority" of Catholics, in a best-selling book, *Catholicism: A Principle of Progress;* very soon he became a victim of Rome's integralist condemnation of modernism. An apocalyptic vision of a two-cultures-and-two-classes society, with educated upper-class Protestants and uneducated lower-class Catholics, was in the air. As could be expected, there was a jubilant resonance among Protestants and liberals of the "we-have-said-this-all-the-time" type and harsh condemnation among Catholic traditionalists. Catholic reformers had to be more than cautious in self-criticism, self-admonition, and pleas for improvement.

In 1901, a kind of affirmative action effort, the appointment of a Catholic historian, Martin Spahn, to a chair in Strassbourg − where there had been fewer than 5 percent Catholics among the full professors − led to an uproar among Protestant liberal academics. Old Theodor Mommsen, then a radical Democrat, took the lead, and

Max Weber was also involved. (Edward Shils has recently published the major articles from this conflict in English in his journal, *Minerva*.) The Catholics were counterattacking Protestant prejudices, and this again brought the interrelation among religion, scholarship, and the educated classes and their social status into the foreground.

Meanwhile, this political and partisan debate was partly transformed into a scholarly debate. Statisticians, the already acknowledged leaders of the rising social sciences, and graduate students took up the problem; the partisan issue became an object of the social sciences. Martin Offenbacher's book, *Konfession und soziale Schichtung* (1901), was but one example of this turn. Since the question of state personnel was more sensitive and more hidden, the scholarly debate concentrated on the disproportional underenrollment of Catholic students. Because this was a well-established fact, the question was how to explain it. In a world fascinated by Social Darwinism and genetics, celibacy was a rather fashionable explanation. Statisticians stressed geographic and socioeconomic causes: the more rural and small-town and the lower-class and traditional middle-class background of Catholics, the fact that Catholics paid on average only half the taxes that Protestants paid. Sociocultural explanations – less motivation toward achievement, rationality, modernity, and even some antimodern resistance – were at first more the matter for speculative journalists than for real scholars. The debate again, however, created its own dynamic. Geographic and economic explanations led to the question of how to explain these differences; conventional wisdom favored the "historical" explanation – that more towns went Protestant in the sixteenth century, and so on – but this was partly a *regressus ad infinitum*, and it did not explain what needed explanation. A certain breakthrough came again from statistical differentiation. If one compared high school enrollment in the traditional *Gymnasium* – with Latin and Greek – and in modern types of high schools, which normally gave broader access to a lower-middle-class, rural, and small-town children, Catholics were even more underrepresented in the new type than in the older one. And in the university system, the picture was similar. The modern areas – technology, science, economics – were the least attractive for Catholic students; among Catholics, less than half as many studied science as among Protestants. Here, apparently, factors of religious culture played a role. Still, scholars remained rather cautious in weighing the different variables. Offenbacher, for example, who discussed the *mentalité* factor, was seemingly inclined to interpret the religious factor in the last resort as a social and historical variable, as a social profile, explaining the Catholic *mentalité* as a product of the specific social surrounding that would decrease in due time in a more urban and modern environment.

At this point, I should add what we know today about the narrow field of student enrollment. There was an enrollment explosion, as Konrad Jarausch has demonstrated, between 1900 and 1914 that led to a much higher inclusion of lower-middle-class students. The percentage of Catholics was increasing and the deficit decreasing, as Offenbacher had predicted; part of the deficit, however, and the disproportion between traditional and modern types of high schools and disciplines remained. So far, the religious factor remained independent.

One last and quite different part of the discussion must be mentioned. That was its tendency to explain world history, and its political and social differences, in terms of religion. This was part of an old European intellectual tradition, exemplified by seventeenth-century explanations of the astonishing success of the Dutch, by referring either to Calvinism or to tolerance, and by eighteenth-century arguments about the decline of societies with a large ecclesiastical sector. Since the French Revolution, such perspectives became especially widespread among European liberals. The philosophers of the Counterrevolution had singled out Protestantism as the real origin and seedbed of revolution against tradition and authority. The liberals turned the argument around: Protestantism is indeed connected with progress and modernity, but Protestantism is not revolution; it is constant reform. The Catholic countries are the ones with these kinds of revolutions, provoked by despotism, corruption, and laziness. This kind of argument colored all historical-political reasoning in the first two-thirds of the nineteenth century. Progress and backwardness were frequently explained in terms of religious categories.

In the last decades of the nineteenth century, however, the rising wave of nationalism changed and weakened this kind of reasoning. French liberals, for example, would no longer praise the Reformation as the origin of modernity, as Guizot and Michelet had done, but would find its origin in the Latin and perhaps the French Renaissance. Weber quoted a relic of the older tradition, Émile Laveleye, a Belgian Catholic anticlerical, whose 1875 book on Catholic and Protestant nations in Europe continued all the stereotypes about the inferiority of Catholic nations in education, culture, wealth, liberty, and even morality. The editor of the German translation, Johann Caspar Bluntschli, a Swiss-German professor of public law and a dignitary among moderate liberals of the time, stressed all these points and added that the pioneers of German industry, the entrepreneurs of the Rhineland, were almost all Protestant, whereas the population at large was mainly Catholic.

In Germany this type of reasoning survived among Protestants. A theologian, Gerhard Uhlhorn, in 1887 coined the phrase that "the machine had something Protestant about it" – Friedrich Naumann loved to quote that slogan. In 1898, German newspapers frequently commented on the war between the United States and Spain in terms of Catholic decline and Protestant progress. The more secular the society became, the more, so it seems, religious categories were used as tools to interpret reality, and liberal nonchurchgoers of Protestant background, as well as liberal Protestants, were particularly addicted to this mixture of universalistic speculations, self-righteousness, and prejudices. Scholars normally remained distant and cool, and a methodological rigorist and nonbeliever like Weber was even more likely to keep aloof. But we should not forget that he and his family set were products of cultural Protestantism; he breathed its air and was shaped by its ascetic moralism.

In transition, we may remark that Weber never mentioned Durkheim's famous study on suicide, in which the religious factor played such a prominent role. Probably at that time he had not read it, but one may also speculate about the strange Weber–Durkheim nonrelation.

We return to Weber's essay. The decisive point is what he did with the somewhat confused questions of his time. After dealing with the more general themes of that discussion, he took up Offenbacher's work as a representative scholarly approach and developed, partly explicitly, partly implicitly, some critical arguments and drew his conclusions. First, he argued against all strategies that reduce the religious factor to geographic and social or historical factors; this kind of reductionism did not explain the explanandum. Second, he rejected all-embracing theories of the universalistic type as a kind of historical metaphysics or as premature for the time being. Third, he turned away from the multidimensional analysis – not because he denied its logic and its legitimacy, but because of its present in-

conclusiveness. Fourth, he turned instead to a one-dimensional analysis of the religious factor to single out a manageable complex and a
strictly empirical enterprise. And he cautiously limited the general
meaning of such an analysis.

In light of his later methodology, we may say (with some reservation) that he constructed an ideal type of a relationship, of a process,
comprehending existing qualities and trends and developing them
into a consequential and logical system – not as an image of reality,
but as a tool to understand reality better. And eventually, as we all
know, he limited his research to the economic sector and in fact to
one single problem, albeit one of overwhelming importance: the rise
of rational capitalism and its religious preconditions, not causes. He
turned away from Germans, Catholic and Lutheran, to the Anglo-
Saxons and the Calvinist world. On the other hand, and in contrast
to these limitations, he broadened the concept of religion, its cultural
meaning (*"Kulturbedeutung" der Religion*). He made explicit what was
until then a not very clear concept of morality or mentality by con-
centrating on the guiding principles of life conduct, the value system
governing patterns of behavior, their religious foundation, and their
social meaning. And he, himself an agnostic, rejected some of the
more trivial explanations of his time. He did not see religion as an
irrational force, diverting humankind from the path of reason and
progress, nor as a kind of imperfect forerunner of modern (and
scientific) culture. He rejected the conventional view that Catholicism was otherworldly-oriented and therefore indifferent to this
world. He tried to establish a more differentiated dialectic relation
between religion, lifestyle, and economic behavior, and his famous
concept of innerworldly asceticism was the main tool for this dialectic. Offenbacher had stated a normal and a rather trite liberal opinion:
that Protestants preferred to eat well and Catholics to sleep undisturbed. Weber developed a theory of how different strategies of
how to sleep undisturbed affect opportunities to eat well; he knew
that the joys of eating were much more widespread among Catholics,
and he would have been unsurprised to learn that Protestants soon –
and until today – became the major consumers of sleeping pills.

My attempt to connect Weber's essay with the previous general
discussion has one major consequence for our understanding of
Weber. Given the broad horizon of the debate around 1900, the more
general question of modernity must be used as a tool to interpret
Weber's essay. It was not only Weber's later writings on the sociology

of religion that did not concentrate mainly on questions of economics, but on the interdependence of religion and society, on lifestyle, on rationalization and disenchantment, on the process of universal history and the grim outlook for the future, the iron cage of bureaucracy. The essay on Protestantism should also be read in this broader context. Weber styled himself sometimes as an economic historian, and as a scrupulous scholar he tried to insulate his research object, but from his starting point on, he was a generalist, pursuing the history of the human being, the process of modernization in a rather encompassing sense, the dialectic of rationalization as a product of what was believed to be irrational at his time, namely, religion. This is already inherent in his early approach of 1903.

The last question I want to raise concerns the history of the problem in the historical disciplines. What happened to the problem of religion and society in Germany? Weber did not take it up, despite his reference to the ongoing debate. His remarks on the impact of Calvinism in Germany were rather weak; in dealing with Luther, he referred to the concept of the "calling" as rather traditional and static, not as a choice, and without the dynamism of Calvinism. The relationship between Protestantism and modernity in Germany, he concluded, must have a more indirect character. But he himself never again pursued this theme. This was partly because of his growing systematic and universalistic interests, partly because of his status as a nonteaching scholar without doctoral students. He left the German theme to his colleague and friend, Ernst Troeltsch, and his classic work on the social teaching of the Christian churches.

But Troeltsch's interests and assumptions were different. He was mainly preoccupied with organizational structures of churches or sects and their social impact; as a devoted liberal, he was not concerned about the modern but about the conservative heritage of Lutheranism in Germany – the absence of voluntary congregations as a base for liberalism and democracy. And as an intellectual historian, he developed his famous concept that it was the Enlightenment and its forerunners – dissenters, spiritualists, humanists – who were the real fathers of our own age, and that Protestantism, Reformation, and Counterreformation belonged much more to the Middle Ages. Troeltsch's was not a perspective that would explain why Protestants were the major segment of the movers and doers in modernizing Germany society, why there was a Lutheran Protestant potential for modernity. Scholarship in the 1920s became even more ideological (such as, for example, Werner Elert's *Morphologie des Luthertums*). Only in recent years have a few scholars from the United States and France taken up the Weber theme in comparative field studies on German villages. The impact of religion upon demography, birth rates, and child mortality, upon social stratification and mobility, and upon education becomes clear beyond any doubt. A Swiss social psychologist, A. Schmidtchen, has shown from all the polls the enormous importance of the two religious cultures in the 1950s and 1960s in shaping the mentality of present-day agnostics as well as of churchgoers. His theory may be a key to further research on German history.

# 4
# Weber the Would-Be Englishman: Anglophilia and Family History

GUENTHER ROTH

Since the Napoleonic period, England had been for many German liberals the "older brother" who could show a way out of the confusions of French history and the frustrations of German history. After German unification in 1871, the number of liberal admirers gradually declined, until the stage was set for Germany's fatal challenge to the British Empire. Max Weber was one of the last to consider England a model for both constitutional reform and *Weltpolitik*. The hatred he felt for his Lutheran heritage and the German authoritarian realities was so great that he modeled his notion of ethical personality and innerworldly asceticism to a considerable extent after an idealized image of English history, especially of Puritanism.

Although a vigorous spokesman of his generation's nationalism, Weber greatly sympathized with the Puritan and liberal traditions of England. Sometimes he sounded as if he were half English. Indeed, more than elective affinity is involved. Weber was a descendant of the cosmopolitan bourgeoisie. His ancestors and relatives were businessmen in Manchester and London, not just in Frankfurt and Bielefeld. Three generations moved back and forth; some members returned to Germany, others stayed on. Weber could view himself, if he wished, as a would-be Englishman and in a romantic dream as one of the admired *Herrenmenschen* (masters), Puritan or not. He too had some links, if tenuously, with the "commercial aristocracy" that made Lancashire the cradle of the modern factory system. By a last stretch of the imagination, he could envisage himself as a liberal

In the text, PE refers to *The Protestant Ethic and the Spirit of Capitalism,* translated by Talcott Parsons (New York: Scribner's, 1958); MWGA refers to *Max Weber Gesamtausgabe,* Horst Baier, M. Rainer Lepsius, Wolfgang J. Mommsen, Wolfgang Schluchter, and Johannes Winckelmann, eds. (Tübingen: Mohr, 1984 –).

party leader in Birmingham or Manchester, a Joseph Chamberlain or a William Ewart Gladstone.

I proceed in two steps. First, I deal with Weber's image of England and its relation to his perception of Puritanism and the Protestant ethic. Second, I treat his entrepreneurial relatives as a negative example for his notion of the spirit of capitalism. Weber's construct appears almost as a counterimage to the speculative capitalism and nonascetic lifestyle that characterized many of them.

### 1. WEBER'S PERCEPTION OF ENGLAND

In the midst of the Great War, late in 1917 and after America's entry, Weber admonished his countrymen: "Only *Herrenvölker* are called upon to be helmsmen of the world's course."[1] The foremost *Herrenvolk* was, of course, England, about which Weber remarked in the face of all the anti-English propaganda: "Is this a 'night-watchman state' [a Manchesterist minimal state] that has managed to attach to itself, despite its small population, the best parts of all continents? How philistine is this hackneyed phrase that betrays so much of the resentment of the *Untertan*" (MWGA, I/15, 472, ES 1407), the German authoritarian personality. With some desperation, Weber wished that the Germans could become the equals of the English in attaining the status of a "master people." Profound admiration for England lay behind his advocacy of German *Weltpolitik*.

In *The Protestant Ethic* Weber stated clearly what was politically attractive to him about English history: "Puritanism enabled its adherents to create free institutions and still become a world power" (PE 261). Here he followed the contemporary Whig interpretations, which treated Puritanism as a predecessor of liberalism and equated the political and religious struggles for liberty. One of Weber's sources was the great historian Samuel Rawson Gardiner, who propagated the

---

1 "By *Herrenvolk* we do not mean that ugly face of a parvenu which is drawn when some people's [distorted] sense of national dignity lets that English turn-coat, Mr. Houston Stewart Chamberlain, tell them and the nation what *Deutschtum* is" (MWGA, I/15, 594). *Herrenvolk* sounds ominous, especially if translated as "master race," and "master people" too is awkward, as is any translation of German compounds with *Herr* in it. But Weber smuggled into a popular rhetoric debased by Social Darwinism and racism a mundane meaning: A *Herrenvolk* is an enfranchised citizenry that participates in shaping the nation's fate. Therefore he demanded democratization so that Germany could "join the circle of the *Herrenvölker*" as a free and mature people (MWGA, I/15, 727). The crucial point was that "only a *Herrenvolk* had the right to pursue world politics" (MWGA, I/15, 396).

notion – no longer popular today – of a "Puritan Revolution."[2] Given this perception of Puritanism, it makes sense that Weber drew such an invidious distinction vis-à-vis Lutheranism – witness his striking statement to Adolf Harnack in early 1906 in an exchange of letters on *The Protestant Ethic:* "The fact that our nation never went through the school of hard asceticism, in no form whatsoever, is the source of everything that I hate about it (and about myself). I can't help it, but in religious terms the average American sect member surpasses our institutional Christians as much as Luther excels, as a religious person-ality, Calvin, Fox et tutti quanti" (MWGA, II/5, 32f).

For Weber one of the main sources of modern individualism de-rived from the biblical injunction (Acts 5:29) that God must be obeyed more than humans, as it had been adapted by the ascetic conventicles and sects in their struggle against the patriarchal and authoritarian powers.[3] He connected this stance to the "traditional American objection to performing personal service" and compared "the relative immunity of formerly Puritan peoples to Caesarism, and . . . the subjectively free attitude of the English to their great statesmen" with the German worship of Bismarck since 1878, with the "naive idea that political obedience could be due anyone from thankfulness" (PE 224f). In a letter to Count Keyserling he called this articulation of the religious postulate the "truly creative element of

2  For the Whig interpretation and its latter-day revision, see Peter Wende, *Probleme der Engli-schen Revolution* (Darmstadt: Wissenschaftliche Buchgesellschaft, 1980), 41ff. For a recent defense of the older notions, see Christopher Hill, "The Place of the Seventeenth-Century Revolution in English History" (1988), in his *A Nation of Change and Novelty* (London: Routledge, 1990), 6–23.

Weber was familiar with the liberal reinterpretation of Oliver Cromwell. See Samuel Rawson Gardiner, *Oliver Cromwell* (London: Goupil, 1899; German ed. 1903). Cromwell had first been rehabilitated by Carlyle, who turned him into "the three-dimensional hero of nineteenth-century Nonconformity, and the spiritual ancestor (ironically, for Carlyle was a great anti-Liberal) of Victorian popular Liberalism. It is hard, at our distance from them, to comprehend the political passions that gave to events of the seventeenth century so profound and immediate a significance for the nineteenth. . . . In Manchester, the capital of industrial Liberalism, the erection in 1875 of the first Cromwellian statue in England caused a minor political sensation." Blair Worden, "Rugged Outcast," *New York Review of Books,* Nov. 15, 1974, 24.

For the German interest in Carlyle and Whig historiography, see especially Weber's Freiburg colleague, Gerhart von Schulze-Gaevernitz, *Zum sozialen Frieden. Eine Darstellung der sozialpolitischen Erziehung des englischen Volkes* (Leipzig: Duncker & Humblot, 1890); on Carlyle, see 77–290; see also idem., *Carlyles Stellung zu Christentum und Revolution* (Leipzig: Marquardt, 1891). Schulze-Gaevernitz repeats some of his favorite themes as late as his 1930 Swarthmore Lectures, *Democracy and Religion. A Study of Quakerism* (London: Allen & Un-win, 1930).

3  "The Protestant Sects and the Spirit of Capitalism," in Hans Gerth and C. Wright Mills, eds., *From Max Weber* (New York: Oxford University Press, 1946), 321.

Western cultural development."[4] Politically, Weber upheld the rights of man against conservative detractors, but he traced them back, with Georg Jellinek, to English and American traditions rather than to the French Enlightenment and the French Revolution. Thus, he could write to Harnack in January 1905, between the publication of the two parts of *The Protestant Ethic and the Spirit of Capitalism:* "We must not forget that we owe to the sects achievements which nobody wants to miss today: freedom of conscience and the most basic rights of man (*Menschenrechte*), which we take for granted today. Only radical idealism could bring them about."[5] Marianne Weber echoed her husband when she wrote in 1907: "Just as freedom of conscience has been the mother of all human rights, so it also stood at the cradle of women's rights."[6]

The struggle against the authoritarian powers had, however, led not only to the Bill of Rights and the rights of man, but also to bloodshed as an act of self-assertion. Weber's political loathing of William II and his authoritarian subjects was so great that he pointedly expressed his approval of the English and French regicides. He told Count Keyserling: "A people which, as we Germans, has never dared to behead the traditionalist powers will never gain the proud self-assurance that makes the Anglo-Saxons and Latins (*Romanen*) ["politically" crossed out] so superior to us in the world. This is true in spite of all our 'victories,' gained through discipline, in war and technology."[7]

Weber, then, affirmed a particular kind of political voluntarism and "radical idealism" as against German constitutional and cultural authoritarianism. His great existential problem – political as well as

4 Letter of June 21, 1911, in Eduard Baumgarten, ed., *Max Weber. Werk und Person* (Tübingen: Mohr, 1964), 429.
5 Letter of Jan. 12, 1905, quoted in Wolfgang J. Mommsen, *Max Weber and German Politics 1890–1920*, tr. Michael Steinberg (Chicago: University of Chicago Press, 1984), 392.
6 Marianne Weber, *Ehefrau und Mutter in der Rechtsentwicklung* (1907; repr. ed. Aalen: Scientia, 1971), 290.
7 Baumgarten, *Max Weber*. Paul Honigsheim remembers Weber exclaiming: "A people that has never beheaded its monarch is not a *Kulturvolk*"; note that Weber here speaks not of *Herrenvolk* but of *Kulturvolk*. See Honigsheim, *On Max Weber*, tr. Joan Rytina (New York: Free Press, 1968), 13 (tr. altered). At the moment of Imperial Germany's collapse, Weber mitigated his formulation: "It has been beneficial to the self-esteem of every nation to have repudiated its legitimate powers at one time or another, even if they were recalled later by the grace of the people, as it happened in England" (MWGA, I/16, 107). When William II fled from Berlin in early November 1918 to seek safety in his military headquarters in Belgium (before ending up in the Netherlands), Weber was immediately reminded of the flight of James II and of the opportunism of many members of Parliament. See Karl Loewenstein, "Persönliche Erinnerungen an Max Weber," in René König and J. Winckelmann, eds., *Max Weber zum Gedächtnis* (Cologne: Westdeutscher Verlag, 1963), 51.

personal – was the connection between self-control and world mastery. This is reflected in his admiration for the "steely Puritan merchants," who were not yet imprisoned in the "iron cage" of modern capitalism. Only iron determination could strengthen the backbone of the German bourgeoisie. Only then was there a chance to democratize the *Kaiserreich* and legitimize its claim to world power, to a place under the sun. (The alliance of "steel and rye," of industrialists and agrarians, undermined the chance for such iron determination.) Weber witnessed Germany's extraordinarily rapid transformation into an industrialized country that increasingly challenged the British Empire. But as a class-conscious bourgeois, he suffered from a pronounced sense of political impotence vis-à-vis Imperial Germany's supreme failing: the lack of self-control (*Unbeherrschtheit*), embodied in the impulsive personality and erratic behavior of William II. Although *Weltpolitik* was conducted in the spirit of a power-conscious *Realpolitik,* the German leadership and public seemed to lack any sense of proportion about what was feasible in the world. The German problem, we might say, was one of "macho impotence."

In view of the fact that Weber remained so ambivalent about Germany's historical capacities in spite of its increasing industrial and military might, it is not surprising that his image of England did not differ fundamentally from that of two generations of liberals preceding him. Moreover, he had close family connections with the older liberals.[8] In his formative years, Weber developed an intensive intellectual relationship with his uncle Hermann Baumgarten (1825–1893), then a historian of the Reformation and Counter-Reformation at the University of Strasbourg. Young Baumgarten, in turn, had been the pupil and collaborator of Georg Gottfried Gervinus, the intimate friend and house companion of his father-in-law, Georg Friedrich Fallenstein, Max Weber's grandfather. Gervinus dared to praise the English parliamentary system even in the reactionary 1850s. When he was indicted for predicting the inevitable advance of democracy despite the failure of the 1848 revolution, Baumgarten, at the behest of Fallenstein, defended him with his first major publication: *Gervinus and His Political Convictions* (anonymous, 1853).

Gervinus (1805–1871), one of the most widely read historians of his time, believed in laws of historical development: In ascending states, intellectual and political freedom spreads from the few to the

8 See the letter to Robert Michels, Aug. 16, 1908, *Briefe 1906–1908,* M. Rainer Lepsius and W. J. Mommsen, eds., with Birgit Rudhard and Manfred Schön, MWGA, II/5, 641ff.

many; in declining states a reversion occurs, threatening caesarism and dictatorship. Within medieval Christianity there had been an antagonism between Romanism and Germanism, universalism and individualism. Echoing Montesquieu, Gervinus believed that individualism came naturally to the Germanic peoples. Democratic freedom grew out of "Germanic-Protestant individualism." He recognized the aristocratic elements in Calvinism and considered, in contrast to Max Weber, the *decretum horribile* a fatalistic doctrine, but he also asserted that the dynamics of Calvinism promoted the democratic evolution of Protestant ideas. Gervinus concluded his famous *Introduction to the History of the Nineteenth Century* (1852) with what he thought was a factual statement and the public prosecutor considered high treason: "The movements of our time are propelled by the instincts of the masses. . . . It is the masses that are beginning to take over politics. . . . They demand that the state pursue the welfare of the many rather than of the few or of a single person; they appeal to a rationale . . . which the Calvinist political theorists had preached warningly long ago: That there can be states without princes, but not without a people."[9] Here was a point of connection with Weber's view about the historical benefits of regicide.

In his generation of Anglophiles, Gervinus moved furthest to the left. Although still widely read in the 1850s and 1860s, he was quickly forgotten after his death in 1871, the year of German unification. No longer did the public want to read Whiggish historiography that predicted the inevitable victory of liberty. Instead, Heinrich von Treitschke, who had begun as a warm admirer of English traditions,[10] became the great nationalist seer and oracle of Bismarck's empire. In the 1870s Baumgarten broke with his erstwhile ally, Treitschke, over Bismarck's increasingly antiliberal course, remembered his old closeness to Gervinus, and himself became an embittered outsider, who filled the ears of the young Max Weber with his jeremiads. But Baumgarten also imparted positive impulses to Weber that later went into the writing of *The Protestant Ethic*. After an active career as a political publicist, Baumgarten became a historian of the Reformation and Counter-Reformation largely for political reasons,

9 Georg Gottfried Gervinus, *Einleitung in die Geschichte des neunzehnten Jahrhunderts,* Walter Boehlich, ed. (Frankfurt: Insel, 1967), 162, 165. See also, Gangolf Hübinger, *Georg Gottfried Gervinus. Historisches Urteil und politische Kritik* (Göttingen: Vandenhoeck & Ruprecht, 1984).
10 Reinhard Lamer, *Der englische Parlamentarismus in der deutschen politischen Theorie im Zeitalter Bismarcks, 1857–1890* (Lübeck: Matthiesen, 1963), 5.

namely his convictions about the world-historical mission of an ethico-political Protestantism. Appointed to the new German university at Strasbourg in 1872, he dreamed of restoring the Protestant glory of the sixteenth century to an Alsace that had long ago been reconquered by the Counter-Reformation.[11]

The struggle of the Protestant *Reich* against the Catholic church – the *Kulturkampf* – had ended, however, in a serious defeat. In 1887, when the second legislative settlement was passed, Baumgarten wrote a polemical pamphlet on "Roman Triumphs." The pope, he noted plaintively, "has forced the dominant power of our times, an essentially Protestant power, which is led by an almost omnipotent and truly ingenious statesman, to bow down before him after a long bitter struggle. He has conquered for his church a position in Germany, the heartland of heresy, that it has not held for a long time. His partisans openly proclaim the certain return of the German as well as the English people and of all other heretics into the bosom of the only saving church. One does not have to go far to hear skeptics, who have not the slightest sympathy for Rome, pronounce: 'Protestantism has no future.' "[12]

Baumgarten offered a set of paradoxical explanations. Prussian

11 In 1894, a year after Baumgarten's death, the right-wing historian Erich Marcks tried to sum up his alienated teacher's political and religious ethos:

> His was a Protestantism, nourished by Lessing and Herder, that understood Christianity in historical terms and history as part of revelation. It was a Protestantism that expressed itself most sharply in struggle against Lutheran orthodoxy and especially Catholicism. On this score Baumgarten was ever more passionate. In his eyes the struggle was crucial for German existence. The whole intellectual history of modern times rested for him on the Protestant idea of the free, self-determined personality. The supreme duty consisted in protecting and enlarging this freedom. His admonition of his contemporaries and his historical sympathies – for Calvinism and political Protestantism as against North German Lutheranism – concerned the fructification of the inner life through the deed, through the political spirit. The challenge lay in uniting the peculiar interiority of our Protestant nature with the powers of the world. . . . In this regard the influence of Dahlmann and Duncker and, it must be conceded, of Gervinus too made a deep impact: The ethical element predominates in all of Baumgarten's utterances, in his whole historical approach.

Erich Marcks, biographical introduction to Hermann Baumgarten, *Historische und politische Aufsätze und Reden* (Strasbourg: Truebner, 1894), lxxxv.

Max Weber's uncle Adolf Hausrath (1837–1909), who was married to Henriette Fallenstein, also was a church historian and shared with his brother-in-law Hermann Baumgarten a sympathy for Calvinism and the conviction that the Alsace would become genuinely German again. On Calvinism and the Jesuits, see his historical novel on sixteenth-century Heidelberg, *Klytia,* written under the English pseudonym George Taylor (Leipzig: Hirzel, 1883; 6th ed., 1894); it was twice published in German in the United States (1884, 1929) and twice translated (1883, 1884); on the Alsace, see "Die oberrheinische Bevölkerung in der deutschen Geschichte," in *Kleine Schriften religionsgeschichtlichen Inhalts* (Leipzig: Hirzel, 1883), 301–328.

12 Baumgarten, "Römische Triumphe," 504f.

Protestantism had unintentionally revitalized German Catholicism through its post-Napoleonic reforms in the Rhineland and through national unification. Like Weber after him, Baumgarten pointed out that "where Protestants and Catholics live together, the former occupy predominantly the higher, the latter the lower rungs of society. . . . Where the Catholic population flees higher education or cannot attain it, the Protestants must inevitably gain a considerable lead in public administration, justice, commerce, industry, and science. This fact is then very effectively held up as the height of injustice by the clerical agitators before the masses of the faithful."[13] Baumgarten linked the sins of the old Lutherans to those of the new. "The Calvinists had dared to defend their faith against a legitimate king with arms, when suffering obedience had become a major tenet of the Lutheran confession. Therefore Lutheran Germany stood by when the brothers in Holland and France bled. Plenty of strife divided the Protestants there as well as in England. But when Spain, backed up by Rome, took on the divided heretics, the lively, spiritually active disunity defeated the rigidly united power."[14] In present-day Germany, Baumgarten recognized again an opportunistic alliance between Protestant orthodoxy and Catholic clericalism: "Rome, this mother of Revolution, looks like a conservative power vis-à-vis the radical tendencies" of the time. Paradoxically, however, "whoever thinks today of pursuing a conservative policy in alliance with Rome will merely promote the cause of radicalism"[15] Rome appeared to him as the mother of revolution because time and again clericalism, especially the Jesuits, had pushed the Catholic peoples to rebellion.

Both Baumgarten and Weber feared the implications of the lost *Kulturkampf*, but the younger man was particularly concerned about the issue of conscience backfiring on the Protestants. In the same year, 1887, the twenty-three-year-old Max Weber wrote a birthday letter to his uncle, who was almost forty years older:

This meek "peace" is sad. If it is said today that the struggle had only "political" reasons from our side, we admit to a grave injustice. If it was indeed for us not a matter of conscience but only of opportunism, then we have violated the conscience of the Catholic people for extraneous reasons, as the Catholics assert. After all, for the masses of the Catholics it was a matter of conscience, and then it was not true that conscience stood against conscience, as we always claimed. In this case we have acted without con-

13 Ibid., 515f.    14 Ibid., 507.    15 Ibid., 517f. See also "Ignatius von Loyola," 498ff.

science, and we are the moral losers. This is the worst aspect of the defeat, because it prevents us from ever renewing the struggle the way it has to be conducted if it is to lead to victory.[16]

If the Protestant empire had violated the conscience of the Catholics, this did not change Baumgarten's and Weber's conviction that historically freedom of conscience was the achievement of radical Protestant individualism, especially of the consistent sects. Yet the homeland of the sect was not Germany but England. Again English history had created a religious and political ideal that threw the German realities into stark relief.

The great liberal Anglophiles, from Karl von Rotteck to Robert von Mohl and Gervinus, idealized English institutions for their own political purposes.[17] They wrote for a broad bourgeois audience and usually did not bother with archival research. It was a paradox of German historiography that the improving scholarship of succeeding generations went together with increasing chauvinism. After 1870 historians became in some respect more professional and academic, yet the growing emphasis on archival research did not lessen ideological commitments – witness Baumgarten's intermediate position between the older liberal publicists and Weber's generation. In fact, serious scholarly research on England seems to have declined as national competition and antagonism increased. Archival research about English institutions no longer promised to be of any relevance for the constitution of the Reich. In the wake of the Spanish-American War of 1898, however, political and academic interest increased vis-à-vis the United States, which appeared for the first time as a possible imperialist competitor. In this situation *The Protestant Ethic* saw print as a scholarly study that had palpable political overtones. If it stood at the end of a long line of liberal preoccupation with England, it was also an early contribution to the rapidly growing interest in the United States as a possible enemy or ally in Germany's competition with the British Empire.

A comparison between Weber and Gerhart von Schulze-Gaevernitz (1864–1943) can further illuminate the ideological context of *The Protestant Ethic*. In 1890 Schulze-Gaevernitz had published his book *On Social Peace*,[18] a study of the critics and reformers of British

16 Letter of Apr. 25, 1887, in Max Weber, *Jugendbriefe* (Tübingen: Mohr, 1936), 234.
17 For a comprehensive treatment, see Charles E. McClelland, *The German Historians and England* (Cambridge: Cambridge University Press, 1971).
18 Schulze-Gaevernitz, *Zum sozialen Frieden* (Leipzig: Drackert Humblot, 1890).

capitalism from Thomas Carlyle to the Christian socialists and the cooperative movement. Schulze-Gaevernitz's interests in British industrialization and welfare politics was undergirded by the fact that his maternal grandfather, Carl August Milde, had learned his trade as a cotton manufacturer in Manchester before becoming president of the Prussian Constituent Assembly in 1848 and Prussian minister of trade. Growing up in a liberal Catholic home, Schulze-Gaevernitz's mother was, in her son's words, a "Christian with the strictest self-discipline, a puritan in the best sense of the word."[19] By 1890 Schulze-Gaevernitz's book and background had blocked his career in the conservative Prussian administration, and he turned to academic life, following in the footsteps of his father, the Heidelberg constitutional theorist Hermann Schulze, who was ennobled in 1888. The young Schulze-Gaevernitz was an Anglophile with a vengeance – adopting a competitive attitude toward the old liberal model. Within a few months of Weber's *Protestant Ethic* he brought out a massive study on *British Imperialism and English Free Trade at the Beginning of the Twentieth Century.*[20] In spite of the difference in title, the two studies parallel one another over long stretches. Schulze-Gaevernitz and Weber held similar views on the legacy of Puritanism and the contemporary rivalry between Great Britain and Imperial Germany. The former spelled out a program of Germany's world mission and thus followed in the wake of Weber's inaugural lecture of 1895 on "Nation State and Economic Policy." Weber, however, did not explicitly connect his essay with his speech at the University of Freiburg, where the two men had been fellow economists and established a family friendship. In a letter to his brother Alfred he even distanced himself from his colleague: "As far as Schulze-Gaevernitz's *Imperialism* is concerned, I agree with you of course *insofar* as *such* exaggerations of views which I too hold must backfire, even though the book is brilliant."[21] Yet the exaggeration of a jointly held position

---

19  See Kurt Zielenziger, *Gerhart von Schulze-Gaevernitz* (Berlin: Prager, 1926), 7f.

20  *Britischer Imperialismus und englischer Freihandel zu Beginn des zwanzigsten Jahrhunderts* (Leipzig: Duncker & Humblot, 1906).

21  MWGA, II/5, 236. Unfortunately, the letter breaks off at this point. Nevertheless, it is clear that Max objected mainly to the exaggeration, not the basic position, whereas Alfred seems to have had greater doubts. In the 1920 version of *The Protestant Ethic,* Weber refers to Schulze-Gaevernitz's "beautiful book" – for him usually an adjective that combines praise with some reservation. For another comment see "Antikritisches Schlusswort" (1910) in Johannes Winckelmann, ed., *Die protestantische Ethik II. Kritiken und Antikritiken* (Gütersloh: . Siebenstern, 1978), 327.

In his necrology of Max Weber, Schulze-Gaevernitz continued to claim him for his own particular reading. He praised Weber's critical attitude toward the shallow and vapid utilitar-

makes it easier for us to understand what was increasingly at stake for a broad German audience. Schulze-Gaevernitz's book turns out to be an anticipation of some of the "ideas of 1914," which Weber criticized strongly during the war and from which Schulze-Gaevernitz partially retreated afterward. But even as a wartime critic of Imperial Germany, Weber was not so far from his colleague's position in his concern with "the quality of the culture of the future," with the political determination to prevent the division of the world "between the rules and regulations of Russian bureaucrats and the conventions of Anglo-Saxon 'society,' perhaps with a dash of Latin 'raison'" (MWGA, I/15, 96). Still, this was milder rhetoric than that of hundreds of German professors, including brother Alfred and, of course, Sombart. In the end, recognition of the inherent political superiority of the Anglo-Saxon world powers seems to have acted as a brake on Weber. If he had shared the outrageous anti-British rhetoric of so many of his colleagues before and especially after 1914, he would probably have been unable to achieve his posthumous fame in England and America. As it was, *The Protestant Ethic* was constructed in such a way that it could ultimately be transplanted into the Anglo-Saxon world. Although once much translated, Schulze-Gaevernitz is forgotten today.

In varying degrees, then, German liberal and even conservative scholars acknowledged a historical connection between English Puritanism and contemporary democracy, world power, and capitalism. In the late 1890s, Weber turned to his theory of the Protestant ethic and the spirit of capitalism at the same time that he supported strongly the first navy budget that opened the naval race with Great Britain; he and Schulze-Gaevernitz did not believe it to be directed against England. Weber considered it imperative that in "the age of cap-

ianism into which religious innerworldly asceticism had deteriorated, thus emptying the modern world of meaning. It appeared to him that Weber could maintain such a critical distance all the more easily because "Anglo-Saxon reserve (*Gehaltenheit*) was alien to his explosive nature. On British soil he would have been conceivable only with a strong admixture of Celtic blood." Schulze-Gaevernitz lamented that "Weber's extraordinary understanding of the Anglo-Saxon soul (*Volksseele*) was not utilized politically, neither before nor during the war. Weber understood what it meant to turn against us that religiously nourished idea of liberty, as it was done in England and even more in America. . . . The benighted German government was blind before the light of his genius." Schulze-Gaevernitz was not capable of facing up to the inherent limitations of his own program of displacing England for the betterment of world civilization. See Schulze-Gaevernitz, "Max Weber als Nationalökonom," in König and Winckelmann, eds., *Max Weber zum Gedächtnis*, 56f. See also Willy Schenk, *Die deutsch-englische Rivalität vor dem Ersten Weltkrieg in der Sicht deutscher Historiker* (Aarau: Keller, 1967), esp. 136ff.

italism" and of increasing military tensions between the bourgeois *Kulturvölker,* Germany, as an *Industriestaat* and a great nation, had "to take responsibility before history," if more for the ethical qualities than the material welfare of future German generations.[22]

Weber's ethical rigorism remained suspended between an attraction to the imagery of ascetic Protestantism and the heady notion of a secular ethic of imperial responsibility. It is well known that in his teens and student days Weber, although he called himself "amusical" in matters religious, read much theological literature, especially with his mother Helene, his aunt Ida Baumgarten (Helene's sister), and his cousin Otto Baumgarten, the young theologian.[23] This included the American Unitarians William Ellery Channing and Theodore Parker.[24] Thus, Weber could write in the first version of *The Protestant Ethic* that Georg Jellinek's *The Declaration of the Rights of Man and of Citizens* (1895) had motivated him to "turn again to Puritanism."[25] It is equally well known that, again with these closest of his relatives, he engaged in the religious and social reform efforts of the Protestant Social Congress and of Friedrich Naumann's Christian Social Party.[26] Yet in this respect, too, Weber remained something of an "agnostic," insofar as such reformist efforts interested him primarily from the viewpoint of *Weltpolitik.*

It is less well known, however, that there was not only a family

22  The phrases can be found, for instance, in Weber's public affirmation of the naval expansion program of 1898, reprinted in *Gesammelte politische Schriften,* 3rd ed., Joh. Winckelmann, ed. (Tübingen: Mohr, 1971), 30f. On the contemporary meaning of Weber's slogan, "Our responsibility before history," and its outdatedness today, see my essay "Max Weber's Ethics and the Peace Movement Today," *Theory and Society,* 13(1984): 491–511.

23  Otto Baumgarten (1858–1934) also was an Anglophile with a high degree of personal engagement. In the early 1880s he married his cousin, Emily Fallenstein, the daughter of Ida's half-brother, Otto Fallenstein, who had married an English woman. Emily grew up in England and Australia. Otto Baumgarten learned to speak English fluently and traveled to England before and during his brief marriage; Emily died in childbed with her son. Much concerned about the deteriorating relationship between England and Germany, Baumgarten wrote *Carlyle und Goethe* (Tübingen: Mohr, 1906) in order to "strengthen the spiritual bond between the two Germanic nations in spite of the increasing tensions" (2). He traveled to England on two ecclesiastic "peace missions" in 1908 and again in 1922. See also his autobiography, *Meine Lebensgeschichte* (Tübingen: Mohr, 1929), 57, 123, 240f., 451ff.

24  Adolf Hausrath satirized his sisters-in-law Helene and Ida for judging people, especially tutors, in terms of their reactions to Channing in his novel *Elfriede. A Romance of the Rhineland* (London: Swan Sonnenschein, 1888), 59, 251.

25  Weber, "Die protestantische Ethik und der 'Geist' des Kapitalismus," *Archiv für Sozialwissenschaft und Sozialpolitik* 21 (1905): 43.

26  On the Congress, see Harry Liebersohn, *Religion and Industrial Society: The Protestant Social Congress in Wilhelmine Germany. Transactions of the American Philosophical Society,* Vol. 76, Part 6 (1986). It was from their inherited wealth that Ida Baumgarten and Helene Weber, the granddaughters of Carl Cornelius Souchay, financed Naumann's candidacy for the Reichstag.

context for Weber's theoretical and practical interests in the future of Protestantism, but also an extended family connection with German as well as English capitalism. It is true that Max and Marianne called attention to their links with the linen merchants and manufacturers of Westphalia, but they volunteered almost no information on the familial ties with London and Manchester. Since so much of our knowledge of Max Weber the person is shaped by Marianne's biography, it is prudent to remember that she apparently not only felt much more ambivalent toward England and the United States but also wrote under the shadow of a lost war and the Versailles Treaty, which she, like almost all political liberals, considered completely unjust. Perhaps this was one reason for her noticeable downplaying of the English connection at the same time that she dramatically elevated the story of Georg Friedrich Fallenstein, the superpatriotic "freedom fighter" against Napoleon in the hour of Germany's defeat.

There is a family background to Weber's academic and political concern with international trade and the international role of stock exchanges, and this may go some way toward explaining why he began his academic career as a student and teacher of commercial law. In fact, Weber made one effort to become practically acquainted with this world of international trade and the securities and commodities exchange.[27] In 1891, he applied for the position of a municipal lawyer in the seaport and city-state of Bremen, a post given up by the young Werner Sombart. When Weber heard about Hermann Baumgarten's disapproval of this plan, he replied to him: "I still believe that it would have been very valuable for me to learn the export/import business thoroughly over several years and especially in a position that would have allowed me to continue scholarly writing. I have an extraordinary longing for a practical position."[28]

Since Weber was unsuccessful in his application, his knowledge about the business of his maternal relatives had to remain theoretical. He learned some of it from his "doctor father," Levin Goldschmidt

---

27 Already as a fifteen-year-old he had seen his first exchange and port when he visited his uncle Otto Weber, a merchant in Hamburg. Somewhat precociously he reported to his cousin Fritz Baumgarten: "The life of such a seaport has its particular fascination for the layman. One sees how thousands of people work for one purpose. I also watched business being transacted on the floor of the exchange, and thus got a glimpse of the world of trade." Letter of Oct. 1, 1879, Max Weber, *Jugendbriefe,* 28. Many years later, during their trip to America, Max and Marianne Weber visited the New York Stock Exchange. See Ernst Troeltsch's letter of Sept. 3, 1904, quoted in Rollmann's essay in this volume.

28 Letter of Jan. 3, 1891, *Jugendbriefe,* 326. For an excerpt, see Marianne Weber, *Max Weber,* tr. Harry Zohn (New Brunswick, N.J.: Transaction, 1988), 164.

(1829–1897), under whom he wrote his 1889 dissertation "On the History of Medieval Trading Companies." Goldschmidt, who worked on his famous *Handbook of Commercial Law* while living in Emilie Souchay Fallenstein's Heidelberg mansion between 1862 and 1870, knew her grandson Max Weber as a Souchay descendant from his earliest childhood on.[29] He furthered his career and apparently envisaged him as his successor in Berlin.

In the mid-1890s Weber approached the securities and commodities exchange along two dimensions, legislative reform and popular education. He participated as an expert in the proceedings of a committee on the exchange in the Imperial Ministry of the Interior. In 300 pages he analyzed "The Results of the Enquete on the German Exchange" in Goldschmidt's *Zeitschrift für das gesamte Handelsrecht* (vols. 43–45, 1895–1896). He also dealt in long articles with "The Technical Function of Futures Trading" and contributed summaries on the new legislation in a handbook. Finally, he tried to explain the beneficial social and economic purposes of the exchange to a presumably skeptical or hostile working-class readership in a sixty-five-page pamphlet for Friedrich Naumann's "Workers Library."

In Berlin he also lectured in Naumann's workers' education course, but before a very small and "inappropriate" audience, according to his mother, who listened to him "about the theme that is as remote from my interests and as incomprehensible to me as can possibly be."[30] At stake in the political battle on exchange reform was the power balance between liberal commercial interests in a free commodities market, especially for grains, and conservative agrarian interests, who wanted to set their own prices. Weber feared that a legislative restraint of commodities speculation would weaken Germany's competitive position. He was, however, in favor of moving in the direction of the English model, a status group of financially strong brokers who were socially homogeneous and could exert social control over one another. But if members of the exchange should be honorable gentlemen, they also had to have "good nerves." For the rest, Weber affirmed that "a strong exchange cannot be a club for 'Ethical Culture,' and the capital of the great banks is as little a matter

29  See Levin Goldschmidt, *Handbuch des Handelsrechts,* Vol. I:1, *Universalgeschichte des Hand-elsrechts* (Erlangen: Enke, 1864); Vol. 1:2, *Die Lehre von der Ware* (1868). The second volume reads like a guide to the activities of the Souchay circle, involving securities, foreign exchange, liens, mortgages, purchase deeds, dead pledges, warehouse receipts, bills of freight, etc. Like Wilhelm Benecke (see footnote 45 of this essay), Goldschmidt also was an expert on maritime insurance. See Levin Goldschmidt, *System des Handelsrechts, mit Einschluss des Wechsel-, See- und Versicherungsrechts,* 2d ed. (Stuttgart: Enke, 1889).
30  Letter of Oct. 7, 1896, in Baumgarten, ed., *Max Weber,* 330.

of 'social welfare' as are rifles and cannons."[31] In these writings, then, Weber still emphasized the heterogeneity of religious ethics and business logic rather than the genetic link between religious belief and the spirit of capitalism.

In contrast to the capitalist role of Weber's Huguenot ancestors and relatives, the literature has often called attention to the religious aspect. Thus, Weber's grandmother has been variously described as a woman of "stern Calvinist morality" (Liebersohn) and a "paragon of sorrowing ethical religiosity" (Mitzman), who handed on a religious rigorism to her daughters Ida and Helene.[32] It should be asked, however, as I do later, how strong this family tradition really was, even for the women. It is true that for Weber the Protestant ethic flourished in the seventeenth century and the spirit of capitalism in the eighteenth, until the Enlightenment, the French Revolution and British utilitarianism ushered in the age of self-sustaining industrial capitalism. Still, it is striking to see that his highly successful relatives seemed so little imbued with the old spirit.

## 2. WEBER'S FAMILY HISTORY: CAPITALISM WITHOUT THE SPIRIT?

Weber chose to begin his exposition of the spirit of capitalism not with an abstract definition but with an illustration from Benjamin Franklin that he considered self-evident. Here was an ethic that prescribed "the earning of more and more money, combined with the

---

31 Weber, "Die Börse" (1894–1896), reprinted in *Gesammelte Aufsätze zur Soziologie und Sozialpolitik* (Tübingen: Mohr, 1924), 321.

32 See Harry Liebersohn, *Fate and Utopia in German Sociology. 1870–1923* (Cambridge, Mass.: MIT Press, 1988), 83; Arthur Mitzman, *The Iron Cage. An Historical Interpretation of Max Weber* (New York: Knopf, 1970), 18. See also similar remarks by M. Rainer Lepsius, "Die Bewohner des Hauses Ziegelhäuser Landstrasse 17 in Heidelberg" (Ms., 1989), 5f. There is no doubt that the women remained more religious than the men, who often separated their personal faith from their business ethics. It seems to me, however, that there was an upsurge of ethical rigorism, rather than a mere continuation of a Huguenot/Reformed tradition, in the generation of Helene Weber and Ida Baumgarten. This is my reading of Otto Baumgarten's account of the religious development of his mother, Ida, in her later years. Writing as a theologian, Baumgarten began his autobiography with a section on "Religious Huguenot Influences" and located his mother and Weber's grandmother, Emilie, in the "old pastoral Souchay tradition." See Baumgarten, *Lebensgeschichte,* 1–9. Although admitting the religious impact of David Friedrich Strauss' radical rationalism within the Fallenstein family, he remained silent on the business side of the Souchay family and did not mention Emilie's father, the cosmopolitan capitalist. Thus, Baumgarten may have construed a more consistent religious heritage than had in fact existed.

A closer study of Marianne Weber would be needed to decide the extent to which she stylized the women's ethical rigorism out of her own moralistic concerns and her own involvement with Max Weber's mother. For a first effort, see my essay "Marianne Weber and Her Circle," introduction to Marianne Weber, *Max Weber,* xv–lx.

strict avoidance of all spontaneous enjoyment of life . . . completely devoid of any eudaemonistic, not to say hedonistic, admixture. . . . Man is dominated by the making of money, by acquisition as the ultimate purpose of his life. . . . This reversal of what we should call the natural relationships, so irrational from a naive point of view . . . at the same time . . . expresses a kind of feeling which is closely connected with certain religious ideas" (PE 53). Weber constructed a homology that would permit him to claim a basic similarity within a crucial historical difference: The spirit of capitalism was identical to Puritan vocational asceticism, but its religious roots had died off by Franklin's time.

Weber's distinction between the form and the spirit of capitalism allowed combinations of traditionalism and rationalism. Franklin appeared to combine the capitalist spirit with a traditional form of handicraft production – his print shop. Weber illustrated the conjunction of capitalist form and traditionalist spirit with the example of his paternal grandfather, Karl August Weber (1796–1872), a linen merchant from the Bielefeld patriciate. Marianne Weber later underlined the absence of any spirit of capitalism on the part of this man who was her great-grandfather: "In those days the linen trade was still carried on by home labor in early 'capitalist' fashion: making money was neither an end in itself nor a sign of grace (*Bewährung*). . . . Accordingly the pace of work was slow."[33] By contrast, Max Weber portrayed his uncle Karl David Weber (1824–1907), the son of Karl August, as the representative of a new capitalist drive: He "went out into the country, carefully chose weavers for his employ, greatly increased the rigor of his supervision of their work, and thus turned them from peasants into laborers . . . he would begin to change his marketing methods by so far as possible going directly to the final consumer. . . . The idyllic state collapsed under the pressure of a bitter competitive struggle, respectable fortunes were made, and not lent out at interest, but always reinvested in the business" (PE 68).

Weber claimed that such sudden eruption of a spirit of capitalism had often nothing to do with "any essential change in the form of organization, such as the transition to a unified factory, to mechanical weaving, etc." (PE 67). Marianne Weber pointed, however, to technological factors that enforced greater entrepreneurial effort on the part of her grandfather, Karl David Weber. When the Bielefeld firm

---

33 Marianne Weber, *Max Weber*, 25.

declined with the coming of mechanical spinning, he moved to the village of Oerlinghausen – Marianne's birthplace – in 1850: "Here Karl Weber, the energetic son of the Bielefeld business house that had suffered because of modern technology, built a new business from scratch. . . . Later on his nephew Max analyzed his novel business methods and his personality as an example of modern entrepreneurship."[34]

Recent research has shown that there was indeed a change in economic mentality but that, as Weber himself had conceded, the new spirit could be understood "purely as a result of adaptation . . . bound up with the conditions of survival in the economic struggle for existence" (PE 72). After the Napoleonic Wars, English textile goods flooded the European market. In the first half of the nineteenth century the German textile industry encountered increasing competition with regard to exports and imports. By the 1830s linen production, the major industry in Bielefeld, had suffered in volume and price, impoverishing the spinners and weavers. Short of changing the product, the merchants could move in two directions to cope with the crisis: (1) mechanization or (2) the putting-out system. Since linen was the most important Prussian export in the early nineteenth century, the government set up trade schools to train a technological elite of mechanical engineers and technical factory directors. Often students were sent to England, Ireland, and Belgium for extended periods. One of them was Ferdinand Kaselowsky (1816–1877), who first went to England in 1840.[35] In Silesia he helped the Prussian government set up model spinning mills. In Bielefeld, however, the government insisted that, apart from some subsidies, the wealthy patricians had to finance the mechanization of the linen industry on their own.[36] The older merchants were traditionalist not only be-

---

34  Ibid., 172. Weber attributed to his uncle sterling entrepreneurial qualities: "Only an unusually strong character would save an entrepreneur of this new type from the loss of his temperate self-control and from both moral and economic shipwreck. . . . But these are ethical qualities of quite a different sort from those adapted to the traditionalism of the past" (PE 69). See also Weber's letter of condolence on his uncle's death, July 21, 1907, in *Briefe*, MWGA, II/5, 335f.

35  Peter Lundgreen, "Ferdinand Kaselowsky," in Jürgen Kocka and Reinhard Vogelsang, eds., *Bielefelder Unternehmer des 18. bis 20. Jahrhunderts, Rheinisch-Westfälische Wirtschaftsbiographien* 14 (Münster: Aschendorff, 1990), 163–187.

36  In 1842 Peter Beuth, the Prussian secretary of commerce, who promoted much foreign travel and sponsored Kaselowsky, wrote to Gustav Delius, who in the 1830s had the highest annual income in town: "As far as Bielefeld is concerned, I have often told you openly that the gentlemen there are merchants who rest on their laurels and money bags, but are not manufacturers." Thus, for Beuth the problem was how to turn established merchants into

cause they preferred their accustomed trading role over a new entrepreneurial one but also because they put quality over quantity at a period when mechanical production was indeed often inferior. But gradually they lost out and were forced to go out of business, as it happened to Weber, Laer & Niemann by 1861. When the changes finally came, it was mainly the sons of leading families rather than the parvenus who succeeded in new ventures. In this sense, Weber's statement must be qualified that the classical representatives of the capitalist spirit "were not the distinguished gentlemen of Liverpool and Hamburg, with their commercial fortunes handed down for generations, but the parvenus of Manchester and Rhineland-Westphalia, who often rose from very modest circumstances" (PE 65).[37] At any rate, the spirit of capitalism Weber discerned was in part an adaption to Prussian government policies, which pressured linen merchants into setting up mechanical spinning mills.

Karl David Weber did not choose the route of mechanization. When his father barely escaped bankruptcy, he took to the countryside in search of cheap labor and set up a putting-out system, ultimately organizing 1,000 pauperized weavers into an effective production unit. Since he could no longer live the life of a patrician merchant, he turned himself into an entrepreneur, but he retained the tradition of quality linen.[38] Economic pressures, then, were para-

technologically innovative manufacturers and how to change a mercantile spirit into an industrial one. Letter of Jan. 10, 1842, cited in Martin Schumacher, *Auslandsreisen deutscher Unternehmer 1750–1851* (Cologne: Rheinisch-Westfälisches Wirtschaftsarchiv, 1968), 218. See also Beuth's critical letter of 1836, quoted in Karl Ditt, *Industrialisierung, Arbeiterschaft und Arbeiterbewegung in Bielefeld 1850–1914* (Dortmund: Westfälisches Wirtschaftsarchiv, 1982), 16; on Delius, see 33f. Ditt provides a detailed account of the outlook of the patrician linen merchants, including the Webers, and the pressure that ultimately resulted in mechanization despite much resistance.

37 In Bielefeld the younger generation finally took the plunge after 1850. In 1852 the first mechanical spinning mill was indeed set up by parvenus, the Hungarian brothers Bozi, who suffered a perpetual capital shortage because of their outsider status. But two years later the young Hermann Delius fetched Kaselowsky, who had become one of the best linen industry experts, from Leeds and made him technical director and major shareholder of the much more successful Ravensberger Spinnerei, which used English machinery until 1902. Kaselowsky, the son of a shoemaker, became very rich and invested much of his wealth in what was considered the most beautiful mansion in Bielefeld, where he lived in grand style. Elected to the Prussian diet in 1877, he died before he could begin his term. Was Kaselowsky one of the parvenus whom Weber so berated for developing "feudal" tastes?

38 His three younger brothers left the home territory for good. Otto (1829–1889) became a merchant and bill broker in Hamburg (see footnote 27 in this essay), Leopold (1833–1876) a well-to-do merchant in Manchester. The youngest, Max Weber's father (born 1836), left the realm of commerce and became a lawyer, higher-ranking civil servant, and parliamentary deputy. He had, however, planned to spend several years abroad to gain practical experience, a plan that was upset when he met Helene Fallenstein. Through Uncle Leopold, Max Weber had three English cousins, who were slightly older than he. See the entry "Weber" in

mount. After contrasting the old spirit of his grandfather and the new capitalist spirit of his uncle, Max Weber was right to stress that "today . . . any relationship between religious beliefs and conduct is generally absent, and where any exists, at least in Germany, it tends to be of a negative sort" (PE 70). It is true that Karl David Weber came from Lutheran Bielefeld and moved to the Reformed (Calvinist) Oerlinghausen, but the religious difference was apparently no longer significant. He was, says Marianne Weber in her own memoirs, "sober, *sachlich* and not religious, at least not in later years. He once told me confidentially that he preferred Islam, that Christianity favored the enjoyment of wine at communion, and directed the common people to eternal salvation in the hereafter instead of encouraging industry in this world."[39] Thus, he was primarily interested in work discipline, but he did not connect it with the Protestant ethic, and although he obviously wanted his workers to be abstemious, he was no teetotaler himself and enjoyed his daily bottle of Moselle.

If Max Weber conceded that in the nineteenth century the spirit of capitalism was largely an adaptation to the economic struggle for existence, he still upheld an ideal type of the capitalist entrepreneur – fudging norm and construct – in the face of what he disapproved most about the "empirical average": "The resort to entailed estates and the patent of nobility, with sons whose conduct at the university and in the officers' corps tries to cover up their social origins – the usual history of German capitalist parvenu families – is a product of the decadence of late-comers" (PE 71).

Weber was already exploring the subject matter of the Protestant ethic when he appealed, at the Eighth Protestant Social Congress in 1897, to the German bourgeoisie "to recall its own identity, to return to the proud pursuit of its own ideals, and to dissolve the unnatural alliance [with the agrarian conservatives] in the interest of a beneficial social development and the country's political freedom."[40] Just before publishing his essay, he launched a vitriolic attack on the entailment bill of 1904 in the new *Archiv*. For years he had opposed the opportunity, popular among rich merchants and industrialists, to buy entailed estates and thus secure a patent of nobility. He also kept

Edmund Strutz, ed., *Deutsches Geschlechterbuch. Quellen deutscher bürgerlicher Geschlechter* (Limburg: Starke, 1962).

39 Marianne Weber, *Lebenserinnerungen* (Bremen: Storm, 1948), 11.

40 See *Die Verhandlungen des achten Evangelisch-sozialen Kongresses* (Göttingen: Vandenhoeck, 1897), 113.

condemning the "feudal" preoccupations with student fraternity membership and reserve officer status as being unsuited "to the hard and somber work without which our bourgeoisie will not be able to maintain Germany's power position in trade and industry around the world." As late as 1911 he professed: "I take my name from Westphalian linen and don't deny my pride in this bourgeois ancestry the way those circles I spoke of are eager to do."[41]

Weber's Oerlinghausen relatives did not buy landed estates and noble patents, but they belonged to the political and social elite of the tiny principality of Lippe-Detmold (which still exists today as a business corporation). A grandson of Karl David Weber, Georg Müller, was not only co-owner of the firm now called Weber and Co., but also president of the German association of linen manufacturers in Berlin. His brother Richard was a member of the diet of Lippe-Detmold. He married the daughter of a wealthy Berlin manufacturer, who brought metropolitan tastes to the small company town, which the family ran in the spirit of benevolent paternalism. In 1913 Müller built an elegant and sumptuous art nouveau villa. Thus, a villa typical of the wealthiest Berlin suburbs took its place incongruously next to the factory complex and the three other Victorian family villas (in what is today called the "Weber park" along Marianne Weber Street). When Karl David Weber died in 1907, he left his granddaughter Marianne the substantial sum of 350,000 marks, about half of which remained invested in the Oerlinghausen firm, which had become a leading supplier of bed and table linens for the ruling houses and the higher nobility.[42]

The other fortune from which Max Weber benefited in indirect ways was made by Carl Cornelius Souchay (1768–1838), one of his great-grandfathers. When his grandmother, Emilie Souchay Fallenstein, died in 1881, his mother's inheritance made feasible a much more opulent lifestyle in the Berlin household, although Helene was clearly troubled by any form of ostentation. Her inheritance was increased once more when her uncle, Wilhelm August Souchay, died in 1887. After her husband's death in 1897, she was free to use her

---

41 "Die Handelshochschulen" (1911), in Edward Shils, ed. and tr., *Max Weber on Universities* (Chicago: University of Chicago Press, 1973), 39.
42 Since Marianne did not take an active part in running the enterprise, her role was more that of a capitalist rentier, a figure so often decried by Max Weber. For the Webers, the part ownership was welcome, because it improved their financial circumstances, which had become somewhat reduced after Max resigned his chair in 1903 for health reasons. About the financial arrangements, see the letter from Max to Marianne, Oerlinghausen, Sept. 3, 1907, in *Briefe*, MWGA, II/5, 385ff.

fortune as she saw fit, and she used it in part to help Max and her other children.[43] Last, the famous Weber salon after 1910 was made possible when Max and Marianne moved into the grand mansion that Fallenstein had built with Souchay money in Heidelberg in 1847.

The Oerlinghausen relatives seem to have come close to Weber's standards for a genuine bourgeoisie, although their lifestyle increasingly transcended the older modes of bourgeois comfort in the direction of grand-bourgeois living. By contrast, it is unclear what Weber thought of the far-flung clan of the Souchays, unless they were in the back of his mind when he referred to patrician merchants, parvenus, and "feudal" aspirants. Here he would have had even greater difficulties identifying the spirit of capitalism, in his sense, despite the family's Reformed (Huguenot) background.

What kind of man was Carl Cornelius Souchay? When he died in 1838, he left behind a fortune of 2 million florins (gulden), one of the largest in Frankfurt. It was accumulated in a period when the city was the commercial and financial center of the Germanys, rivaled only by Hamburg and not yet by fledgling Berlin, and also was the most important and most profitable German distribution point for English manufactures.[44] Together with a close network of relatives, friends, and associates, Souchay ran an import-export firm, traded in futures, and acted as discount banker, bill broker, commission and shipping agent, and industrial investor, primarily in Frankfurt, London, and Manchester. His operations extended to the Near East, the Far East, and Russia. He was (in Weber's term) an "adventure capitalist" in the

43 While Alfred managed Helene's money, Max was the real paterfamilias, making the financial decisions with Helene's concurrence. See *Briefe,* MWGA, II/5, 36, 52f., 263, 270, 277, 282f., 304, 338, 385f., 404, 420, 526, 682, 686.
44 See Alexander Dietz, *Frankfurter Handelsgeschichte,* Vol. 4 (1925) (repr. Glashütten: Auvermann, 1973), 331. Dietz lists the great fortunes from 1556 to 1812 and includes the later Souchay figure because of its great size. This fortune amounted to about 300,000 pounds sterling, a sum very large also by English standards. On the kind of trade conducted by the Souchays, see a study produced in Weber's Heidelberg seminar, Hugo Kanter, *Die Entwicklung des Handels mit gebrauchsfertigen Waren von der Mitte des 18. Jahrhunderts bis 1866 zu Frankfurt a. M.* (Tübingen: Mohr, 1902); also see the Heidelberg dissertation by Veit Valentin *Politisches, geistiges und wirtschaftliches Leben in Frankfurt am Main vor dem Beginn der Revolution von 1848/49* (Stuttgart: Deutsche Verlagsanstalt, 1907). On the general importance of Frankfurt, see the lively narrative by Werner Sombart, *Die deutsche Volkswirtschaft im Neunzehnten Jahrhundert* (Berlin: Bondi, 1903), esp. 225ff. On the rise of international capital markets and the capital flight from the French Revolution that helped finance the British Industrial Revolution, see Larry Neal, *The Rise of Financial Capitalism. International Capital Markets in the Age of Reason* (Cambridge: Cambridge University Press, 1990). On the general role of the cosmopolitan bourgeoisie, see Charles A. Jones, *International Business in the Nineteenth Century. The Rise and Fall of a Cosmopolitan Bourgeoisie* (New York: New York University Press, 1987).

tumultuous years of the French Revolution, the Napoleonic Wars, and the Continental Blockade (1806–1813), a successful smuggler of English goods, a great wartime profiteer, a lucky speculator, and one of the few entrepreneurs who managed to perpetuate his gains in the postwar decades.[45] In the 1830s, his firm, Schunck, Souchay & Co., was the richest German merchant house in Britain.[46] When Weber contrasts the "dare-devil and unscrupulous speculators, economic adventurers such as we meet at all periods of economic history" with the representatives of the new spirit of capitalism, "men who had grown up in the hard school of life, calculating and daring at the same time, above all temperate and reliable, shrewd and completely devoted to their business, with strictly bourgeois opinions and principles" (PE 69), then this distinction is hard to maintain in the case of the Souchay circle. In fact, its spirit of capitalism turns out to be Lujo Brentano's, not Weber's.

Both men were not only among the last liberal Anglophiles but also had in common Frankfurt family roots.[47] Brentano (1844–1931) defined the capitalist spirit as the striving for the largest possible profit, a natural propensity that did not exclude the pursuit of happiness and pleasure. This striving originated with long-distance trade and was often connected with the diaspora status of religious minorities. Brentano only had to remember his own family history to understand that "as a stranger the foreign merchant was not inte-

---

45  His daughter Henriette's future father-in-law was Wilhelm Benecke, an international authority on maritime insurance and risk ventures, matters especially critical during the Blockade. See Wilhelm Benecke, *System des Assekuranz- und Bodmereiwesens*, 4 vols. (Hamburg: Selbstverlag, 1805–1810); on the effects of the Continental Blockade, see the supplemental fifth volume (1821), 158ff. For an English version of the widely translated work, see *A Treatise on the Principles of Indemnity in Marine Insurance, Bottomry, and Respondentia* (London: Baldwin, 1824).

46  See Stanley Chapman, *Merchant Enterprise in Britain. From the Industrial Revolution to World War I* (Cambridge: Cambridge University Press, 1992), 91. An important source for the various partnerships of the Souchays, Schuncks, Beneckes, and related families is the forty-five volumes of printed trade circulars from 1829 to 1934 in the Nottingham University Library (Brandt Collection). I am much obliged to Dr. Chapman for directing me to these and other materials.

47  In contrast to Weber, Brentano had close academic connections with England, and he also encouraged his student Gerhart von Schulze-Gaevernitz to go for extended stays and work in the British Museum. As a teenager (1861–1862), Brentano was sent by his very conservative and orthodox mother, perhaps by miscalculation, to his Irish brother-in-law Peter Le Page Renouf (1822–1897), who turned out to be one of the leading liberal Catholics in Great Britain. When Germany was unified under Prussian dominance in 1871, Brentano even thought of emigrating to England. At the time, as he recalled in his autobiography, "I remained in my heart an aggrieved Frankfurter." See Lujo Brentano, *Mein Leben im Kampf um die soziale Entwicklung Deutschlands* (Jena: Fischer, 1931), 41; see also James J. Sheehan, *The Career of Lujo Brentano* (Chicago: University of Chicago Press, 1966), 10, 24.

grated into the domestic status hierarchy. What then was his justifiable standard of living? What was the right level of profit and the just price?"[48] Not just the status order but also religious control failed. Even when the Catholic church tightened its regulations, it was in fact compelled to relax them in practice. For Brentano, the empirical lesson of economic history – and political economy was for him an empirical science – was not the isolated effectiveness of a religiously fortified economic ethos, but the power of "natural" economic forces to change ethical evaluations in the long run. Therefore, "it made no difference for the accumulation of capital whether a pious Catholic made big profits and then secured a place in heaven through great donations and alms-giving, or whether a Calvinist sought great profit and then did good works, because great profit and good works were visible signs of his faith and his state of grace."[49] Thus did Brentano the *Kulturkatholik* respond to Weber the *Kulturprotestant*.

By 1800, the Souchays and Brentanos had risen to the Frankfurt patriciate, even though religious discrimination against Huguenots and Catholics had only recently been removed under the impact of Enlightenment reform and the French Revolution. The Brentanos belonged to a group of Italian families from the Lake Como area that had struggled for a century to rise from rags to riches. Unlike some other Italian families, they did not come as urban patrician merchants or, contrary to some later family mythology, as rural noblemen.[50] In the mid-seventeenth century they appeared in Frankfurt as street vendors of citrus fruits. They differed from Weber's Puritans by being not only hard-working and frugal, but also unscrupulous, violating formal legality – concretely, the many legal restrictions placed on them by the Lutheran city government. Around 1700 the Frankfurt grocers viewed them as their most dangerous competitors and, according to Alexander Dietz, "the burghers hated them more than the Jews."[51]

48 Excursus III of Lujo Brentano, *Die Anfänge des Kapitalismus* (Munich: Akademie der Wissenschaften, 1916), 122.
49 Ibid., 133.
50 Dietz, *Frankfurter Handelsgeschichte*, 240. In *Mein Leben*, 4ff., Brentano reacted with some irritation to Dietz's claim of the lowly origins of the Brentanos, but he admitted that some proofs of noble descent might be spurious, and for the rest he declared that he did not care one way or another.
51 Dietz, *Frankfurter Handelsgeschichte*, 240. Efforts by the city government to expel the Italians failed completely, but the city managed to obstruct for many years an imperial rescript of 1706 that ordered it to make economic and political concessions. The Brentanos fought back by disregarding ordinances and court decisions and by recourse to legal subterfuges. The major one consisted in keeping the firm undivided upon the death of a formal head

Before the mid-nineteenth century the basic business unit was still the family enterprise.[52] Young men clerked in the firms of their own family or those of relatives, neighbors, and business friends. Intermarriage with partners (*associés*) and clerks (*Kommis*) was the social cement of private enterprise; divorce and illegitimacy were its nemesis. Carl Cornelius Souchay too followed the usual path. His fortunes were intertwined with those of several other families, especially the Mylius family. The central figure in the group's capital accumulation was Isaac Aldebert (1762–1817), a great speculator. The story begins in 1776, when Jonas Darfeldt, one of the leading merchants, married the twenty-three-year-old Katherina Elisabeth Mylius (1753–1832), who was thirty years younger. In 1784 he founded Darfeldt and Brothers Mylius with his brothers-in-law Peter Friedrich and Johann Jakob Mylius (1756–1835). They traded linen wholesale and also ran a commissions and shipping business. But the firm broke up within a few years, probably in connection with the failure of Darfeldt's marriage. In 1786 Darfeldt and Peter Friedrich Mylius left the firm, whereupon Johann Jakob Mylius went into partnership with Isaac Aldebert, who married the divorced Mrs. Darfeldt (nine years his senior). Introduced by Pastor Souchay, Aldebert had been Darfeldt's favorite clerk and, according to Emilie Souchay Fallenstein, even became his heir. The Aldebert marriage remained childless, but the couple later brought up two children of Johann Jakob Mylius, Carl (1790–1870) and Susanna ("Nanny") (1793–1884). In 1793 the twenty-five-year-old Carl Cornelius

who had acquired a residency permit – a "green card," so to speak – when in fact there was a constantly changing number of secret associates. Profits were distributed on a discretionary basis by the patriarchal head of the family firm. The breakthrough came with Peter Anton Brentano, born in Tremezzo in 1735, who gained Frankfurt citizenship through marriage in 1762, set up his own firm in 1771, and was rich enough by 1785 to hand his business over to his son Franz and become financial counsellor and tax administrator for the Elector of Trier. He died a millionaire (in florins) about 1800. The family had "arrived." Among the thirteen surviving children, who shared in the inheritance, two became famous in the history of German literature: Bettina and Clemens Brentano.

A sister, Kunigunde, married the renowned jurist and later Prussian minister of justice, Friedrich von Savigny, and a brother, Christian, was Lujo Brentano's father. Christian became a close friend and fellow student of Henry Crabb Robinson; see footnote 55 in this essay. In his critique of *The Protestant Ethic,* Brentano pointed out that since Weber had drawn on his entrepreneurial ancestors, "I may perhaps be permitted to do the same" (133). Just as Weber had portrayed his uncle Karl David, so Brentano eulogized his uncle Franz, who had continued the paternal firm as a banking house until the 1840s. Brentano, *Die Anfänge des Kapitalismus,* 134.

52 See the comprehensive treatment by Jürgen Kocka, "Familie, Unternehmer und Kapitalismus. An Beispielen aus der frühen deutschen Industrialisierung," *Zeitschrift für Unternehmensgeschichte* 24 (1979): 99–135. Kocka deals with many families, but not the Souchay clan or the Bielefeld Weber family. Hence, the following information supplements Kocka's larger analysis.

Souchay, who also had been apprenticed to Darfeldt, became a partner in the rapidly growing firm Mylius and Aldebert, investing 1,000
pounds. As early as 1788 Aldebert operated in London; by 1802 he
lived in Manchester. By that time he had sent his brother-in-law
Heinrich Mylius (1769–1854) to Milano, and the linen business had
been replaced by English manufactures. When Heinrich Mylius was
jailed there by the French for his English connections, Johann Jakob
Mylius, a prestigious Frankfurt senator, sprang him free from Paris,
where he was negotiating with the French government about commercial debts and war contributions. In June 1806, five months before the beginning of the last and most severe blockade, Souchay
pulled out his investment, which had grown to 7,000 pounds, and,
together with his childhood friend Franz Perret, set up the firm of
Souchay and Perret, with a warehouse in Manchester and a banking
office in London. In view of Perret's particularly risky speculations,
Souchay dissolved the partnership in 1811, but Perret remained his
London representative. In the same year, Mylius and Aldebert was
also dissolved. Until 1821 Souchay's Frankfurt firm dealt in "overseas foods" (such as tea, coffee, cocoa) and commissions, partly from
English yarns and textiles, but after 1825 the aging Souchay limited
himself to the exchange banking business and discount operations.
By that time his Manchester firm, first called Schunck, Mylius and
Co. and later Schunck, Souchay & Co., had successfully weathered
the postwar economic turbulence, and the family fortune had grown
to several hundred thousand pounds. During the Napoleonic Wars
and especially during the last blockade, many firms in Frankfurt and
Hamburg had failed and many businessmen fled to England. There
they took advantage of distressed English textiles and smuggled
them at great risk and enormous profit to the Continent. Their
quickly acquired wealth tempted many of these German businessmen to overreach themselves after the war and join the ranks of
business failures.[53]

53 In 1900, Edgar Jaffé, whose family fortune was also made in Manchester (and who used it to
   buy the *Archiv für Sozialwissenschaft und Sozialpolitik* for Weber and to build a villa for his
   wife, Else von Richthofen, in Heidelberg), sketched the historical development of the
   German merchant's relationship to the Lancashire textile industry: "Die englische Baum-
   wollindustrie und die Organisation des Exporthandels," *Schmollers Jahrbuch für Gesetzgebung*
   24 (1900): 193–217, esp. 200. Among several nationalities, French, Greek, Armenian,
   Danish, and Dutch in particular, German firms predominated. "In volume and number,"
   Jaffé pointed out,
   the German houses rank first, but we must emphasize that in spite of their German
   origin and even though some of the owners were still born in Germany, they mostly
   do not consider themselves German. By inclination and citizenship most of them have
   become English, and this is true of them much more than of the members of other

In what spirit, we may now ask, did the Souchay circle conduct its business? What was its lifestyle? Two daughters of Carl Cornelius left memoirs for their children: Emilie Fallenstein (1805–1881), Max Weber's grandmother, and Henriette Benecke (1807–1893), his great-aunt.[54] Written when Henriette was fifty-eight (in 1865) and Emilie was in her late sixties (between 1872 and 1875), these memoirs were printed for private circulation and handed on to the grandchildren in their teens on such occasions as their confirmation. Although vivid and intimate, the memoirs leave out, of course, what Henriette and Emilie considered inappropriate for posterity, especially for younger eyes and ears. For a more balanced view of the triumphs and failures, and especially the family conflicts and family secrets, we must turn to the extraordinary record of the literary critic, journalist, and lawyer Henry Crabb Robinson (1775–1867), who in his long life came to know intimately three generations of the Souchay circle.[55] Before

nations. Thus, the German firms have been most intimately linked with the flourishing of the textile exports. A very prominent role was played by a firm that was established early in this century and owed the foundation of its enormous wealth to the profits from the days of the Continental Blockade. The story has it that the first owner was quite satisfied if one of the five ships that tried to run the blockade from Helgoland in his behalf managed to get through. The profits from one ship easily outweighed the losses of the other. (p. 200)

If Jaffé did not have Souchay in mind, he came pretty close to his case. During the Napoleonic period, English wares were acquired very cheaply at distress sales and auctions, since the Blockade forced many manufacturers and traders into selling below cost or into outright bankruptcy. Even during the Blockade (1806–1813) there were some 20 German firms in Manchester; they numbered 28 by 1820, 84 by 1840, and 118 by 1861. See Otto-Ernst Krawehl, *Hamburgs Schiffs- und Warenverkehr mit England und den englischen Kolonien 1814–1860* (Cologne: Böhlau, 1977), 258f, 495. Krawehl mentions Schunck, Souchay & Co. (495).

Only recently has significant progress been made toward a history of the textile exporters and merchant bankers, although Edgar Jaffé's Heidelberg dissertation was a significant early treatment of the merchant bankers, *Das englische Bankwesen* (Leipzig: Duncker & Humblot, 1904). See Stanley Chapman, *The Rise of Merchant Banking* (London: Allen and Unwin, 1984); on the Souchay firm, see 11, 13, 139f., 151; for an older overview, see idem., *The Cotton Industry in the Industrial Revolution* (London: Macmillan, 1972).

54 See Emilie Fallenstein (anonymous), *Erinnerungsblätter an meine Kindheit und Jugend. Für meine Kinder aufgezeichnet in den Winterabenden 1872–1875* (Stuttgart: Guttenberg, 1882); Henriette Benecke (anonymous), *Alte Geschichten* (Heidelberg: Avenarius, n.d.), written in 1865; 2d ed., Denmark Hill (London, 1872). Beyond the anecdotal genealogical information contained in the two memoirs, I have relied on Otto Döhner, *Das Hugenottengeschlecht Souchay de la Duboissière und seine Nachkommen*, Vol. 19, *Deutsches Familienarchiv* (Neustadt: Degener, 1961). A brother of Emilie and Henriette, Johann Souchay, wrote "Familienaufzeichnungen," but their whereabouts are unknown to me. The two sisters wrote their memoirs shortly after bereavements, Henriette after her husband's death and Emilie after the death, in quick succession, of her three stalwart brothers.

55 See *Diary, Reminiscences and Correspondence of Henry Crabb Robinson*, 3 vols., Thomas Sadler, ed. (Boston: Fields, 1869); Edith Morley, ed., *Crabb Robinson in Germany 1800–1805. Extracts from His Correspondence* (London: Oxford University Press, 1929); Hertha Marquardt, ed., *Henry Crabb Robinson und seine deutschen Freunde. Brücke zwischen England und Deutsch-*

Carlyle, Robinson was instrumental in introducing the German classical and romantic writers to an English audience. His diaries, reminiscences, and letters deal not only with Goethe and Schiller, the Wordsworths, and Coleridge, but also, until his last days, with the fortunes of the Souchay family. In 1800, quite by accident, Aldebert took Robinson, an eager young Germanophile, home to Frankfurt and introduced him to the Souchays and their circle. In time Robinson became not only a family friend, but also a family lawyer and fellow investor.

Marianne Weber described Carl Cornelius Souchay all too briefly as a "cheerful, amiable and cultured man, who by his own efforts and by his marriage acquired considerable wealth, which he spent generously."[56] She erred when she claims that he married into wealth but states correctly that his motto was "to live and let live." Albeit an extraordinarily successful businessman, Souchay was innocent of Weber's spirit of capitalism. Quite capable of the "spontaneous enjoyment of life," he did not let himself be "dominated by the making of money, by acquisition as the ultimate purpose of his life" (PE 53). This is how Henriette saw him: "He interrupted his business activities for a long time to pursue his beloved music, even though in that regard he had little success. His kitchen and cellar were always well-stocked for his friends. He supported many artists in public and in his home. He was successful with most things he undertook in his life. It was easy to please him, and he had an open heart for everything beautiful, good and gay. He had begun with little and died a well-off man."[57] (Both Henriette and Marianne discreetly play down the sheer wealth.)

His religious outlook was far removed from Weber's Protestant

---

land im Zeitalter der Romantik. Nach Briefen, Tagebüchern und anderen Aufzeichnungen, 2 vols. (Göttingen: Vandenhoeck, 1964 and 1967). On June 30, 1866, the ninety-one-year-old Robinson wrote to Nanny Mylius Schunck after reading Henriette's memoirs:

> It is a singular circumstance, that my life, insignificant as it has been, and my qualities, altogether inferior to those of the Schunck-Mylius connection, have nevertheless had, on one occasion, an important influence on the affairs of the family. I had the satisfaction to know that influence had been exercised usefully and happily. I propose, one of these days, to draw up a short narrative of my German life. It will be, in the first place, connected with Mrs. William Benecke's narrative, which I have read with interest. The more, perhaps, because I could connect with Mrs. William Benecke's history other facts within my own knowledge, and in which I was an agent, which would modify the consequences drawn from those.

*Diary, Reminiscences*, 496f. Robinson died soon afterward. It took a century before Hertha Marquardt reconstructed the story of the families involved and discovered what Robinson was alluding to.

56 Marianne Weber, *Max Weber*, 8.    57 Benecke, *Alte Geschichten*, 53.

ethic. "He considered it right," continued Henriette, "to thank God through cheerful, grateful and shared enjoyment (*Genuss*) of his blessings. . . . The extreme parsimony of some rich merchants was not father's habit." She recalled him saying: "I have always lived like a rich man, and I have managed to do so with God's help. The skinflints around me have always thought I was rich, even when that was not yet true."[58] The two sisters themselves experienced a warm relationship with a benign God. Henriette ended her memoirs with the declaration that "I have retained my faith in the lovingness of God the father, who likes to see his children gay and happy." And Emilie began her memoirs with the confession that "God guides the individual and he also leads all of humanity in a thousand inscrutable ways toward an ever richer development and perfection – slowly, it is true, but with a steady fatherly hand. The eternal God is a God of limitless forbearance and mercy."[59] Returning from one of her early visits to England, Emilie felt "happy about the progress as I wished it for the world,"[60] and she became an ardent partisan of Louis Philippe when she watched him enter Paris during the July Revolution.

It is true that Carl Cornelius' father was a Huguenot minister in Frankfurt, in fact the first resident one, strictly speaking, since until 1789 services had to be held outside the city gate in Bockenheim on Hanau County territory; full civic equality was granted only in 1806. Since 1722 the family had been settled in the nearby court residence of Hanau, where they had been admitted as goldsmiths by the Count, after a stay in Geneva in the wake of the revocation of the Edict of Nantes in 1685. They produced goldware and traded at the Frankfurt fair. Although not as rich as some of his relatives, the pastor was a man of means, and at least one of his four wives had brought a large dowry from Holland. The young Carl Cornelius freed himself from the orthodox and intolerant views of his father during the French Revolution and especially under the influence of his closest and lifelong friend Franz Perret, whose family had "a spirit that was more oriented toward the enjoyment of life (but only in a good sense)," as Emilie puts it cautiously.[61] It is also indicative of his nonascetic outlook on life that at twenty-seven Souchay married the impecunious and barely literate Helene Schunck (1774–1851), practically on sight, for her extraordinary beauty. This demonstrates

58 Ibid., 54; Marianne Weber, *Max Weber*, 8.
59 Benecke, *Alte Geschichten*, 129; Fallenstein, *Erinnerungsblätter*, 3.
60 Fallenstein, *Erinnerungsblätter*, 15.      61 Ibid., 29f.

how far removed he was from an inner-worldly asceticism for which marriage "contracted for purely erotic or external reasons was, from an ethical standpoint, concubinage" and even marriage "entered for purely economic reasons preferred (because after all it is inspired by rational motives) to one with erotic foundations" (PE 263). There are two independent witnesses for Helene's appearance. The court painter Joseph Karl Stieler (1781–1858), who painted her portrait when she was already the mother of four children, called her "the most beautiful woman in Germany," an episode recounted by Marianne Weber.[62] For Henry Crabb Robinson she was "the most beautiful woman I have ever seen."[63]

A letter in English from Souchay to Robinson dated Dec. 24, 1802, is one of the very few instances where we can hear his own voice. After acknowledging a monetary transaction on Robinson's behalf, he congratulates him on his studies at the university of Jena, adding: "I cannot but find your situation a happy one, as it entirely tends to your moral improvement, while we men of business very often live and die as very great ignorants."[64] In view of this good-humored self-deprecation, it is striking, however, that this group of entrepreneurs managed to combine business with artistic and intellectual interests. Where Souchay had his music, Henriette's later father-in-law, Wilhelm Benecke, discussed his interpretation of the Christian God of love, and others discovered and collected *altdeutsch* paintings from the fifteenth and sixteenth centuries.[65] Still, success in business determined the range of alternatives and the possibility of early retirement. In this "era of speculation," according to Emilie, the three

62  Benecke, *Alte Geschichten*, 46f; Marianne Weber, *Max Weber*, 8. A tinge of Marianne's nationalist sentiment is revealed in the curious observation that Helene Schunck was "of entirely German descent" and that therefore "the grace and noble beauty of Max Weber's mother . . . were more a German than a French heritage." Why would she care?

63  *Reminiscences* (Ms. I, 148), cited in Marquardt, *Henry Crabb Robinson*, 27. Robinson's initial judgment makes all the more poignant his observations on her gradual aging and her final thirteen-year struggle against ever more crippling strokes.

64  Marquardt, *Henry Crabb Robinson*, 88. Many letters from the Souchay circle lie today in the Robinson Collection of the famed interdenominational library, "Dr. Williams's Trust," in London.

65  Next to unpublished musings on the philosophy of religion, Wilhelm Benecke published his commentary, *Der Brief Pauli an die Römer* (Heidelberg: Winter, 1831), tr. by his son Friedrich Wilhelm Benecke, *An Exposition of St. Paul's Epistle to the Romans* (London: Longman, 1854). [Not available to me was *Grundzüge der Wahrheit* (Berlin: Nicolai, 1838).] As a young woman, Emilie Souchay was excluded from the regular discussions with Wilhelm Benecke in the London home of Heinrich and Elise Schunck because she was considered "too young to understand the latitudinarian (*frei-religiös*) tendency of the work." See Fallenstein, *Erinnerungsblätter*, 14. See also Wilhelm Benecke, *Lebensskizze und Briefe als Ms. gedruckt*, 2 vols. (Dresden, 1850).

friends Aldebert, Perret, and Souchay tested their luck time and again. She acknowledges that her father made much money especially during the Continental Blockade, and Henriette adds that "father went to the theater in his accustomed manner when everything depended on some ships getting through, and he told my mother only after their safe arrival how much had been at stake. My mother, who was very different from him in this regard, often became very upset about his equanimity."[66] Thus, many of the early profits came from taking advantage of the wartime conditions. "My father was a young beginner, without wealth of his own," says Henriette, "and he owed the basis of his later fortune to his quiet confidence and his luck (as he called it) in wartime."[67]

Souchay kept a lavishly open house in Frankfurt and at his vineyard in Eltville-on-the-Rhine, which he had bought as a birthday present for his wife. On his regular trips to England he sometimes took his daughters to Paris and bought them "magnificent silk dresses."[68] There he hired carriages and servants and chose the most expensive seats in the opera – being himself a frustrated musician. Almost every summer the family traveled to spas or for sightseeing. In the last decade of his life, Souchay moved every year for several months to England, "the country he liked so much."[69] His Anglophilia was drastically matched by that of his wife Helene, who came from a rustic background. Upon seeing southern England for the first time, she is supposed to have exclaimed: "If God had wanted to create me as an animal and had given me a choice which animal I wished to be, I would have called out without hesitation: 'A cow in England!' "[70]

The Anglophilia of these men and women had both a cultural and a commercial component, and it was, of course, usually connected with disappointments about the French Revolution and bitterness about the economic threats posed by French nationalism. Aldebert,

66 Fallenstein, *Erinnerungsblätter*, 32; Benecke, *Alte Geschichten*, 54.
67 Benecke, *Alte Geschichten*, 49. As the only son of a well-to-do pastor, Carl Cornelius was, of course, not really a "self-made man." Through his mother, Lily Baumhauer, he seems to have inherited or acquired his large residence and warehouse, Am Fahrtor, near the Main River.
68 Fallenstein, *Erinnerungsblätter*, 124.   69 Benecke, *Alte Geschichten*, 92.
70 Fallenstein, *Erinnerungsblätter*, 102. Emilie Fallenstein's own Anglophile judgment, expressed as late as the 1870s, emphasized ethical aspects: "The more time passes, the more I have come to the conviction that in terms of duty, faithfulness, and self-sacrifice in those regards in which it furthers the good, the English nation stands higher than any other, even the Prussians not excepted" (110).

for instance, barely managed to hide 1,000 pounds worth of English goods from the French occupiers in Hamburg in 1807, an episode he lived through with Robinson, then war correspondent of the London *Times*. Although calling Aldebert "one of the most excellent men I ever knew," Robinson added critically that "his greatest fault is an extravagant and irrational predilection for England in all points. He has been naturalized, and seems to have no taste for anything that is not 'British Sirs from top to toe.' "[71] A rational motive, we may add, may have been that citizenship allowed him to operate on the Manchester and London exchanges.

Like Souchay, Aldebert and his partner in England, Carl Christian Becher (1770–1836), liked to live in grand style. In 1805, Aldebert resided with his wife, Katherina Mylius, and their two adopted children, Carl and Nanny, in a sumptuous villa in Stamford Hill (near London), with seven servants and a carriage. Becher, whose brother, Dr. Georg Becher, married Caroline Schunck in Manchester in 1803, was such an exuberant speculator that Robinson once said to him: "It seems to me that you are not so much a merchant as a gambler in goods."[72] By 1814 both Aldebert and Becher had gone bankrupt twice. Using his excellent social connections, Aldebert recovered quickly each time. Becher, however, ended up in debtor's prison after a third bankruptcy and finally had to flee to the Continent.

But the real challenge to notions of bourgeois probity occurred when Aldebert died in 1817, leaving behind an elegant mistress and three children, whom he wanted to be provided for.[73] Robinson, Souchay, and Heinrich Mylius (the Younger) became executors of Aldebert's will, a task not finished until the 1850s. Souchay spent months in London straightening out Aldebert's complicated affairs, while Helene visited Mrs. Krukenberg and her children, who grew up without knowing about their illegitimacy. From Mrs. Aldebert, who had gone back to Frankfurt during the Continental Blockade, to the Souchays and Myliuses, the families involved acted rather decently, but the complications never ended and they occupied Robinson until the last week of his life. Although it appears that Souchay was more cautious with his business deals, he never abandoned his old friends Aldebert and Perret and, together with the Mylius family,

71 Morley, ed., *Crabb Robinson in Germany*, 126.
72 Marquardt, *Henry Crabb Robinson*, II:20.
73 Ibid., II:43ff. In later years, it turned out that Jonas Mylius in Hamburg, a brother of Heinrich and Nanny Mylius, also had a mistress and children whom he wanted to legitimate.

acknowledged how much his own fortune had benefitted from their speculations as long as they were successful.

The active cooperation of a group of families that pooled their capital was crucial to the success of this form of family capitalism before the advent of the joint stock company. In expanding his operations across Europe, Souchay relied especially on his wife's siblings, whom he first trained as clerks (*Kommis*) in his Frankfurt counting house. He sent Heinrich Schunck, after stays in Vienna and Trieste, to London to take Aldebert's place. Schunck retired in 1832 with 60,000 pounds to Frankfurt, where after his death this fortune became the object of a long and bitter conflict between his wife's family, the Harniers, and the Schunck-Souchay families. Martin Schunck (1788–1872) was delegated to Manchester, where in 1816 he married Nanny Mylius, who, when living there as a child, spoke English "almost like a native," as Aldebert reported to Robinson in 1802.[74] Martin Schunck left an estate of about 300,000 pounds.

Souchay set up Philip Schunck in Leipzig, where he made a fortune through his English connections without being formally part of Schunck, Souchay & Co. In 1802 Souchay's sister-in-law, Friedericke Schunck, married one of Aldebert's acquaintances, John Middleton Pickford, who made so much money in his Manchester spinning mill over ten years that he retired early to Heidelberg and built a mansion (which was used as a residence by Tsar Alexander at the end of the Napoleonic Wars). But he lost most of his fortune when a partner's speculations went sour. Brought up in the Souchay household, the son of Wilhelmine Schunck, another of C. C. Souchay's sisters-in-law, Dr. Fritz Schlemmer, became tutor to the Rothschild children in London in 1828. (Nathaniel Rothschild had gone to Manchester as early as 1798 before moving on to London.) Finally, Souchay sent Jakob Hartmann, the son of his sister-in-law Sannchen Schunck, to Riga, where he became a well-off merchant.[75]

The second generation of English residents consisted mostly of

---

74 Marquardt, *Henry Crabb Robinson,* I:74.

75 Beyond this network of in-laws, Souchay cooperated closely with the Milano firm of the elder Heinrich Mylius, who began at age nineteen as a traveling salesman and died as a very rich banker. In England, Souchay was in partnership with the son of Johann Jakob Mylius, the younger Heinrich Mylius (1792–1862). The younger Heinrich became a naturalized citizen as head of the London house, from which he is said to have retired with 160,000 pounds. His brother Carl, who had grown up in the Aldebert household, also was a Souchay partner, but their brother Georg Melchior (1795–1857) joined the firm Enrico Mylius in Milan. At his death he left behind 400,000 pounds, which seem to have passed into the hands of the younger Heinrich Mylius. Some of the figures provided here come from Robinson, who in turn got much of his information from Souchay's son-in-law

Souchay's own children and their spouses. In 1817 John (Jean, Johann) Souchay (1798–1871) became a partner in Manchester and also in London. He married his Leipzig cousin Thekla Schunck (1809–1876) and retired with her to Dresden, where he built a great English mansion and was known as a munificent English benefactor. (Emilie Fallenstein inherited one-tenth of his estate of more than 2 million Prussian thalers.) Charles (Carl) Souchay (1799–1872) went to London in 1817 to help, in the long run unsuccessfully, rescue Perret's business, which failed in 1824–1825. He then joined the Souchay firm in Manchester and there married Adelheid Dethmar (1809–1890); they stayed on in England and were buried in Withington near Manchester. He too left an estate of about 300,000 pounds. Another member of the second generation was Henry Edward Schunck (1820–1903), whose father, Martin Schunck, had acquired and expanded a calico-printing and dyeing works in Belfield – chemicals being of crucial importance to the textile industry. Trained to run the dye works, Edward Schunck became one of the leading chemists in England. A pupil of Justus von Liebig, he was a member of the Royal Society and for twenty years president or vice-president of the Manchester Literary and Philosophical Society, a center of British science and of the movement of the "civil scientists."[76]

In 1826 Henriette married Friedrich Wilhelm Benecke (1802–1865), who had arrived in England as a refugee child when his father, Wilhelm (1778–1837), fled from Hamburg in 1813 (upon the second arrival of the French). When Wilhelm Benecke retired from his chemical plant in London-Deptford in 1827 in order to devote himself fully to his studies in the philosophy of religion in Heidelberg, his son continued to run the plant on his own. But when Heinrich Schunck retired from Schunck, Mylius & Co. in 1832, Souchay replaced him with his son-in-law. Wilhelm August Souchay (1810–1887) worked in England as a chemist before going to Fresenius in Wiesbaden (still a well-known firm after World War II).

Before and after her marriage to Georg Friedrich Fallenstein, Emilie Souchay visited her relatives in England for extended stays (first in 1823–1824) and even sheltered her Prussian husband there when he became unpopular in Heidelberg during the 1848 revolution. Only

Friedrich Wilhelm Benecke. Another important source is the wills, which I consulted at the Principal Registry at Somerset House in London.

76 See Robert H. Kargon, *Science in Victorian Manchester. Enterprise and Expertise* (Baltimore: Johns Hopkins University Press, 1977), 95–101 and passim. Henry Edward Schunck left about 150,000 pounds as late as 1903.

Elisabeth (1796–1871) and Eduard (1800–1872) did not leave their native Frankfurt. At age twenty-four Elisabeth returned permanently to her father's big house, Am Fahrtor, as the widow of the Huguenot pastor Franz August Jeanrenaud. Eduard, who called himself again Souchay de la Duboissière, became more prominent than his father in the public life of Frankfurt, but at a period when the city's political and economic fortunes were declining. First as senator and then as junior mayor, Eduard tried to take a mediating position in the long and ultimately futile struggle to preserve the city state's independence. Early on, in the 1830s, Souchay had recognized the inevitability of having to join the Prussian *Zollverein* (Customs Union). In 1848–1850 he was on the losing side, caught between the positions of the doomed liberals and the victorious reactionaries. In the 1850s he turned to the writing of history, composing a four-volume *History of the German Monarchy from Its Beginnings to Its Decline*.[77] Embittered at the Prussian annexation and ill treatment of Frankfurt in 1866, he and his children, as well as other patrician families, withdrew to their country estates, signaling the political end of the Frankfurt patriciate. A number of firms and individuals, such as Francis Joseph Schuster, emigrated to England.[78] This course of events made the entrenchment of the Souchay enterprises in England even more important than before.[79]

In the third generation the German–English nexus remained intense, before the fourth generation blended into English society, with the pattern of close intermarriage loosening and English family names appearing. The third generation produced two noteworthy episodes in cultural and political history. In 1837 Elisabeth Souchay

77 See Eduard Franz Souchay, *Geschichte der deutschen Monarchie von ihrer Erhebung bis zu ihrem Verfall* (Frankfurt: Sauerländer, 1861–1862). See the review by Gustav Freytag, reprinted in *Vermischte Aufsätze aus den Jahren 1848 bis 1894* (Leipzig: Hirzel, 1903), 137ff.

78 On Eduard Souchay and the decline of Frankfurt, see Richard Schwemer, *Geschichte der Freien Stadt Frankfurt (1814–1866)*, 3 vols. (Frankfurt: Baer, 1910–1918), and Helmut Böhme, *Frankfurt und Hamburg. Des Deutschen Reiches Silber- und Goldloch und die allerenglischste Stadt des Kontinents* (Frankfurt: Europäische Verlagsanstalt, 1968); much material on Souchay is also contained in Franz Lerner, *Bürgersinn und Bürgertat. Geschichte der Frankfurter Polytechnischen Gesellschaft 1816–1966* (Frankfurt: Kramer, 1966). On the retreat of Frankfurt patricians, see the letter of Karl Mendelssohn Bartholdy to Alexander Freiherr von Bernus, Berlin, Oct. 19, 1868, in Felix Gilbert, ed., *Bankiers, Künstler und Gelehrte. Unveröffentlichte Briefe der Familie Mendelssohn* (Tübingen: Mohr, 1975), 199ff. On the emigration of businessmen to England, see Chapman, *The Rise of Merchant Banking*, 136.

79 The Italian firm Enrico Mylius also continued to flourish. Much of its wealth ultimately flowed back to Frankfurt to shore up its cultural status. The famous Senckenburg Museum was endowed with bequests from Heinrich Mylius, who lost his acquisitive drive when his only son died. The museum was built by the architect Carl Jonas Mylius (1839–1883), a son of Carl Mylius.

Jeanrenaud's daughter Cecilia (1817–1853), who had inherited her grandmother Helene's beauty, married Felix Mendelssohn Bartholdy, just in time for the music-loving Carl Cornelius Souchay to give his blessings before he died in 1838. During his triumphal appearances in England, the composer stayed for extended periods with the London and Manchester relatives.[80] In 1864 Charles (Carl) Souchay's daughter Juliet married Robert Lucius von Ballhausen (1835–1914), a Catholic, at the Souchay estate in Withington near Manchester: "a Frankfurt Souchay with a dowry of five million," as Gustav Freytag wrote to Duke Ernst of Coburg (Queen Victoria's brother-in-law).[81] Lucius was to become a Reichstag deputy and leader of the Free Conservatives, as well as a close ally and table companion of Bismarck, whom he served as minister of agriculture from 1879 to 1890.[82] Here was, in Weberian terms, an impressive example of the "feudalization" of the German bourgeoisie, with a dash of English gentrification. Juliet called herself again Souchay de la Duboissière, the full name of her Huguenot ancestors. The family's assumption that this pointed to an aristocratic lineage was disproved only later, but it served its purpose at the time. Lucius reached the highest rung of bourgeois ennoblement when Emperor Friedrich made him a *Freiherr* in 1888, together with the notorious industrialist Karl Ferdinand von Stumm – the third industrialist, Friedrich Alfred Krupp, actually turned down the honor. At the time, the twenty-four-year-old Max Weber reported to Hermann Baumgarten the privately expressed opinions of Lucius von Ballhausen on the difficult political constellation of the "three emperors year" (when William I was succeeded by Frederick III, only to be quickly followed by William II).[83] About 1890, when Weber went to the polls for the first time, he seems to have voted conservative, against his father's affiliation. Later, however, Weber turned left again, when "King Stumm" gave his name to the reactionary period after 1894, and launched some of his sharpest attacks on the "feudal" pretensions of the "in-

---

80  When Cecilia's sister Julie married Julius Schunck in Leipzig in 1839, the famous "Wedding March" was supposedly played for the first time. For an account from the Mendelssohn side, see Sebastian Hensel, *Die Familie Mendelssohn 1727 bis 1847. Nach Briefen und Tagebüchern* (Berlin: de Gruyter, 1921).

81  Letter of Jan. 30, 1867, in Eduard Tempeltey, ed., *Gustav Freytag und Herzog Ernst von Coburg im Briefwechsel 1853 bis 1893* (Leipzig: Hirzel, 1904), 215. If the currency unit referred to was the Prussian taler (dollar), the sum appears to me exaggerated. The occasion was Freytag's victory over Lucius in gaining the Liberal nomination for the new North German diet.

82  See Freiherr Lucius von Ballhausen, *Bismarck-Erinnerungen* (Stuttgart: Cotta, 1921).

83  Weber, *Jugendbriefe*, 292.

dustrial nobility attained by letters-patent." From Max Weber's point
of view, family matters must have been made worse when Juliet
Souchay's son, Lucius von Stödten, married Bertha Freiin von
Stumm, a daughter of the "King" in 1896.[84]

The father of Lucius von Ballhausen was plain Sebastian Lucius
(1781–1857). He had turned his father's small firm, Johann Anton
Lucius, in Erfurt into a prosperous textile and shipping business,
merchant bank, putting-out enterprise, and textile mill. Trading in
Manchester products, he knew the Souchays from his stays in England in 1825 and 1832. His Anglophilia had a practical bent: "In
England, this land of wonders, a new world opened up to me. I saw
much that enriched my knowledge and saved me in my business
from making big errors." His capitalist spirit was in the Catholic
mold. In the face of the family's financial troubles, "I didn't lose
courage and trusted God. . . . I struggled to save every dollar (*Taler*)
in order to increase our trading fund and make us more independent.
Because of my efforts I succeeded so well that we accumulated sur-
plus as never before."[85] After so much saving, he lived in grand style,
bought his title with the entailed estates of Stödten and of Klein-
Ballhausen in 1851, and finally endowed a Catholic Hospital and
home for the aged. Significantly, in his autobiography Lucius von
Ballhausen mentioned neither the occupation of his father and father-
in-law nor the commercial source of his wealth, which allowed him
to choose politics as a vocation and fox hunting as his avocation.[86]

In the same year in which Juliet Souchay and Lucius von Ballhausen married in Manchester, Max Weber was born in Erfurt. From
1862 until 1868, Max Weber Sr. was a salaried city magistrate in
charge of the municipal bank, poor relief, and public education in the
very city in which the Lucius family was a leading economic and
political force.[87] It is still not fully established that his appointment

---

84  By contrast, Lucius von Stödten's English cousin Ida Benecke (1851–1934) was a feminist
    and socialist.
85  Quoted in Katharina Trutz, "Sebastian Lucius," *Mitteldeutsche Lebensbilder,* Vol. 3, n.d.
    (before 1938), 368, 365.
86  See *Selbstbiographie des Staatsministers Freiherrn Lucius von Ballhausen* (privately printed in
    1922). This short autobiography was apparently written in connection with the *Bismarck-
    Erinnerungen.* A copy is in the Deutsche Bibliothek in Leipzig.
87  See the privately published family history, *Die Erfurter Familie Sebastian Lucius* (Berlin 1894).
    On the dominance of the Lucius family in Erfurt and its influential political role in Prussia
    during the *Kaiserreich,* see Willibald Gutsche, "Die Veränderungen in der Wirtschaftsstruk-
    tur und der Differenzierungsprozess innerhalb des Bürgertums der Stadt Erfurt in den
    ersten Jahren der Herrschaft des Imperialismus," *Jahrbuch für Geschichte* 10 (Berlin:
    Akademie-Verlag, 1974), 362ff. I thank Hubert and Ulrike Treiber for procuring these
    materials from Erfurt.

was promoted by the Lucius family, whose members served during the period as unsalaried magistrates and members of the city parliament. At any rate, Max Sr. first met Helene Fallenstein, Emilie Souchay's daughter, in the Berlin home of Hermann and Ida Baumgarten in 1861, where the sixteen-year-old had fled after the fifty-five-year-old Gervinus, a close family friend and private tutor, had become erotically obsessed with her. It came naturally to the son and brother of Westphalian linen merchants to marry the granddaughter of a wealthy textile trader and merchant banker. Unless there were prior ties between the Weber and Lucius firms, the relationship of the Weber family to the Lucius family was established through the siblings Emilie Fallenstein and Charles Souchay and the cousins Helene Fallenstein and Juliet Souchay. Here the English–German family connection came full circle.

The Manchester and London firms continued to prosper under the third generation when Victor Benecke (1831–1908), who married the Mendelssohn Bartholdy daughter Marie, and Otto Benecke (1837–1922) became partners in 1865 in what was now named Benecke, Souchay & Co.;[88] the last male Souchay in England, a son of Charles, had died at age thirty in 1863. But in 1894, a hundred years after Carl Cornelius had joined his first partnership, the London firm of Benecke, Souchay & Co. was acquired by Blyth, Greene & Jourdain, a private Far Eastern house, whereas the Manchester and Leeds branches continued as Schunck, Souchay & Co. until 1905 and thereafter as Schunck & Co. into World War II.[89] In the London firm's last year and just a few months after Henriette's death, Max and Marianne Weber came to London on their honeymoon in the fall of 1893. But nothing is known about a family meeting. In her biography Marianne proved exceedingly reticent about this first of their three England trips – the others were in 1895 and 1910 – and only remarked, without even mentioning their destination, on Weber's explosive anger that was directed at her for the first time.[90] As a tourist,

---

88 At their elegant home in London-Lambeth, Marie and Viktor Benecke assembled musicians, writers, actors, and painters. See the vivid description by the banker Franz Mendelssohn in a letter of July 2, 1883 in Gilbert, ed., *Bankiers, Künstler und Gelehrte*, 229ff. Marie's brother Paul Mendelssohn Bartholdy, who had been apprenticed to Schunck & Co. in Leipzig from 1857 to 1859, became a founder (1867) and first director general of Aktiengesellschaft für Anilinfabrikation (AGFA), just as the Erfurt Lucius family cofounded Meister Lucius & Co., known today as Hoechst. (In 1925 the two chemical enterprises were combined into IG Farben.)

89 See Chapman, *The Rise of Merchant Banking*, 151.

90 Only when she described the second trip in August and September 1895 at great length did Marianne mention in one sentence that "the couple whizzed over the asphalt of London in

Weber viewed England through the spectacles of his preoccupation
with the "denationalization" of the German East, where the Junkers
were replacing the settled German rural laborers with Polish migrant
labor. While traveling on the "Flying Scotchman" to Edinburgh, he
looks out of the window and "thinks of the possible future of the
German East," recalled Marianne.[91] She also claimed that Weber's
reactions in 1910 were similar. Apart from the magnificent cathedrals
and Shakespeare's birthplace, "the other aspect of British civilization
that most intensely occupied the Webers was, as it had been years
ago, the distribution of land. . . . An area that could have given
sustenance to hundreds of thousands provided the livelihood for a
few hundred servants. No complaints were to be heard in these
empty spaces, for anyone who could have complained had long ago
been driven into the slums of the giant city [London] and no longer
belonged in the country. The free peasant had been wiped out."[92]
Weber saw the ruins left behind by Oliver Cromwell in the Irish
countryside. It seems he also saw the ghosts of Gerrard Winstanley
and of the Diggers crying for land and freedom.

By 1910 the political tensions between Great Britain and Imperial
Germany had become serious. During the Great War a great-
grandchild of Henriette Souchay, Robert Beckh, a student at Jesus
College in Cambridge, and Martin Schunck's great-grandson, Roger
Schunck, died in France, just as a grandchild of Emilie Souchay and
brother of Max Weber, Karl, was killed in the East a year earlier. If
Emilie Souchay had married and stayed in England, as her sister
Henriette did, her grandson might have ended up on the English
side. A fanciful speculation about Emilie? Not really. In 1856, when
at the age of eighty-one Henry Crabb Robinson paid one of his many
visits to Heidelberg, he recalled her in his diary as having been "a
very delicate little creature when my nephew Thomas was almost in
love with her."[93]

But the man Max Weber was fated to be a German nationalist. We
have seen that his Anglophilia was a legacy of German liberalism and
that he had closer links to the cosmopolitan bourgeoisie than has

---

dainty-two-wheel 'hackneys' in order to say a quick hello to the historical sites with which
they had become acquainted on their first trip together." Marianne Weber, *Max Weber*, 207.
   More research is needed on this score. It turns out that Ida Baumgarten and her ailing
daughter Emmy, who was considered "promised" to her cousin Max Weber, visited the
English relatives as late as the summer of 1888: Marie and Viktor Benecke, Henriette
Souchay Benecke, and Alfred and Adelheid Souchay Benecke. I thank Dr. Max Weber-
Schäfer for giving me access to Ida's letters.
91 Ibid.     92 Ibid., 495.     93 Marquardt, *Henry Crabb Robinson*, II:479.

generally been realized. Yet it was too late for a member of his political and intellectual generation to turn himself into an Englishman. Even the most avowed liberals suffered from the nationalist fevers that ravaged Wilhelmian Germany. It is true that Weber fought the antimodernist romanticism that grew so wildly in this period, but if he was a would-be Englishman, he was so out of modernist nostalgia. His own romanticism led him to glorify English Protestantism in its heroic age – largely a Whig reconstruction – for the sake of promoting German modernization. He wished Imperial Germany to be like Great Britain in political liberty and world power, if without its rural depopulation. At the beginning of his career, in 1893, Weber told his elders in the *Verein für Sozialpolitik* that "tremendous illusions had been necessary to create the German Reich."[94] His Anglophilia, I conclude, was his own illusion insofar as *The Protestant Ethic and the Spirit of Capitalism* reflected his wishful political thinking. If only the Germans had had a Puritan legacy to make them great like the English!

94 "Die ländliche Arbeitsverfassung," reprinted in *Gesammelte Aufsätze zur Sozial- und Wirtschaftsgeschichte* (Tübingen: Mohr, 1924), 468.

# 5
# Weber's Historical Concept of National Identity

HARRY LIEBERSOHN

Max Weber was a vehement nationalist all his public life, from his Freiburg Inaugural Address and other writings of the 1890s to his political speeches of the First World War. I wish to explore a paradox that emerges from his *scholarly* writings, above all *The Protestant Ethic and the Spirit of Capitalism:* The advocate of German political and cultural hegemony radically undermined his era's conventional definitions of nationhood. Neither linguistic nor ethnic nor racial categories had more than marginal significance for Weber's understanding of national identity, which he defined in critical opposition to them.[1]

National identity is not a major theme in *The Protestant Ethic,* which is, after all, primarily an essay on religion and economics. Yet in the course of asserting the historical significance of religion, Weber compares it to other possible determinants of culture, and one of the foremost candidates in the minds of his contemporaries was national identity. When Weber compares Puritanism and Lutheranism in his chapter on Luther and the concept of the calling, he opens up the possibility that the contrast between his examples of Milton's *Paradise Lost* and the chorales of Martin Luther and Paul Gerhard is just an expression of differences between English and German temperament. Before undertaking his analysis of the contrasting religious psychologies, he needs to eliminate this rival explanation:

It is now our task to replace this vague feeling [of difference between the mood of Puritanism and Lutheranism] by a somewhat more precise logical

---

1  When I first proposed the topic of national identity for the conference preceding this volume, the Berlin Wall was still firmly in place and the topic of German national identity had not yet made headlines. My interest arose then from a larger study of definitions of culture in Germany, and my motive is still to understand Weber's notion of national identity in this larger context. Two recent critiques of conventional notions of nationhood and culture that have influenced my approach are Richard Handler, *Nationalism and the Politics of Culture in Quebec* (Madison, Wis., 1988), and Daniel Segal, "Nationalism, Comparatively Speaking," in *Journal of Historical Sociology* 1 (1988): 300–321.

formulation, and to investigate the fundamental basis of these differences. The appeal to national character is generally a mere confession of ignorance, and in this case it is entirely untenable. To ascribe a unified national character to the Englishmen of the seventeenth century would be simply to falsify history. Cavaliers and Roundheads did not appeal to each other simply as two parties, but as radically distinct species of men, and whoever looks into the matter carefully must agree with them. On the other hand, a difference of character between the English merchant adventurers and the old Hanseatic merchants is not to be found; nor can any other fundamental difference between the English and German characters at the end of the Middle Ages, which cannot easily be explained by the differences of their political history. It was the power of religious influence, not alone, but more than anything else, which created the differences of which we are conscious to-day.[2]

This was a radical denial of essential or even long-standing national identity. Weber here excludes the possibility of German national identity as something *Urgermanisch,* any derivation of it from the time of Tacitus, any identification of it with the medieval mystics, any interpretation of the Reformation as an expression of a preexisting self. Note the fine inversion of categories in his treatment of Cavaliers and Roundheads: Englishmen who on national criteria should be alike actually appear at a moment of political and religious conflict to be distinct species; historically contingent factors create illusions of *natural* difference. Weber takes issue with the confusion of appearance and nature and pushes his reader toward an understanding of *historical* causes.

This passage introduces Weber's general position. We may dig deeper by examining his assumptions and method in dealing with the categories of ethnicity, language, and race. We shall see that although in principle he allows some room for theorists of natural origins, he consistently attacks their claims to having achieved plausible results.

First, language: Weber came at the end of a century in which philology had increasingly linked discrete languages to discrete peoples. The historical linguistics of the late nineteenth century assumed that languages grew organically out of a specific group of roots, and it assumed that these roots expressed the essential character of a continuous group of speakers.[3] Weber's historical method

---

2 Max Weber, *The Protestant Ethic and the Spirit of Capitalism,* trans. Talcott Parsons (New York, 1958), 88–89.

3 For two recent evaluations of nineteenth-century linguistics, see Jonathan Culler, *Ferdinand de Saussure* (New York, 1977); and Hans Aarsleff, "Introduction" to Wilhelm von Humboldt, *On Language: The Diversity of Human Language-Structure and Its Influence on the Mental Development of Mankind* (Cambridge and New York, 1988), vii–lxv.

of analyzing the concept of calling departs from both assumptions. The concept is not organically rooted in any language at all, but is a historical innovation that first appears in Luther's translation of Ben Sirach. If it has any forerunner, it is not Indo-European; Weber goes to great pains to document the absence of anything comparable from Latin or Greek. The only similar concept in an ancient language is in Hebrew, a so-called Semitic language, hence the wrong choice for nineteenth-century linguistic genealogies. The absence of any comparable concept from Catholic cultures breaks with any scheme of Christian or European continuity. Rather, Weber argues that concepts of calling appear in the languages of all the Protestant peoples of Europe. This, too, could have a ready connection to ethnicity; the linguistic peculiarity could be a mark of the folk character of the Germanic peoples. Weber rules out precisely this conclusion, writing with reference to the Protestant locus of the concept: "It may further be shown that this is not due to any ethnical peculiarity of the languages concerned. It is not, for instance, the product of a Germanic spirit, but in its modern meaning the word comes from the Bible translations, through the spirit of the translator, not that of the original."[4] The act of translation disrupts the continuum of culture and introduces a new concept. The search for origins does not lead to a primordial linguistic past but is arrested at a specific moment in Luther's work. Weber's survey of linguistic evidence goes on the assumption of the *instability* of linguistic meaning over time; he delineates how social and political institutions provide the proper frame of reference for the interpretation of words, whose meaning depends not on linguistic essence or folk spirit, but on social convention.

Turning to the categories of ethnicity and race, we find that Weber considers them separately, as did the scholarship of his time. His appraisal of ethnography is decidedly positive. Although he does not explicitly address the use of ethnographic material in the first edition of *The Protestant Ethic,* he reflects on his omission in the 1920 Introduction to the essay on the world religions:

Some justification is needed for the fact that ethnographical material has not been utilized to anything like the extent which the value of its contributions naturally demands in any really thorough investigation. . . . We are here necessarily dealing with the religious ethics of the classes which were the culture-bearers of their respective countries. Now it is quite true that this can only be completely known in all its details when the facts from eth-

---

4 Weber, *Protestant Ethic,* 79.

nography and folk-lore have been compared with it. . . . This is a gap to which the ethnographer will legitimately object.[5]

Weber recognizes the value of ethnography, and not just in principle – not just as a theoretical possibility – for he acknowledges the valuable results of *existing* ethnographies and goes on to promise to make use of ethnographic material in his sociology of religion. Ethnography has a valid methodology for studying a genuine empirical subject matter.[6]

I emphasize Weber's appreciation of ethnography in order to draw out the contrast to his evaluation of the category of race, which he also discusses in the Introduction. The mutually independent appearance of certain types of rationalization in the West, and only there, might lead one, he notes, to suspect that the reason lies in heredity. Weber admits to a personal inclination to think the importance of biological heredity very great. "But," he continues, "in spite of the notable achievements of anthropological research, I see up to the present no way of exactly or even approximately measuring either the extent or, above all, the form of its influence on the development investigated here."[7] A social and historical investigation, he continues, must first examine all the environmental causes and influences. Despite what he calls their "in many ways very promising beginnings," he sees no value yet in "comparative racial neurology and psychology." He concludes the Introduction by calling the appeal to racial difference a renunciation of knowledge attainable and a shift of the problem to factors at present still unknown.[8] How are we to read this passage? To what extent should we take it to be inclining toward a natural explanation of Western rationalization, in contrast to the emphasis on social and cultural explanations that we have encountered so far?

First, a word is in order about the actual state of physical anthropology in early-twentieth-century Germany. Like physical anthropology elsewhere in Western Europe and North America, it was

---

5 Ibid., 29–30.
6 A recent study beautifully fulfills the ethnographic task: James L. Peacock and Ruel W. Tyson, Jr., *Pilgrims of Paradox: Calvinism and Experience among the Primitive Baptists of the Blue Ridge* (Washington, D.C., and London, 1989). Peacock and Tyson describe a group of Calvinists (including descendants of the kinsmen Weber himself visited on his trip to the United States) who continue to adhere strictly to the Westminster Confession. Though Peacock's and Tyson's ethnography is far more than an illustration of the "Weber thesis," it does, among other things, discover primitive Baptist daily practice to be a "Weberian" working out of anxiety over salvation.
7 Weber, *Protestant Ethic*, 30.   8 Ibid.

in a state of transition from an older, classificatory science of racial types to evolutionary models attempting to determine the statistical frequency of inherited characteristics. Many of its practitioners were racists, but their research was not necessarily so. For example, Franz Boas, already well advanced in his critique of racial assumptions in physical anthropology, admired the 1909 study of Hottentot [Herero] intermarriage that established Eugen Fischer's reputation, and Boas remained in touch with his German colleagues until the 1930s. We should not read back from the role of Fischer and his colleagues in the Third Reich to the reputation of their earlier work, parts of which were credible by the highest critical standards of the time. Weber's endorsement of physical anthropology's achievements was not in itself an endorsement of racial "science."[9]

Even so, Weber's Introduction admits the hypothetical possibility of using race as a category of analysis. Yet what *The Protestant Ethic* "is," or better, what it does as a work of social science, is not in any way determined by a hypothetical possibility, which the author may insert as a rhetorical move to be modified by the actual execution of the work. What is his practice in *The Protestant Ethic?* A footnote to Weber's observations about Lutherans and Puritans, cited earlier, gives a further glimpse of his evaluation of racial explanation.

One who shared the philosophy of history of the Levellers would be in the fortunate position of being able to attribute this in turn to racial differences. They believed themselves to be the defenders of the Anglo-Saxon birthright, against the descendants of William the Conqueror and the Normans. It is astonishing enough that it has not yet occurred to anyone to maintain that the plebeian Roundheads were round-headed in the anthropometric sense![10]

Weber's joke contains a serious assertion. The actual practice of the anthropometricians, their body measurements and typologies of race, was a misplaced materialism, which he evokes here by carrying their logic to the point of absurdity. For racial theorists, as parodied here, the physical contrast between Roundheads and Cavaliers calls for a biological explanation of origins. The Roundheads related themselves to a mythical ancestry in unbroken historical descent instead of examining the verifiable factors – here Civil War and religious controversy – that account for differences in *appearance* such

9 See Robert Proctor, "From *Anthropologie* to *Rassenkunde* in the German Anthropological Tradition," in George Stocking, ed., *History of Anthropology*, Vol. 5: *Bones, Bodies, Behavior: Essays on Biological Anthropology* (Madison, Wis., 1988), 138–179.
10 Weber, *Protestant Ethic*, 216–217.

as, in this case, plebeian cropped hair versus aristocratic flowing locks. Elsewhere Weber makes a point that is an important logical extension of this one: The social psychology of religions actually explains physical appearance; religious difference, not racial type, accounts for the supposedly tense, alert appearance of Anglo-Saxons versus relaxed Germanic *Gemütlichkeit*.[11]

The concluding paragraph of *The Protestant Ethic* suggests by omission the place of heredity or race in Weber's thinking. Weber writes that after his tracing of a religious causal sequence, one would need to investigate "how Protestant Asceticism was in turn influenced in its development and its character by the totality of social conditions, especially economic." Religion and society mark the boundaries of the inquiry. As for heredity, Weber simply omits it – hardly the procedure of someone seriously tantalized by the possibility of racial explanation. And then comes a final reference to national identity: "Modern man is in general, even with the best will, unable to give religious ideas a significance for culture and national character which they deserve."[12] If Weber reaches beyond the knowable in order to account for national character, it is not in the direction of a hereditary unknown; rather, his pathos ultimately lies with religion, or rather with the limits to understanding when members of a modern, secular culture attempt to comprehend their own religious predecessors.

So far I have cited evidence for Weber's views on national identity and race from two moments, 1904–1905 and 1920. Weber's lengthiest consideration of the subject, to my knowledge, falls roughly between these dates of the two editions of *The Protestant Ethic*, in his comments at the two prewar meetings of the German Sociological Association in 1910 and 1912. At the first meeting Alfred Ploetz gave a paper on "The Concepts of Race and Society." Ploetz, like most practitioners of physical anthropology in Germany a physician, was the founder of the racial hygiene movement in Germany and chairman of the Society for Racial Hygiene. Weber's judgment of Ploetz and his variety of social biology was ambivalent. Its mixture of social reform and social science made it especially provocative at a time when he was determined to keep the Sociological Association strictly free of reform propaganda. Yet he made a considerable effort to keep Ploetz and his fellow racial theorists in the Association; as the corre-

11 Ibid., 127–128.    12 Ibid., 183.

spondence in the papers of the Association make clear, he wanted the biological dimension of social science to be represented in an organization that was supposed to give shape to the nascent discipline of sociology. But Weber's criticisms in the discussion following Ploetz's paper refuted everything the racial theorist had to say. Ploetz's fundamental presupposition, his belief, directly antithetical to Weber's methodological principles, in a collective social totality, met with attack. In attacking Ploetz, Weber repeatedly turned to the alternative concept of *culture:* Rome decayed, not as Ploetz supposed, because of racial decline, but because of the introduction of new *cultural* values; racial relations in the United States were primarily a *cultural* problem, not in need of racial explanation.[13] One exchange will give something of the flavor of the whole discussion:

Ploetz: Wouldn't it be much better if present-day Greece were still inhabited by the ancient Greeks and not by those who live there today, or if it at least were inhabited by men who acted like the ancient Greeks!
Weber: They wouldn't have the same culture!
Ploetz: But then another culture! If the men had the same brains. . .
Weber: Maybe they do![14]

The exchange captures a decisive point of difference: Ploetz ignored environment with his fantasy of latter-day Hellenes, who would be the same as their pagan ancestors if endowed with the same brains.

---

13 *Verhandlungen des deutschen Soziologentages* I (19–22 October 1910) (Frankfurt am Main, 1969), 152, 154. The day after his comments on Ploetz's paper, Weber underlined his interest in racial research. The newspapers had reported that, according to him, sociology had no interest in racial problems. Weber replied that this was never his view: "Ich habe gesagt, dass ein bestimmter, ein sehr bestimmter, von mehreren möglichen Rassenbegriffen meines Erachtens nicht diejenige Fruchtbarkeit für *unsere* – wohl gemerkt – Untersuchungen hat, die ihm vielfach zugeschrieben wird." He emphasized his plan to found a social biology section of the organization. Ibid., 215.
   Commenting on the sections being planned for the Association, Weber wrote to Hermann Beck, secretary of the Association: "Von dem Gedanken an die Bildung einer Abteilung für Anthropologie wird schon deshalb Abstand zu nehmen sein, weil Herr Dr. *Ploetz* in der Tat mit Recht geltend macht, dass seine Doppelstellung in unserer und der von ihm präsidierten Gesellschaft unmöglich würde, falls eine *Konkurrenz* beider entstünde. Für uns besteht das Bedürfnis, eine solche Konkurrenz zu machen, gewiss nicht. Die Gesellschaft für Soziologie muss die biologische Seit ihrer Probleme pflegen, aber sie kann dies innerhalb des Rahmens der *allgemeinen* Veranstaltungen tun. Sie wird unbedingt in die Lage kommen – falls sie sich lebensfähig zeigt – auch *Arbeiten* machen zu lassen, welche jene Probleme mit berühren. Aber sie braucht nicht *jene* Gesichtspunkte zu behandeln, welche schon von anderer Seite bearbeitet werden. Unbedingte Voraussetzung ist freilich, dass der Gesellschaft mehr *Mitglieder* aus naturwissenschaftlichen Kreisen beitreten und in dem Versuch, solche heranzuziehen, wird ja Herr Dr. *Ploetz* auch keinesfalls eine 'Konkurrenz' erblicken." Weber to Beck, Heidelberg 4 Oct. 1910, papers of the German Sociological Association, Ferdinand-Toennies-Nachlass, Schleswig-Holsteinische Landesbibliothek, Kiel, Cb54.61:1.1.
14 *Verhandlungen des deutschen Soziologentages* I, 159.

Weber's point in reply was that they might very well have the same brains and would *still* have a different culture. Again, as in his critique of Roundhead anthropometrics, physical appearance is only a condition for the possibility of sociocultural interpretation. Weber made similar remarks in response to Sombart's defense of racial theory at the second meeting of the Sociological Association two years later. Once again he discoursed on the Romans, this time pointing out, among other things, that precisely barbarians could become the most assimilated "Romans" of all when they assimilated into the Empire's *culture*. And he made the general observation that before racial theories could be worthy of discussion at all, two things would be needed: exact measurable differences of provably inherited responses to stimuli and proof that these qualities made a difference for *cultural* causality. The results: "Not a single fact of this kind is available so far."[15] Throughout the discussions of both years, Weber's refrain was the specificity and variability of *culture* as a source of social explanation.

The concept of nationhood was the general theme of the 1912 meeting of the Sociological Association. The first plenary session began with a paper by Paul Barth on "The Sociological Significance of Nationalities," which so exasperated Weber, with its confusion of description and value judgments, that he declared it to be the last meeting he would attend.[16] He then delivered a speech that may serve as a final document of Weber's views on national identity, for it both summarizes and rounds out his remarks in *The Protestant Ethic*. "Do we have any reason at all," he asked, "to treat these concepts [of nation and national feeling] as special realities?" There was no essential causal factor, according to Weber, leading to nationhood. A common language was neither a necessary nor a sufficient defining quality. The most heterogeneous peoples could be welded together into a single nation; hence ethnicity was also in no way decisive. On race, Weber commented: "We would do well to ignore completely the mystical effects of blood community," and he went on to describe race relations in the United States entirely as a consequence of social relations. What, then, was left? Weber shifted the discourse entirely to the realm of politics. The nation was "a community of feeling whose adequate expression is a state of one's own and which normally has the tendency inherently to bring forth one (*einen solchen aus*

---

15  *Verhandlungen des deutschen Soziologentages* II (10–22 Oct. 1912) (Frankfurt am Main, 1969), 188, 190.
16  See the report in *Frankfurter Zeitung* 3. Morgenblatt, Nr. 293, 2–3.

*sich hervorzutreiben*)." Weber specified that the contents of community feeling resided in collective memory – a remark that took it out of the realm of abstractions and grounded it in collective practices. The relevant pages of *Economy and Society* argue along the same lines.[17]

Two features of Weber's understanding of national identity call for comment. First, Weber's position in the Sociological Association and in *Economy and Society* differs notably from that of *The Protestant Ethic*. There he gives priority to religion, here to politics, in his definition. On this as on other issues, *The Protestant Ethic* is a one-sided book, and one needs to piece it together with other writings for a full account of his position. Second, a more general point. Weber completely emptied national identity of essentialist contents: Jews were not excluded, Alsatians were not included by definition in the German nation. National identity referred neither to any specific content, nor even to any predetermined empirical category such as language or ethnicity, for it was a dependent concept shaped by its relationship to political events and the state. Weber could be, and of course was, a political nationalist; but his use of the concept of national identity in *The Protestant Ethic* and his other scientific writings deflated any and every attempt to remove it from the vagaries of history.

17 See Max Weber, *Economy and Society,* ed. Guenther Roth and Claus Wittich (Berkeley, Los Angeles, and London), 395–398.

# 6
# Nietzsche's Monastery for Freer Spirits and Weber's Sect

The concept of "elective affinity" is particularly useful in discussing Nietzsche and Weber, and it has been chosen deliberately because it leaves open the question of causality that has recently been discussed so much in the literature.[1] In searching for elective affinities, I would like to use Weber to demythologize Nietzsche. Looking for such affinities implies comparison, and comparing Nietzsche means relativizing his uniqueness. Both Weber and Nietzsche developed ideal types of "sect" and "monastery," and both were concerned with the process of self-education that produces "strong natures" ("free thinkers") or "personalities" (rationalistic "supermen"), in essence, exemplary religious individuals.[2] But they also differed very much

*I would like to express my warm thanks to Dr. Anna Bankowska (Edinburgh) for her work as translator.

The following abbreviations are used throughout the footnotes to this essay:

On Nietzsche: KGB      *Kritische Gesamtausgabe. Briefwechsel* (Berlin and New York, 1975–1987)

           KSA      *Kritische Studienausgabe* (Munich, Berlin, New York, 1980), vols. 1–15

           KSA, letters      *Kritische Studienausgabe. Sämtliche Briefe Nietzsches* (Munich, Berlin, New York, 1986), vols. 1–8

On Weber:      GARS I      *Gesammelte Aufsätze zur Religionssoziologie* (Tübingen, 1920; 6th ed., 1972), Vol. I

           WL      *Gesammelte Aufsätze zur Wissenschaftslehre*, 4th ed. (Tübingen, 1973)

1 Robert Eden, *Political Leadership and Nihilism. A Study of Weber and Nietzsche* (Tampa, 1984); Harvey Goldman, *Max Weber and Thomas Mann. Calling and the Shaping of the Self* (Berkeley, Calif., 1988); Wilhelm Hennis, *Max Weber. Essays in Reconstruction*, Keith Tribe, tr. (London, 1988); Lawrence A. Scaff, *Fleeing the Iron Cage. Culture, Politics and Modernity in the Thought of Max Weber* (Berkeley, Calif., 1989); Wolfgang Schluchter, *Religion und Lebensführung*, Vol. 1, *Studien zu Max Webers Kultur- und Werttheorie* (Frankfurt, 1988); and *Rationalism, Religion and Domination. A Weberian Perspective*, Neil Solomon, Tr. (Berkeley, Calif., 1989).

2 Harvey Goldman speaks of "empowered selves" in his essay in this volume, and to this extent we complement one another. However, I differ from Goldman in one important respect. So far as the meaning of asceticism is concerned, I put Nietzsche closer to Weber. This is because I have drawn exclusively on extracts from Nietzsche's fragments that have been published posthumously. These fragments make a slightly different impression, and

133

methodologically, and Weber's *Sachlichkeit* threatens Nietzsche's position. The differences are well known, but they become ever clearer when we look at issues and concepts of Nietzsche's generation and that of his teachers. I would like to follow here Montinari's suggestion by attempting to reconstruct part of Nietzsche's "ideal library" and to present "the contemporaries with whom he engaged in argument as well as his ties to individuals and groups of his time."[3] Although this brings out the great difference from Weber, it also moves, surprisingly, figures like Jhering, Tönnies, and Simmel closer to Nietzsche and, for all their differences, places them in a paradigm that asserts a successful union of the natural sciences and the humanities in the study of language, at least for the period in question.

Nietzsche conceived the idea for a "monastery for freer spirits" in December 1870. The key to the whole plan can be found in a letter from Erwin Rohde to Nietzsche.[4] Nietzsche may also have been stimulated by a pamphlet published in 1869 by Afrikan Spir.[5] Spir promoted the idea of a Protestant monastery in which kindred spirits and "like-minded men," who thus called themselves friends, could meet for joint discussion and reading in order to strive for "inner perfection" in strict isolation, guided by strict dietary rules. The educational ideal of this male community was summed up in the following slogan: "Think and act in harmony with one's self (with one's true nature)."

The monastery for freer spirits first came into being in Basel in 1873. The monastery, later known as Baumannshöhle (formerly Schützengraben 45, now 47), provided to the friends who grouped around the "twins,"[6] Nietzsche and Franz Overbeck, a stable focal

they differ to some extent from the third paragraph in the *Genealogy of Morals*, "What do ascetic ideals mean?". See also Goldman, "The Problem of the Person in Weberian Social Theory," in Murray Milgate and Cheryl B. Welch, eds., *Critical Issues in Social Thought* (New York: Academic Press, 1989), 59–73.

3 Mazzino Montinari, *Nietzsche lesen* (Berlin, 1982), 6.

4 KGB, second section, II, 280; KSA, letters, III, 165f.

5 This pamphlet, entitled *Vorschlag an die Freunde einer vernünftigen Lebensführung* (*Suggestion to Friends on Rational Conduct*), was published in Leipzig in 1869. It was discussed in the *Zeitschrift für exacte Philosophie* 9 (1871): 211–214. On Spir, see Hubert Treiber, "Nietzsche's 'Kloster für freiere Geister'. Nietzsche und Weber als Erzieher," in Peter Antes and Donate Pahnke, eds., *Die Religion von Oberschichten* (Marburg, 1989), 117–161, 121. I do not know whether Nietzsche took the name from the late medieval sect called the "Brothers and Sisters of the Free Spirit."

6 Nietzsche wrote the following dedication on the copy of *Thoughts out of Season* destined for Franz Overbeck:

| Ein Zwillingspaar aus Einem Haus | Twins from one house |
|---|---|
| ging muthig in die Welt hinaus, | went courageously out into the world |
| Welt-Drachen zu zerreissen, | to slay world-dragons |

place. Among those who lived there were Heinrich Romundt, who had been a friend of Nietzsche since their student days in Leipzig and who was then a *Privatdozent* at the university of Basel, and Paul Rée, who had been in Basel since April 1873 to visit Romundt, whom he had known in Leipzig. Nevertheless, the monastery for freer spirits was not made up merely of this "gang of four."[7]

The idea of the monastery was also a blueprint for friendship.[8] However, at the time, the friends were also bound by an idea that was described in an extremely vague fashion by the epithet the "society of the hopeful."[9] The concluding remarks in Nietzsche's second *Unzeitgemässe Betrachtung,* a work that met with Ferdinand Tönnies' immediate approval, are also directed at this invisible community of the hopeful.[10] In certain respects, Tönnies was to fulfill what Nie-

| | |
|---|---|
| Zwei-Väterwerk! Ein Wunder war's! | A two father work! It was a miracle |
| Die Mutter doch des Zwillingspaares | The mother of the twins |
| *Freundschaft* ist sie geheissen! | was called *Friendship!* |

Karl Pestalozzi, "Overbecks 'Schriftchen' 'Uber die Christlichkeit unserer heutigen Theologie' und Nietzsches 'Erste unzeitgemässe Betrachtung . . . ,'" in Rudolf Brändle and Ekkehard W. Stegemann, eds., *Franz Overbecks unerledigte Anfragen an das Christentum* (Munich, 1988), 91–107, 92; KSA VII, 410: 17 (10).

7 Pestalozzi, "Overbecks 'Schriftchen,'" 91–107, 93:
　There is a visual record of who belonged to the group in the form of a shallow bowl described as a *monumentulum amicitiae* which was painted by Carl von Gersdorff in the style of *Giulio Romano* and given to Overbeck in 1876 on the occasion of his wedding. Depicted on the bowl, along with initials and symbolic representations, are, in addition to Overbeck, his bride, Nietzsche, and Gersdorff himself, the ancient philologist Erwin Rohde, who had advertised Nietzsche's *Birth of Tragedy* and defended it from Wilamowitz' scathing critique, the philosopher Heinrich Romundt . . . , who . . . had also resided in Baumannshöhle since the summer of 1872.
　Richard Wagner and Heinrich von Treitschke, Overbeck's friend from his university days, are also immortalized on the bowl. Wagner is portrayed as a winged head depicting a genius (*Geniuskopf*) and Treitschke by the symbol of the German empire, the eagle. Ibid. The bowl was no longer quite appropriate: Romundt had left Basel in 1875 but nevertheless remained in close contact with those with whom he had been in Baumannshöhle. On the other hand, Treischke had begun to distance himself from Overbeck since 1873.

8 There are astonishing parallels between the cult of friendship as it was cultivated by Friedrich Hölderlin and his friends, described by Hubert Cancik, " 'Freundschaftskult' – Religionsgeschichtliche Bemerkungen zu Mythos, Kult und Theologie der Freundschaft bei Friedrich Hölderlin," in Christoph Elsas and Hans G. Kippenberg, eds., *Loyalitätskonflikte in der Religionsgeschichte. Festschrift Carsten Colpe* (Würzburg, forthcoming), and the friendship association cultivated or proselytized by Nietzsche. On Nietzsche, see "Freundschaft in der Wüste," chapt. 3 of Ross's biography of Nietzsche. Werner Ross, *Der ängstliche Adler: Friedrich Nietzsches Leben* (Munich, 1984), 212ff. The strong pedagogical impetus that is a distinguishing feature of the "School of Educators," and that above all was aimed at friends, can be interpreted as sublimation, according to Hans Kelsen, "Die platonische Liebe," in Ernst Topitsch, ed., *Aufsätze zur Ideologiekritik* (Neuwied and Berlin, 1964), 114–197. I would like to thank Hubert Cancik for showing me the manuscript of his essay on Hölderlin.

9 Pestalozzi, "Overbecks 'Schriftchen,'" 93; KSA VII, 512 19 (300, 301, 302, 317).

10 "I bought it and was deeply moved." See Ferdinand Tönnies, "Ferdinand Tönnies," in Raymund Schmidt, ed., *Die Deutsche Philosophie der Gegenwart in Selbstdarstellungen* (Leipzig, 1922), 199–234, 204.

tzsche had expressed to Rohde in 1870: "We are each other's teachers, our books are merely the hooks with which we gain someone else for our monastic-artistic society."[11] The hooks that the "fishers of men" threw out of Baumannshöhle in August 1873 were Overbeck's polemic, *Über die Christlichkeit unserer heutigen Theologie,* and Nietzsche's *Unzeitgemässe Betrachtung, Erstes Stück: David Strauss, der Bekenner und Schriftsteller.* The occasion of both these polemics was the publication of two works that he had made the "general question of the future of German culture one of the future of religion in Germany."[12] The works in question were David Friedrich Strauss's *Der alte und der neue Glaube. Ein Bekenntniss* and Paul de Lagarde's *Über das Verhältnis des deutschen Staates zu Theologie, Kirche und Religion.*[13] In Overbeck's and Nietzsche's dispute with the "cultural philistine" Strauss, three post-Christian life forms and attitudes toward religion, which were later received favorably by the bourgeoisie, become apparent.[14] One of these was Strauss's idea of a "secular Sunday and leisure culture," whose devotees had a grounding in the natural sciences and in history and consumed cultural products, but whose way of life was not affected by this "new faith." Another is the understanding shared by Nietzsche and Wagner that it is "taking art and language seriously in an absolute religious manner" that makes it possible to adopt an attitude toward the world (in the sense of a world view). Lastly, there is Overbeck's antimodernist stance of a "Christian faith that has lost its faith," a faithless faith that can still provide guidelines as a "Christian way of looking at the world and at life."[15] If one wanted to specify a fourth basic attitude, then it would be that of a "patriotic state religion" (Overbeck), as represented in Heinrich von

11 KSA, letters, III, 165f.    12 Pestalozzi, "Overbecks 'Schriftchen,' " 95.

13 Lagarde's book was published in Göttingen in 1873. Its appearance made such an impression on Overbeck that he described it in a fulsome letter to Lagarde dated February, 1, 1873; see Fritz Stern, *The Politics of Cultural Despair: A Study in the Rise of the Germanic Ideology* (Berkeley, Calif., 1961), 400. Overbeck recommended Lagarde's work to Nietzsche, who further recommended it to Rohde (January 31, 1873) and Wagner (April 8, 1873), respectively. Nietzsche was later (1877) to call Lagarde "a pompous and sentimental crank."

Max Weber had read David Friedrich Strauss's *Der alte und der neue Glaube* (Leipzig, 1872) in May 1882 and was somewhat disappointed by it; Max Weber, *Jugendbriefe* (Tübingen, 1936), 44; Marianne Weber. *Max Weber. Ein Lebensbild. Mit einem Essay von Günther Roth* (Munich, 1989), 71. He had previously described Strauss's *Leben Jesu* as a "great success"; Max Weber, *Jugendbriefe,* 205. On David Strauss, see Friedrich Wilhelm Graf, *Kritik und Pseudo-Spekulation. David Friedrich Strauss als Dogmatiker im Kontext der positionellen (!) Theologie seiner Zeit* (Munich, 1982).

14 See Georg Simmel, "Tendencies in German Life and Thought since 1870," *The International Monthly* 5 (1902):93–111, 166–184, 172ff.; Thomas Nipperdey, *Religion im Umbruch. Deutschland 1870–1918* (Munich, 1988), 124ff.

15 Pestalozzi, "Overbecks 'Schriftchen,' " 107.

Treitschke. The mainstay of this fourth attitude, and the element that imbued it with sense, was Germany's greatness and national unity.

Tönnies had also read the *Der alte und der neue Glaube* with interest, just as in the summer of 1880 he had read Lagarde "repeatedly with deepest sympathy."[16] In the case of Tönnies too, the critique of and disillusionment with the "abominable present" led to a crisis of identity and of the meaning of life against which he struggled in a characteristic manner by seeking refuge with friends[17] and by undergoing an education comparable to a religious awakening (*Erweckungserziehung*):

Whoever wants to be a philosopher should turn his back on the spirit of our time with disgust! This should be our motto. With it we must form a tightly-knit sect, one that acts and writes of one accord and that is organized and disciplined. We must not look to people, to the masses – we have not enough faith for that and must wait for the Messiah to provide it – but to the educated.[18]

Whoever wants to be listened to sets great store by the power of words: In this case a "philosophizing newspaper" published by Schmeitzner (Chemnitz) with Nietzsche, Overbeck, Paulsen, Rée, Lagarde, and others was to help free them from "the nineteenth century tide of restoration" (Paulsen).[19] This sign of involvement in worldly affairs was followed in 1881 by another brainchild, which this time involved taking refuge from the world: the idea of a home for philosophers "in the country," away from the university and far away from the "smoky cities," held together by "trust, community, friendship."[20]

Even if, as will be shown later, the monastery for freer spirits was to a large extent aimed at education for spiritual awakening, nevertheless, from 1873 on, it had a side that was completely devoted to studies in particular branches of knowledge. These studies were not only aimed at treatises concerning science and the philosophy of nature, as Karl

16 Rainer Polley, ed., "Ferdinand Tönnies – Lebenserinnerungen aus dem Jahre 1935 and Kindheit, Schulzeit, Studium und erste Dozententätigkeit (1855–1894)," *Zeitschrift der Gesellschaft für Schleswig-Holsteinische Geschichte* 105 (1980):187–227, 213; Olaf Klose, Eduard Georg Jacoby, and Irma Fischer, eds., *Ferdinand Tönnies – Friedrich Paulsen. Briefwechsel 1876–1908* (Kiel, 1961), 95.

17 See the passage from *Gemeinschaft und Gesellschaft. Kommunismus und Sozialismus als empirische Kulturformen* (Leipzig, 1887; reprint ed., Darmstadt, 1979), 13, on friendship: "Spiritual friendship, on the other hand, forms a type of invisible place, a mystical town and assembly, which comes to life through artistic intuition and creative will."

18 Klose et al., eds., *Tönnies-Paulsen Briefwechsel*, 95, October 1880.

19 Ibid., 75, beginning of 1880.    20 Ibid., 120.

Schlechta and Anni Anders have shown;[21] what is particularly interesting about the focus on the natural sciences shown in Basel (and afterward) – and this has been overlooked until now – is the fact that it was the new science of the comparative study of languages that provided the framework for this approach to the natural sciences. This also determined the study group's interest in empirical moral science.

The key figure to this realism [or "ré(e)alism"] in reflections on moral and legal norms is Paul Rée.[22] His specific interest in the "English way of thinking," which he shared with Tönnies and Friedrich Paulsen, can be demonstrated by the fact that he read and reviewed George Henry Lewes's two-volume *Geschichte der Philosophie von Thales bis Comte* in Basel.[23]

Rée is an ideal guide through Nietzsche's ideal library for the period from 1873 to the end of 1882. His marginal position as a perennial private scholar saved him from becoming entangled as a university lecturer, which would have ensured him a certain continuity and conformity within his field. His position as an outsider made him an unconventional thinker, as can be seen in his approach to methodology. Rée is thus an ideal guide to the period from 1870 to 1885, the period when he himself was most intellectually active.

Rée's writings, in this case *Der Ursprung der moralischen Empfindungen* and *Die Entstehung des Gewissens,* contain key passages, two of which we will look at briefly here. The first extract is from *Der Ursprung:*

This is a purely theoretical work. Just as the *geologist* first of all seeks out and describes the various formations and then searches for what *caused* them to develop in that way, so the writer first of all grasped moral phenomena from *experience* and then inquired into the *history . . . of their development.*[24]

The second example comes from *Die Entstehung:*

We use the *comparative method* and also investigate *genetic development.* The *comparison* of different cultural *stages* shows that they are governed by differ-

---

21  *Friedrich Nietzsche. Von den verborgenen Anfängen seines Philosophierens* (Stuttgart-Bad Cannstatt, 1962), esp. 60ff.

22  See also Cornelius Bickel, "Ferdinand Tönnies' Weg in die Soziologie," in Otthein Rammstedt, ed., *Simmel und die frühen Soziologen. Nähe und Distanz zu Durkheim, Tönnies und Max Weber* (Frankfurt, 1988), 86–162, 97.

23  George Henry Lewes, *Geschichte der Philosophie von Thales bis Comte* (Berlin, 1871) (Vol. I: *Geschichte der alten Philosophie;* Vol. II: *Geschichte der neueren Philosophie*). The review appeared in *Das Ausland* (1879), 957. See also Werner Sombart, "Die Anfänge der Soziologie," in Melchior Palyi, ed., *Hauptprobleme der Soziologie. Erinnerungsgabe für Max Weber* (Munich, 1923), I:5–19, for more on the English naturalist-monist tradition.

24  Paul Rée, *Der Ursprung der moralischen Empfindungen* (Chemnitz, 1877), Foreword, emphasis added.

ent consciences. An *investigation of the genesis* of phenomena reveals the *reasons* why the conscience of one *cultural stage evolved* out of another. Ethics is thus essentially a *historical science*. The *history* of conscience is its explanation. The man who has no knowledge of the moral standards of others has no knowledge of his own, – just as he who has no knowledge of a foreign language, or another religion has no knowledge of his own language or religion.[25]

These extracts contain key concepts (marked by emphasis) referring to a range of sciences that William Whewell described as *Palaetiological Sciences:* "All these sciences are connected by this bond; – they all endeavour to ascend to a past state, by considering what is the present state of things, and what are the causes of change."[26] Whewell included among the palaetiological sciences such disciplines as geology, the comparative study of languages, the (comparative) study of religion, ethnology, and anatomy. The common feature of these sciences was that they made claims to empiricism, were interested in regularities (*Gesetzmässigkeiten*), preferred the comparative method, and inclined toward a historical, genealogical approach (which was susceptible to evolutionistic constructs).

Rée was confronted with these sciences during his student days in Leipzig (summer term 1869/winter term 1870–1871) and Berlin (winter term 1871–1872). Among his teachers in Leipzig were the philologist and linguist Georg Curtius and the mathematician and philosopher Moritz Wilhelm Drobisch. Of Rée's teachers in Berlin, Robert Hartmann stands out.[27] Hartmann was a respected anatomist, zoologist, and ethnologist who knew linguistics.[28]

During his time in Berlin, Rée also attended, by personal invitation, the experimental lectures on chemistry by August Wilhelm von Hofmann, who had been a pupil of Liebig. Von Hofmann then put together this series of lectures on inorganic chemistry and published a textbook entitled *Einleitung in die Moderne Chemie*.[29] Hofmann had

25  The concluding sentence copies an expression first used by Max Müller, who is not quoted. Müller's wording provided a constant stimulus for variations on this theme. Paul Rée, *Die Entstehung des Gewissens* (Berlin, 1885), 32; italics added.

26  William Whewell, *The Philosophy of the Inductive Sciences, Founded upon Their History* (London, 1840, 1847), I:638.

27  See Karl Heinz Ciz, *Robert Hartmann (1831–1893). Mitbegründer der deutschen Ethnologie* (Gelsenkirchen, 1984).

28  Today Hartmann has slipped into oblivion; few people remember that he had founded the *Zeitschrift für Ethnologie* together with Bastian in 1869. Hartmann is not even mentioned in the detailed monograph on Adolf Bastian by Klaus-Peter Koepping, *Adolf Bastian and the Psychic Unity of Mankind. The Foundations of Anthropology in Nineteenth Century Germany* (St. Lucia, London, and New York, 1983). Hartmann played a leading role in the Berlin Society for Anthropology, Ethnography, and Ancient History; he was also a leading light in the Geography Society.

29  Braunschweig, 1866; first ed. London, 1865.

succeeded in producing aniline from benzene and preparing aniline dyes synthetically. One is reminded in this context of the first aphorism in *Menschliches, Allzumenschliches: "Chemie der Begriffe und Empfindungen,"* as well as of a terminological borrowing from Rudolph von Jhering's *Geist des römischen Rechts auf den verschiedenen Stufen seiner Entwicklung:*[30]

> All that we need and all that can be derived from the present state of development of the individual sciences is a chemistry of moral, religious, and aesthetic conceptions and perceptions . . . : how would it be if this chemistry concluded that in this realm too the most splendid colors were derived from base, indeed despised, materials?[31]

Drobisch and Curtius, who at first glance appear to have had nothing in common, must be considered together. Curtius is regarded as the founder of modern historical-comparative linguistics, which evolved alongside classical philology. In his inaugural lecture in Leipzig in 1862, Curtius asserted that the two disciplines were essentially concerned with different things:

> The domain of the general linguist is the natural side, that of the philologist, as it were, the cultural side of the language. However, because every language forms a whole, it is impossible to separate one side from the other.[32]

This "division of labor" also described two competing research orientations. One, indebted to Jacob Grimm, emphasized the cultural side of the language and assigned it to the humanities, viewing it as history. The other tended toward a scientific (*naturwissenschaftliche*) examination of language. Curtius was a major proponent of the latter approach with his explanation of sound shifts that could be subsumed under general laws, even if he was not prepared to accept the early

---

30 First ed., Leipzig 1852 (Vol. I), 1854 (Vol. II. 1), 1858 (Vol. II. 2), 1865 (Vol. III. 1); the citations here are drawn from: "Geist," Zweiter Theil, Zweite Abt. 1923 6–7, 335; "Geist," Erster Theil, 1924 7–8, 25ff., esp. 25–27, 48ff.

31 KSA II, 24; see also KSA X, 257f.: 7 (48). Rée attended Karl Bogislaus Reichert's practical sessions and lectures on cerebral anatomy. Reichert, one of Müller's successors, had been a pupil of von Baer and was one of the most distinguished anatomists of the nineteenth century. Rée also attended courses by the philosopher Friedrich Adolf Trendelenburg (1802–1872), who was to give lectures for the last time in the winter term of 1871–1872. On the importance of Trendelenburg, see Klaus Christian Köhnke's excellent study *Entstehung und Aufstieg des Neukantianismus. Die deutsche Universitätsphilosophie zwischen Idealismus und Positivismus* (Frankfurt, 1986), 23ff. Trendelenburg's *Logische Untersuchungen*, 3rd ed., 2 vols. (Leipzig, 1870) also had a considerable influence on Rudolph von Jhering's *Der Zweck im Recht*. On the achievements of the scientists whose lectures Rée attended in Berlin, see Ernst Mayr, *Die Entwicklung der biologischen Gedankenwelt. Vielfalt, Evolution und Vererbung* (Berlin, 1984), esp. 104.

32 Georg Curtius, "Philologie und Sprachwissenschaft," in Hans Helmut Christmann, ed., *Sprachwissenschaft des 19. Jahrhunderts* (Darmstadt, 1977), 67–84, 80.

Neogrammarians' views on the subject.[33] Most of the Neogrammarians had at one time been his pupils but had begun to dissociate themselves from him in the mid-1870s.[34] The "principle" was to be found in Curtius' most important work, *Grundzüge der griechischen Etymologie:*

Only the regular and inwardly coherent can be studied scientifically, the arbitrary can at best be guessed at, never conclusively revealed. However, in my view the situation is not as grave as it might appear. Rather, fixed rules can most reliably be recognized in the life of sounds and these rules can be brought to bear almost with the consistency of natural forces.[35]

The culmination of this line of thought was the thesis put forward by the Neogrammarians, namely, that sound laws were absolute (the principle of exceptionless sound laws).[36] Drobisch, who conducted statistical examinations of antique rhyme structures in the 1860s, was also part of this line of development. All of this has been forgotten today, although the importance of Drobisch was recognized by a prominent contemporary, Friedrich Albert Lange, who described him in his *Geschichte des Materialismus und Kritik seiner Bedeutung in der Gegenwart.*[37]

If there had been a best-seller list at the time, Lange's *Geschichte des Materialismus*[38] would certainly have been at its top, and it would

33 Olga Amsterdamska, "Institutions and School of Thought: The Neogrammarians," *American Journal of Sociology* 91 (1985):332–358, 335f.
34 Kurt R. Jankowsky, *The Neogrammarians. A Re-Evaluation of Their Place in the Development of Linguistic Science* (The Hague and Paris, 1972), esp. 93ff., 124ff., 190ff.; Han Helmut Christmann, ed., *Sprachwissenschaft des 19. Jahrhunderts* (Darmstadt, 1977); T. Craig Christy, *Uniformitarianism in Linguistics* (Amsterdam and Philadelphia, 1983).
35 Part 1 (Leipzig, 1858).
36 See Hans Henrich Hock, *Principles of Historical Linguistics* (Berlin, New York, and Amsterdam, 1988), 2, 34ff., 629ff.
37 3rd ed. (Iserlohn, 1877), vol. II, 446f.
38 The reactions of Nietzsche, Tönnies, and Weber to reading Lange's *Geschichte des Materialismus* are detailed in the following paragraphs: Nietzsche (1866): "The most important philosophical work to appear in recent decades is undoubtedly Lange's *Geschichte des Materialismus,* about which I could write a page-long eulogy. Kant, Schopenhauer and this book by Lange – I do not need any more"; KSA, letters, II, 184; see also 159f. and 257f.; Tönnies (1878): "I have recently purchased Lange's *Geschichte des Materialismus* (third edition) and I am reading it with great pleasure; it is indeed an honest and serious work. When reading Lange, it saddens me at times to think that this excellent fellow who could restore honor to the notion of the professor of philosophy has had to give up so early while the air is still ringing with the cries of his colleagues with their immortal souls"; Klose et al., eds., *Tönnies-Paulsen Briefwechsel,* 16; Weber (1882): "We gave up on Lotze's *Mikrokosmos,* enraged at its lack of scientific rigor, foolish attempts at 'Poetisiererei' and soulful philosophizing, and began a history of materialism by Lange instead. The eminently methodical approach adopted by Lange is a real tonic after the chaos created by Lotze"; Max Weber, *Jugendbriefe,* 52, 75. Lange had featured on the list of books that Weber wanted for Christmas 1882; ibid., 65.

indeed have remained so for many years. Here is how Friedrich Paulsen saw it:

By chance [winter term 1867–1868] I got hold of a copy of F. A. Lange's *Geschichte des Materialismus,* which was published not long ago. It is the first book that I have read with lively, indeed passionate interest. It came just at the right time. . . . As a result of reading it I pursued the issues it raised further . . . ; besides the historical material, I found the parts on *geology* and on the *history of evolution* interesting.[39]

This extract was chosen because it contains two key concepts. Their meaning is made clear by an essay, "Zur Naturgeschichte der menschlichen Sprache," that discussed Lazarus Geiger's book *Der Ursprung der Sprache*[40] in the February 1870 edition of the periodical *Das Ausland:*

By giving his work this title [i.e., his *Lectures on the Science of Languages*], Max Müller wanted to make clear what he had already explicitly stated in the opening pages, namely that comparative philology had become a *science* in the true sense of the word since it had adopted the techniques of observation that are part of all rigorous scientific method. And indeed, the way in which the new linguists go about their task and attempt to solve their problems is very similar to the methods adopted by *natural scientists.* Indeed their approach bears the closest resemblance to the investigative methods adopted by *geologists* since the appearance of Sir *Charles Lyell* on the scene. . . . Just as geologists explain how existing formations have emerged from older formations, so present-day linguistics has shown us how languages undergo certain transformations, and how old formations are continually being replaced by new ones. The method adopted in both cases is one of *comparison* and *historical observation.*[41]

39  Friedrich Paulsen, *Aus meinem Leben. Jugenderinnerungen* (Jena, 1909), 147; emphasis added.
40  Stuttgart, 1869.
41  *Das Ausland* (1870), 121f. The periodical *Das Ausland,* which since 1865 had been subtitled *Überschau der neuesten Forschungen auf dem Gebiete der Natur-, Erd- und Völkerkunde,* offers a fascinating insight into the age. As far as I am able to judge, this excellent source has until now been overlooked. The "Jubilee edition," no. 53 of December 31, 1877, which was issued to commemorate *Das Ausland*'s first fifty years, was given over to a presentation of the periodical. *Das Ausland* had appeared weekly since 1852–1853. Since Oscar Ferdinand Peschel took over the editorship at the end of 1854 [Peschel's *Völkerkunde* (Leipzig, 1874) was regarded as a classic], the periodical was largely dedicated to the natural sciences, particularly geology, and thus gave extensive coverage to the works of Lyell. *Das Ausland* prided itself in its Jubilee edition on having included an in-depth discussion of Darwin's *Origin of the Species* under Peschel's editorship in 1860.

 If one wants to determine what themes or recent publications occupied Rée's and Nietzsche's contemporaries in the field of ethnology, geology, philosophy, religion, the study of language, and the natural sciences generally, one could do worse than take a look at the contents of *Das Ausland.*

 Incidentally, in *Das Ausland* (1869), 768, there is a brief reference to an author by the name of Coffin under the heading "Moral Obstacles to Railroad Construction in China." Coffin's argument is reminiscent of points made by Weber in *The Religion of China* (New York: Free Press, 1951), 199, and in *Economy and Society,* 429.

The claim made in the critique of Geiger's *Ursprung der Sprache* was that the study of language represented the successful union of the natural sciences and the humanities.[42] As a result of this, in the 1870s the study of language became a leading discipline and showed the way for a whole range of other disciplines that were seeking a new methodology, either because they were undergoing a period of crisis[43] or because the process of differentiation had had the effect of freeing them from their conventional approaches. In order for the study of language to be able to assume the function ascribed to it, it first had to follow the lead of the natural sciences. The new trends in geology, the major proponent of which was Charles Lyell, served the purpose exactly. The title of his book, *Principles of geology, being an attempt to explain the former changes of the earth's surface by reference to causes now in operation,*[44] precisely described the regulatory principle that was to govern the study of language: the temporal uniformity of geological processes and their causes.[45] This book split geologists into two camps: the "catastrophists" and the "quietists," as readers of *Das Ausland* discovered.[46]

This is not the place to examine in detail how Lyell's theories were received. We must content ourselves here with a brief reference. Max Müller was one of the first to apply the principle of uniformity to the study of language, with specific reference to Lyell, who had quoted him in his *Geological Evidence of the Antiquity of Man.*[47] Moreover, ethnology undoubtedly played a major role in disseminating Lyell's views, since the domain of knowledge and the object of inquiry were often the same in both ethnology and the study of language.

In the present context, it is not possible to describe how the intellectual framework provided by geology and linguistics was taken up by authors who were taken note of in their day, for example,

---

42 For more information on this, see Lange, *Geschichte des Materialismus,* 3rd ed. (Leipzig, 1877), II:390f.

43 An example of this is the Leipzig jurist Emil Kuntze's treatise entitled, significantly, *Der Wendepunkt der Rechtswissenschaft: Ein Beitrag zur Orientierung über den gegenwärtigen Stand- und Zielpunkt derselben* (Leipzig, 1856). Kuntze was also acquainted with the "more recent research on language." At the time, this took the lead from the leading discipline of comparative anatomy and used the concept of the organism; see Kuntze, *Der Wendepunkt,* 69, and Hartmut Schmidt, *Die lebendige Sprache. Zur Entstehung des Organismuskonzepts* (Berlin, 1986).

44 Three vols. (London, 1830–1833).

45 See Wolf von Engelhardt and Jörg Zimmermann, *Theorie der Geowissenschaft* (Paderborn, Munich, Vienna, and Zurich, 1982), 350ff.

46 (1870), 260ff.

47 (London, 1863). See Joachim Gessinger, *Charles Lyells (nicht-) evolutionistische Theory der Sprachevolution* (MS Hannover, Homburg, 1989), 1–23.

Rudolph Jhering, Max Müller, and Albert Hermann Post. The fact remains that it helped to constitute what could be described as a research program for an empirical and comparative-oriented moral science.

Rée also viewed this research program for an "ethics of the future," for a "realistic and historical ethics" (Jhering), with interest. Despite obvious differences, Nietzsche's *Naturgeschichte der Moral*[48] is also part of this tradition. Jhering outlined this research program and the individual disciplines best suited to implement it in an article on the historical and social foundations of ethics published in *Schmollers Jahrbuch* in 1882:[49]

The study of language belongs there. I have already made clear elsewhere the immense value of this discipline for providing information about ethical views. Let us now turn to mythology. Next to etymology it is the oldest and most reliable testimony to the ethical views of peoples; taken together they can be described as a paleontology of ethics. By examining the actions of the gods, what they permitted themselves and were allowed to permit themselves without forfeiting the right to the veneration of the people, we may determine the ancients' view of what is ethically permissible. It reveals the ethical canon of the time, the gods are the petrified archetypes of the ethical people of antiquity.[50]

There are echoes of Jhering's research guidance in Rée's *Die Entstehung des Gewissens,*[51] especially in the two passages in *Die Entstehung der Strafsanktion durch die Gottheit* (131–144) and on *Der historische Ursprung moralischer Gebote und Verbote: Paragraph 22: Die christliche Ethik* (145–167). Rée's line of argument will not be described here; in the present context, we shall limit ourselves to citing Rée's main sources in the area of religious studies. The following works would also appear in the ideal library in Montinari's sense of the term – Max Weber was also very familiar with them:

1. Abraham K. Kuenen, *The Religion of Israel to the Fall of the Jewish State* (London, 1874–1875), 3 vols.;
2. Hermann Oldenberg, *Buddha: Sein Leben, seine Lehre, seine Gemeinde* (Berlin, 1881);

---

48 In Friedrich Nietzsche, *Jenseits von Gut und Böse. Vorspiel einer Philosophie der Zukunft* (Leipzig, 1886) and *Zur Genealogie der Moral. Eine Streitschrift* (Leipzig, 1887).

49 Later published in *Der Zweck im Recht,* Vol. 2 (Leipzig, 1883), quoted after the fourth edition, 1905, Vol. II, 74ff.

50 Rudolph von Jhering, "Die geschichtlich-gesellschaftlichen Grundlagen der Ethik," *Schmollers Jahrbuch für Gesetzgebung, Verwaltung und Volkswirtschaft* 6 (1882):1–21, 17.

51 Berlin, 1885.

3. Cornelius Petrus Tiele, *Histoire comparée des anciennes religions de l'Egypte et des peuples sémitiques* (Paris, 1882);
4. Edward Burnett Tylor, *Die Anfänge der Kultur. Untersuchungen über die Entwicklung der Mythologie, Philosophie, Religion, Kunst und Sitte* (Leipzig, 1873), 2 vols.[52]

The type of religious scholarship pursued by Kuenen, Tiele, and Tylor follows the line described earlier and makes use of the comparative method, integrating linguistic and ethnological knowledge, as well as the constructs of evolutionary theory (which are individually very different from each other). How Rée learned of Kuenen and Tiele is not known. Max Müller, whom Rée does not quote, although some of his wording and arguments suggest that he was familiar with his work, mentions both authors in his *Einleitung in die vergleichende Religionswissenschaft*.[53] We also learn from Lou von Salomé's lecture notes that Max Müller and Tiele were among the authors that Alois E. Biedermann had recommended for further study in his Zurich lectures (1880–1881) on *Allgemeine Religionsgeschichte auf philosophischer Grundlage*.[54] Paul Rée had been acquainted with Lou von Salomé since the spring of 1882.[55]

Until this point, the emphasis has been on the output side, that is, on the result of thought processes. By looking at particular texts – albeit a highly selected few – we were able to judge which disciplines played a leading role. These disciplines could, in turn, be associated with particular authors. In this way we can now take the first tentative steps toward outlining an intellectual inventory of a particular age, drawing up the theoretical and methodological paradigms. We get a fuller picture if we take a close look at the input side and establish what works were read as preparation for the writing of others. We can furnish this evidence for the monastery for freer spirits in Baumannshöhle because the record of borrowers has recently been rediscovered in the university library in Basel. We can

---

52 On Weber's familiarity with these sources, see Gottfried Kuenzlen, "Unbekannte Quellen der Religionssoziologie Max Webers," *Zeitschrift für Soziologie* 7 (1978):215–227.
53 Second ed. (Strassburg, 1876).
54 *Nach einer Vorlesungsmitschrift von Lou von Salomé* (Zurich, 1880–1881).
55 On Alois E. Biedermann and the origins of the science of religion, see Kurt Rudolph, *Die Religionsgeschichte an der Leipziger Universität und die Entwicklung der Religionswissenschaft. Ein Beitrag zur Wissenschaftsgeschichte und zum Problem der Religionswissenschaft* (Berlin, 1962), esp. 9–66. I would like to express my warm thanks to Mrs. Dorothee Pfeiffer (Göttingen) for allowing me access to documents in the Lou von Salomé archive.

now see that Romundt, who had introduced Nietzsche to Rée, had read an impressive amount since he had stayed in Baumannshöhle in 1872.[56]

It is clear from the borrowing record that Nietzsche had read Lange's *Geschichte des Materialismus* and had become familiar with these authors and trends in scientific research. These titles give some indication of how Nietzsche's scientific interests evolved between the summer of 1872 and the spring of 1873, while he was lecturing on the pre-Platonic philosophers (summer term 1872; summer term 1873).[57] It is notable that Romundt borrowed certain scientific books before Nietzsche, for example, Hermann von Helmholtz, *Physiologische Optik, Bd. 9 der Allgemeinen Encyclopädie der Physik;*[58] Albert Ladenburg, *Vorträge über die Entwicklungsgeschichte der Chemie in den letzten 100 Jahren;*[59] and Mathias C. S. Pouillet, *Eléments de Physique experimentale et de Météorologie.*[60] Nietzsche only got hold of these books shortly before Rée's arrival in Basel. We may thus suppose that it was Rée who had become acquainted with these scientific texts during his studies in Berlin and who drew Romundt's attention to them. However, Nietzsche also displayed a general interest in the natural sciences. Just before he accepted a professorship, he had expressed to Rohde his desire to study chemistry rather than to teach philosophy.[61] He later repeated this desire on several occasions. His reading of Gustav Gerber's *Die Sprache als Kunst*[62] was one of the reasons Nietzsche's interest in the study of language took another

56 I would like to express my warm thanks to Curt Paul Janz (Muttenz), who, in response to my persistent requests, made inquiries as to the whereabouts of the borrowers' record of the university library in Basel and was so kind as to compile a list of the books borrowed by Rée and Romundt after it was eventually found. Romundt borrowed, for example, works by Büchner, Darwin, Fechner, Helmholtz, Lamarck, Lewes, Lyell, Moleschott, Tyndall, Whewell, and Wundt.

57 See Schlechta and Anders, *Friedrich Nietzsche,* esp. 60ff., 80ff.

58 Ed. by G. Karsten (Leipzig, 1867).     59 (Braunschweig, 1869).

60 Sixth ed., 2 vols. (Paris, 1853).     61 KSA, letters, II, 360.

62 Nietzsche borrowed Gustav Gerber's *Die Sprache als Kunst* (Bromberg, 1871) from the university library in Basel in September 1872. Anthonie Meijers, "Gustav Gerber und Friedrich Nietzsche," *Nietzsche-Studien* 17 (1988):369–390, and Martin Stingelin, "Nietzsches Wort-Spiel als Reflexion auf poet(olog)ische Verfahren," *Nietzsche-Studien* 17 (1988):336–349, hold that Nietzsche was directly influenced by Gerber, whereas Claudia Crawford, *The Beginnings of Nietzsche's Theory of Language* (Berlin and New York, 1988), esp. chap. 14, 199ff., considers that Gerber influenced Nietzsche only indirectly. Gerber's *Die Sprache als Kunst* (1884) was well reviewed by Georg Simmel in the *Deutsche Literaturzeitung* VI (no. 32, August 8, 1885), column 1138f. In February of the same year, in the same periodical (no. 8, February 21, 1885, col. 259–261), Simmel had written a long appreciation of Gustav Gerber's *Die Sprache und das Erkennen* (Berlin, 1884). For more on this, see Klaus Christian Köhnke, "Von der Völkerpsychologie zur Sociologie," in Heinz Jürgen Dahme and Otthein Rammstedt, eds., *Georg Simmel und die Moderne. Neue In-*

turn.[63] Nietzsche was nevertheless familiar with the positions adopted by the Neogrammarian school, as shown by the fact that he borrowed Wilhelm Scherer's *Zur Geschichte der deutschen Sprache*[64] in November 1870. He had also taken note of the theoretical magnum opus of the Neogrammarian school, Hermann Paul's *Principien der Sprachgeschichte,*[65] even if he got the title wrong.[66] August Leskien, whom Nietzsche had described in a letter to his sister as the "leader of the anti-Curtians,"[67] was a frequent visitor in Sils-Maria.[68]

Nietzsche's attitude toward the line of research represented by Rée is characterized in *Distanz und Nähe*. In the summer of 1883, in the year in which *Zarathustra* was published and immediately after the rift with Rée and Lou von Salomé, he noted:

Even free-thinking jurists still sometimes fail to recognize the oldest mean-ing of punishment – it simply is not known: and as long as legal science fails to move on and take on board the lessons of a *historical* and *comparative* approach, it will continue to pit one false abstraction against another. These abstractions put themselves forward as "philosophy of law" and are ex-clusively developed from the people of today (of our cultural sphere). . . .[69]

This is a clear reference to Albert Hermann Post.[70] One of Post's early works, *Untersuchungen über den Zusammenhang christlicher Glaubenslehre mit dem antiken Religionswesen nach der Methode ver-gleichender Religionswissenschaft,*[71] gives a clearer idea of his basic ori-entation. Here the study of religion is almost equated with the com-parative study of language.[72] A discussion of John Lubbock's second

*terpretationen und Materialien* (Frankfurt, 1984), 388–429, 391f., who nevertheless overlooks Gerber's importance for Nietzsche. See also Paul Honigsheim, "A Note on Simmel's An-thropological Interests," in Kurst H. Wolff, ed., *Georg Simmel, 1858–1918. A Collection of Essays, with Translations and a Bibliography* (Columbus, 1959), 175–179.

63 See esp. the essay *Ueber Wahrheit und Lüge im aussermoralischen Sinne* in KSA I, 875ff.
64 Berlin, 1867.   65 (Halle, 1880).   66 KSA XI, 336:29 (2) – 1884–1885.
67 KSA, letters, VII, 88f. – August 1885.
68 There is a critical discussion of Paul by Nietzsche's former colleague Franz Misteli (Basel) in the *Zeitschrift für Völkerpsychologie und Sprachwissenschaft* (1882), 376ff. A brief note that dates from the time when Nietzsche read Scherer is a clear indication that he was well acquainted with the discussion of the Neogrammarians on sound laws: "Regularity in the use of sounds demonstrates great powers of logic, great powers of abstraction? Or does it not . . . ?" (KSA VII, 249f:8 (72).
69 KSA X, 334: 8 (13); emphasis added.
70 See Hans-Jürgen Hildebrandt, "Nietzsche als Ethnolog. Ein Beitrag zur Klärung der Quellenfrage," *Anthropos. Internationale Zeitschrift für Völker- und Sprachenkunde* 83 (1988):565–571, 570.
71 (Bremen, 1869).
72 It was in fact Rée who put Nietzsche on to Post. Three of Post's publications are quoted in *Die Entstehung des Gewissens* (1885), namely, *Die Geschlechtsgenossenschaft der Urzeit und die Entstehung der Ehe. Ein Beitrag zu einer allgemeinen vergleichenden Staats- und Rechtswissenschaft*

edition of his *Prehistoric times as illustrated by ancient remains and customs of modern savages*[73] provides us with a vivid description of that line of thought described by Treitschke as "disgust for metaphysics:"

The speculative philosophers of the barren past invented their "systems" which were fit for nothing better than being demolished by their successors. They in their turn set about constructing a new house from the bits of card that had been knocked down, only for it to be blown down again. While this vain fooling was going on there arose a new breed of seekers after truth. They adopted a strictly scientific method and set to work like an examining magistrate whose task it is to track down the perpetrators of a sinister crime. They gathered together the silent witnesses of the deeds and events that had taken place in order to present them to their like-minded contemporaries as before a jury.[74]

Jhering, Nietzsche, Paulsen, Post, Rée and, Tönnies were not the only ones who went along with this line of thought for a time. What drew them together was a common interest in an empirical moral science (*empirische Moralwissenschaft*) or, as Tönnies put it in a letter to his friend Paulsen dated May 27, 1881, in an "empirically modified

(Oldenburg, 1875), *Die Anfänge des Staats- und Rechtslebens. Ein Beitrag zu einer allgemeinen vergleichenden Staats- und Rechtsgeschichte* (Oldenburg, 1878), and *Bausteine für eine allgemeine Rechtswissenschaft auf vergleichend-ethnologischer Basis,* 2 vols. (Oldenburg, 1881–1882). The last two works were also discussed at some length in *Das Ausland* (1878), 241ff., and *Das Ausland* (1880), 951ff. Very helpful to identify those authors who were read most by academic outsiders at that time is Ferdinand Tönnies, "Entwicklung der Soziologie in Deutschland im 19. Jahrhundert," in idem., *Soziologische Studien und Kritiken. Zweite Sammlung* (Jena, 1926), 63–168. Tönnies was quite close to Rée when the latter finished his manuscript on *Die Entstehung des Gewissens* during their common stay in Switzerland (Flims and Schuls) in the summer of 1883; Klose et al., eds., *Tönnies-Paulsen Briefwechsel,* 191; see also Hubert Treiber, "Gruppenbilder mit einer Dame," *Forum* 35 (1988):40–54, esp. 50ff.

    In April 1879 Rée informed Nietzsche of his intention to write a book about the "History and Critique of the Conscience": "the main part of the work is a history of punishment and it did *not* arise out of a vendetta, but out of the struggle against it"; Ernst Pfeiffer, ed., *Friedrich Nietzsche, Paul Rée, Lou von Salomé. Die Dokumente ihrer Begegnung* (Frankfurt, 1970), 57. Post also makes an appearance in Nietzsche's *Zur Genealogie der Moral* in his "glimpse" into the arsenal of punishments used by the Teutons; KSA V, 296; KSA X, 326: 8 (5); see also Mazino Montinari, "Nachricht zur siebenten Abteilung. Erster Halbband: Nachgelassene Fragmente. Juli 1882–Winter 1883, 1884," in Giorgio Colli and Mazzino Montinari, eds., *Nietzsche Werke. Kritische Gesamtausgabe. Siebente Abteilung, Vierter Band,* unter Mitarbeit von Marie-Luise Haase (Berlin and New York, 1984), 180–195. The Webers were also acquainted with Post. Marianne Weber recommended two of Post's books in her book *Ehefrau und Mutter in der Rechtsentwicklung. Eine Einführung* (Tübingen, 1907), 79 and 80, namely, his *Geschlechtsgenossenschaft der Urzeit* (1875) and his *Afrikanische Jurisprudenz. Ethnologisch-juristische Beiträge zur Kenntnis der einheimischen Rechte Afrikas* (Oldenburg, 1887). According to Paul Honigsheim, "Max Weber in Heidelberg," in René König and Johannes Winckelmann, eds., *Max Weber zum Gedächtnis,* Sonderheft 7 der *Kölner Zeitschrift für Soziologie und Sozialpsychologie* (Cologne, 1963), 161–271, 216, "Max Weber had no direct relationship to ethnology." But Weber referred to Post in the city chapter in *Economy and Society* (Berkeley, Calif., 1978), 1240.

73 (London, 1869).    74 *Das Ausland* (1870), 222.

ethics." By this he meant an ethics modified by the help of evolutionary theory.[75] Georg Simmel was another whose interests lay in this direction. His essay *Psychologische und ethnologische Studien über Musik*[76] provides evidence of this interest. This treatise, which followed in the intellectual tradition of Moritz Lazarus and Heymann Steinthal,[77] was originally presented by Simmel as a dissertation (1880). In it he attempted to refute Darwin's thesis that language developed out of the capacity for the expression of musical sounds.[78] Hermann von Helmholtz decisively rejected the dissertation handed in by Simmel: "The subject seems to me to be entirely unsuitable for this dissertation, especially for an author who does not know and cannot apply the important main points (*Anhaltspunkte*) from the physiology of the senses."[79] However, Helmholtz made the proposal to admit Simmel to the examination with his thesis on Kant, which shortly before had received an award. This proposal was approved.

Helmholtz himself deserves special attention because of his singular position as an intermediary. In his inaugural speech as rector of Heidelberg University on November 22, 1862, he drew a fundamental distinction between the humanities and the natural sciences, but he made exceptions for a range of important disciplines:

If we view the range of sciences with reference to the way they arrive at their results we become aware of a fundamental difference between the natural sciences and the humanities. In the natural sciences it is generally possible to formulate explicit rules and laws by induction. On the other hand in the humanities the primary concern is to formulate judgements on the basis of psychological tact (*psychologisches Tactgefühl*).[80]

Helmholtz also referred to this form of induction as "artistic induction" (*künstlerische Induction*), a term reminiscent of Wilhelm

---

75 Klose et al., eds., *Tönnies-Paulsen Briefwechsel*, 120.
76 Which was published in 1882 in the *Zeitschrift für Völkerpsychologie und Sprachwissenschaft* (261–305).
77 Nietzsche also seems to be familiar with this thesis of Darwin; see KSA VII, 267:8 (119). On Lazarus' and Steinthal's idea, see their programmatic essay in the first number of the first year of the periodical that they edited, the *Zeitschrift für Völkerpsychologie und Sprachwissenschaft* (1860), 1–73. The *Volksgeist* of the historical school is now entrusted to the "exact" disciplines for "processing" and appears as psychology of peoples (*Völkerpsychologie*).
78 For more on this, see the various expositions in *Das Ausland* (1871), esp. 389ff.
79 Michael Landmann, "Bausteine zur Biographie," in Kurt Gassen and Michael Landmann, eds., *Buch des Dankes an Georg Simmel. Briefe, Erinnerungen, Bibliographie* (Berlin, 1958), 11–33, 16f.
80 Hermann von Helmholtz, "Ueber das Verhältniss der Naturwissenschaften zur Gesamtheit der Wissenschaft," Akademische Festrede, gehalten zu Heidelberg am 22. November 1862, republished in H. v. Helmholtz, *Das Denken in der Naturwissenschaft* (Darmstadt, 1968), 3–29, 16.

Windelband's distinction between nomothetic and idiographic sciences.[81] According to Helmholtz, grammar is an exception to this rule:

The laws of grammar are established by an act of human will, even if they did not develop as the result of some well thought-out plan but evolved gradually in response to needs. They thus appear to the person who is learning the language as commands, as laws that have been established by some external authority.[82]

Similarly, this process applied to theology and jurisprudence. According to Helmholtz, subsumption under "grammatical, legal, moral, and dogmatic laws" happened in the same way as the application of a natural law to a particular instance in the form of conscious logical deduction.

Jhering, Paulsen, Rée, Simmel, and Tönnies participated in that line of thought that raised the comparative study of languages to a leading discipline. They participated directly through their studies (principally in Berlin and Leipzig) and thus through direct contact with the major exponents of this line of thought. Nietzsche was only involved in this intellectual movement through his intermittent friendship with Rée and his reading of Lange's *Geschichte des Materialismus*.

Max Weber also read Lange's *Geschichte des Materialismus* with enthusiasm. His motives were, however, largely historical, and his primary interest was to familiarize himself with the issues and concepts of a bygone age. Weber's ideal library would probably have been rather different, even if it had some elements in common with the library we are talking about here.[83] Weber was also in the fortu-

---

81  "Insofar as in Windelband 'law' and 'event' coexisted as incommensurable dimensions of our view of the world." It must also be borne in mind that Windelband was comparing the achievements of historians with creative achievements in art.

82  Ibid., 17.

83  Tönnies' "reservoir of literature" (Cornelius Bickel) of the time represents a list of titles that did not form part of the canon of books that found favor in the university. Some of these titles also appear in Rée, for example, William Edward Hearn (1826–1888), *The Aryan Household, Its Structure and Its Development; an Introduction to Comparative Jurisprudence* (London and Melbourne 1879; 2nd ed., 1891). Tönnies also names Alfred Lyall's (1835–1911) *Asiatic Studies, Religious and Social* (London, 1882; 2nd ed., 1883), to which Max Weber had also referred; see Hermann Kulke, "Orthodoxe Restauration und hinduistische Sektenreligiosität im Werk Max Webers," in Wolfgang Schluchter, ed., *Max Weber Studie über Hinduismus und Buddhismus. Interpretation und Kritik* (Frankfurt, 1984), 293–332, 332, note 49; also *Max Weber Gesamtausgabe* (MWG I/19), Max Weber, *Die Wirtschaftsethik der Weltreligion. Konfuzianismus und Taoismus. Schriften 1915–1920*, ed. by Helwig Schmidt-Glintzer with the collaboration of Petra Kolonko. *Max Weber Gesamtausgabe*, Vol. 19 (Tübingen, 1989), 131.

nate position of being able to take stock, of being able to contemplate the grand evolutionary theories of the nineteenth century with cool detachment. For Weber and others of his generation, the legacy of this period was the antithesis between the natural sciences and the humanities. The comparative study of language had once purported to bridge the gap between these. This "mood of natural monism which expresses belief rather than science" was completely alien to Weber.[84] His concept of the ideal type is an attempt to overcome this monism.[85]

The more Nietzsche thought exclusively about the idea of a monastery for freer spirits (without putting it into practice anymore), the purer his vision of a "forcing house for exotic and exquisite plants" became.[86] He developed his experiences and the episodes that occurred in the Protestant monastery in Schulpforta into principles designed to guide people toward a form of spiritual awakening. This type of spiritual awakening should be total and should take place in "total institutions" (Goffman). "In our society, they are the forcing houses for changing persons; each is a natural experiment on what can be done to the self."[87]

Nietzsche also appeared to reflect more and more upon what had become of him inside the total institution of the Protestant monastery in Schulpforta, an institution not unlike a Prussian officer training school. By "Protestant monastery," I mean that the Schulpforta had to a large extent retained the monastic way of life of the Cistercians who had once lived and worked there.[88] In this way, the young Nietzsche became acquainted with the discipline of time and with a methodical way of life at an age when – as he himself pointed out – people are most receptive to education.[89] He was the first to acknowledge the value of his experience.[90] Nietzsche seemed to suspect that the utility of discipline is based on regularity and practice

---

84  See also Werner Sombart, "Die Anfänge der Soziologie," in Melchior Palyi, ed., *Hauptprobleme der Soziologe. Erinnerungsgabe für Max Weber* (Munich and Leipzig, 1923), I:5–19, 12f.
85  Wolfgang Schluchter, *Religion und Lebensführung.* Vol. I: *Studien zu Max Webers Kultur- und Werttheorie* (Frankfurt, 1988), 53ff.
86  KSA XII, 426:9 (153) – autumn 1887.
87  Erving Goffman, *Asylums. Essays on the Social Situation of Mental Patients and Other Inmates* (Harmondsworth, 1968), 22.
88  Martin Pernet, *Das Christentum im Leben des jungen Friedrich Nietzsche* (Opladen, 1989), 67ff.
89  KSA XIII, 346; KSA VIII, 315f.: 18 (11).
90  KSA, letters, I, 37; KSA XIII, 346: 14 (161).

(*Übung*) – in the sense of "mechanical performance."[91] By "making men increasingly small,"[92] it is possible to achieve great things.

If it was Schulpforta that had given Nietzsche an insight into the monastic way of life, it was two friends of his youth, Wilhelm Pinder and Gustav Krug, who acquainted him with the inspirational piety of "serious Christians."[93] When the monastic life comes into contact with a form of Protestantism tinged with Pietism, there are bound to be some consequences, as indeed was the case with Nietzsche. The result is a heightened feeling for "inner states," a tendency toward self-analysis and introspection that is expressed in the Pietist practice of keeping a diary.[94]

According to Nietzsche, the ascetic exertion of self-control, its "natural utility," and its absolute necessity in the service of the education of the will"[95] were completely bound up with monastic practices. These were part of the monastic way of life, even if the church had "abused" them. However, he did not see any link between these practices and Puritan sects. This might have occurred to him when he consulted a book on the subject while preparing a lecture on the religious situation of Germans in North America for the Gustav-Adolf Association in Bonn in March 1865.[96] The book in question was Philipp Schaff's *Die politischen, socialen und kirchlich-religiösen Zustände der vereinigten Staaten von Nordamerika mit besonderer Rücksicht auf die Deutschen*.[97] Schaff, a Protestant theologian working in Pennsylvania, provided enough clear pointers to the relation between Protestant sects and self-control.[98] He also pointed out that this faculty was extolled as a virtue and was held in high esteem, and that the tendency toward "versatility and ceaseless activity" went hand in hand with the sect mentality.[99] On the other hand, Schaff noted the absence of the "charming blend of sincerity and congeniality, true

---

91  KSA IX, 453; KSA XII, 460.
92  KSA XII, 425.
93  Pernet, *Das Christentum im Leben des jungen Friedrich Nietzsche*, 52ff.
94  Nietzsche as a pupil in Schulpforta and Leopold von Wiese as a trainee cadet displayed the same tendency toward introspection. On Nietzsche see Curt Paul Janz, *Friedrich Nietzsches Biographie* (Munich, 1981), I:72f.; on von Wiese, see Leopold von Wiese, *Kindheit – Erinnerungen aus meinen Kadettenjahren* (Hannover, 1924; reprint ed., Ebenhausen, 1978), 24. See also Leopold von Wiese, "Ueber militärische Erziehung," in idem., *Spätlese* (Cologne and Opladen, 1954), 39–50.
95  KSA XII, 552 f. – autumn 1887.
96  Friedrich Nietzsche, "Die kirchlichen Zustände der Deutschen in Nordamerika," in Hans Joachim Mette and Karl Schlechta, eds., *Historisch-Kritische Gesamtausgabe der Werke (HKGW). Schriften der Studenten- und Militärzeit 1864–68* (Munich, 1935), III:84–97.
97  (Berlin, 1854).    98  Schaff, *Zustände*, 10.    99  Ibid., 17; 8, 72.

mysticism," in the religious life of America.[100] It was precisely this element of Schaff's critique that Nietzsche adopted word for word.[101] The result of this was that he overlooked the more interesting aspects of Puritanism, partly because of the nature of the theme he was addressing and partly because of his youth; he was only twenty-one at the time.[102]

Nietzsche's occasional predilection for the French moralists, which Rée to some extent shared,[103] can also be related to his biography, and once again this means Schulpforta. This approach invites comparison between the ascetic Puritan and the courtier, whom the French moralists had singled out as an object of study. Both are "in control of their feelings, self-controlled and disciplined."[104] The purpose of self-control in the courtier is primarily disguise, since to expose his weak points would spell an end to his chances of gaining prestige in the competitive struggle. He thus has to control the game by resorting to pretense. The person who adopts a disguise for reasons of self-interest has to know himself and others very well. Self-analysis and self-control are thus as inextricably linked as the observation of self and of others. This is particularly true when the analysis of roles is based on intimate knowledge of the role play that forces the agent to adopt a detached attitude toward the role that has been imposed upon him. Total institutions like Schulpforta furnish this knowledge and provide opportunities for practice; it is the "forcing houses" for practices of "secondary adaptation" (Goffman) that constitute the underlife of these institutions and that are supported by a display of feigned conformism. Thus a virtue is made of necessity:

100 Ibid., 79f.    101 Nietzsche, "Die kirchlichen Zustände," 86f.
102 See the comparison between Methodism and Pietism in Schaff, *Amerika*, 125:

> Methodism is entirely lacking in the congenial warmth that typifies German Pietism, its sense for the mystical and contemplative, its vigorous and deep theology, rich in ideas. On the other hand it is far superior to Pietism in its energy, which is directed outwards and aimed at conquest.

> Nietzsche also read Tocqueville; KSA, letters, VIII, 28. Tocqueville served as a model for his sketch of the "last man." Later, in 1887, Nietzsche went into the relation between "asceticism and culture" in some depth (KSA, letters, VIII, 28), albeit with particular reference to monastic asceticism and culture; see also Franz Overbeck, "Pessimismus, Buddhismus, Askese," in idem., *Christentum und Kultur, Gedanken und Anmerkungen zur modernen Theologie*, aus dem Nachlass herausgegeben von Carl A. Bernoulli (Darmstadt, 1963), 29–34. Like Weber, Nietzsche was of the opinion that the basis of Puritanism was a highly "pessimistic view of the 'nature' of the average individual"; Marianne Weber, *Max Weber*, 382; on Nietzsche see KSA XI, 218:26 (261).

103 Brendan Donnellan, *Nietzsche and the French Moralists* (Bonn, 1982).
104 Alois Hahn, "Zur Soziologie der Beichte und anderer Formen institutionalisierter Bekenntnisse: Selbstthematisierung und Zivilisationsprozess," *Kölner Zeitschrift für Soziologie und Sozialpsychologie* 34 (1982):407–434, 426.

the capacity for self-control and the game of dissimulation (*Spiel mit der Maske*)! One could thus claim that Nietzsche's interest in psychology developed as a direct result of his experiences of the Protestant monastery in Schulpforta: *Die Geburt des Psychologen in Nietzsche aus dem Geist des protestantischen Klosters* (*The Birth of the Psychologist in Nietzsche Out of the Spirit of the Protestant Monastery*)!

The type of spiritual formation aimed at by Nietzsche is based on sound principles, namely, selection and isolation. The monastery for freer spirits sets standards and aims to be selective. The selection process was "regulated" by Nietzsche's circle of friends. Admission to the circle of friends was based upon spontaneity and was subject to the principle of selection. This was true for the simple reason that in our culture it is believed that one can only have a limited number of true friends. The principle of selection was moral capability, which was tested in the following way: The person who was to be admitted to the circle of friends had to demonstrate his willingness to identify with conceptions of value that were out of tune with the times and that were represented by particular individuals. The primary representatives of these values were Schopenhauer, Wagner, and, of course, Nietzsche himself. Viewed in this way, the monastery for freer spirits is an elite union of friends and like-minded people on a higher level of institutionalization.[105] Friendship and praise of friendship[106] help secure social cohesion, and it is the friends who are entrusted with the task of ensuring commitment by training themselves to be free spirits. A system of particularistic loyalties with dyadic relations as the basic structure ensures cohesion and offers the "stabilization of existence" in the face of a social environment that is perceived to be disorganized and unstable. This has been considered the ideal form of friendship since antiquity. In this respect, Nietzsche can be said to have been part of the great era of friendship that came to an end in Germany about 1850.[107]

Isolation is required in addition to being selected and tested according to the strongly ethical ideal of friendship.[108] Isolation means

---

105  The mode of address "my friend and brother in arms" is significant here; see KSA, letters, IV, 142 – April 1873 – and KSA, XI, 195:26 (173).

106  KSA, letters, II, 356ff. Friendship was a theme that was to dominate nearly all of Nietzsche's compositions in the 1870s. The history of the origin and rise of the "hymn to friendship," which was so important to Nietzsche, also falls into this period. In highly personal relations, music was the most important means of expression.

107  Friedrich H. Tenbruck, "Freundschaft. Ein Beitrag zu einer Soziologie der persönlichen Beziehungen," *Kölner Zeitschrift für Soziologie und Sozialpsychologie* 16 (1964):431–456, 441.

108  KSA XII, 425:9 (153).

building up distance and cutting oneself off from the spirit of the age in order to "escape the paralyzing educational ideal of the time." Cutting oneself off does not mean fleeing from the world, but it is one of the preconditions for constructing an alternative. For monks, a life of asceticism withdrawn from the world was "a royal road to the supernatural."[109] In the same way, Nietzsche appeared to want to construct a "royal road" to the "superhuman" from the fundamental principles of monasticism when the otherworldly "vanishing point" has ceased to exist.[110] Even the "strong men of the future" need isolation so that they can get the feel of "inverted values."[111] Like the monk who lives his life in a methodical and purposeful way, exercising a degree of self-control in order thus to overcome humanity's natural propensity to sensuality, the free thinker has to inculcate in himself the capacity to lead a purposeful life and to commit himself to his chosen path. Whoever wants to build anew has to destroy, has to subject the "old" self to a process of mortification (Goffman) that is easier to accomplish in isolation:

I dream of a society of men who are free from all restraint, who know no mercy and want to be known as "destroyers:" They apply their critical standards to everything and sacrifice themselves to the truth.[112]

This is the most precise characterization of the free spirit, a description that could equally well be applied to a monk as to a member of a Puritan sect. Both have to free themselves from established traditions and mundane values. Total devotion is required of both groups, and both have to adopt a conscious value orientation and adhere to it rigidly. This is why Nietzsche claimed that "the *free-thinker* [is] the *most religious* person that exists *today.*"[113]

Weber defined a sect as the voluntary association of religious (morally) qualified individuals. It represents a religious elite that makes evidence of moral qualities a condition of admission and of membership. The obligation constantly to "prove one's worth" in the "circle of associates" turns out to be an objective task that is in keeping with the "cool objectivity of the sociation" in the form it takes within the sect. Using Tönnies' terminology, Weber argues that a sect is not a *Gemeinschaft* but a *Gesellschaft* and is not to be confused with "that undifferentiated peasant-vegetative 'geniality' without

---

109 Werner Bergmann, "Das frühe Mönchtum als soziale Bewegung," *Kölner Zeitschrift für Soziologie und Sozialpsychologie* 37 (1985):30–59, 37.
110 KSA XII, 552f.: 10 (165).    111 KSA XII, 424f.    112 KSA VIII, 48:5 (30).
113 KSA, X, 30:1 (74); emphasis added.

which (as Germans are accustomed to believe) there can be no community."[114] On the contrary, the dominant orientation toward objectivity (*Sachlichkeit*) and the cultivated inner habitus imply the complete overcoming of humankind's instinctual nature. The process of learning to assert oneself in the circle of sect members, which entails the endeavor to establish control over oneself and others is, according to Weber, an ideal school for the formation of the personality.

Puritanical – like very "rational" – asceticism worked on enabling the individual to assert the value of his "constant motives," particularly those "inculcated" by ascetism, as against the "emotions:" – its aim was to train him to develop a "personality" in the formal-psychological sense of the word![115]

One of the consequences of solemn acceptance into the sect is the formation of a definable support group (*Trägergruppe*) that underpins the claim to recognition of specific values in the actual behavior of the members of the sect. This happens in such a way that their whole lives are permeated by the ideas imposed on them.[116] In this respect, the mechanism of socialization into the sect holds the answer to the question that Nietzsche had in mind when he conceived his idea of the monastery: "How can one implant new values in people and how can one bind them securely to this new system of values?"[117] And the answer to that question is as follows: People are wrenched out of the social and evaluative networks of their previous existence through a process of selection and isolation and put into a new social context that demands total commitment from them: "The fact that the conduct of each individual in small groups is clearly visible means that eduction can go on indefinitely and direct control can be established."[118] In this respect, the member of a sect and the free thinker represent the archetype of the religious person, one who is prepared to devote his entire life to his "cause," to submit his life to a methodical control that presupposes the highest degree of self-referential

114 Max Weber, "'Churches' and 'Sects' in North America," tr. Colin Loader, *Sociological Theory* 3 (1985):7–13; see also "The Protestant Sects and the Spirit of Capitalism," in Hans Gerth and C. Wright Mills, *From Max Weber* (New York: Oxford University Press, 1946), esp. 320ff.
115 PE, 119.
116 M. Rainer Lepsius, "Interessen und Ideen. Die Zurechnungsproblematik bei Max Weber," *Kölner Zeitschrift für Soziologie und Sozialpsychologie,* Sonderheft 27: *Kultur und Gesellschaft* (Cologne, 1988), 20–31, 23; reprinted in idem, *Interessen, Ideen und Institutionen* (Opladen, 1990), 35.
117 Stephen D. Berger, "The Sects and the Breakthrough into the Modern World: On the Centrality of the Sects in Weber's Protestant Ethic Thesis," *Sociological Quarterly* 12 (1971):486–499.
118 Lepsius, "Interessen und Ideen," 24.

spiritual alertness. The monastery for freer spirits, the "school for educators where the educators educate themselves," is thus synonymous with the "school of hard ascetism."[119]

In both cases, we are dealing with models of "selection" and breeding of "strong natures" (Nietzsche) or "personalities" (Weber) who are able to handle "everyday demands" in a disenchanted world. Although there is undoubtedly a biological element in Nietzsche – in contrast to Weber, where there is not a hint of biological terminology – breeding (*Züchtung*) means essentially the same thing in both Nietzsche and Weber. It is a moral concept that refers to being well-bred, in the sense of having a disciplined upbringing (*Zucht*) and *Bildung*.[120] In the same way, *Bildung* contains religious and neo-humanistic elements. The conception of "inner growth" and "personal development" is bound up with the concept of *Bildung*. The phrase "become who you are," so dear to both Nietzsche and Weber, mirrors this precisely.

For Weber the exhortation to educate oneself is also an exhortation to become a personality by adhering to a constant set of values. If, like Ann Swidler,[121] one considers that the essence of Weber's concept of rationality resides in the methodical control over the individual's life, then the high degree of affinity between Weber's concept of personality and the archetype of the ascetic Puritan becomes apparent. One can then understand why Weber – going against the spirit of his age – established a connection between religion and rationality.

Weber put forward the idea of a rational individualism, and this

119 Max Weber, *Briefe 1906–1908,* ed. by M. Rainer Lepsius and Wolfgang J. Mommsen, with Birgit Rudhard and Manfred Schön, MWGA, II/5 (Tübingen, 1990), 33.
120 In Max Weber's copy of Spengler's *Decline of the West,* there is one significant positive marginal note among many highly critical ones. Weber called "by and large correct" the following passage: "Nietzsche notices that the Darwinist idea of the superman requires breeding, but he does not go beyond colorful phrases. Shaw goes further and demands that society be turned into a stud farm. This is merely Zarathustra's consistency, for which Nietzsche did not have the courage, even the courage of bad taste. Breeding is an extremely materialistic and utilitarian notion if it is meant to turn marriage into a sexual institution in the interest of society and of a physiological program. In this case one owes an answer to the question who is to do the breeding, of whom, where and how. Yet Nietzsche's romantic disinclination to draw highly prosaic social conclusions, and his fear of exposing poetic utopias to any reality test, made him silent before the fact that his whole positive program, as it derives from Darwinism, presupposes socialism [underlined by Weber], the socialist dictatorship." *Der Untergang des Abendlandes,* Vol. 1 (Munich, 1919), 520.
121 "The Concept of Rationality in the Work of Max Weber," *Sociological Inquiry* 43 (1973):35–42, 39.

rational individualism "is his ultimate value."[122] This form of individualism, expressed through Weber's concept of personality, is fundamentally religious in origin and is largely indebted to the moral culture of the educated Protestant bourgeoisie in Germany.[123] However, Weber's "royal route" to personality leads to an impasse. As Harry Liebersohn has pointed out, Weber sought "in the Protestant past a spiritual dignity lacking in contemporary bourgeois individualism. Weber's quest into the past was a useless triumph. He had found the spirituality he sought, but could not bring it into the present."[124] Nietzsche's friend Franz Overbeck – a theologian in a world forsaken by God – stated the consequences of this dilemma clearly:

Whoever tries to become completely self-reliant in the world has to find the courage to rely on *nothing*. . . . He must no longer talk about God. . . . The strict individualist has to be able to do without God. . . . Only without God can the individualist be able to live *freely*. If he cannot renounce God, then this individualism is either not true individualism or has not flourished to its full extent.[125]

Overbeck also can help us recognize a revealing difference between Nietzsche and Weber. If in the case of Nietzsche the aphorism is the embodiment of his individualism, with Weber it is the concept of the ideal type:

The ideal-type construct is motivated by the stand taken by a person who has lost his illusions, who finds himself in a world that has become objectively meaningless and very sober, and who, thrown back on himself, is forced to conceive the meaning of things and even man's relationship to reality as, basically, his own problem, and to "create" meaning, both practical and theoretical.[126]

The ideal type is not merely an elaborate intellectual construct that presupposes the availability of specialized knowledge of the "reality" to be analyzed. It also forms an elaborate intellectual arrangement of adequacy relations, which give a "general direction" to the logical

---

122 Kurt Beiersdörfer, *Max Weber und Georg Lukacs. Uber die Beziehung von Verstehender Soziologie und Westlichem Marxismus* (Frankfurt and New York, 1986), 80.
123 Paul Honigsheim, "Max Weber: His Religious and Ethical Background and Development," *Church History* 19 (1950):219–239.
124 Harry Liebersohn, *Fate and Utopia in German Sociology, 1870–1923* (Cambridge, Mass., 1988), 104.
125 Franz Overbeck, *Christentum und Kultur. Gedanken und Anmerkungen zur modernen Theologie.* Aus dem Nachlass herausgegeben von D. A. Bernoulli (Basel, 1919; reprint ed., Darmstadt, 1963), 286; emphasis added.
126 Karl Löwith, "Die Entzauberung der Welt durch Wissenschaft. Zu Max Webers 100. Geburtstag," *Merkur* 18 (1964):501–519, 513.

operation of "causal attribution" (*kausale Zurechnung*).[127] These elaborate steps serve to explain "cultural phenomena" that are of interest to us.

Nietzsche's aphorisms, on the other hand, do not take the time (and leave the reader no time) to indulge in "more elaborate intellectual justifications." As Overbeck perceptively put it:

The sword of Damocles of refutation that hangs over everything that one tries to justify is not as dangerous as the congenital handicap with mere assertion comes into the world like the flash of meteor. Through the aphorism the individual also claims more efficacy in the world than is humanly possible, despite all exertion.[128]

We should take Overbeck's doubts seriously.[129] However, we should not overlook that Nietzsche made a strenuous effort to go on reading until almost the end. He continued to do the hard labor, remaining true to his philological training and to his origins in the Protestant monastery in Schulpforta: "A painstaking attention to detail and the exercise of self-control that is typical of the religious person was a preschool for the scientific character: Above all the way of thinking that takes problems seriously, without considering what it means for one personally."[130]

127 See Gerhard Wagner and Heinz Zipprian, "Methodologie und Ontologie. Zum Problem kausaler Erklärung bei Max Weber," *Zeitschrift für Soziologie* 14 (1985):115–130.
128 Franz Overbeck, *Christentum und Kultur. Gedanken und Anmerkungen zur modernen Theologie* (Darmstadt, 1963), 183.
129 Such doubts may also have motivated Schluchter's sharp critique of Hennis's effort to move Weber close to Nietzsche. Wolfgang Schluchter, *Religion und Lebensführung*. Vol. I: *Studien zu Max Webers Kultur- und Werttheorie* (Frankfurt, 1988), esp. 191.
130 Friedrich Nietzsche, *Werke IV. Aus dem Nachlaß der Achtzigerjahre*, ed. by Karl Schlechta (Frankfurt, Berlin, and Vienna, 1979), 400 (III), 808.

# 7
# *Weber's Ascetic Practices of the Self*

HARVEY S. GOLDMAN

Beginning with *The Protestant Ethic,* Max Weber's *oeuvre* contains an implicit discourse concerning what we can call the "empowerment" of the "self" that informs many of his works, as well as his interpretations of what he takes to be the crisis of modern society and politics. Weber analyzes the shaping of subjects or selves in religions and the traditional economy in the past, as well as in bureaucracies, systems of rationality, and traditions of education in the present. Despite this concern with the empowerment of the self, however, Weber rarely mentions the self directly. Instead he analyzes disciplines of the self like the "calling" and charismatic education, conceptions of the transformed self like the "personality" and the *Ordnungsmensch,* and the different "roles" empowered selves occupy, like the scientist or politician with a calling, the entrepreneur, and the charismatic leader. I also argue that Weber, who was convinced of the significant historical role played by the Puritan concept of calling, brought a secular version of that concept into social theory as an ethos and a discipline for action, defending an ascetic notion of personhood against the failures of the tradition of *Bildung* and the ideals of the *Bildungsbürgertum.* This was his only model for a fortified self that could accomplish the tasks of German society and culture under conditions of rationalization. The capacity of a calling like the Puritan's to empower the self made it a unique vehicle, in Weber's view, for mastering the rationalized world. His called individuals are all patterned on the portrait of Puritan entrepreneurs in *The Protestant Ethic.*

Weber's belief in the need for a contemporary discipline of the self as a source of power derives from his analysis of modern history. Numerous arguments have been made that Weber's fundamental problematic and governing theme is the nature and advance of ra-

161

ad its contribution to the uniqueness of the West.[1]
claim is only part of the story, for Weber believes not
West's uniqueness rests on rationalization, but also that
ed historically by its capacity to create what I call em-
lves with a unique power to master conditions and over-
stance, permitting fundamental innovation in society and
poin. That is, Weber's analysis of modern society cannot be construed simply in terms of the progress and difficulties of rationalization, inevitable or otherwise. His work reveals instead a dialectic between "practices of the self" and the imperatives of institutions and social order, a conflict between innovation and creation, on the one hand, and conformity and compliance, on the other, set in objective conditions the self has both created and inherited. His work also contains the story of a search for forms of strength and sources of motivation that would give modern Western selves the power to overcome social and institutional resistance and the resistance of others, as well as inner obstacles, permitting them to innovate.[2]

Thus Weber has a significant, historically grounded microsociological dimension, not just a macrosociological one. The institutionalization of rationalization is for him the newest objective condition, the most contemporary form of social power in the context of which to pose the problem of the person and the situation of actors, of character and social structure. This is not meant to imply that Weber's work is not centrally concerned with structures and institutions as objects of analysis, but in certain places in his work the question of institutions often leads to the question of the type of person they make possible and then to the question of what created them or might have held them back, then sometimes to the question of *who* created them and what inner and outer obstacles they had to overcome, and invariably back to the question of what *enabled* such creators to overcome obstacles and innovate. The ultimate question is about what it would take to control and master existing institutions and create new ones.

Weber's investigation of practices of the self is not surprising, for

1 See, for example, Wolfgang Schluchter, *The Rise of Western Rationalism. Max Weber's Developmental History*, trans. with an introduction by Guenther Roth (Berkeley and Los Angeles: University of California Press, 1981).
2 This has some similarities with the view of Jeffrey Alexander that Weber's work can be seen as a "dialectic of individuation and domination." See Alexander, "The Dialectic of Individuation and Domination: Weber's Rationalization Theory and Beyond," in Sam Whimster and Scott Lash, eds., *Max Weber, Rationality and Modernity* (London: Allen & Unwin, 1987), 185–206.

the interest in such practices had been strong in German culture since the late eighteenth century, when formal religious practice and Christian belief lost much of their appeal among intellectuals in Germany as sources of ideals and models for the shaping of identity and the guidance of action. This weakening led to the generation of non-religious techniques and codes for shaping and legitimating the self: Kantian conceptions of moral law and personality, the ethos of *Bildung* or self-cultivation through scholarship, the ideal of *Kultur*. In Norbert Elias's words, the German middle-class intelligentsia legitimized itself to itself through its possession of *"das rein Geistige,* in books, scholarship, religion, art, philosophy, in the inner enrichment, the intellectual *Bildung* of the individual, primarily through the medium of books, in the personality."[3] By the late nineteenth century, however, the new techniques and practices that had aided in shaping and equipping bourgeois individuals for lives and roles in nation, culture, and class were seriously weakened and persistently challenged by the pressures of a rapidly developing capitalist society. Nietzsche, who criticized servility toward the lessons of history; Simmel, who warned about the overwhelming of "subjective spirit" by "objective spirit"; Troeltsch, who feared society was turning away from impersonal ideals to personal masters; and Thomas Mann, who feared the overcoming of *"Kultur"* by "civilization" all testify to the widespread concern with this problem. Weber's approach too is a response to the pressures of rational capitalism and to the undermining of these practices and other ideals within bourgeois circles.

In an essay of 1932 entitled "Karl Marx and Max Weber," Karl Löwith, the first major analyst of Weber's conception of rationalization, tried to shed light on the concept by comparing Marx on alienation with Weber on rationalization.[4] But despite its subtlety and insight, Löwith's comparison obscured the issue, for he juxtaposed a concept in Marx that concerns the undermining of human powers with a concept in Weber meant to grasp a larger systemic, and impersonal, social dynamic. In fact, if any comparison is to be done with Weber on rationalization, then it must be done with Marx on *capitalism,* not on alienation, and if a comparison is to be done with

3 Norbert Elias, *The Civilizing Process: The Development of Manners,* trans. Edmund Jephcott (New York: Urizen Books, 1978), 27.
4 Karl Löwith, "Karl Marx und Max Weber," in Löwith, *Gesammelte Abhandlungen* (Stuttgart: W. Kohlhammer Verlag, 1960), 1–67.

Marx on alienation, then it must be done with the correlate in Weber to Marx's notion of the estrangement of human powers in commodity society. This correlate is what I call "disempowerment," for the parallel to alienation in Weber's work is found in the ways persons are rendered inwardly powerless by social orders and in the forms of weakness and deprivation imposed specifically by rationalization.

The purpose of the practices of the self that Weber proposes for modern Germany is the generation of power, empowerment of the self for innovation in and mastery of the rationalized world, which not only disenchants but also disempowers. Indeed, in its proliferating discipline, rationalization "increasingly reduces the significance of charisma and individually differentiated action."[5] Though Foucault once argued that the self is shaped *by* relations of power in institutions and social practices, Weber wants to shape selves *for* power and generate selves *with* power. It is Nietzsche who mediates Weber's concern with power. Nietzsche believed that "the fundamental instinct of life . . . aims at *the expansion of power*."[6] Life is grounded on a will to power, on "a desire to overcome, a desire to throw down, a desire to become master, a thirst for enemies and resistances and triumphs." Indeed, the " 'development' of a thing . . . [is] the succession of more or less profound, more or less mutually independent processes of subduing." Thus, "[e]very animal . . . instinctively strives for an optimum of favorable conditions under which it can expend all its strength and achieve its maximal feeling of power."[7] It is necessary, says Nietzsche, to recognize the will to power even behind the strivings of the weak and to create a caste of sovereign individuals with power over themselves, their fate, and their world. "Something living wants to *release* its strength – life itself is *will to power*."[8] For Nietzsche, this will is natural, innate, instinctive, especially in the noble type of human being, as long as certain ideals teaching weakness do not prevail. But for Weber the will to power is, in general, not natural, nor is it embodied especially

5 Weber, "Charismatic Domination and Its Transformation," *Wirtschaft und Gesellschaft*, 5th ed., ed. Johannes Winckelmann [hereafter WG] (Tübingen: J. C. B. Mohr [Paul Siebeck], 1976), 687.

6 Nietzsche, *The Gay Science*, in Nietzsche, *Kritische Studienausgabe* [hereafter KSA], ed. Giorgio Colli and Mazzino Montinari (Munich: Deutscher Taschenbuch Verlag; Berlin: Walter de Gruyter, 1988), Vol. 3, 583.

7 Nietzsche, *On the Genealogy of Morals*, in Nietzsche, KSA, Vol. 5, Essay I, section 13, 279; Essay II, section 12, 314; and Essay III, section 7, 350.

8 Nietzsche, *Beyond Good and Evil*, in Nietzsche, KSA, section 13, 27.

in aristocracies; it is rooted in specific social and cultural, usually religious practices, and Western culture generally and Calvinism specifically, in his view, generated a will to power among certain groups, whereas other cultures did not. Weber implies that in their normal functions social orders "educate and create," or produce and reproduce, subjects adapted to their needs through a process of selection and material incentives or coercion. But, at unpredictable times, ideal interests of different kinds may arise to which certain individuals orient themselves, interests that place those individuals in tension with the social order and sometimes lead to the creation of a new kind of self to challenge, master, or overcome the order.

To Weber, rationality increasingly provides the limits within which social orders, institutions, and individuals may develop, providing new techniques of control and administration but weighing on individual actors and undermining other cultural forms that generated practices of self-shaping in the past – tradition, religion, cultivation, charismatic education, and so on. To regain the vitality it once had, the West, in Weber's view, now requires, first, new means of self-mastery and forms of empowerment to permit it to remaster the institutions it has created. Second, it requires a new, individualist "metaphysics," that is, an acceptance of the "polytheism" of the modern world, coupled with the willingness of individuals to posit or recognize their ultimate values as "gods." These gods give them a "mission" and make demands that put the self in tension with the existing order and provide the basis of an empowering form of service to lead the self to master the world. Though the West must rely on rational means and techniques to gain world mastery through self-mastery, it also needs a source of *inner* power to mobilize in confrontation, not with tradition, as the Puritans had done, but with rationality, and not to overcome it, as the Puritans had overcome tradition, but to control and use it. Weber's account of this confrontation is replete with metaphors of war and the battlefield. Newly fabricated selves must dedicate themselves to war and battle on behalf of their gods in order to create meaning and find a model ethos for a new self. But it is not only rationalization that must be confronted: The type of self shaped by excessive submission to rational norms must also be overcome, both within oneself and among the defenders of the bureaucratic ethos.

Rationalization, of course, must not be construed *only* as an obstacle to the self's power, for the Puritan example alone shows its role as a *tool* of power, an aid to and form of mastery over nature, economy, politics, salvation. But its nature and its institutionalization make *it* master over the modern world, and Weber argues that society needs those who can use and control it at the same time, rather than be mastered by it. In Weber's view, rationalization threatens to impose itself totally on self and society, depriving them of the capacity to posit anything but their own submission. Yet Occidental rationalization is partly a creation, however unintended, of the unified, ordered self of Puritanism, whose spirit once provided an ethos that empowered individuals to rationalize the world on behalf of sacred tasks. Its creations, however, now control their creators. Rationality promised mastery of the world but has come back to master the self, shaping it to its own demands through the pressure of material needs and social order, undermining and eliminating the original preconditions that had allowed innovation and empowerment of the self.

The disempowerment of the self produced by the advances of rationalization has weakened the West's ability to confront its political and social struggles. The problem is especially acute for Germany, because Weber was convinced that there, both the will to power and the paradigms of self-shaping and training for rule "carried" by leading classes of the past and potential leading classes of the future could no longer be relied upon to produce autonomous subjects. He wished to create instead a discipline to fashion selves empowered to master the institutions fabricating submissive and obedient selves. His practical critique of buraucracy is thus joined to a cultural critique of a society fabricating a bureaucratic self.

The notion of the "power of the self" is not an explicit concept in Weber's work, though innovative power always appears as an attribute of the "man of vocation," the "Occidental personality," and the "charismatic leader." Even power as a concept is not given a central role in *Economy and Society,* where it is defined as "the chance within a social relationship to carry out one's own will even against resistance, no matter on what this chance rests." Indeed, because Weber considers the concept of power to be "sociologically amorphous," even in concrete social relations, he prefers "domination" as a category for describing relations of power, since it is more precise, though it refers, more narrowly, to "the chance of a *command* to find obedience." But Weber moves toward a broader, more Nietzschean conception of the self's power when he adds: "All conceivable qualities of a person and all conceivable constellations can put someone in the position of carrying out his will in a given situation."[9] The issue is what inner qualities equip a person for power, how they may be generated, and what premiums must be put on action to orient it to systematic, rational control of the world.

For Weber, the powers of the self are not a question merely of endurance or persistence or of the capacity to execute commands. Those are the strengths he associates with the Lutheran calling in the past and with contemporary German culture. It is the capacities to initiate, overcome resistance, and attract followers that are the crucial aspects of the self's power, the kinds he associates with the Calvinist calling and with formerly Puritan peoples. This type of power links his project on religion and the spirit of capitalism to his proposals for coping with rationality and mastering modern politics. Foucault seems to recognize this when he remarks: "Max Weber posed the question: If one wants to behave rationally and regulate one's action according to true principles, what part of one's self should one renounce? What is the ascetic price of reason? To what kind of asceticism should one submit?"[10] But Foucault formulates Weber's goal incorrectly, for though Weber did analyze the renunciation that enabled the Puritans to rationalize the world, and though he did try to specify the kind of asceticism to which he thought the self should submit, he did not do so on behalf of submission to reason or rationality abstractly understood, but rather on behalf of the need for power, to master rationalization itself, submitting to its requirements but conquering its capacities for the realization of the transformed self's ultimate values.

Weber's proposals for modern self-fashioning are cast, as we know, in a vocabulary we would not normally associate with supposedly disenchanted life: "service in a calling," "creaturely worthlessness," "becoming a personality," "devotion" and "submission" to a "holy" cause or object, "deadly sins" against the "holy spirit" of the calling, contracting with "diabolic" forces and powers, the "salvation" and fate of the soul, the "serving" of "gods." In these terms, Weber is speaking figuratively, of course. But this language reveals the extent to which his treatment of the modern self relies on his earlier analysis of the Puritan calling and the form of personhood it shaped, as well

---

9 Weber, "Fundamental Concepts of Sociology," WG, 28–29.
10 Michel Foucault, "Technologies of the Self," in Luther H. Martin, Huck Gutman, and Patrick H. Hutton, eds., *Technologies of the Self. A Seminar with Michel Foucault* (Amherst: University of Massachusetts Press, 1988), 17.

as on Kantian conceptions of autonomy. Weber wants to create an ascetic leadership elite to enter and master the rationalized institutions of society, a band of virtuosos whose quasi-religious devotion to the service of their cause will lead to a form of empowerment similar to Puritan empowerment.

Weber proposed his solution because he believed that in *The Protestant Ethic* he had discovered not only an element contributing to the development of a unique spirit of modern capitalism but a spiritual discipline of enormous consequence that transformed and fortified the natural self of the Puritan believer into a hardened tool of divine purpose in a way never before seen in worldly action on such a scale. Indeed, I have argued elsewhere that the explanatory heart of *The Protestant Ethic* has less to do with the historical linkage of Calvinism and the spirit of capitalism than with Weber's positing of the existence and action of a unique type of self newly constituted in the Reformation. In effect Weber argued that for capitalism to have developed in the West, there was a need not only for the separation of classes, accumulation, and the circulation and use of money as capital in pursuit of ever-renewed profit, all of which Marx had already recognized. There was also a need for a mode of power found not in techniques or rationality *outside* the self as material preconditions, but a mode of power found and engendered *inside* the self: In Weber's view, a new kind of person must have existed before capitalism was established, a person with special capacities and a restless inclination for the new kind of rationalized labor that capitalism as a system would bring with it, and whose appearance changed the destiny of the Occident. This power was rooted in ascetic triumph over the natural self and in the need to discharge anxiety about salvation through a search for proof of grace in world mastery for God's purposes. Weber's conclusions are based on the crucial role he ascribes to the idea of calling in modern culture and to the extraordinary powers and "taming of the soul" with which, he claimed, the Calvinist calling endowed what we can call "the first great entrepreneurs." Weber calls the Puritan calling "a powerful unconsciously refined arrangement for the breeding of capitalist individuals" that "has existed in no other church or religion."[11] The ways in which *other* cultures and religions contributed to forming persons, and whether or not they empowered them for innovative action and

---

11 Weber, *Wirtschaftsgeschichte,* ed. by S. Hellmann and M. Palyi (Munich and Leipzig: Duncker & Humblot, 1924), 314.

resistance to an established ethos or set of institutions, became a central concern of his later sociological work.

This type of the first great entrepreneur – later refined through comparison with ideals and practices of the self in other cultures – is, in its essence, the same as the type of those other strong figures who reappear in Weber's writings. Aloneness, inclination to ascetic labor, devoted service to an ultimate value, self-denial and systematic self-control, a unified inner center or core, and a capacity to resist their own desires and the desires and pressures of others – these are the qualities all of Weber's strong selves possess, whether their goals are worldly action or religious renewal based on prophecy. This archetypal innovative individual is called the "man of vocation" in *The Protestant Ethic,* the "Occidental personality" in the sociology of world religions, and the "politician and scientist with a vocation" in the late essays.[12] Indeed, the "charismatic" individual in Weber's studies of economy and society is also such a person, because, Weber says, authentic charisma "where it appears constitutes a 'calling' in the emphatic sense of the word: as 'mission' [*Sendung*] or inner 'task.' "[13]

Rooted in the discoveries of *The Protestant Ethic,* Weber's work thus reveals a theory of historical innovation in which innovative social change depends not only on necessary material and political conditions, but also on the emergence and mediation of empowered actors whose strength is rooted in an ascetic character, and whose spirit is capable of overcoming resistance and commanding obedience. Other cultures have contained empowered selves, but in Weber's view, no culture other than the modern West contains widespread *practices,* whether produced by religious or other ideal motivations, that empower the self *from within* to undertake systematically innovations against the strength and resistance of inner and outer obstacles.[14]

12 According to Friedrich H. Tenbruck, "Max Weber and the Sociology of Science: A Case Reopened," *Zeitschrift für Soziologie* 3 (1974), 318: "There cannot be the slightest doubt that *Science as a Vocation* is the authentic offspring of *The Protestant Ethic,* inasmuch as that essay shows us the genuine Puritan of *The Protestant Ethic.*" See also Paul Honigsheim, *On Max Weber* (New York: Free Press, 1968), 114; and "Max Weber: His Religious and Ethical Background and Development," *Church History* 18–19 (1949–1950), 235–237.
13 Weber, "Types of Domination," WG, 142. According to Luciano Cavalli, "charisma constitutes a 'calling' in a strong sense." See Cavalli, "Charismatic Domination, Totalitarian Dictatorship, and Plebiscitary Democracy in the Twentieth Century," in Carl F. Graumann and Serge Moscovici, eds, *Changing Conceptions of Leadership* (New York: Springer-Verlag, 1986), 67–81, here 61.
14 On this subject, see Harvey Goldman, *Max Weber and Thomas Mann: Calling and the Shaping of the Self* (Berkeley: University of California Press, 1988).

There are, of course, many rich and complex practices of the self in premodern Occidental as well as non-Occidental cultures, embodied in systems of education and in religious technologies for creating ethical and moral subjects, and they are a principal concern of his sociology of religion. But, according to Weber, these do not create systematic worldly innovators, nor do they rival the substance or the scale of Western practices. Wolfgang Mommsen has remarked that the "rationalization of the conduct of life" has often led, in the West to a situation where "the individual or the group to which he belongs, accumulates a capacity for action whose force under certain conditions can have revolutionary consequences for the existing social system of which he is a part."[15] Indeed, it is urgent, according to Weber, to restore power to the West to rescue it from being depleted by its own creations, and this restoration can only come, he believes, through a secular revival of the calling.

In Weber's conception, the calling is a mode of asceticism for legitimating the self by sacrificing it in its natural form and building a new and higher self devoted to an ultimate value or cause. It sanctifies the person through service, creating a sense of meaning, purpose, and personal value in a world that rationalization has emptied of meaning. But whereas Nietzsche aimed his attack on Western culture *at* asceticism, seeing it as the sign of a *weak* will, Weber wants to *restore* an ascetic source of meaning and value. In the discourse of calling, value is not located in the self and its development or in the discovery of what the self is or contains, or in what it creates, or in the world as it is given. Value lies, rather, in the capacity to discipline oneself in work for ideals on behalf of which one makes oneself a tool and a servant. The calling thus serves the needs of self-definition and self-justification through devotion and service. Indeed, too great an involvement with others pulls one away from ascetic accomplishment in the service of the cause. "With every task of a *calling* the *object* as such demands its right and wants to be carried out according to its own laws. With every task of a calling he to whom it is assigned has to restrict himself and to exclude what does not belong strictly to the *object,* and most of all, his own love and hate."[16] In Weber's view, the empowered self cannot seek a witness or companion in others. In-

---

15 See Mommsen, "Personal Conduct and Societal Change," in Whimster and Lash, eds., *Max Weber, Rationality and Modernity,* 40.
16 Weber, "The Meaning of the 'Value Freedom' of the Social and Economic Sciences," in Weber, *Wissenschaftslehre* [hereafter WL], 5th ed., ed. Johannes Winckelmann (Tübingen: J. C. B. Mohr [Paul Siebeck], 1982), 494.

deed, it is formed *against* others. All personal or popular witnesses, all outside acclaim, except as a means to the power of the self, must be excluded as threatening the self and its task. The empowered self of the calling must perform its tasks "as objective duty of the calling and not on account of a concrete personal relationship."[17] Thus Weber's self is not an interactional or a socialized self, but rather a countersocialized self. One must resist the temptations of others as much as the desires of self.

To Weber, the outcome of subjection to the calling is the transformation of the natural self into a "personality," a concept with roots in Kant and in the neo-Kantians of Weber's time, and that Durkheim, Simmel, Troeltsch, and others drew on as well. Puritanism, Weber argued, *created* the Occidental form of personality, which is always essentially ascetic.[18] It first strengthened the believer's "constant motives" or impersonal purposes, or, in Weber's later formulation, "ultimate values," and gave them hegemony within the person, subjecting the natural self to them. Then the ascetic person worked to realize them in impersonal service, extending their hegemony from inside the self outward into the world. To Weber, becoming a personality requires hierarchically unifying the self. It demands a "striving toward unity from within [*von innen heraus*]" and "moving outward from a center which the individual has himself achieved." The person must become a "systematic unity," a "whole," not just "a combination of useful particular qualities." The Occidental personality has "an inner core [*einer 'von Innen heraus'*], unity from a center, an above all regulated unity of life conduct, deriving from some central point of view [*Stellungnahme*] of one's own."[19]

To Weber, the source of personality today can be found only in self-limitation, specialization, and narrowing of focus. "[T]here is only one way to become . . . [a personality] . . . : the unreserved submission to an 'object' [*Hingabe an eine 'Sache'*]."[20] Personal conduct in a rationalized world built on specialization of tasks

17 Weber, "Sociology of Religion," WG, 361.
18 Weber, "The Protestant Ethic and the Spirit of Capitalism," in *Gesammelte Aufsätze zur Religionssoziologie,* Vol. I [hereafter GRS, I] (Tübingen: J. C. B. Mohr [Paul Siebeck], 1920), 117.
19 Weber, "Sociology of Religion," WG, 339–340; "Confucianism and Taoism," GRS, I, 521, 518; "Hinduism and Buddhism," in *Gesammelte Aufsätze zur Religionssoziologie,* Vol. II [hereafter GRS, II] (Tübingen: J. C. B. Mohr [Paul Siebeck], 1921), 371.
20 Weber, "Value Freedom," WL, 494. See also Ernst Troeltsch, *Christian Thought. Its History and Application* (London: University of London Press, 1923), 51: "Out of the flux and confusion of the life of the instincts, the unity and compactness of personality has first to be created and acquired. . . . No man is born a personality; everyone has first to make himself

must accept these new terms of action: It must have "the character of 'service' vis-à-vis an impersonal *objective purpose* [*sachlichen Zweck*]."[21] Indeed, in discussing the vastly different ethos of conduct appropriate to personal, nonrational kinds of rule, Weber makes the claim that "only the ethic of the calling of inner-worldly asceticism is truly inwardly adequate to the commitment to impersonal objects characteristic of the coercive structure of domination [*Versachlichung der Gewaltherrschaft*]."[22] To Weber, whereas the providential interpretation of profit making once gave the Puritan businessman an ethical justification for his activities, in a parallel fashion in the present, "the enjoining of the ascetic meaning of the firm calling ethically transfigures [*verklärt*] the modern *specialists*."[23]

But despite the apparent adaptability of the ascetic calling to the rationalized world, Weber believed modern German culture was principally fashioning as its cultural product and prototype a "bureaucratic self," what he calls the *Ordnungsmensch,* the person dependent on order, a product of society's emphasis on diplomas, technical training, expertise, growing demands for administration, admiration for the "high moral standard" of German bureaucracy, and socialization and habituation to functional, obedient action on the basis of rational norms.[24] Modern society, in fact, idolizing the "bureaucratic ideal of life," is producing officials "in the spiritual sense of the word."[25] The power embodied in rationalization's social and political structures produce a disempowered self, adjusted "to the observation of accustomed norms and rules" and "to obedient accommodation cultivated in the officials on the one hand *and* the ruled on the other."[26] It is "as if we *should* become, with knowledge and will, men who need 'order' and nothing but order, who become nervous and cowardly if this order wavers for a moment, and helpless if they are

---

into a personality by obedience towards another instinct, which leads to unity and homogeneity." Also, see 71, 79, 80.
21 Weber, "Political and Hierocratic Domination," WG, 709; see also 710.
22 Weber, "Sociology of Religion," WG, 362.
23 Weber, "The Protestant Ethic," GRS, I, 178.
24 Weber, "Diskussionsreden auf der Tagung des Vereins für Sozialpolitik in Wien 1909," in Weber, *Gesammelte Aufsätze zur Soziologie und Sozialpolitik,* 2d ed., ed. Marianne Weber [hereafter GSS] (Tübingen: J. C. B. Mohr [Paul Siebeck], 1988; 1924), 414; "Bureaucratic Domination," WG, 560.
25 Weber, "Diskussionsreden auf der Tagung des Vereins," GSS, 414; and "Parliament and Government in a Reconstructed Germany," in *Gesammelte Politische Schriften,* 3d ed., [hereafter GPS], ed. Johannes Winckelmann (Tübingen: J. C. B. Mohr [Paul Siebeck], 1971), 335.
26 Weber, "Bureaucratic Domination," WG, 570, 553, 558.

wrenched out of their exclusive adaptation to this order."[27] In Robert Merton's terms, rules and submission have gone beyond the functional to become symbolic, *not* just *within* the structure, but rather throughout society.[28] Thus, one must find something *"to set against this machinery to keep a remnant of humankind free from this parcelling out of the soul, from this exclusive mastery of the bureaucratic ideal of life."*[29]

In Germany's past, of course, though bureaucracy was often idealized, it was less highly developed, and its influence on education and socialization was weaker. Indeed, humanist cultivation had been the traditional prerequisite for official careers. The advance of capitalism and administration, however, pushed education in the direction of technique and specialization, and self-fashioning in the direction of adaptation and submission. Further, leadership in society and state was then aristocratic, and the aristocracy's economic independence and traditions enabled it to produce types of character appropriate for the tasks of society and politics. But under the influence of capitalist development, "the landed aristocracy undergoes a serious inner transformation, which completely alters the character of the aristocracy inherited from the past."[30] They "have done their work and lie today in an economic death struggle, out of which no state economic policy can lead them back to their former social character."[31]

Weber believed that new social and political leaders to replace the aristocracy, master rationalization, and lead the nation in international economic and political competition could not easily emerge from the current economically leading class, the bourgeoisie, because it had become too submissive to the state and narrowly oriented to its own interests, even aping the habits and seeking the privileges of the nobility, weakening its class identity. The reason for this submissiveness, he thought, lay in the historical peculiarities of German unification and bourgeois political defeat but also in a culture shaped by Lutheranism and Pietism, quite unlike the culture of Puritanism, which had shored *up* the British bourgeois classes in *their* struggles

27 Weber, "Diskussionsreden auf der Tagung des Vereins," GSS, 414.
28 Robert K. Merton, "Bureaucratic Structure and Personality," in Merton, *Social Theory and Social Structure,* rev. and enlarged ed. (New York: Free Press, 1957; 1949), 195–206.
29 Weber, "Diskussionsreden auf der Tagung des Vereins," GSS, 414.
30 Weber, "Capitalism and Rural Society in Germany," in H. H. Gerth and C. Wright Mills, eds., *From Max Weber: Essays in Sociology* (New York: Oxford University Press, 1946), 369, 373.
31 Weber, "The National State and Economic Policy," GPS, 19.

with aristocratic rule. In fact, Weber says, "the power of religious movements first – not alone, but principally – has created here those differences that we sense today."[32] As he wrote in 1906: "that our nation has never in *any* form gone through the school of hard asceticism is . . . the source of all that I find hateful in it (as in myself)."[33] Weber was even willing to consider the potential of the working class for leadership in state and society, but through its trade unions and party it had become too bureaucratically disciplined to be capable of action, initiative, and responsibility. Thus, in Weber's analysis, classes can no longer empower the self on the basis of their economic power or position, nor can they generate autonomous empowered selves through any inherited cultural norms. Economic change, political culture, and class relations have combined to undermine what we can call "socialization for mastery." Weber proposed instead to transform a self-selected group of persons through submission to the discipline of the calling, who would adhere not to others but to their cause alone and would thus be in tension with the existing order, empowered to struggle for their mission: to use David Riesman's terminology, a group of "inner-directed" types against "tradition-directed" and "other-directed" ones.[34]

It is important for us to note, however, that the aristocratic self that was so capable in its time was not ascetic and self-denying. The aristocratic sense of self-worth, as Weber often remarked, rested on "the consciousness of their qualitative 'being,' residing in itself, not referring beyond itself," and independent of any sense of mission or task.[35] Thus, the adequacy of forms of self-empowerment should be understood relative to the concrete social and economic order whose tasks they must accomplish, and a single, universal model of the strong self and its sources, especially an ascetic one, must be rejected. But Weber believed, unlike Nietzsche, first, that the old aristocratic qualities were irretrievably gone, along with any form of collective social identity that rests on a shared sense of "being," and, second, that the burden imposed by the contemporary rationalized world

---

32 Weber, "The Protestant Ethic," GRS, I, 81.
33 Quoted in Wolfgang Mommsen, *Max Weber und die deutsche Politik, 1890–1920,* 2d ed. (Tübingen: J. C. B. Mohr [Paul Siebeck], 1974), 100.
34 See David Riesman, with Nathan Glazer and Reuel Denny, *The Lonely Crowd,* abridged ed., with a new forward (New Haven, Conn.: Yale University Press, 1961; 1950), chap. I; and David Riesman, in collaboration with Nathan Glazer, *Faces in the Crowd* (New Haven, Conn.: Yale University Press, 1952), chap. I.
35 Weber, "Sociology of Religion," WG, 298–299; "Political Communities," WG, 536; "Introduction" to "Economic Ethics of the World Religions," GRS, I, 248.

could in any case be dealt with only by a radically different kind of self.

Weber rejected the possibility that nonascetic modes of self-fashioning could adequately empower the modern self for mastery and innovation: "the service of a *cause* . . . must not in any way be lacking, if action is . . . to have inner firmness [*Halt*]."[36] To confront the demands of rationalization and disenchantment, Weber thought, a self must accept the strictures of technical expertise and strict specialization, for strength in action requires devotion solely and systematically to the object the calling serves. "The restriction to specialized work, with the renunciation of the Faustian universality which it involves, is above all the presupposition of worthwhile action in today's world." Thus, " 'deed' and 'renunciation' unavoidably imply one another today."[37] This is why Weber rejects the tradition of *Bildung,* enshrined among the educated classes. It had originally been a *counter*aristocratic ideal oriented toward being, toward the development and unfolding of the self and the creation of *its* version of personality. Its goal was for the person "to form himself in himself" according to the "inward" pattern and "law" of his own self and to strive for "the unity of his whole being."[38] The *"cultivated* personality" was distinguished by its possession of a "cultural quality" rather than by possession of privileged birth, specialized knowledge, or bureaucratic position.[39] But to Weber, the self cannot be fortified by reliance on *Bildung.* Though Humboldt believed that primacy of the will and force of self derive from first forming the self in accordance with its own inner law and then affecting others, Weber implies, to the contrary, that *Bildung* – concerned with growing and developing, rather than elevating and taming – does not empower. It rejects specialization and task-oriented devotion, orienting the self toward self-perfection and away from self-denying, worldly action. Yet without empowered individuals, life will drift into rigid, impersonal rationalization with no values or purposes to motivate it. Only the self's domination and mobilization in ascetic service can strengthen human beings for mastery of the rationalized world.

Precisely because Weber believes that systematic social and political

---

36 Weber, "Politics as a Vocation," GPS, 547.
37 Weber, "The Protestant Ethic," GRS, I, 203.
38 Wilhelm von Humboldt, quoted in Rudolf Vierhaus, "Bildung," in Otto Brunner, Werner Conze, Reinhart Koselleck, eds. *Geschichtliche Grundbegriffe* (Stuttgart: Ernst Klett Verlag, 1972), Vol. I, 520.
39 Weber, "Bureaucracy," WG, 578.

innovations are possible only by the action of called individuals acting on behalf of a higher cause, his work can discover or acknowledge no other sources of innovation, autonomy, and action, collective or otherwise. Collectivities cannot be empowered, but only used as the tool of charismatic domination. It is impossible within Weber's scheme to envision, for example, the public creation of purposes and goals or innovative social and political action originating in social movements, mass efforts, or associations. Further, there can be no individual strength except in some variant of an ascetic calling. "Where all reaching beyond this world is lacking, so must all independent weight against the world be wanting."[40] To be sure, strong and empowered selves appeared before the Reformation and elsewhere than in the West, but Weber interprets them in terms of the structure of self he found in the Puritans, because he understands his model as the *essence* of the empowered self. By severely restricting the conception of the kind of person capable of acting in innovative and commanding ways and restricting the understanding of what demands and processes of self-fashioning *make* the self such an actor, Weber makes it impossible to conceive of an autonomous and strong self not structured identically to the ascetic Puritan's.

Some consequences of Weber's logic of self and power can be seen in his interpretation of German political development and in his project for German democratization at the end of World War I. Weber's conviction about the necessity for creating a specific kind of self for the tasks of German politics led him into two serious errors. First, he misinterpreted and misappropriated the model of British prime ministerial politics. Weber thought of Gladstone, an unquestionably "called" politician, as the ideal type of the empowered modern leader, constrained only by his own charisma, inspired only by his political cause, consulting no others, and dominating a fully tamed Parliament. In this purist vision of politics, purged of the play of social classes and interests, of political culture, other personalities, and the motivations, ideologies, and coalitions of diverse constituencies, Weber attributed to Gladstone a more authoritarian power and to the British Parliament a more submissive role than they had. He imagined a politics inspired only by higher causes, where leaders have unrestricted responsibility to their idea of the nation, unlimited by the demands and needs of the real nation except during elections,

---

40 Weber, "Confucianism and Taoism," GRS, I, 521.

where lone champions struggle against one another at the head of armies of followers to impose visions of national greatness. He thus ignored many aspects of the social foundation and complexities of British politics, isolating the leader's capacity to win a constituency through the force of personality, and substituting a single compelling vision of *leadership* for a comprehensive analysis of politics. And he did this because of his dependence on the notion of an ideal, ascetic leader that he projected onto Britain.

Second, in his proposals for the transition of Germany from authoritarianism to democracy, Weber focused too much on leaders, failing to reckon with the social and cultural bases of the existing order; inadequately confronting the hostility, conservatism, and political bias of institutions like the army, judiciary, and bureaucracy; and ignoring the problem of building mass support for parliamentarism. These forces were among the many factors contributing to the eventual collapse of Weimar. Indeed, Weber's inadequate attention to the social foundations of contemporary political order and the importance of mass political culture underlies his excessive reliance on the notion of domination as the principal tool for thinking about politics and social order. The one-sidedness in his use of Britain and his program for Germany reveal the excessive influence on his thought of the German problem of leadership, the limits imposed by his conception of the self and its power, and the need to pay more attention to the social bases of modern politics and the interaction of politics, culture, and institutions.

# 8
# The Protestant Ethic versus the "New Ethic"

KLAUS LICHTBLAU

In his methodological essays, Max Weber declared that one of the main prerequisites of historical interpretation and explanation are the scholar's own value commitments (*Wertbeziehungen*) and the main cultural issues of his period.[1] Weber shared this insight with men such as the philosopher and sociologist Georg Simmel, who first elaborated a kindred theory of interpretation in a systematic way in 1892, as Weber freely acknowledged.[2] In 1908, Simmel refined his argument by saying that all individuals are only *fragments* who need a glimpse of the "general other" to complete the picture of their own selves. But if another human being appears as a generalization and typification of our own self, he or she is also a fragment that we shape into a whole. Thus we interpret our inner world with reference to the outer world and symbolize them both as if in a mirror image.[3]

Rather than discussing this core problem of the hermeneutic process of "interpretation" (*Verstehen*) in general, I first ask what the main problems of Max Weber and his period were at the time when he wrote his study about the religious background of the modern capitalist professional ethics. This involves the modern gender issues, that is, the crucial development of the modern family structure and the "sexual question" at the turn of the century. Reading Weber's study about the genealogy of the ascetic roots of the modern lifestyle in the light of his own "family story" (*Familienroman*) and its close relationship to the modern feminist movement and the "erotic reb-

1 See Max Weber, *The Methodology of the Social Sciences*, trans. and ed. by Edward A. Shils and Henry A. Finch (New York, 1949), esp. 72–112.
2 See Georg Simmel, *The Problems of the Philosophy of History. An Epistemological Essay*, trans. and ed. by Guy Oakes (New York, 1977), 56ff. For a comprehensive discussion of Simmel's theory of interpretation, see Guy Oakes' introduction to Georg Simmel, *Essays on Interpretation in Social Science*, trans. and ed. by Guy Oakes (Manchester, 1980), 3–94.
3 See Georg Simmel, *Soziologie: Untersuchungen über die Formen der Vergesellschaftung*, 5th ed. (Berlin, 1968), 24–25.

ellion" also means locating his work within a cultural context that not only gave rise to Freud's "discovery" and decoding of the language of the unconscious, but also to Simmel's "philosophy of money" as a general theory of a symbolizing process. According to these theorists, it seemed that modern culture required a fundamental *sacrifice* of human nature and of the personal desires of the individual.[4] One of the starting points for my interpretation of Weber's *Protestant Ethic,* therefore, is to reconstruct his own answer to those cultural questions about the ascetic roots of the capitalist money economy and the personality structure of the modern individual. Without resorting to a psychoanalytic framework,[5] I deal with some striking "elective affinities" between the works of Simmel, Weber, and Freud with regard to the main issues of the cultural crisis of the bourgeois society at the turn of the last century.

Weber's own nervous illness was not only a personal disaster, but was symptomatic and representative of the "nervous" character of his period that gave rise to many formulas describing the nature of this cultural crisis, and to very different therapeutic programs for solving the problems that were specific to it. In his inaugural lecture of 1895, Weber characterized his own generation as one of epigoni who were condemned to carry on the work that their fathers had started so successfully.[6] His own "generational rebellion," therefore, can be interpreted as an attempt to gain a new platform for renewing the energies that had not only led modern capitalism to its worldwide victory but had also made possible the founding of the new German Empire. Distancing himself from the dominant Wilhelmine aristocracy and those "liberal" politicians who, like his own father, had made peace with the "personal regime" of William II and the Junkers, Weber searched for some *historical* forerunners of those liberals whom he described as the real "heroes" of the German bourgeoisie and the true "founding fathers" of the new Empire. Lack of

4 According to Simmel, the economic exchange itself is based on the renunciation of the immediate personal consumption of an object. Simmel therefore used the notion of "sacrificing exchange" (*aufopfernder Tausch*) to characterize the peculiarity of modern money economy. See Georg Simmel, *The Philosophy of Money,* trans. by Tom Bottomore and David Frisby (London, 1990), 79ff.; 2d enlarged ed., with a new introduction by David Frisby, xv–xli.
5 Such an interpretation has been proposed by Arthur Mitzman, *The Iron Cage: A Historical Interpretation of Max Weber* (New York, 1970), and by Nicolaus Sombart, *Nachdenken über Deutschland: Vom Historismus zur Psychoanalyse* (Munich, 1987), 22–51.
6 See Max Weber, *Gesammelte politische Schriften,* 4th ed., ed. by Johannes Winckelmann (Tübingen, 1980), 1–25.

heroic *action* and subordination to the authority of William II and the Junkers' regime were major charges in Weber's critique of the contemporary bourgeois politicians of his nation.[7]

The diversion of action in favor of a subjectivist culture of hedonism, consumerism, aestheticism, and eroticism also was a main topic of Weber's critique of the bourgeois culture of his period as a whole. The search for "inner experience" (*inneres Erleben*) and the cult of a highly personal conduct of life appeared to him as symptoms of a general "decadence" that gave rise to severe "pathologies" in modern culture. It also led to some tensions within his own personality and conduct.[8] That "modernism" is a source and symptom of many cultural pathologies and human diseases is one of the most striking critiques inaugurated in the nineteenth century by such influential philosophers and poets as Schopenhauer, Kierkegaard, Baudelaire, Tolstoy, and Nietzsche. The notion of *décadence* and *dégénérescence* also was one of the stereotypes used by psychiatric and sexual scientists to describe the "anomalies" and "pathologies" deeply rooted in the "modern" lifestyle. The imposing "career" of such mental "diseases" as hysteria and neurasthenia in the 1880s and 1890s was not only a matter for psychiatry and medicine, but also a ubiquitous topic in cultural and literary criticism that treated the central features of modern culture. There were close intellectual relationships between the different "orders" of the psychiatric, medical, literary, and aesthetic discourse, which also gave rise to some common key issues concerning the modern "gender question."[9]

In his *German History,* Karl Lamprecht had characterized his own culture as a *subjectivistic* and *impressionistic* one that was closely intertwined with the decline of the *symbolic, typical,* and *conventional* character of the Middle Ages and that gave rise to a mental state that

7 On Weber's "generational rebellion" and his critique of the political leaders in Wilhelmine Germany, see Christoph Stedin, *Politik und Wissenschaft bei Max Weber* (Breslau, 1932); Guenther Roth, "Max Weber's Generational Rebellion and Maturation," in Reinhard Bendix and Guenther Roth, *Scholarship and Partisanship: Essays on Max Weber* (Berkeley, Los Angeles, and London, 1971), 6–33; Wolfgang J. Mommsen, *Max Weber and German Politics, 1890–1920* (Chicago, 1984).

8 On Weber's own psychic depression, see Mitzman, *The Iron Cage,* 148–163, and Sombart, *Nachdenken über Deutschland,* 27–42.

9 See Wolfgang Drost, ed., *Fortschrittsglaube und Dekadenzbewusstsein im Europa des 19. Jahrhunderts* (Heidelberg, 1986); Jens Malte Fischer, *Fin de siècle: Kommentar zu einer Epoche* (Munich, 1978), 11–93; Wolfdietrich Rasch, *Die literarische Décadence um 1900* (Munich, 1986); Andreas Steiner, *'Das nervöse Zeitalter': Der Begriff der Nervosität bei Laien und Ärzten in Deutschland und Österreich um 1900* (Zurich, 1964); Regina Schaps, *Hysterie und Weiblichkeit: Wissenschaftsmythen über die Frau* (Frankfurt and New York, 1982).

Lamprecht called the "period of nervousness" (*Periode der Reizsamkeit*).[10] Georg Simmel also interpreted the nervous character of his time as a consequence of the vitalistic character of the money economy and the modern urban lifestyle. The search for "new impressions" seemed to him necessary for a human being confronted with the continuous acceleration of "modern times" and his own desire for a truly authentic, personal lifestyle.[11] In contrast to this value-neutral description of cultural modernism, Willy Hellpach asserted in 1902 the genuinely pathological character of modern culture and pointed to the "elective affinities" between the aesthetic, erotic, religious, and medical issues of the period. The "phantasmagoric apperception," which according to Hellpach was a specific character of the medieval mind, had now returned in the symbolic and ornamental character of the hysterical body that not only was a peculiarity of the female but that symbolized femininity, as well as cultural modernism as a whole.[12]

In the work of Otto Weininger, the antagonism between male and female appeared as the core of this "crisis of culture" that now was decoded as a return of oppressed femininity. The destabilization of the male personality could therefore be ascribed to a loss of the traditional role ascriptions and the division of labor between the sexes.[13] Unsurprisingly, one of the most important aims of the anarchist movement at this time was to overthrow the ascetic and repressive character of capitalism and patriarchalism in favor of restoring the power of ancient "mother right" (*Mutterrecht*) and the tradition of "holy prostitution," as well as the *ars amandi* of aristocrat-

---

10 Karl Lamprecht, *Deutsche Geschichte. Erster Ergänzungsband: Zur jüngsten deutschen Vergangenheit. Erster Band: Tonkunst – Bildende Kunst – Dichtung – Weltanschauung* (Leipzig, 1901), VII f., 53–66, 379–389, 464–471.

11 Simmel, *Philosophie des Geldes*, 519–552; Simmel, "Tendencies in German Life and Thought Since 1870," *International Monthly* 5 (1902): 93–111, 166–184; Simmel, "The Metropolis and Mental Life" (1903), in Donald Levine, ed., *Georg Simmel on Individuality and Social Forms* (Chicago, 1971), 20–339.

12 Willy Hellpach, *Nervosität und Kultur* (Berlin, 1902), 127–158; see also Hellpach, *Grundlinien einer Psychologie der Hysterie* (Leipzig, 1904), 469–494. Already in the first edition of *The Protestant Ethic*, Weber had referred to these studies. See Max Weber, "Die protestantische Ethik und der 'Geist' des Kapitalismus II: Die Berufsidee des asketischen Protestantismus," *Archiv für Sozialwissenschaft und Sozialpolitik* 21 (1905): 1–110, 45, 61. See now also Weber's letters to Hellpach in *Briefe 1906–1908*, MWGA, I/10. For a lucid interpretation of this topic, see Manfred Schneider, "Hysterie als Gesamtkunstwerk: Aufstieg und Verfall einer Semiotik der Weiblichkeit," *Merkur* 39 (1985): 879–895.

13 See Otto Weininger, *Geschlecht und Charakter: Eine prinzipielle Untersuchung* (Vienna, 1903); Jacques Le Rider, "Modernisme – féminisme/modernité – virilité: Otto Weininger et la modernité viennoise," *L'Infini* 4 (1983): 5–20; Jacques Le Rider and Norbert Leser, *Otto Weininger: Werk und Wirkung* (Vienna, 1984).

ic society. That eroticism also could be regarded as a surrogate for religious experience was recognized by Gertrud Bäumer, one of the most influential leaders of the German women's movement, who observed in 1904:

A sensual and artistic epoch of history that desires to experience the intoxicating power of all natural drives is dawning. People have become attuned to the vibrations of the sensual energies in the balance of pleasure and pain. Eroticism has become vitally important. Ellen Key goes so far as to claim that love is for people in the present what religion was in the past. Love becomes the object of a restless interest that drags all its mystical secrets into the lime light . . . and multiplies its power through ever greater auto-suggestion.[14]

For women like Gertrud Bäumer, the glorification of eroticism appeared, however, as an exaggeration that eviscerated the theoretical and literary expression of this life experience. "The first female enthusiasts for the rights of man," she continued,

held womanhood in almost ascetic disdain. But today we encounter a mood for which all *Weltschmerz*, all dissatisfaction with life, is attributed to unfulfilled erotic desires. Ricarda Huch is right when she says in her essay on Gottfried Keller that people are overestimating the importance of love. "In modern life as in modern art love occupies too much space, and this is one of the most important causes of the sickliness and weakness of our time."[15]

In fact, the question of eroticism and the demand for free love was one of the main issues discussed in some influential intellectual circles and within the women's movement. In Munich some members of Ludwig Klages' Cosmic Round championed the idea of a "new paganism" as spokesmen of the Schwabing *bohème.* They advocated radical sexual liberation from all ascetic ideals and patriarchal forms of domination. Their paganism attacked not only the values of occidental rationalism, but also the standards of bourgeois sexual morality. Already a cult figure, the Countess Franziska zu Reventlow played the role of the new hetaera who disdained the bluestockings of the bourgeois women's movement and demanded the reestablishment of an erotic culture in the sense of *l'art pour l'art.*[16] This sort of

14 Gertrud Bämer, *Die Frau in der Kulturbewegung der Gegenwart* (Wiesbaden, 1904), 5f.
15 Ibid., 20.
16 On Franziska Gräfin zu Reventlow, see Marianne Weber, *Die Frauen und die Liebe* (Königstein and Leipzig, 1935), 180–195; Johannes Székely, *Franziska Gräfin zu Reventlow: Leben und Werk* (Bonn, 1979); Helmut Fritz, *Die erotische Rebellion: Das Leben der Franziska Gräfin zu Reventlow* (Frankfurt a.M., 1980); Regina Schaps, "Tragik und Erotik – Kultur der Geschlechter: Franziska Gräfin zu Reventlows 'modernes Hetärentum'," in Wolfgang Lipp, ed., *Kulturtypen, Kulturcharaktere: Träger, Mittler und Stifter von Kultur* (Berlin, 1987), 79–96.

*Kulturkritik* was radicalized by Freud's pupil Otto Gross, who was also influenced by Bachofen and Nietzsche. Gross raised the sexual revolution to the level of a political program. The revolutionary force of free love, he believed, had a socially therapeutic function and could transform society.[17] Such ideas entered the German's women's movement in 1904 when the Association for the Protection of Motherhood was founded and began to play a crucial role within the divisions of the bourgeois women's movement during the following years.

The original purpose of this league was to help unmarried women and their illegitimate children solve their moral and material problems within an oppressive patriarchal society. For a time, some progressive liberals like Friedrich Naumann, Werner Sombart, and Max Weber himself supported this union founded by Ruth Bré. Other supporters were such active combatants of the women's movement as Adele Schreiber, Henriette Fürth, Lily Braun, Hedwig Dohm, Marie Stritt, Rosa Mayreder, and Ellen Key. But soon Helene Stöcker and her circle began using this forum to propagate their own convictions about the emancipating nature of free love and the illegitimate love child, and forced the members of the association to take sides on a "new ethic," which in fact was an old one.[18] In 1909 Gertrud Bäumer pointed out that among the crucial inspirations for this new ethic of sexual liberation was not only the Nietzschean doctrine of the *Übermensch* but the declaration of the power of love by the early German romantic movement around 1800, especially in the works of Friedrich Schlegel and Schleiermacher.[19] But in contrast to these romantics, the new individualism of love gave rise to a new sexual ethic that also proclaimed the emancipation of love from the traditional con-

---

17 See Arthur Mitzman, "Anarchism, Expressionism and Psychoanalysis," *New German Critique* 10 (1977): 77–104; Josef Dvorak, "Kokain und Mutterrecht: Die Wiederentdeckung von Otto Gross," *Neues Forum* 295–296 (1978): 52–61; Emanuel Hurwitz, *Otto Gross: "Paradies"-Sucher zwischen Freud und Jung* (Zurich and Frankfurt a.M., 1979).

18 See Richard J. Evans, *The Feminist Movement in Germany 1894–1933* (London, 1976), 115–143; Amy Hackett, "Helene Stöcker: Left Wing Intellectual and Sex Reformer," in Renate Bridenthal, Atina Grossmann, and Marion Kaplan, eds., *When Biology Became Destiny: Women in Weimar and Nazi Germany* (New York, 1984), 109–130; Ilse Kokula, "Der linke Flügel der Frauenbewegung als Plattform des Befreiungskampfes homosexueller Frauen und Männer," in Jutta Dalhoff, Uschi Frey, and Ingrid Schöll, eds., *Frauenmacht in der Geschichte* (Düsseldorf, 1986), 46–64.

19 Gertrud Bäumer, "Die neue Ethik vor hundert Jahren," in Gertrud Bäumer et al., *Frauenbewegung und Sexualethik: Beiträge zur modernen Ehekritik* (Heilbronn, 1909), 54–77; see also Helene Stöcker, "Neue Ethik in der Kunst," *Mutterschutz: Zeitschrift zur Reform der sexuellen Ethik* 1 (1905): 301–306, and Heinrich Meyer-Benfey, "Lucinde," *Mutterschutz: Zeitschrift zur Reform der sexuellen Ethik* 2 (1906): 173–192.

jugal restrictions. This revolutionary claim for a genuinely free love and the woman's right to the illegitimate child was one of the most important challenges to the marital values that Max and Marianne Weber had taken for granted in respect of their own personal lives. Their controversy with the representatives of the new ethic helps us to understand the way the Webers tried to legitimate not only their own marriage, but also the historical traditions and cultural values related to it.[20]

At the time, Max and Marianne Weber defended bourgeois sexual morality from the standpoint of a Christian world view that was anchored in the tradition of ascetic Protestantism. Sexual fidelity was for them a taken-for-granted ascetic ideal that binds the "beautiful moment" to the rule of the moral law, which determines the mutual responsibility of the partners "up to the pianissimo of old age."[21] Law, duty, and asceticism constitute the ideals of a monogamous community, which demands sacrifice and subordinates unbridled eros to the ethical norms of a puritanical union of souls. The demand for free love and a child out of wedlock appears as a "desecration of monogamy" that amounts to "killing something divine." According to this ascetic ethic of responsibility, sensual enjoyment must not become "an end in itself, not even in the form of an aesthetically sublimated eroticism."[22]

Here we encounter the spirit of ascetic Protestantism, which not only shaped the Webers' marital understanding but also influenced the comprehensive study *Wife and Mother in Legal Development,* which Marianne wrote during the years of Max's illness and con-

20 For a more exhaustive discussion of this controversy and the personal involvement of the Webers within the erotic movement, see Marianne Weber, *Max Weber: A Biography,* trans. and ed. by Harry Zohn (New Brunswick, N.J., 1988), 371–390, and Guenther Roth's introduction to this edition of Marianne Weber's biography, ibid., xv–lx; Mitzman, *The Iron Cage,* 256–296; Martin Green, *The von Richthofen Sisters: The Triumphant and the Tragic Modes of Love* (New York, 1974); Sombart, *Nachdenken über Deutschland,* 22–52; Wolfgang Schwentker, "Passion as a Mode of Life: Max Weber, the Otto Gross Circle and Eroticism," in Wolfgang J. Mommsen and Jürgen Osterhammel, eds., *Max Weber and his Contemporaries* (London, 1987), 483–498; Ingrid Gilcher-Holtey, "Max Weber und die Frauen," in Christian Gneuss and Jürgen Kocka, eds., *Max Weber: Ein Symposium* (Munich, 1988), 142–154.

21 See Marianne Weber, *Max Weber,* 371–390. The phrase "up to the pianissimo of old age," a maximum of an ethic of responsibility, occurs at the very end of Marianne Weber, *Ehefrau und Mutter in der Rechtsentwicklung* (Tübingen, 1907), 572, and in the last version of the "Zwischenbetrachtung" (1920), published under the title "Religious Rejections of the World and Their Directions," in H. H. Gerth and C. Wright Mills, eds., *From Max Weber: Essays in Sociology* (New York, 1946), 350; it also appears in the dedication to Marianne Weber in the first volume of the *Gesammelte Aufsätze zur Religionssoziologie* (Tübingen, 1920).

22 Marianne Weber, *Max Weber,* 371, 374.

valescence.[23] Weber's 1904 essay on the elective affinity between ascetic Protestantism and the modern capitalist ethos not only provided her with a theoretical framework but also guided her substantive interest in the development of marriage law from archaic communities to the bourgeois marriage and its Puritan morality. Like her husband, Marianne was interested in identifying the noneconomic, purely spiritual determinants in the emergence of modern secular conduct. As against the monistic approach of the economic interpretation of history, she emphasized the multiple influences that shaped the development of marriage law and marital conduct. Again, like her husband, she concluded that bourgeois marital morality resulted from the religious radicalism that began with the Reformation and continued through Calvinism, English Puritanism, and the Baptist sects. Let us now turn to Weber's text.

In The *Protestant Ethic and the Spirit of Capitalism,* Weber attempted to reconstruct the purely religious motives at the root of the capitalist sense of vocation. The religious conviction of the world's sinfulness demanded an inner-wordly asceticism that aimed at destroying any "spontaneous sensual enjoyment of life" (PE, 119). Sexual intercourse appeared at most acceptable in marriage and only for the sake of procreation, and in the selection of partners, erotic attractiveness was subordinated to sober, rational choice. Like his wife, Max Weber believed that a sexual morality that rested basically on a rationalist affirmation of abstinence had led to an ethical transformation of marital relations and thus to the "flowering of a chivalry" that helped bring about the modern "emancipation of woman" (PE, 264).[24] The idea of a universal priesthood, the demand for freedom of conscience for both sexes, and the rejection of any kind of militarism favored the formal equality of women in the Puritan communities. But what was the price?

In vivid imagery, Weber sketches the fundamental rejection of all sensual culture (*Sinnenkultur*) in its consequences for practical conduct and its relation to cultural values that have no immediate religious relevance. On the one hand, the impersonality of charity and the distrust of friendship appear as the logical consequence of every

---

23 Marianne Weber, *Lebenserinnerungen* (Bremen: Storm, 1948), 124.
24 The phrase "emancipation of woman" is an insert from 1920. For a similar discussion of Puritan sexual morality, see Marianne Weber, *Ehefrau und Mutter,* and the formulation: "Just as freedom of conscience was the mother of 'the Rights of Man,' so it was the cradle of women's rights" (290).

ascetic ethic that perceives in all purely emotional and personal relations the danger of the "idolatry of the flesh." On the other hand, this attitude must in principle oppose the aesthetic sphere insofar as the latter retains any elements of sensuality (*Sinnenkunst*). Therefore, Puritan England sacrificed most art forms. This was accompanied by the emergence of a uniform and standardized lifestyle. Together with the industrial mode of production, this process eventually led to the iron constraints on conduct and the tragedy of modern professionalism of which Weber spoke with such pathos.

It is not difficult to see that Weber, in depicting the rejection of sensual culture as well as the treatment of positive science as the only explicitly approved nonreligious value, also portrays his personal ethos. This originally religious stance, to which the Webers still tried to adhere, was challenged to the core by the erotic movement and the literary-aesthetic avant-garde of the time. The challenge from a free love that eluded ethical and religious regulation, and had affinity with an aesthetic and expressive lifestyle, deeply affected Weber and finally made him modify decisively his views on the cultural significance of a purely ethical and religious value position. He came to develop three strategies toward the erotic question. First, with Marianne, he continued to uphold the unconditional validity of the ethical ideal of monogamous marriage, but he became willing to allow persons unable to live up to it a practical dispensation under certain preconditions, a dispensation that he claimed in the end for himself.[25] Second, given his conviction of the autonomous value of sexual abstinence, Weber now became strongly interested in the effects of a norm-free eroticism on the personality. This interest is reflected in his reception of Freud's works and in his virulent critique of Otto Gross. Weber repudiated the latter's plea for a sexual ethic that embraced the therapeutic function of sexual release, but he accepted the lasting contribution of Freud's studies insofar as they succeeded in creating an "exact casuistry."[26] Third, Weber was troubled and fascinated by the notion that ethical values are not the only normative ones, since the spheres of the erotic and the aesthetic each possess a value of its own (*Eigenwert*). In Nietzsche's terms, they are "beyond good and evil" and thus have a close elective affinity. Weber even began to plan a sociology of

---

25 See Marianne Weber, *Max Weber*, 371.

26 Ibid., 376. On the relation to Freud, see Tracy B. Strong, "Weber and Freud: Vocation and Self-Acknowledgement," in *Max Weber and His Contemporaries*, 468–482.

art, but he managed to write only the fragment on the sociology of music. He also developed an avid interest in the various efforts to found a specifically modern aesthetics.

From modern aesthetics Weber also expected a clarification of eroticism as a particular value sphere. For instance, he wrote to Georg Lukács after reading the first instalment of his *Heidelberg Philosophy of Art*:

> I am very eager to see what happens when you turn to the concept of "form." After all, form is not only found at the value level that rises above the level of the experiential. The erotic sphere, which reaches deep down into the "cage," also has form. It shares the fate of bearing the guilt common to all formed life. It stands close to the aesthetic attitude by virtue of its opposition to everything that belongs to the realm of "form-free" divinity. The topographic location of the erotic must be established, and I am very interested to find out where you will place it.[27]

Unfortunately, Lukács' aesthetic theory also remained a fragment. Thus we must determine the topographic location of the erotic and the aesthetic elsewere. Weber's sociology of religion provides us with a key, in particular through the three versions of the "Intermediary Reflections." Together with the two speeches on science and politics as vocations, the last version became Weber's ultimate legacy to us. Not surprisingly, much of the recent Weber literature has dealt with these last writings.[28]

Weber sketched the cultural autonomy of the aesthetic and the erotic in a typology and sociology of rationalism that lays out the range of fundamental conflicts among the various orders of life (*Lebensordnungen*). In the great salvation religions and their image of a transcendental God, the basic tension between religious ethics and the world becomes radicalized through the opposition of a "cosmos of natural causality" and a "cosmos of ethical, retributive causality."[29] The sublimation of salvation in the direction of an ethic of conviction (*Gesinnungsethik*) exacerbates the conflict with the world, because the religious rationalization of conduct also leads to a greater comprehension of the logic inherent in the other value spheres, and thus to a

27  Weber to Georg Lukács (March 10, 1913) in Eva Karádi and Eva Fekete, eds., *Georg Lukács: Briefwechsel 1902–1917* (Stuttgart, 1982), 320. The *Heidelberger Philosophie der Kunst* appeared as Volume 15 of the Lukács *Werke*.
28  On the controversial interpretations of the three versions with regard to their significance for Weber's *oeuvre*, see Wolfgang Schluchter, *Rationalism, Religion, and Domination: A Weberian Perspective*, trans. by Neil Solomon (Berkeley, Los Angeles, and London, 1989), chap. 12.
29  *From Max Weber: Essays in Sociology*, 355.

greater awareness of the tensions between them. In Weber's scheme, the rise of a universalist ethic of brotherhood is of crucial importance for the differentiation of the other spheres.

The logical precondition for the "universalism of love" and "acosmistic" (unspecific) love is the emergence of religious congregations that differentiate themselves from the household and the sib and gain support from the authorities in the politically pacified empires. But the universalist claims of this ethic of love are directed against the extended family and the neighborhood association no less than against the sphere of political power proper. Thus the moral "slave revolt" organized by the priests reveals itself also as an "ethic of the ruled." Since "women had everywhere shown a particular susceptibility to religious stimuli," Weber observed, "this domestication provided ever stronger grounds for assigning religious value to the essentially feminine virtues of the ruled."[30] The more political authority became institutionalized in its own right, the greater was the likelihood that subjects would "take flight into the irrationality of apolitical sentiment," especially into the erotic sphere.[31]

Weber was especially concerned with the tension between the universalist ethic of brotherhood and the secular spheres of economy, politics, and science, on the one hand, and the spheres of sexual love and art, on the other. The latter two stood in particularly sharp opposition to the salvation religions because of their close similarities with mystical religiosity. The psychological similarity between the highest forms of eroticism and the "sublimated forms of heroic piety" and their "mutual psychological and physiological substitutibility" explain why these two spheres became sharpest rivals in the rationalized and intellectualized world of modernity.[32] Only a culture that claimed to be able, in principle, to rationalize all spheres could provoke the emergence of "irrational" subjective experience as an autonomous sphere.

Religiosity, however, came to share a retreat into the private experience of the extraordinary with erotic intimacy and with subjective enjoyment of *l'art pour l'art*. The sublimation of sexuality into eroticism, in the sense of a "consciously cultivated, extra-mundane sphere," was possible only in a purely intellectualist culture that embraced ascetic professionalism. Extramundane, especially extra-

---

30 From the first version of the "Intermediate Reflections" in Max Weber, *Economy and Society*, 591f.
31 Ibid., 601.   32 *From Max Weber: Essays in Sociology*, 348.

marital, sexuality thus could appear as "the only tie connecting human beings with the natural source of all life," opening "a gate into the most irrational and thereby real kernel of life, in opposition to the mechanisms of rationalization."[33]

In recognizing the autonomy of "love for love's sake" and of "art for art's sake," Weber decisively modified the conceptual framework of *The Protestant Ethic* in relation to his theory of modernity. Thus Weber's *oeuvre* linked up with the cultural avant-garde, which identified the distinctiveness of modern culture with a systematic differentiation of the aesthetic-expressive sphere from the purely cognitive-instrumental and moral-practical spheres.[34] This theory of modernity took up central motifs of the early romanticist critique of reason, which had endeavored to defend the "internal infinity of the subject" (Hegel) against the logical and substantive imperatives of theoretical and practical rationalism, and to rehabilitate the spheres of aesthetics and of sexual love as matters of authentic expressiveness.[35] By acknowledging the autonomy of the erotic and the aesthetic value realms, Weber integrated this aesthetic-expressive modernism into a theory of rationalization and modernization that had begun with a massive historical process of religious disenchantment and now conjured up the return of the gods. As a "praise of polytheism," Weber's theory can be understood as "myth (*Mythos*) directed against itself," a posthistorical attitude to history.[36] Weber thereby anticipated the break between modernism and modernity that Daniel Bell later described as a cultural contradiction of capitalism. Demanding limitless self-fulfillment for the individual, the postmodern counterculture represents an aesthetic-hedonist, consumption-oriented, expressive

---

33 Ibid., 345f. A lucid analysis of Weber's theory of erotic love and of its possible significance for feminist theory today is found in Roslyn Wallach Bologh, "Max Weber on Erotic Love: A Feminist Inquiry," in Scott Lash and Sam Whimster, eds., *Max Weber: Rationality and Modernity* (London, 1987), 242–258. See also Roslyn Wallach Bologh, *Love or Greatness: Max Weber and Masculine Thinking – A Feminist Inquiry* (London, 1990).

34 Weber himself recognized the elective affinity between the postulate of value freedom in science and the postulate of autonomy in aesthetics, and in this connection mentioned Baudelaire and Nietzsche. See "Science as a Vocation" in *From Max Weber: Essays in Sociology*, 148.

35 On the "modernism of romanticism," see Hans Sedlmayer, "Ästhetischer Anarchismus in Romantik und Moderne," in *Scheidewege* 8 (1978): 174–196; Hauke Brunkhorst, "Romantik und Kulturkritik: Zerstörung der dialektischen Vernunft?" *Merkur* 39 (1985): 484–496; Karl Heinz Bohrer, *Die Kritik der Romantik* (Frankfurt a.M., 1989).

36 This phrase refers to a modernist rejection of any history founded on the Judeo-Christian tradition and of any philosophy of history related to it. See Theodor W. Adorno, *Ästhetische Theorie*, ed. by Gretel Adorno and Rolf Tiedemann (Frankfurt a.M., 1970), 41f.; see also Wolfgang J. Mommsen, "Rationalization and Myth in Weber's Thought," in *The Political and Social Theory of Max Weber: Collected Essays* (Chicago, 1989), 133–144.

culture. But the institutional core of modern society, which found its historical paradigm in the Protestant ethic, still rests on a conventional ethic.[37]

In the two versions of *The Protestant Ethic,* however, Weber rejected any allusions to the possibility of a reconciliation of eros and culture in a more liberal or aesthetic way of life. Sombart's critique of Weber's thesis concerning the ascetic roots of modern capitalism, and his rehabilitation of the aristocratic "mistress economy" (*Mätressenwirtschaft*) as one of the main sources of capital accumulation, is countered by Weber with the argument that it is not decisive to *have* money but *how to deal with it.*[38] Like Simmel and Freud, Weber seeks the origins of modern Western culture in a fundamental repression of desire (*Triebverzicht*) that leads to the emergence of a new world and destroys the wasteful, traditional, aristocratic one. In Weber's mind, this act of *purification* and *disenchantment of the world* is the real "heroic" one. Sombart's praise of the "merchant adventurers" and the luxury of the *grand seigneurs* fails, according to Max Weber, as an explanation of why the spirit of modern capitalism and professional ethics appeared for the first time in regions far from the vast capital accumulation in the European centers of mercantile trade and ostentatious consumption. The ethical reglementation and calculability of personal conduct through innerworldly asceticism appeared to him as one of the main sources of modern individualism and professionalism even though they had destroyed their own spiritual roots. But Weber personally accepted the *form* of this intellectual and cultural heritage that is conserved not only in the routines and constraints of very day life but also in modern science and in a secular work ethic as a quasi-transcendental value.

Like Karl Kraus, Arnold Schönberg, Adolf Loos, Ludwig Wittgenstein, and Otto Weininger, Max Weber belonged to that ascetic faction of the "antimodernist modernists" that opposed the revival of the medieval allegories, ornaments, and mysticisms within modern culture and looked for an act of purification in order to maintain the notions of form, distance, and asceticism as a medium of intellectual and aesthetic therapy. Weber's sharp distinction between intellectualism and aestheticism, and his condemnation of all theoretical

---

37 See Daniel Bell, *The Cultural Contradictions of Capitalism* (New York, 1976) and "Beyond Modernism, Beyond Self," in Quentin Anderson et al., eds., *Art, Politics and Will: Essays in Honor of Lionel Trilling* (New York, 1977), 213–253.
38 See Werner Sombart, *Liebe, Luxus und Kapitalismus* (Munich, 1967); this book originally appeared in 1913 under the shortened title *Luxus und Kapitalismus.*

fashions, is an expression of the asceticism that he identified as one of the main historical sources of modern capitalism and culture. His preference for *action* as a central sociological notion over *inner experience* (*Erleben*) may be viewed as a therapeutic device recommended as an antidote to depression in the contemporary medical literature. His preference for *asceticism* over *mysticism* may also mean that he was looking for a way of life that was able to avoid the personal risks and the political indifference that could result from getting lost in the labyrinth of "inner experiences." And his sympathy for the "English Hebrews," as well as his disdain for the political submissiveness of the Lutherans, suggests that he was searching for those "heroes" who generated the modern workmanship described by Thomas Carlyle in a more literary than historical style. "Work, and don't despair" was a formula that not only was a frequently given piece of medical advice at the turn of the last century or after the decline of the German Empire but also was the core of the ascetic Protestantism that itself has been seen as the expression of a *depressive world view.*[39] Thus Weber may have had felt some close connection or elective affinity with his *own* depressive and pessimistic worldview.

It is therefore the form of *tragedy* that characterizes both his study about the origins of modern capitalism and his own way of life. For tragedy, according to Nietzsche and Simmel, is that kind of downfall in which an individual or a whole culture destroy their own presuppositions. The paradoxical effect of innerworldly asceticism made the "heroic" foundation of modern culture vanish. And we might say that the virtues of ascetic Protestantism trapped Weber in an iron cage from which he was released only by the "reenchanting" power of ("nonlegal") erotic love that made him now work as intensively as many years ago.[40]

Weber rejected any claim of an "aesthetic of style" (*Stilästhetik*) with respect to his own work. "Aestheticism" and "mysticism" are metaphors of an irrational and chaotic force that is symptomatic of the *décadence* of culture as a whole. These notions are also metaphors and analogies for *femininity* and the "feminist" character of *cultural modernism* that menaced the traditional gender roles of the patriarchal

---

39 See Werner Stark, "Die kalvinistische Ethik und der Geist der Kunst," in Justin Stagl, ed., *Aspekte der Kultursoziologie: Aufsätze zur Soziologie, Philosophie, Anthropologie und Geschichte der Kultur* (Berlin, 1982), 87–96, 95.
40 See Gilcher-Holtey, "Max Weber und die Frauen."

era.[41] The crucial methodological claim in Weber's *Protestant Ethic* and in his later studies on the world religions lay in the rejection of any historical and social "laws" in favor of the "infinite causal regressus" and the simultaneous "interactions" (*Wechselwirkungen*) between the different cultural spheres. In this context, Weber often made use of the literary *topos* of "elective affinities" (*Wahlverwandtschaften*). In his novel of that title, Goethe intended a "chemical analogy" (*chemische Gleichnisrede*) in order to characterize the different relations between his four *dramatis personae*. The artificial notion of elective affinities implies in this context a natural determinism or a magical attractiveness of love that tends to destroy the legal and moral base of the bourgeois institution of marriage. Weber criticized Simmel for enthroning the notion of "interaction" (*Wechselwirkung*) as the fundamental sociological concept and for using "symbols" and "analogies" in a quasi-aesthetic manner.[42] But in spite of his critique, Weber himself often made use of a literary metaphor that Walter Benjamin in his Goethe study decoded as a *mythical* way of thinking.[43] It seems to be no accident that this metaphor also symbolizes the tragic decline of marriage as an institution. But it is also surprising to see that Weber employed an alchemistic metaphor for the historical genesis of modern capitalism, when Sombart had contrasted the old alchemistic ways of searching for wealth with the new capitalist spirit.[44] Talcott Parsons "solved" this "overcoded" problem by mistranslating the German term *Wahlverwandtschaften* as "correlations," instead of the more precise "elective affinities," and by favoring a term that is closer to Simmel's terminology than to that of Weber. Isn't this an interesting displacement within Parsons' *own* "discourse of the other" (*discours de l'autre*)?[45]

41 See Jacques Le Rider, "Das Werk des Weiblichen in der (Post-)Moderne," in Jacques Le Rider and Gérard Raulet, eds., *Verabschiedung der (Post-)Moderne? Eine interdisziplinäre Debatte* (Tübingen, 1987), 133–147.

42 See Max Weber, "Georg Simmel as Sociologist," *Social Research* 39 (1972): 155–163.

43 See Walter Benjamin, "Goethes Wahlverwandtschaften," in *Gesammelte Schriften I* (Frankfurt, 1974), 123–201; Benjamin also speaks of a "mythical play of shadows" (*mythisches Schattenspiel,* 140).

44 See Werner Sombart, *Der moderne Kapitalismus I: Die Genese des Kapitalismus* (Leipzig, 1902), 385–388.

45 On Parsons' relation to Simmel, see Donald N. Levine, *Simmel and Parsons: Two Approaches to the Study of Society* (New York, 1980).

# 9

# The Rise of Capitalism: Weber versus Sombart

HARTMUT LEHMANN

On February 21, 1990, in a speech to both houses of Congress, the Czechoslovak playwright elected president, Vaclav Havel, explained that his country needed a great deal of assistance from the United States, not financial aid primarily, but help in other areas. Assistance, for example, in "how to educate our offspring," "how to elect our representatives," and "how to organize our economic life so that it will lead to prosperity and not to poverty." In return, Havel remarked, Czechoslovakia could offer the United States its "experience and the knowledge that has come from it," in particular "specific experience," "one great certainty," namely, that "consciousness precedes being, and not the other way round, as Marxists claim." For this reason, Havel continued, "the salvation of this human world lies nowhere else than in the human heart, in the human power to reflect, in human meekness and in human responsibility."[1]

One hundred years ago, in the decade before the turn of the last century, young scholars like Werner Sombart, born in 1863, or Max Weber, born in 1864, were not so certain about Havel's "one great certainty." Weber and Sombart attempted to look into the historical background of the Marxist theory of history, and they set out to determine the relationship between the factors that Havel labeled "consciousness" and "being." In those years, both Sombart and Weber published a number of works in which they discussed the relationship between what Marxists called the "material basis" and the "nonmaterial superstructure," thus trying to explain the course of human development in general and the emergence of modern capitalism in particular.

By 1900, despite impressive scholarly achievements, the careers of

1 *The Washington Post*, February 22, 1990, A28.

both Sombart and Weber had not developed as either had probably imagined. As a result of his publications on German economic history, Sombart was considered a leftist by his peers and not fit for one of the chairs in his field at any major German university. Because of unexpected illness, Weber had been forced into what may be called semiretirement. Each in his own way believed himself to be an outsider; each struggled to gain recognition.

In the first decade of the twentieth century, through a series of important studies, Sombart and Weber managed to shape the content and determine the course of the debate about the emergence of modern capitalism. The outsiders had become insiders, or opinion leaders. The impact of their arguments on the origin of capitalism was felt well into the 1920s, and one may even argue that they influenced the debate on the history of capitalism well into the period after the Second World War.

Werner Sombart published his two-volume work, *Modern Capitalism,* in 1902.[2] Capitalism had come about, as Sombart explained in the first edition of this work, as a result of many factors and several developments, of which he considered the accumulation of capital income by landowners and merchants in the Middle Ages to be the most important. In the third part of this work, Sombart discussed "the genesis of the capitalistic spirit," dealing first with the awakening of the urge to earn and then with the development of economic rationalism. It is in these chapters that Sombart elaborated on what he called the "strange idea" that money should and could be multiplied through economic activities. In Sombart's view, this attitude was typical for Europeans, but it could not be explained by climate, or race, or by pointing to certain religious groups, as Eberhard Gothein had done in his *Economic History of the Black Forest.*[3] Rather, Sombart continued, it was during the Middle Ages that people had come to cherish the value of money, and secularization and urbanization had strongly supported this notion. By the end of the Middle Ages, he argued, the desire to earn and possess money, especially gold, had turned into a mass phenomenon.

According to Sombart, it was this desire that led people to search feverishly for gold, by digging or through alchemy, and it was in this context that he believed some people discovered that money could

---

2 Leipzig 1902. Vol. 1: *Die Genesis des Kapitalismus;* Vol. 2: *Die theorie der kapitalistischen Entwicklung.*
3 Strassburg 1892.

also be won through economic activity. No one knew, Sombart continued, who had made this discovery first. He suspected, however, that it must have been people of modest means; people who were sober and cool-minded, who calculated and understood business matters in a sharp, rationalistic way, but who were at the same time well acquainted with doing everyday financial transactions because they were lending money to others. In short, as Sombart explained in 1902, the spirit of capitalism could be found first among small shopkeepers and retailers, among profiteers of limited means, and, as Sombart went on to say, among those who did business among foreigners and not among their own people. Sombart concluded, therefore, that the rapid rise of the urge to make money had developed in Western Europe among foreigners living there, that is, among the Jewish part of the population, although, as he added, one should not overestimate their influence. Very often, as Sombart argued, doing business with outsiders had served the same purpose, that is, to develop the spirit of making money.

When discussing the impact of religion, Sombart made several statements. First, he observed that the rise of capitalism could not be explained fully by pointing out that the economically productive groups had been affiliated with certain religious communities. Then he remarked that the role of specific religious groups in the early history of capitalism, in particular the role of Protestant groups such as the Calvinists and the Quakers, was "too well-known a fact to require detailed explanation." Should anyone dispute this (by citing the example of Italian cities of the High Middle Ages or of German cities of the Late Middle Ages, which both possessed a highly developed capitalistic spirit) and insist that the Protestant religion was not the cause but the result of modern capitalist thinking, Sombart added, one could disprove such a view only by providing "empirical proof of concrete historical circumstances."[4]

After reading this paragraph, Weber, it seems, was unsatisfied by the inconsistent manner in which his friend and colleague had depicted the influence of religion. As an admirer of Eberhard Gothein, who had described the way the "Calvinist diaspora" had shaped the early history of capitalism and whom Sombart had cited, Weber set out to take a closer look at the "concrete historical circumstances" that Sombart had mentioned without having made an effort to clarify

---

4 Vol. 1, 380–381.

them. I agree with Bernhard vom Brocke, who calls Weber's essays on *The Protestant Ethic and the Spirit of Capitalism* Weber's reply to Sombart's explanation of the genesis of the capitalistic spirit in his *Modern Capitalism*.[5] In my view, we should not be misled by the fact that Weber mentioned Sombart only two or three times in the first version of his essay, that is, in 1904 and 1905, and that those places were quite insignificant. As I point out later, Weber mentioned Sombart much more often in the second version of his text in 1920. As far as the first version of Weber's essay is concerned, his arguments show how much he was stirred, or disturbed, by Sombart's explanations. In his essay, therefore, Weber not simply squarely refuted Sombart's account, but he did so by citing a wealth of sources on the importance of Protestantism for the development of the modern world in general and the spirit of capitalism in particular. Weber quoted extensively from seventeenth-century authors such as Richard Baxter, and, most important, he presented, step by step, the development of the spirit of capitalism from Luther's conception of the notion of calling, via the religious foundations of worldly asceticism, to the relationship of asceticism and the spirit of capitalism. What Weber offered in 1904–1905, it seems, was the empirical proof of concrete historical circumstances that Sombart had advocated in 1902.

Certain other aspects of Weber's essay can be mentioned here only briefly. Weber no doubt relied on his own earlier studies on the interdependence of various factors in history. He used and applied to his topic Georg Jellinek's path-breaking work on the importance of seventeenth-century pious dissenters for the development of basic political rights and personal liberties. He further enriched his insights with the help of the results of recent works on religious affiliation and social stratification, and he shaped his remarks and observations into more general theories of modernization.[6]

As Edgar Jaffé remarked some years later, Weber's essay, in turn, inspired Sombart to look into the matter again. "Undoubtedly stimulated by Max Weber," as Jaffé puts it,[7] Sombart published his *Die Juden und das Wirtschaftsleben* in 1911 and his *Der Bourgeois. Zur Geistesgeschichte des modernen Wirtschaftsmenschen* in 1913. In both of

---

5 Bernhard vom Brocke, ed., *Sombart's 'Moderner Kapitalismus.' Materialien zur Kritik und Rezeption* (Munich, 1987), 36.
6 See Hartmut Lehmann, "Ascetic Protestantism and Economic Rationalism: Max Weber Revisited After Two Generations," *Harvard Theological Review* 80 (1987): 307–320.
7 Edgar Jaffé, "Der treibende Faktor in der kapitalistichen Wirtschaftsordnung," *Archiv für Sozialwissenschaft und Sozialpolitik* 40 (1915): 4.

these works, and in some others, Sombart took issue with Weber's essay. As Sombart pointed out in an article in 1909, it was not only justifiable to uncover the influence that certain religious ideas had had for the rising class of capitalistic entrepreneurs, as Weber had done, but also, as he set out to do, to explain other factors in this process and to demonstrate how Puritanism had been shaped by historical forces. According to Sombart, Weber would be the last to object against the attempt to complement his work in this manner.[8]

Let us now examine what Sombart considered necessary in order to complement, or complete, Weber's argument. In his preface to *Die Juden und das Wirtschaftsleben,* Sombart wrote that he had wanted to dig "some tunnels deeper" than he had done previously, and in so doing he had discovered that Jewish influence in the history of capitalism was far greater than he had previously anticipated. Giving these matters a closer look, he had gained, with much certainty, the insight that the Jews were the ones who had caused economic progress wherever and whenever they had appeared, and had caused economic downfall wherever and whenever they had disappeared. As Sombart phrased it in another passage, the Jews had moved across Europe like the sun: Where they arrived, new life had blossomed; where they left, whatever had been in bloom had fallen into decay.[9]

In his 1911 book, Sombart set out to explain in detail the role of the Jews for modern economic development and the special qualifications of Jews for capitalistic enterprise. In large sections he discussed topics such as "The Objective Fitness of Jews for Capitalism," "The Relevance of Jewish Religion for Economic Life," "Jewish Identity," "How Jewishness Came about: the Problem of Race," and "The Destiny of the Jewish People." Furthermore, in this book, Sombart made some very controversial statements, for example, "America, in all her parts, is a Jewish country" and "What we call Americanism is, in large part, nothing but coagulated, clotted Jewish spirit." Further, in the language of popular Darwinism: "The homo Judaeus and the homo capitalisticus are members of the same species, as both are homines rationalistici artificiales."[10]

It is in this context that Sombart argued that he found an almost complete agreement between the basic ideas of the Puritans and the basic ideas of the Jews. Specifically, Sombart believed to have ob-

8 Werner Sombart, "Der kapitalistische Unternehmer," *Archiv für Sozialwissenschaft und Sozialpolitik* 29 (1909): 754–755.
9 *Die Juden und das Wirtschaftsleben* (Leipzig 1911), vi, 15.    10 Ibid., 31, 44, 281.

served the almost total agreement between Puritan and Jewish views
with regard to the rise of capitalism as discussed by Weber and himself: the preponderance of religious interest; the idea of spiritual certainty; the rationalization of daily life; innerworldly asceticism; the
merging of religious ideas and financial interest; the attempt to calcu-
late matters of sin and salvation. Sombart concluded: "Puritanism is,
means, represents, Judaism." On the basis of his own and Weber's
work, it was now possible, Sombart continued, to establish the spiritual linkage, even the spiritual conformity, between Puritanism and
Judaism.[11]

Sombart then posed the question of whether one could prove how
Puritanism had been influenced by the Jewish religion. He referred to
examples from seventeenth-century England, such as Cromwell's
veneration for the Old Testament, but he made no real effort to dig
"some tunnels deeper." Rather, he simply postulated that one could
probably derive Puritan thinking directly from Jewish doctrine and
then added that he left the clarification of the details to specialists in
the field of church history.[12]

In evaluating Sombart's argument, I think we should keep two
matters in mind. First, Sombart linked Puritanism and Jewish influence by associating them very closely, without clarifying in detail,
however, how he believed them to be linked. Second, by giving what
he considered ample proof for the role of Jewish influence in the
history of the rise of capitalism, he de facto replaced Weber's explanation and introduced an explanation of his own. Abstract rationalism
was typical of Jewish thinking, according to Sombart, as much as it
was typical of capitalism. It was in the wish to make money that the
innermost elements both of Jewish identity and of the spirit of capitalism converged and expressed themselves in perfection.[13] With
this, Sombart believed he had moved beyond Weber.

In the years that followed, Sombart articulated an ever-growing
number of arguments that undoubtedly were meant to supplement
(but that could be understood to be meant to undermine) Weber's
position on the historical causes of the rise of capitalism. In *Der
Bourgeois,* Sombart repeated much of what he had written earlier on
the relationship between the urge to make money and entrepreneurial
spirit, as well as on the role the Jews. At the same time, he included
large sections on the development of national economies, on what he

---

11 Ibid., 292, 293.    12 Ibid., 294.    13 Ibid., 329.

termed the biological foundations of *"Bourgeoisienaturen,"* and on the predisposition of certain peoples for capitalism. He even reintroduced topics that he had dismissed some years before, such as the role of religion in the rise of capitalism, including specifically a chapter on persecuted Christian minorities, especially Protestants.

Nevertheless, the differences between Sombart's and Weber's positions remained quite clear. When discussing the role of religion, for example, Sombart implied that there existed similarities among Catholics, Protestants, and Jews, thus blurring distinctions Weber had made. More important, when looking at Protestantism, Sombart argued that the Puritan ethic had been strongly influenced by early Christian ideals of poverty, that Baxter had condemned wealth, and that with him all Puritans had condemned the capitalistic spirit of making a profit in business, while neglecting to mention Luther or the teachings of Calvin that Weber had stressed in his study. Also, when he discussed "the migration of persecuted Christians, especially Protestants," Sombart used an argument that Weber had explicitly excluded, namely, that the struggle of persecuted religious minorities to make a living resulted in extraordinary economic activity, which, in turn, was one of the major causes for the rise of capitalism.

In the same work, Sombart reiterated some of what Weber had written about the relationship of the Puritan ethic and the rationalization of innerworldly life: that Puritanism demanded thrift and industry, as well as the use of time as a God-given opportunity to work for salvation, while condemning luxury and idleness. Even in these parts of his work, however, Sombart never followed Weber very closely. Rather, he seemed to attempt to incorporate parts of Weber's argument into his own line of thought without giving credit to the meaning of Weber's explanation.

Also in 1913, Sombart published two volumes on what he labeled studies on the history of the development of modern capitalism, one on war and capitalism, the other on luxury and capitalism. In the former volume, he discussed the various ways in which war had stimulated the production of and trade in goods over the centuries. In the latter, he explained how luxury consumption was related to the rise of capitalism.[14] Both studies were supposed to add new points of view, Sombart wrote, without mentioning Weber, but there can be

14 *Studien zur Entwicklungsgeschichte des modernen Kapitalismus,* Vols. 1 and 2 (Munich and Leipzig, 1913).

no doubt that especially Sombart's work on *Luxus und Kapitalismus* implicitly contradicted Weber's views. There was no way to combine or harmonize Weber's careful reflections on *The Protestant Ethic and the Spirit of Capitalism* with Sombart's rather straightforward exposition on "The Birth of Capitalism out of Luxury."[15] Weber's scrupulous Puritans and Sombart's luxury-minded courtiers lived in two different worlds.

Finally, in 1915 Sombart added yet another aspect. In his *Händler und Helden. Patriotische Besinnungen,* he contrasted what he called the "English trading mentality" with "German heroism." What the German fatherland needed, he wrote, was "a race of bold people with broad chests and light blue eyes. . . . Women with broad hips so that they could bear courageous warriors, and daring, courageous, tenacious men with strong bones so that they were capable of making war."[16] With remarks like these, it seems that Sombart embarked on a voyage that led him far away from his earlier works on the origins of modern capitalism, away also from the interests that he had shared with Weber, toward what may have been his most controversial work, that on *Deutscher Sozialismus,* published in 1934. A few years ago, Jeffrey Herf examined this embarrassing route in the chapter on Sombart in his *Reactionary Modernism.*[17]

Considering the direct and indirect ways in which Sombart had criticized Weber's views, and remembering the sharp manner in which Weber replied to other critics of his essay, the way Weber reacted to Sombart's various publications on the origins of capitalism appears almost moderate, although he was absolutely clear in the distinctions that he made. In defending his views against the attacks by H. Karl Fischer and Felix Rachfahl, Weber mentioned Sombart's studies two or three times, and in all instances in an approving manner. Differences that existed, Weber wrote in a footnote to his answer to Rachfahl, were differences of terminology and not differences of substance.[18] In a letter to Robert Michels written in 1906, Weber called Sombart the most likeable person if you are alone with him, while the presence of others would create for him, in Weber's view, an "audience."[19] In another letter, written to his brother Alfred

15 This is the title of chapter 5 of *Luxus und Kapitalismus.*
16 *Händler und Helden. Patriotische Besinnungen* (Munich and Leipzig, 1915), 121.
17 *Reactionary Modernism: Technology, Culture, and Politics in Weimar and the Third Reich* (Cambridge, 1984), 130–151, chap. 5: "Werner Sombart. Technology and the Jewish Question."
18 Max Weber, *Die Protestantische Ethik. II. Kritiken und Antikritiken,* ed. by Johannes Winckelmann (Munich and Hamburg, 1968), 28, 55–56, 170, 184.
19 Max Weber, *Briefe 1906–1908,* ed. by M. Rainer Lepsius and Wolfgang J. Mommsen (Tübingen, 1990), 173 (MWGA II/5).

Weber in 1907, Weber commented on a critical review that Hans Delbrück had published about Sombart's *Modern Capitalism*. Weber deplored the fact that Delbrück had reviewed the author as a person and not the book as a piece of scholarship. In the same letter he excused the "few blunders" that could be found in Sombart's work.[20] When Sombart lamented in 1908 that he had failed in his career completely, Weber reminded him that academic positions were not all that important and tried to console him by referring to the merits of his *Modern Capitalism*.[21]

All of these examples show one thing. Weber fully accepted that Sombart's views differed from his own without discounting Sombart's merits as a scholar; quite the reverse. Compared to the way Weber criticized his other critics, it seems that he believed that Sombart and he were analyzing and describing simply two sides of the same coin, thus complementing far more than contradicting each other.

Of course, a certain degree of rivalry seems to have shaped their relationship as scholars much more than Weber admitted in the letters in which he defended Sombart against attacks by others. Just as Sombart attempted to replace Weber's analysis of the origins of capitalism by referring to the role of the Jews, Weber came forth with arguments that served to contradict Sombart's explanation. Weber took issue with Sombart's views in treatises that were to become part of *Wirtschaft und Gesellschaft*. First, he stated that no one should deny that the Jews had played an important role in shaping economic development in the modern era, but he then went on to point out that the Jewish contribution had not been characteristic for those factors that shaped modern capitalism. "Neither those elements that are specifically new in the modern economic system, nor those specifically new in the modern economic ethos," were in his view "specifically Jewish." What was characteristic of the Jews was their status as a "pariah people," which led to a double ethical standard. According to Weber's interpretation, Jews used economic practices vis-à-vis others that they would never have used among themselves. In his opinion, this was the decisive difference: Whereas pious Puritans performed in the economic field with the best of conscience, their status as outsiders permitted Jews to employ business practices that Puritans abhorred.[22] In Weber's view, therefore, perhaps the only way the

20 MWGA II/5, 233.  21 Ibid., 605.
22 *Wirtschaft und Gesellschaft*, ed. by Johannes Winckelmann. (5th rev. ed. Tübingen, 1976), 370–374. See also S. Z. Klausner, *Introduction to Werner Sombart, The Jews and Modern*

Jews influenced the modern capitalistic ethic was by the fact that the Puritans had accepted and internalized some Jewish (that is, Old Testament) laws that served to strengthen the sense of legality within Puritan ethical thinking. In Weber's opinion, this, in turn, had to be related to modern bourgeois economic ethics.[23]

Moreover, just as Sombart was very sensitive when someone criticized his work, Weber also tended to look at scholarly matters in a highly personalized way. As Else Jaffé-Richthofen wrote to Sombart in a letter after Weber's death, she remembered very well "how in the summer of 1919, on the occasion of re-editing the "Spirit of Capitalism," he [Weber] borrowed "The Bourgeois" from Edgar [Jaffé] (his library had still not arrived [in Munich]) and half in jest, half in annoyance said: Sombart thinks I am also a 'bourgeois,' you know." This led Lawrence A. Scaff to the conclusion that "with respect to *Der Bourgeois,* Weber suspected that the study was about him."[24] Whether this interpretation is correct or not, we should recall that the inconsistencies in Sombart's study had not escaped Weber's attention, and that his remark may have implied that he was very well aware of how much Sombart's interpretation was different from his own, and in fact quite inferior. As Weber wrote in a letter to Sombart in 1913, "insofar as religion was concerned," in Sombart's *Die Juden und das Wirtschaftsleben,* "nearly every word was wrong."[25]

In the second version of his essay, *The Protestant Ethic and the Spirit of Capitalism,* prepared in 1919 and published in 1920, Weber included a number of footnotes in which he contrasted Sombart's views with his own. Through a number of changes in the text, by omitting certain sentences, by changing certain words, and especially by adding a number of paragraphs, Weber changed the tone of the revised version of his essay considerably. In the first version of the text he sounds as if he is presenting an interesting argument: He proceeds as if conducting an experiment. By contrast, in the second version, Weber appears to speak with an authoritative voice: He writes as if presenting the final results of a study that allow no objection. It is in this assertive manner that Weber in the second version called *Der*

*Capitalism.* (New Brunswick, N.J., 1982), lxxiv–lxxxv; Hans Liebeschütz, *Das Judentum im deutschen Geschichtsbild von Hegel bis Max Weber* (Tübingen, 1967), 310–315; Paul Mendes-Flohr, "Werner Sombart's The Jews and Modern Capitalism", *Leo Baeck Yearbook* 20 (1976): 87–107.

23 *Wirtschaft und Gesselschaft,* 717–719.
24 *Fleeing the Iron Cage. Culture, Politics, and Modernity in the Thought of Max Weber* (Berkeley, Los Angeles, and London, 1989), 202.
25 Quoted by Scaff, *Fleeing the Iron Cage,* 203.

*Bourgeois* "by far the weakest of his [Sombart's] larger works" and Sombart's theses, "completely untenable."[26] However, he did not discuss *Die Juden und das Wirtschaftsleben* in detail. In another footnote Weber remarked that Sombart had "by no means neglected" the "ethical aspects of the capitalistic entrepreneur," but he stressed that in Sombart's view of the problem, the entrepreneurial ethic appeared as "a result of capitalism," whereas he assumed "the opposite as an hypothesis."[27] Weber also inserted a long footnote in which he defended his use of Benjamin Franklin and denied the similarities that Sombart claimed to have detected between Franklin and the Renaissance writer Alberti. "The essential point of the difference," Weber remarked in this footnote, "is [to anticipate] that an ethic based on religion places certain psychological sanctions [not of an economic character] on the maintenance of the attitude prescribed by it, sanctions which, so long as the religious belief remains alive, are highly effective and which mere worldly wisdom like that of Alberti does not have at its disposal." Furthermore, "such an ethic" gained "an independent influence on the conduct of life and thus on the economic order" only "in so far as these sanctions work, and above all, [only] in the direction in which they work, which is very often different from the doctrine of the theologians." This was, Weber concluded, "the point" of his whole essay, and he had not expected that it would be so "completely overlooked."[28] Not all the footnotes of the second edition of *The Protestant Ethic* in which Weber criticizes Sombart can be cited here. Weber noted, for example, that Sombart had "completely misrepresented the significance of the prohibition of interest."[29] In Weber's view, both Sombart and Lujo Brentano had "badly misunderstood" the reasons why he had introduced Puritan ethical writers, as they cited them "as codifications of rules of conduct without ever asking which of them were supported by psychologically effective religious sanctions."[30] Specifically, they had not understood the way he had interpreted Baxter. They had overlooked the fact that he had "attempted to show how, in spite of its antimammonistic doctrines, the spirit of this ascetic religion nevertheless, just as in the monastic communities, gave birth to economic rationalism because it placed a premium on what was most important for it: the fundamentally ascetic rational motives."[31] Finally, in yet another

---

26 *The Protestant Ethic and the Spirit of Capitalism,* trans. by Talcott Parsons, ed. by Anthony Giddens (New York, 1976), 191.
27 Ibid., 193.  28 Ibid., 194–198.  29 Ibid., 201.  30 Ibid., 217.  31 Ibid., 259.

footnote, Weber did not fail to repeat "that Jewish capitalism was speculative pariah–capitalism, while the Puritan was bourgeois organization of labour."[32]

If we compare the views that Weber and Sombart expressed on the causes, and the rise, of capitalism in the years between 1905 and 1920, three observations seem in order. First, whereas Sombart's publications sought to dispute the results of the one work that Weber had written after his illness, and that he defended as if it was valid proof of his regained capacity as a scholar, Weber, despite all differences, remained loyal to Sombart. In a footnote in the second version of his essay, Weber mentioned that Sombart had written important works and that even those "who feel themselves continually and decisively disagreeing" with him, "and who reject many of his theses, have the duty to do so only after a thorough study of his work."[33] Even though he disagreed with Sombart on many points, Weber, the outsider, it seems, retained a high regard for the scholarship of the other outsider, Sombart, whom he called his friend. Second, although the correspondence between the two, to my knowledge, is scanty, and although scholarly matters were not discussed at length in the letters that we do have, we can be certain that each one read and responded to what the other one wrote almost to the point that the sequence of their works on the rise of capitalism between 1902 and 1920 can be called a dialogue. In the course of this dialogue, Sombart introduced and employed various arguments, whereas Weber attempted to clarify, to defend, and thus to solidify, the position he had taken in 1904–1905. Sombart's position, therefore, seems to waver; he is inconsistent to the point of being eclectic, whereas Weber's position appears firm and well founded. Third, the difference in scholarly style between Sombart's texts on the rise of capitalism and Weber's text is striking. Certainly, both agreed that the rise of capitalism could not be explained in a monocausal way, that multiple factors had to be taken into account, and that there were no laws of development based on race, or climate, or religion, or class. In analyzing the rise of capitalism, however, Weber and Sombart used different techniques and operated on a different level of precision. Weber can be compared to an anatomist who dissects a vital nerve; Sombart can be seen as a painter of landscapes who uses color plentifully and changes his style

---

32 Ibid., 271. See also Max Weber, *Wirtschaftsgeschichte. Abriss der universalen Sozial- und Wirtschaftsgeschichte* (Munich, 1932), 307.
33 *The Protestant Ethic*, 198.

according to trends. Bernhard vom Brocke thinks that frequent mistakes, unsound theories, and imprecise proof in Sombart's works should be judged of secondary importance if compared to the richness of his historical vision, the boldness of his synthesis, and his impressive overview.[34] I disagree. If one checks Sombart's texts closely, one can observe that he fails to answer the decisive questions. By contrast, Weber is much more precise in his arguments, no less bold in his vision, and operates on a level of theoretical insight never reached, and not even imagined, by Sombart. In this sense, therefore, it is a fortunate turn in the development of scholarship that Weber, and not Sombart, inspired future generations of historians and social scientists to dig "some tunnels deeper."

In examining the works of Sombart and Weber on the rise of capitalism, Lujo Brentano criticized both. In Brentano's view, Weber had ignored the significance of Catholicism; he had exaggerated the interest of Protestant believers in economic matters, he had overlooked that those Puritans who had become rich also left Puritanism; and above all, he had failed to take into consideration the emancipation from traditionalism that originated in Italy. According to Brentano, Benjamin Franklin stood in line with empirical philosophers and was a friend of physiocrats like Adam Smith. By contrast, Brentano called Sombart's book of 1911 one of the most depressing matters in German scholarship, and went on to label Sombart frivolous, arrogant, irresponsible, ruthless, and arbitrary. Beyond that, Brentano took great care to disprove and refute Sombart's view of the role of Jews in the history of capitalism.[35] Although he could not dispel the prejudice that Sombart helped to spread, in light of German history since Brentano, one is inclined to praise his farsightedness.

Although there can be no doubt that Brentano had also come forth with arguments that served to undermine Weber's thesis, Weber was even more cautious in his reply to Brentano[36] than in the way he responded to Sombart. Obviously, there were personal ties that have to be taken into account. In 1919, when Weber decided to become Brentano's successor at the University of Munich, he had been a friend of Brentano for many years and called him "our honored master" in the second edition of the *Protestant Ethic*.[37] In fact, Weber

---

34 Vom Brocke, *Sombarts 'Moderner Kapitalismus,'* 49.
35 Lujo Brentano, *Die Anfänge des modernen Kapitalismus* [1913] (Munich, 1916), 78–199 (III. Exkurs: Handel, Puritanismus, Judentum und Kapitalismus).
36 *The Protestant Ethic,* 187, 190, 192–193, 198, 205, 209–210, 217, 259, 283.
37 Ibid., 185.

probably used Brentano's former office at the University of Munich when he revised the text of the *Protestant Ethic* in 1919–1920. It seems, however, that personal elements such as these are only part of the story. Weber liked to exchange arguments and to look at the different aspects of scholarly matters. In the debate on the origins of capitalism, he seems to have accepted both Sombart and Brentano as partners. We should not overlook, however, subtle differences that he makes. Through Weber's handling of the criticism of Sombart and Brentano in the revised version of *The Protestant Ethic,* he demonstrated that he was equal, if not superior, to Sombart[38] and nothing less than the "honored master" Brentano's peer.

38 Differences in personal evolution and in character between Sombart and Weber are analyzed in Alfred Mitzman's "Personal Conflict and Ideological Options in Sombart and Weber," in *Max Weber and His Contemporaries,* ed. by Wolfgang J. Mommsen and Jürgen Osterhammel (London, 1987), 99–105.

# PART II

*Reception and Response*

# 10
# The Longevity of the Thesis:
# A Critique of the Critics

MALCOLM H. MACKINNON

## 1. INTRODUCTION

The Weber thesis controversy has been one of the most significant and well-publicized disputes of twentieth-century scholarship. The multidisciplinary background of those who have engaged the thesis is a mark of this significance: Sociologists, historians, economists, and theologians have in one way or another taken up Weber's famous claim that the Protestant ethic was in some fashion responsible for the spirit, then the form, of capitalism. My purpose is to trace selectively the career of only one side of this debate, the side that has challenged Weber's claim on the causal efficacy of religious ideas. The purpose in doing so is to demonstrate why the thesis has shown such remarkable durability, surviving relatively intact for over eighty years. It can claim such an achievement, despite the fact that the ideal-religious assumptions upon which the thesis is predicated are incorrect, as I have recently demonstrated.[1] The current undertaking therefore seeks to enlarge upon this earlier work, showing in the process that three generations of critics must be held substantially answerable for the longevity of Weber's venerable polemic.

When selectively following in the footsteps of these critics, we shall see that they can be held responsible on two counts, the first an error of omission, the second an error of commission: (1) The earliest critics failed to take up and resolve Weber's theological mistakes, creating an inviting opening that Weber readily exploited in his replies to their commentary; (2) the critics erroneously assumed that Weber is all idealism and no materialism, again conceding the high ground, which allowed Weber to respond effectively to their sallies.

1 M. H. MacKinnon, "Part I: Calvinism and the Infallible Assurance of Grace," *British Journal of Sociology* 39 (1988): 143–177; M. H. MacKinnon, "Part II: Weber's Exploration of Calvinism," *British Journal of Sociology* 39 (1988): 178–210.

211

He was able to do so because of his causal pluralism, his receptivity to both ideal and material factors as agents of social change. Weber thus succeeded in deflating his adversaries by the simple expedient of recognizing their material counterclaims, adroitly showcasing the other side of his causal chain in the process. Weber accepted such counterclaims to the extent that the causal weight assigned to them was not necessary and sufficient for capitalism triumphant. For Weber, material preconditions were necessary and sufficient only when combined with his ideal precondition: sanctified works in a calling. From the other direction, ideal preconditions were necessary and sufficient only when combined with relevant material preconditions.[2] This is Weber's pluralism.

The critics' error of omission was that they failed to identify, and hence to challenge, the spiritual footing upon which Weber's thesis rested. The critical point in Weber's argument was that seventeenth-century dogmatic-predestinarian Calvinism confronted the believer with a crisis of proof on his prospects for salvation. Yet so deeply felt was the need for redemptive assurance by the doubt-stricken soul that the pastoral literature of Puritan divines responded to this cry by inserting good works in a mundane calling as a sign of grace. Private profit is hereby the recipient of Weber's "psychological sanction" and is equated with eternal bliss, creating an "ideal" stimulus for capitalist acquisition. Such a line of thought creates a critical problem for Weber. Whereas, on the one hand, the pastoral literature recommends asceticism in an earthly calling as an indicator of deliverance, on the other it savagely rebukes the pursuit of wealth as the mark of the Beast. Weber resolves this difficulty by introducing unintendedness. In this situation, ideal interests are best served by ignoring antimammonistic doctrines and following instead those injunctions calling for earthly accumulation.

Weber's argument is wrong for two reasons. First, there is no crisis of proof in dogmatic Calvinism that tenders an absolute guarantee of assurance from the use of good works and introspection. Second, works in dogma and pastoral advice have nothing to do with earthly toil but are spiritual duties that call for the enactment of the Law. Hence, there is then no unintendedness, no call for devotion to a workaday pastime, but only exhortations to follow one's heavenly

2  The origin of this insight into Weber's causal reasoning must be accorded to N. M. Hanson, "The Protestant Ethic as a General Precondition for Economic Development," *Canadian Journal of Economics and Political Science* 29 (1963): 462–474.

calling. In consequence, the calling of Calvinism is not in possession of any unique properties and did not contribute to capitalism in the way that Weber claims.

The paramount problem for the critics here is that they fail to understand and question Weber's crisis of proof and are thereby unable to develop an accurate measure of Christian works, although Samuelson is able to gain a glimmer of their otherworldly constitution from another direction. Without the benefit of this understanding, the critics, although able to marshal some telling observations, are unable to make them stick, because Weber is able to reply that his argument has been misunderstood. Thus the critics correctly observe that the Catholic calling is similar to the Calvinist calling; that there were many elements in the medieval church favorable to capitalism; that the great merchant princes of the Renaissance and the medieval period were fully capitalist; and that capitalism thus antedated the Reformation. Still oblivious to the heart of Weber's argument on the calling, the critics also accurately charge that the antimammonism of the Puritan literature made it antipathetic rather than favorable to capitalist expansion. As such, Sombart argues that the religious character of Judaism was more favorable in this respect, that it gave greater encouragement to rational acquisition.

Despite the fact that considerable evidence supports these views, Weber is able to repulse them effectively by erroneously falling back on the properties he has assigned the Puritan calling. Although Catholicism and Judaism, for that matter, also may well have counseled the scrupulous performance of worldly toil, Weber counters, these religions did not generate a spiritual sanction for labor, which is a different matter altogether. Weber's conception of capitalism as unique follows from these deliberations. The spirit of capitalism as the offspring of such a sanction is the crucible of this singularity, a spirit that other religions of the world have been unable to muster. Thus "authentic" capitalism could not and did not exist in the Middle Ages or the Renaissance, since the ultramundane motivations for its creation were lacking. Weber handles commentary on Puritan antimammonism in much the same way. His tactic of unintendedness is to admit that the ethical observations of Calvinists were replete with condemnations of wealth. Yet these curses of cupidity were simply ignored by the laity, who followed instead the direction of their ideal inclinations, good works in a calling as the seal of grace.

Combined with their error of omission, the critics' error of commission renders their position even more untenable. Their second deficit of credibility stems from the fact that they claim, either explicitly or implicitly, that Weber is an ideal monist, that his causal analysis is confined to ideal factors. In the commission of this error, the critics have pointed the finger at structural factors and their causal contribution to bourgeois capitalism. One side of this argument features the impact of the Discoveries, with the subsequent increase in European stocks of bullion and hence the money supply, with inflation as a result. Yet Weber's pluralism is not hostile to these or related lines of thought. It in fact agrees with the causal weight of these factors, but in the limited sense that although structural factors may well have been necessary for the capitalist spirit, they could not become the sufficient cause without the necessary ideal supplement from the calling. From the other direction, Weber uses the same line of reasoning to handle the charge that in some historical situations the victory of Calvinism was not always associated with the victory of rational accumulation. The calling was necessary but not sufficient for formal rationality, Weber reasons. The addition of material preconditions was also required to realize the final result.

Another tactic of the critics is to claim that Calvinism's main contribution to the modern world lay in another direction, its impact on democracy in particular. Once again, Weber concurs, for the causal efficacy of his religious ideas was broad enough to see the rationalization of life proceed on several fronts in addition to the economic sphere.

The Weber thesis has thus endured because the critics make these two strategic blunders: (1) They have failed to address and thus resolve the theological substructure upon which the thesis rests, and (2) they have groundlessly assumed that Weber is an ideal determinist. In my critique of the critics, I first correct their error of omission, delineating the theological backdrop as Weber sees it while demonstrating its inaccuracy. I then trace the criticism of Weber's thesis in three temporal stages, showing in the process that the protagonists of each stage commit anew the oversights of their predecessors. Rachfahl's polemics constitute the first stage; those of Sombart, Brentano, and Simmel the second; and those of Samuelson, Robertson, Tawney, Trevor-Roper, and others the third. Whereas Weber was able to reply directly to the critics of the first two stages, the third is post-Weber, subsequent to his untimely death. Nevertheless, this third stage raised nothing new in substance, tabling issues that

Weber had already addressed in his replies to the first and second stages. Some new points of detail were raised in the third stage, but Weber had anticipated them and responded effectively to them.

## 2. WEBER'S THEOLOGICAL FOUNDATION FOR THE CALLING AND ITS REBUTTAL

The theological-ideal link to the calling – the link so widely misunderstood by Weber's detractors – takes the following form. The mid-sixteenth century predestinarian basis of Calvin's soteriology survives intact into the seventeenth century in the synods of Dort, Westminster, and Savoy.[3] The thrust of Calvin's system, one with momentous historical consequences for Weber, is the crisis of proof it presents to the true believer. Synodal doctrine is one of utter gloom and despair, complete with an omniscient and vengeful deity who has decreed for eternity the fortunate few for election, whereas the unfortunate majority has been doomed to perdition. Weber thus sees dogma in much the same way as Calvin, reporting that one's standing before God is made impossible by Calvin's system, of which Anglo-dogma is a complete reflection. Calvinism is unable to incorporate knowledge of assurance because of the complete transcendentality of its God and the inability to fathom His secret decrees.[4] By Weber's account, unadulterated predestinarianism of this sort spurns the use of means (works): Man is the passive recipient of salvation.[5] In Weber's mind the "pure doctrine of predestined grace" was never entirely eliminated from Calvinism, inasmuch as acts of the individual could in no way influence God's election.[6] By extension, the devout can never know their calling, which is "both impossible to pierce and presumptuous to question";[7] personal salvation always remains "above the threshold of consciousness,"[8] forever shrouded in divine mystery. "The elect are and remain God's invisible church."[9]

The wall behind which Calvin and thus dogma conceal the ultimate reward provided precious little solace to the believer. How did theological circumstances respond to this redemptive impasse in dogma? According to Weber, it came to pass that God became perceptible to the Puritan "only" in the sense that he became aware of

---

3 M. Weber, *The Protestant Ethic and the Spirit of Capitalism* (New York, 1958), 99, 102, 226.
4 M. Weber, *Economy and Society* (Los Angeles, 1978), 541–544, 548.
5 Weber, *The Protestant Ethic*, 103, 105.    6 Weber, *Economy*, 575.
7 Weber, *The Protestant Ethic*, 103.    8 Ibid., 223.    9 Ibid., 110, 114, 232.

His inner presence through worldly activity.[10] So deep was the motivational yearning for salvation that Baxter and other Puritan divines brought pastoral advice to the rescue. More sensitive to the ideal needs of parishioners, pastoral advice stands in muted contrast to dogma, creating works in a mundane calling as a "sign" of grace.[11] Pastoral works constitute "the technical means, not of purchasing salvation, but of getting rid of the fear of damnation."[12] For Weber, it is a worldly calling alone that "disperses religious doubt and gives the certainty of grace."[13] "Baxter's principal work," Weber tells us, "is dominated by the continuously repeated, almost passionate preaching of hard, continuous bodily and mental labour."[14] So it follows that "the Puritan idea of the calling and the premium it placed on ascetic conduct was bound directly to influence the development of a capitalist way of life."[15] The Protestant ethic that is the calling in this sense promotes the spirit of capitalism because it represents the pursuit of "private profitableness," which "is not only morally but actually enjoined."[16] Providential purpose, or, in Weber's terminology, a "psychological sanction," is here bestowed on the profit motive, giving a divine stamp of approval to the "activities of the business man."[17]

Yet Weber faces a critical problem in the pastoral literature – a problem that he seeks to resolve by introducing the notion of "unintendedness." A conceptual by-product of the crisis of proof, unintendedness has not been grasped by those who have grappled with the Weber thesis. Weber used unintendedness to explain away an apparent contradiction in ministerial writing. On the one hand, this writing exhorts followers to pursue profit assiduously in a worldly calling; on the other hand, this same writing is crammed with cries of antimammonism, that the accumulation of riches is evil in the eyes of the Lord. Weber's strategy is to concede the antimammonism of the pastoral literature but to circumvent it with unintendedness: "I have attempted to show in spite of its anti-mammonistic doctrines, the spirit of ascetic religion nevertheless . . . gave birth to economic rationalism."[18] "Of course this was not the purpose of the Puritan ethic, especially not the encouragement of money-making; on the contrary, as in all Christian denominations, wealth was regarded as dangerous and full of temptations."[19]

10 Ibid., 113–114.    11 Ibid., 228.    12 Ibid., 115.    13 Ibid., 112.    14 Ibid., 158.
15 Ibid., 166.    16 Ibid., 163.    17 Ibid., 163.    18 Ibid., 259.
19 Weber, *Economy*, 1200.

Weber further admits that the Puritan literature is less tolerant of Mammon than the medieval church.[20] Yet this strident opposition is effectively overcome because the cultural consequences of the Reformation were "unforeseen" and even unwished-for results of the reformers.[21] Salvation of the soul was the primary concern of the founders of Calvinism as well as other Puritan sects, in spite of which the capitalist spirit flourished anyway.[22]

Why was this religious opposition to accumulation simply brushed aside by the nascent Puritan capitalist? Weber never fully elaborates his position on this score, which may be responsible, at least in part, for the critics' repeated reference to Puritan contempt for covetousness as a fatal flaw in Weber's argument. To apprehend Weber's thinking on unintendedness, some appreciation of his "ultimate value" (itself a residue of Kant's categorical imperative) should clarify the issue. Not unreasonably, Weber cites the seventeenth century as an age in which concern for the afterlife was paramount in the minds of men.[23] This Kantian command of reason thus sought to establish with certainty its state of grace: How can I be certain of my salvation?[24] was the overriding question of the age. Yet dogma – and this point is critical – rather than giving some kind of reassurance to the ultimate value, responds instead with the proverbial "kick in the teeth." Shunned by dogma's *decretum horrible,* the ultimate value then begins to cast about frantically, looking for some way out of the existential impasse. At this point of desperation, pastoral advice provides a flotation device for the drowning victim. In contrast to dogma, pastoral writing tacitly counsels that eternal blessedness can be sealed by the effective performance of good works in an earthly calling. Yet at the very time that the pastoral literature provides for this yearning, it also warns against wholesale immersion in things of this world, the lust for riches in particular. Faced with this dilemma, the ultimate value in search of redemption at any cost simply ignores these antimammonistic doctrines, for works in a calling hold the greatest allure. In this way, Calvinism unintentionally provides a psychological sanction for profit making.

By Weber's reckoning, Calvinism is unique precisely because it unintentionally generates this psychological sanction for accumulation. Among other reasons, this is why capitalism first developed in England, a conclusion that Weber's comparative studies of world

20 Weber, *The Protestant Ethic,* 157.    21 Ibid., 90.    22 Ibid., 89.
23 Ibid., 109–110.    24 Ibid., 110, 229.

religions mean definitively to establish. Neither Islam, Judaism, Taoism, Confucianism, Hinduism, nor Buddhism give the search for
salvation a this-worldly direction. In these religions, divine approval
instead derives from different salvation methodologies, such as con-
templative bliss, gnosis, and other alternatives. Calvinism is also
unique in the Occident, which again in part accounts for England
as the leading capitalist power. Because neither Catholicism nor
Lutheranism confronts the believer with a crisis of proof, neither is
able to impart Calvinism's motivational powerhouse to a this-worldly calling. Instead, Catholicism and Lutheranism direct the ultimate
value, the search for the certainty of salvation, in an other-worldly
direction: sacramental solace for the Catholic and the *unio mystica* for
the Lutheran. Lutherans can obtain absolute certainty of their election through contemplation, a salvation methodology that seeks
mystical union and fusion with the deity. Weber notes that these
circumstances make it impossible for Lutheranism to attach religious
significance to "external activity."[25] Besides, Lutheranism specifically decrees practical conduct to be *adiaphora,* spiritually indifferent,
with no bearing on salvation whatsoever.[26]

In a similar way, the Catholic offer of grace through the sacraments
steers the ultimate value away from the world. Unlike Lutheranism,
Catholicism is more this-worldly in the sense that it recognizes the
importance of works in its methodology of redemption. Yet it is
unable to impart to these works the motivational sinew of Calvinism,
the sacraments, the confessional, extreme unction, and the like,
which provide for the needs of the ultimate value. As a result of this
motivational deficit, Catholic works are atomized, not rationally unified, by the ascetic determination of the Puritan.[27] Furthermore, the
Church regards work in the world with dogmatic indifference, Aquinas preaching its utility only for the maintenance of individual and
community.[28] On those occasions when Rome does lend its support
to an ascetic calling, the believer is led down the corridor of monastic
seclusion, not into the world but in flight from it.[29]

There are two fundamental theological flaws in Weber's line of
reasoning, flaws that mean that Calvinism did not give a divine
stamp of approval to earthly toil: (1) There is no crisis of proof in the
*Westminster Confession of Faith,* the dogmatic culmination of seventeenth-century Calvinism upon which Weber so heavily relies, and

25 Ibid., 113.   26 Ibid., 84, 160, 215.   27 Ibid., 115–116.
28 Ibid., 211.   29 Ibid., 80, 121.

(2) in Christianity generally and Calvinism in particular, works have nothing to do with mundane activities. As soteriologically conceived in relation to salvation, works are spiritual activities that call for obedience to the Law.

On the first point, and to Weber's credit, he does give a good account of Calvin, stating that his predestinarianism makes it virtually impossible for the believer to seal his state of grace psychologically. Calvin reveals in his *Institutes of the Christian Religion* that the search for election is looking through a glass darkly, imperceptible to the powers of fallen man who is "sunken in infinite filth!"[30] Not by works can anyone plumb his deliverance – works that, in the last resort, belong to that great Antichrist of Rome;[31] not by "knowledge" can we know our salvation because the Spirit works secretly and mysteriously in connection with predestination;[32] not by human powers of perception or rational proof either, whose dubious utility is restricted to temporal squalor;[33] and not by internal examination, introspection, and contemplation, which bring fear, consternation, and damnation rather than assurance.[34] Forever beyond our corrupted natures, we can never discern true saving faith in ourselves, for God alone is privy to this eternal secret.[35] The only hope for the believer is Calvin's *sola fide,* justification by persevering faith alone.

Yet if Weber hits the mark on Calvin, he errs in the degree to which his predestinarianism is preserved by the *Westminster Confession of Faith.* Covenant theology, of which the *Westminster Confession* is the dogmatic exemplar, virtually obliterates Calvin's predestinarianism and its crisis of proof, substituting in its stead an anthropocentric rather than a God-centered divinity. It invites the believer to validate his election infallibly through the use of good works and internal examination. The opening passages of the *Westminster Confession,* which appear to give ringing endorsement to unadulterated predestinarianism, no doubt were a source of confusion for Weber (and the critics, too). In fact Weber approvingly cites some of these passages in *The Protestant Ethic,*[36] not realizing that had he carefully read on, he would have discovered that God's so-called immutable decrees are nothing more than window dressing. In the first of many frontal assaults on Calvin, the *Westminster Confession* explains that this

30 J. Calvin, *Institutes of the Christian Religion* (Philadelphia, 1960), 763.
31 Ibid., 264, 286, 288–289.
32 Ibid., 537–542.    33 Ibid., 559.    34 Ibid., 746, 749, 759, 765–766, 786–787.
35 Ibid., 280, 542–543, 580–581.    36 Weber, *The Protestant Ethic,* 100–101.

"mysterious doctrine" must be accorded special care so that "men may be assured that they have been eternally chosen from the certainty of their effectual calling."[37] The way to secure this certainty was to perform good works, as they have been set forth by God's commandments, rather than to search for mundane spoils. Believers "should diligently attempt to identify what good works God has commanded in His word and then try their best to do all of them."[38]

Significantly, the *Westminster Confession* admits that some things are destined by "secondary causes,"[39] which dumps Calvin's immutable decree into the dustbin of history. The voluntarism, the dedication, and the sincerity of the true believer mobilize these secondary causes, albeit with the helping hand of God: He through Christ "is pleased to accept and reward what is sincerely done."[40] Not only would Calvin totally reject the use of works in this way, but he would also reject the use of introspection to seal election. For it is upon the devout performance of good works that the Westminster divines recommend introspection to establish the certainty of grace. The certainty gleaned from introspection, they state, is based not on the "fallible hope of guesswork or probabilities" but on the "infallible assurance of faith," whose acquisition is forthcoming from the "ordinary working of the Spirit."[41] There is no crisis of proof here. Salvation is there for the taking for those who cherish it. "[T]hose who truly believe in the Lord Jesus, who honestly love him and try to walk in good conscience before him, may in this life be assured with certainty that they are in a state of grace."[42]

Without the dogmatic crisis of proof, Weber's psychological sanction for a worldly calling in the pastoral literature and the ultimate unintendedness of it all comes crashing earthward. But how does Weber arrive at the conclusion that ministerial reflection counsels earthly toil? He does so by misinterpreting the meaning of works in this context. For there is no hiatus between dogma and the pastoral sphere. Both preach the spiritual instrumentality of good works to secure election. This is particularly so for Baxter, Weber's pastoral paragon for works in a calling. In contrast to Weber's earthly interpretation, Baxter's "true doctrine of good works" is spiritual obedience to the Law, simply to do the best we can that is pleasing to God. And though all our works must remain ultimately imperfect, Baxter states, "Christ hath so fulfilled the Law of Works, as to merit

37 *The Westminster Confession of Faith* (Greenwood, S.C., 1981), 8.
38 Ibid., 25.   39 Ibid., 10.   40 Ibid., 25.   41 Ibid., 25.   42 Ibid., 28.

for us."[43] Thus Baxter's use of works as other-worldly labor mirrors their employment by dogma, just as his experimentalism, testing the purity of faith in ourselves, is a reflection of dogmatic thought. To ensure passage from this life to the next, Baxter provides a list of instructions on how to make thoughts "effectual through meditation,"[44] to "make sure" of our election by introspection.[45] There is not a word in Baxter that urges the pursuit of private profit as a way of earning favor from God.

What then is the Puritan doctrine of the calling of which Weber makes so much? First, there is a spiritual (often called "effectual") calling that alone carries redemptive significance; and, second, there is a temporal calling or callings that are indifferent in divine calculations of spiritual worth. On these matters, Perkins advises that Christian freedom was purchased by the blood of Christ and the covenant of grace. Freedom under grace means that acts not expressly commanded or forbidden by God in the Decalogue are called "things indifferent" or "natural activity," in contrast to "spiritual activity," which remains a Christian duty.[46] Christ's sacrifice in purchasing our freedom signals remission of the ceremonial law of the Old Testament whereupon the Redeemer now merits for our imperfect obedience only on those elements of the Law still binding, namely, the Decalogue. Perkins' views are ultimately legitimated into creed by the *Westminster Confession,* which affirms that good works are only those performed by Him and His holy word and do not include other works, no matter how well intentioned or passionately promoted by men.[47] As far as they go, which is not very far, Weber's thoughts on the Puritan calling are marked by ambivalence, and in one instance they admit the standpoints of Perkins and the *Westminster Confession.* We are told that the sects, specifically Baptists and Quakers, held workaday activity to be *adiaphora,* as did "some" Calvinist denominations.[48] This is virtually all Weber has to say on the matter, and the reader is left to presume that, like money making, the psychological sanction is enough to negate these doctrines of indifference unintentionally.

True to Scripture and to the theological climate that he inhabited, Baxter's reflections on the calling take this form: There is a heavenly

---

43 R. Baxter, *A Christian Directory* (London, 1678), 21–30, 107.
44 Ibid., 255–261.    45 Ibid., 3.
46 W. Perkins, *William Perkins, 1558–1602: English Puritanist* (The Hague, 1966), 44.
47 *Westminster,* 25.    48 Weber, *The Protestant Ethic,* 150, 257–258.

calling and an earthly calling or callings, the latter disqualified from making a positive contribution to our deliverance. Baxter notes that the apostle uses the calling to distinguish an unmarried from a married person, a servant from a freeman or from an individual who adopts a trade or assumes an office.[49] Adopting this temporal pluralism, Baxter speaks of a calling to occupation in one instance, to public affairs in another, and to service in the church in yet another.[50] Above all else, the devout must ensure that their mundane callings in no way impede the prosecution of the greatest good of all: their heavenly calling. Baxter states: "Choose that employment or calling . . . in which you may be most serviceable to God. Choose not that in which you may be most honorable in the world; but that which you may do most good and best escape sinning."[51]

Baxter repudiates riches precisely because they invariably reverse these priorities: Wealth as the singular pursuit of life leaves precious little of ourselves to devote to the highest good, namely, effectual calling and the heavenly duties attendant to it. For these reasons, the poor are held to be more receptive to the glad tidings of the Gospel whereas "the rich are proud and obstinate and will not endure the conduct of the ministry."[52] So, although our worldly labors are of themselves indifferent, they become sinful as substitutes for pure worship. For Baxter, love of the world is the most common cause of damnation, and he pleads to "labor to feel the great wants which worldly wealth will not supply."[53] Thus there is no theologically constructed unintendedness at work here, no pastoral contradiction between the urgency to accumulate, on the one hand, and antimammonistic doctrines, on the other. On these matters we are merely required to follow Baxter's words: "Above all, God and Mammon cannot be reconciled."[54]

With no crisis of proof in dogma, once Weber's misunderstanding of the doctrine of works is corrected, his interpretation of the Puritan calling collapses. Because it awaits all who are disposed to accept it, redemption for Calvinism, as for Lutheranism, and Catholicism, carries the ultimate value in an other-worldly direction to the Spirit, where it there reposes in the lap of the Lord. Also, as for Lutheranism and Catholicism, work in the world is *lex naturae,* for the Calvinist incapable of making a positive contribution to our justifica-

49 Baxter, *Directory,* 110.    50 Ibid., 110.    51 Ibid., 110.
52 R. Baxter, *The Autobiography of Richard Baxter* (London, 1931), 82.
53 Baxter, *Directory,* 218–219.    54 Ibid., 13.

tion but negatively capable of leading us away from true devotion in two ways: in the first place by sloth, for he that refuseth to work, as Baxter cites Scripture, shall be forbidden to eat;[55] and, in the second place, by the reverse, by the immersion of self in earthly futility to the inevitable exclusion of dedicated worship. Unqualified commitment to things of this world leads the sensuous down the primrose path of cupidity, where damnation is their fate. In spiritual terms, therefore, the earthly calling is a form of double jeopardy, in two ways capable of casting the wayward into the bottomless pit: Believers incur a heavenly deficit by not doing the calling at all, just as they incur a heavenly deficit by doing the calling too much. Again, the significant point here is that temporal obligations are at best indifferent and at worst sinful; they cannot make a contribution to the realization of celestial paradise. It is a grim twist of irony that Weber would choose such a spiritually worthless vehicle to realize his causal ambitions.

### 3. WEBER'S "ANTICRITICAL LAST WORD" TO RACHFAHL

Rachfahl as principal of the initial stage of Weber thesis criticism is eager to score four points, the first three committing the error of omission and the fourth the error of commission: (1) Motives such as power, honor, and security are more important impulses for accumulation than religious motives; (2) attacking the singularity that Weber assigns to the Puritan calling, Rachfahl counters that the Catholic laity was also charged to work in the world and thereby was the beneficiary of the Puritan's inner-worldly asceticism; (3) the great capitalists rather than the petit bourgeoisie are the carriers of the capitalist spirit, of which Jacob Fugger is one among many; and (4) capitalism in seventeenth- and eighteenth-century Holland had almost nothing to do with the sects, whereas in England capitalism and enterprise antedated the sects.[56] Weber is able to deflect the first three objections simply because they fail to engage the crisis of proof and workaday works; Weber repulses the fourth with his pluralism, simply recognizing the importance of structural preconditions.

In his rejoinder to Rachfahl, note that Weber does not restate his

---

55 Ibid., 111.
56 F. Rachfahl, "Kalvinismus und Kapitalismus," in J. Winckelmann, ed., *Die Protestant Ethik II* (Hamburg, 1972), 57–148; and, F. Rachfahl, "Nochmals Kalvinismus und Kapitalismus," in Winckelmann, *Protestant Ethik,* 216–282.

"Religious Foundations" and the crisis of proof found in Chapter IV of *The Protestant Ethic,* confining his observations instead to the remoter corollaries of the premise. Weber states that the primary intention of his Puritan deliberations was to elucidate a specific notion of "vocation," one produced by the elective affinity between Calvinism and capitalism.[57] Weber goes on to observe accurately that Rachfahl fails to grasp this special conception of vocation, revealed by Rachfahl's observation that the Catholic laity also had inner-worldly asceticism. Here Weber alludes to the indifference of the Catholic calling, wherein practical activity ("conscientious work") is "required" or "valid" in church theory. Conscientious work has been praised and recommended to the laity of every epoch, Weber wryly observes. Calvinism is unique precisely in its creation of a "psychological vehicle" or a "psychological premium" for work ethics that created typical modes of conduct.

Catholicism cannot achieve such results because its theology is differently conceived, which time and time again allowed the person to begin anew, cleansed of all spiritual transgressions. By contrast, atonement is foreign to Calvinism and the sects, which were thereby able to create specific psychological premiums for the ascetic regulation of life, not only life in general but particularly on vocation as the subjective guarantee of the *certitudo salutis.*[58] Protestant asceticism thus creates a "work holiness," for which the pastoral writings of Baxter and Spener are in part responsible.[59] In this way, ascetic Protestantism produced a *habitus* among individuals that prepared them for a way of life suited to early modern capitalism.

This entrepreneur was filled with the conviction that Providence had shown him the road to profit not without particular intention. He walked it for the greater glory of God, whose blessing was unequivocally revealed in the multiplication of his profit and possessions. Above all, he could measure his worth not only before men but also before God by success in his occupation as long as it was realized by legal means.[60]

Decisive for Weber – again taking his cue from Kant's categorical imperative – is that the inner ethical core of the personality can be unified only by a transcendental ideal. The practical vocational ethic of the Middle Ages and its great merchant princes, by contrast, did not obtain this unity of purpose from the personality because such "a

---

57 M. Weber, "Anticritical Last Word on the Spirit of Capitalism," *American Journal of Sociology,* 83 (1978): 1112.
58 Ibid., 1115.   59 Ibid., 1122–1124.   60 Ibid., 1124.

spiritual bond was lacking."[61] Thus capitalism, as Weber understands it, can arise only from a transcendental cause of reason, in this case its quest for an eternity of perfection. Accumulation driven by power and honor, by contrast, can be found in all epochs where they uniformly failed to produce either the spirit or the form of capitalism.

Weber's rejoinder to the fourth point is to remind Rachfahl that he is not a determinist on the ideal side of things, that the Protestant ethic was not necessary and sufficient for the spirit of capitalism. The full-blown emergence of *homo economicus,* Weber reports, is not the sole product of ideas but also the result of specific objective conditions: geographical, political, social, and other elements of culture located in the Middle Ages, in contrast to those of antiquity.[62] Among those conditions were the political and organizational characteristics of the medieval city, as well as new forms of production like cottage industry.[63] Weber also acknowledged the contribution of the Renaissance and the rationalist, antitraditionalist spirit that it fostered.[64]

Weber concludes his essay by again correctly charging that Rachfahl simply misunderstands both the religious grounding that the calling receives from Calvinism and Weber's own causal pluralism. Part of his hope in writing *The Protestant Ethic,* Weber tells us, was for the theological community to take his work seriously. But such scrutiny so far had been lacking, except for the approval of Weber's friend, Ernst Troeltsch:[65] "This was my hope, and I now await fruitful and informative criticism from the theological side, but not from dilettantish, bungling polemicists such as Rachfahl."[66]

### 4. WEBER'S RESPONSES TO BRENTANO, SOMBART, AND SIMMEL

Simmel cannot be considered an active critic of the Weber thesis: His book on the *Philosophy of Money* merely equated money with cap-

---

61 Ibid., 1124–1125.   62 Ibid., 1125.   63 Ibid., 1128.   64 Ibid., 1129.

65 Weber is right. Troeltsch approved of his thesis, but for reasons that were inconsistent with Weber's line of thought on the calling. Tawney also agreed with Weber on this score for reasons that Weber would find rather strange. Otherwise, Tawney was a critic of Weber's work. See M. H. MacKinnon, "Part II: Weber's Exploration of Calvinism: The Undiscovered Provenance of Capitalism," *British Journal of Sociology* 29 (1989): 200–204. As it was with the critics, so it went with Weber's supporters who misunderstood his work. Their support stemmed from reasons that were inconsistent with the thesis's premises. All the same, it would hardly be appropriate to criticize Weber's apologists for the longevity of the thesis.

66 Weber, "Anticritical Last Word," 1127.

italism, too closely for Weber's liking. Brentano and Sombart more actively engage Weber but, like Rachfahl, never fully grasp the inner spiritual essence of the calling and the crisis of proof whence it comes. Weber's responses to these critics recognizes the ubiquity of the Calvinist calling. This is the case when Weber rejects the causal efficacy of the Catholic calling as Brentano presents it; it is similarly so when Weber repudiates Brentano's characterization of Jacob Fugger and Sombart's characterization of Alberti as respective bearers of the capitalist spirit. It can also be found in Weber's dismissal of Brentano's claim that his pre-Reformation Italian banker ancestors were authentic capitalists. Weber also deflects the Brentano–Sombart focus on the antimammonism of the Puritan literature by means of the calling, as well as Sombart's claim that the medieval church and the Jews contributed to rational growth. The significance of the calling assumes a different shape as Weber qualifies Sombart and Simmel on the importance of the Discoveries and the consequent increase in the money supply. Weber's causal pluralism is quite prepared to recognize the contribution of these factors, and that their additive impact upon glorified works in the world was causally adequate to launch a modern economy.

In connection with the calling, Brentano maintains that Latin translations of the Bible speak of the calling or *vocatio* in much the same way as Luther's German version speaks of *Beruf:* Work is a duty in the eyes of God. The Vulgate refers not only to "work" but also to "work of the calling" or "thy commissions" in conjunction with the "deadly Sin" of sloth.[67] As noted earlier, Weber would not disagree with Brentano on this score; rather, he would contend that Catholicism could not and did not foster a psychological premium for labor, although it recommended conscientious labor and repudiated the sin of indolence. The Catholic calling is indifferent precisely because it sees sloth as sinful, just as it sees preoccupation with earthly things as sinful. Our temporal responsibilities can lead to damnation in these ways but can score no points for us in the great game of salvation. There is no sign here of the psychological premium that Calvinism assigns to labor. Weber makes the same point when taking up Brentano's charge that capitalism existed well before the Reformation in the Italian cities but more specifically in the personage of Jacob Fugger, merchant prince and banker to popes. Fugger as exemplar of the

---

67 L. Brentano, *Die Anfänge des modernen Kapitalismus* (Leipzig, 1916), 134, 136.

capitalist spirit (the making of money for its own sake) is said to be revealed in an exchange with his nephew George Thurzo, who asked Fugger if he ever wished to retire. Fugger's reply was that he wished to continue making as much as possible for as long as possible. Weber's *Verstehen* of Fugger's accumulative motives see them in a light quite different from those of Franklin. The spirit of capitalism is nowhere to be found in Fugger, Weber counters, because his ambition is one of "commercial daring," not an "ethically colored maxim for the conduct of life," as we see in Franklin.[68] Weber accuses Brentano of not recognizing this "moral neutrality" in Fugger.[69]

The same set of circumstances come to the fore when Sombart raises the case of Leon Battiste Alberti. Alberti was a Florentine money changer and cloth merchant of the Renaissance whose views, Sombart insists, are remarkably similar to those of Benjamin Franklin. According to Sombart, Alberti stresses in his *Government of the Family* (circa 1450) the absolute necessity of balancing income against expenditure.[70] In Puritan-like fashion, Alberti speaks of the profitable use of time and the avoidance of idleness that corrupts.[71] Similarly, he proclaims the virtues of honesty in business, for honesty brings higher profits.[72] Above all, Alberti recommends the value of thrift, of asceticism in business, which Sombart identifies as the cornerstone of middle-class capitalist activity. Alberti holds thrift in great reverence: "Thrift is holy."[73] Not without sounding somewhat forced, Weber rejects the possibility that Alberti and Franklin hold identical ethics. Weber argues that Alberti nowhere says that time is money (Alberti in fact does say this), and nowhere do we find that characteristic ascetic streak in his methods of acquisition.[74] The clincher for Weber, though, is that Alberti failed to use religious motives to justify the manner of life he advocated. In the final analysis, Alberti did not attach salvation and damnation to the pursuit of profit.[75] Forced as Weber's response may be, Sombart cannot effectively counter it unless he is prepared to engage Weber's theological premises.

Brentano thinks that he has detected another crack in Weber's argument. Calling to witness his own family, Brentano claims that his Italian ancestors were pre-Reformation banker-capitalists who were

---

68 Weber, *The Protestant Ethic*, 51–52.   69 Ibid., 192–193.
70 W. Sombart, *The Quintessence of Capitalism* (New York, 1967), 105.
71 Ibid., 108.   72 Ibid., 122–123.   73 Ibid., 106.
74 Weber, *The Protestant Ethic*, 194, 196.   75 Ibid., 196, 197.

forced to move north when trade routes shifted away from the Mediterranean and the Levant to the North Sea. Weber's reply seeks to establish that bourgeois accumulation is unique, the product of a special religious impulse that flows from the calling. He argues that as an economic species, bankers have been historically ubiquitous; they are not peculiar to modern capitalism, and least of all the bearers of the capitalist spirit. As Weber sees it, Brentano's problem is that he has thrown all struggle for gain into one pot, refusing to differentiate and thereby unable recognize the uniqueness of such a struggle under modern capitalism.[76] History can show us all sorts of ways of acquiring wealth, Weber continues: There has been adventure capitalism, booty capitalism, political capitalism, and a variety of other capitalisms, but nowhere else have we seen capitalism based on the rational organization of free labor.[77] Speaking directly to Brentano, Weber says that not all types of acquisition are representative of the spirit of capitalism; acquisition by booty is quite different from acquisition by management of a factory.[78]

The failure of Brentano and Sombart to grasp the essence of the Weber thesis, particularly the unintendedness that is its by-product, can be seen in their citation of the antimammonistic doctrines of the Puritan moralists. Sombart observes that Puritanism was less favorable to capitalism than Catholicism.[79] Sombart goes so far as to cite a source from Baxter's *Directory* to bring the point home.

Remember that riches do make it harder for a man to be saved. . . . Remember that riches are no part of your felicity. . . . It is not for nothing that Christ gives so many terrible warnings about riches.[80]

Weber's rejoinder is to reestablish the fact that he is concerned not with prohibitions of riches, but only with the "psychological sanctions" generated by religious belief that "gave direction to practical conduct and held the individual to it."[81] In a footnote, Weber goes on to observe accurately that Brentano and Sombart have badly misunderstood this point in their citations of ethical writers, "(mostly those of whom they have heard through me)." Both observe certain codifications of rules of conduct, particularly antimammonism, "without ever asking which of them were supported by psychologically effective religious sanctions."[82]

Still neutralized within the purview of Weber's calling, Sombart is eager to establish the causal contributions of the medieval church and

76 Ibid., 198.   77 Ibid., 17–21.   78 Ibid., 185.   79 Sombart, *Quintessence*, 259.
80 Ibid., 252–253.   81 Weber, *The Protestant Ethic*, 97–98.   82 Ibid., 217.

the Jews to the advent of capitalism. There were many elements in Catholicism favorable to the growth of capitalism, Sombart states, especially the way it rationalized the pace of life, placing strict control over the passions.[83] Sombart goes on to demonstrate that many influential church fathers developed doctrines favorable to the ultimate victory of capital. For example, Aquinas differentiates between borrowing for unproductive purposes (the pompous parading of self) and borrowing for productive purposes (to create capital). To obtain funds for the first is impious, whereas seeking funds for the second is perfectly legitimate. Both Antonine of Florence and Bernard of Sienna understood capital in this way, "and what they have to say about it, political economy has learned afresh from Karl Marx."[84]

Weber agrees that certain elements in the Church were favorable to capital, yet the dominant trend of thought was to oppose it. Yet the decisive factor was that Catholicism lacked the soteriological means to give divine encouragement to the creation of capital. The Jesuits were sympathetic to capitalist practice, Weber admits, even more so than "Protestant writings."[85] Anthony of Florence and Bernard of Sienna, who were Scotists, were also kindly disposed, permitting the payment of interest when the loan was used for the productive investment of capital.[86] Furthermore, both saw the profit of the merchant as a reward for his *industria*.[87] Yet Weber charges that these "latitudinarian" writings were exceptional rather than conventional, the product of ethically lax thinking opposed by the strictest disciples of the Church.[88] An ethical stigma attached to business activity, so that those who pursued it were perceived as less than strict enthusiasts of the Church.[89] The ethos of medieval Christianity can be summed up in the old judgment passed on the merchant: *homo mercator vix aut numquam potest Deo placere;* he may conduct himself without sin but cannot be pleasing to God.[90] This opposition was incorporated into dogma and canon law and is reflected by Aquinas's characterization of the desire for gain as *turpitudo*. Antonine of Florence's applause of *industria* did not overcome this opposition, yet the Church for purely practical reasons, Weber concludes, still had to make some concessions to the financial power.[91]

For Weber, the critical reason Calvinism *could* and Catholicism

83 Sombart, *Quintessence*, 237, 239.   84 Ibid., 248.
85 Weber, *The Protestant Ethic*, 269.   86 Ibid., 201.   87 Ibid., 202.
88 Ibid., 269.   89 M. Weber, *The Sociology of Religion* (Boston, 1969), 220.
90 M. Weber, *General Economic History* (New York, 1961), 262.
91 Ibid., 262; Weber, *The Protestant Ethic*, 73.

*could not* create a capitalist calling is that whereas the Puritan businessman was ethically devout in the pursuit of gain, his Catholic
counterpart was ethically lax. The Protestant idea of the calling
placed the true ascetic believer in the service of capitalist acquisition
in order to gain "the *certitudo salutis* in a calling which gave *industria* a
psychological sanction. Catholicism does not do this because its
means of salvation are different."[92]

Sombart's studies, which he candidly admits were stimulated by
Weber's investigations,[93] lead him to conclude that the Jews made a
pivotal contribution to capitalist modes of acquisition. Judaism is a
sober, unemotional religion, Sombart advises, which banned mystical fusion with the Godhead and developed in its stead a regulated,
contractual relationship amounting to a spiritual form of bookkeeping.[94] This admirably suited the Jews to profit making, as did the fact
that they were "outsiders" deeply involved in the European re-
distribution of bullion pillaged from the New World.[95] The outsider
is on "intimate" terms with impersonality, reinforced by Jewish familiarity with money and money lending, caused by the prohibition
of Jews owning land. Borrowing perhaps from Simmel's *Philosophy
of Money,* Sombart argues that money as a mobile and liquid form of
wealth produces a quantified, abstract conception of life so central to
the capitalist temper, in contrast to a qualitative, natural view.[96]

Weber viewed the outsider ("pariah") status of the Jews as a handicap rather than as contributory to capitalism. The strong ethnic,
triballike identity of the Jews resisted integration into the host society
throughout the postexilic period. It was a self-imposed segregation
that had significantly adverse social consequences and ultimately resulted in the failure of the Jews to carry economic activity in a capitalist direction. The historical refusal of the Jews to integrate, Weber
tells us, stems from religious motives to maintain ritual purity and
was largely responsible for their status as a "pariah people."[97] The
Jews had to endure terrible consequences for taking this religious
stand in the face of the world: expulsion, confiscation of property,
denial of land-holding rights, persecution by the Inquisition, and, at
worst, the pogrom. Self-segregation also produced what Weber calls

92 Weber, *The Protestant Ethic,* 203.
93 W. Sombart, *The Jews and Modern Capitalism* (New York, 1962), 188.
94 Ibid., 200–204.
95 W. Sombart, *The Jews and Modern Capitalism* (New York, 1969), 37, 118–121.
96 Ibid., 188–189, 276, 344, 346.
97 M. Weber, *Ancient Judaism* (Glencoe, Ill., 1952), 406; Weber, *Economy,* 417.

an "ethical dualism," which meant that shady economic dealing with the outsider was acceptable, but that such practices were strictly forbidden in dealings with a fellow Jew. Within these circumstances, the Jews pursued irrational economic practices ("pariah capitalism"), which include state and booty capitalism, pure money, usury, and trade, precisely what the Puritan abhorred.[98]

The pariah status of the Jews created external barriers to their participation in industry, excluding them from economic activity consistent with the continuous, systematic, and rationalized industrial enterprise with fixed capital and its bourgeois organization of labor.[99] Ethical dualism, Weber continues, meant that the Jews could not find morally directed motives for economic transactions. Dividing the economic world into "us" and "them" short-circuited the possibility of developing an "inner-worldly asceticism," or proving oneself ethically worthy by the "disreputable" pastime of reserving sharp practice for the exploitable mass of the unwashed and commercial altruism for the insider. In contrast, seventeenth-century Quakers and Baptists took great pride in the honesty and fairness that marked their trade with the godless: Honesty was reciprocated bountifully by the repeated return of the satisfied buyer.[100] In short, the Jews did not develop capitalistically because they were unable to lift the ethical barrier between the internal and external economies.

Apart from calling-related issues, Sombart explicitly and Simmel implicitly[101] see the Discoveries and their fallout as taking Europe in a capitalist direction. Sombart sees the primary stimulus for entrepreneurial acquisition as flowing from the shift in the economic center of gravity inaugurated by the Discoveries: away from the Mediterranean and the Levant to the North Sea, to Holland and England.[102] In the process, Europe was deluged by precious metals, which increased the supply of money, which in turn increased the demand for commodities. Simmel's claim that a money economy is the fundamental feature of a capitalist economy, is relevant in this connection, assuming as it does that the Spaniards' bullion-related

---

98 Weber, *Judaism*, 345; Weber, *General Economic History*, 264, Weber, *The Protestant Ethic*, 271.

99 Weber, *Sociology of Religion*, 250; Weber, *The Protestant Ethic*, 271.

100 Weber, *Judaism*, 333–334; Weber, *Sociology of Religion*, 252.

101 G. Simmel, *The Philosophy of Money* (New York, 1978). It is the pervasiveness of money that creates a capitalist mentality, according to Simmel: "The money economy enforces the necessity of continuous mathematical operations in our daily transactions. The lives of many people are absorbed in such evaluating, weighing, calculating and reducing the qualitative values to quantitative ones" (444).

102 Sombart, *Quintessence*, 316.

pillage of the New World contributed to the creation of this money economy.

Weber's causal pluralism is prepared to concede that other agents played a role in the creation of the modern age. Yet they were necessary but not sufficient for the capitalist spirit; the addition of a sanctified calling is sufficient to produce such an outcome. Thus Weber does not deny the centrality of money to capitalism but is unprepared to accept the claims of Simmel and Sombart that they are synonymous.[103] Money is important to capitalism because it is a necessary precondition for Weber's "formal rationality." Formal rationality of economic action is the degree to which the provision of needs can be expressed in numerical, calculable terms. "When this is expressed monetarily," Weber states, "the highest degree of formal rationality is reached."[104] Yet a large supply of money alone is not enough to produce formal rationality, although it certainly does help; Weber notes that the influx of precious metals in the sixteenth century produced more stable relations in the field of coinage.[105] The case of Ptolemaic Egypt is similar: Although the widespread use of money was associated with the considerable development of production and market demand, the Ptolemies nevertheless employed budgetary accounting rather than capital accounting.[106] Weber also raises the example of India, which, during the period of Imperial Rome, experienced an enormous influx of precious metals – some 25 million *sestertii* annually. Yet the greatest part of this influx disappeared into the hoards of the rajahs rather than being converted into cash and applied to enterprise.[107]

### 5. THE POST-WEBER CRITICS: ROBERTSON, SAMUELSON, TAWNEY, TREVOR-ROPER, AND OTHERS

The level of debate conducted by the critics in the third stage does not significantly advance beyond those issues raised during Weber's lifetime. It fails to do so because none of this criticism grasps or questions pastoral works in a calling as the unintended result of dogmatic closure. The conceptual foundation upon which these objections rest is thus "old news," already raised and successfully handled in Weber's

---

103 Weber, *General Economic History*, 259, Weber, *The Protestant Ethic*, 185.
104 Weber, *Economy*, 85.     105 Weber, *General Economic History*, 188.
106 Ibid., 59; M. Weber, *The Theory of Social and Economic Organization* (New York, 1969), 218.
107 Weber, *General Economic History*, 259.

replies to Rachfahl, Sombart, and Brentano. The writings of Robertson and Samuelson, who mount the most trenchant but still ultimately unsuccessful critique of Weber's Puritan calling, reveal the failure to grasp the core of Weber's argument. They fail, that is, according to Weber's ground rules, but they succeed in the final analysis. Because the leading spokesmen of the opposition movement fail to grasp and then dismember Weber's line of reasoning, we are given old wine in new bottles: the antimammonism of Puritan divines; the resuscitation of Alberti and Fugger as manifestations of the capitalist spirit; the argument that Calvinist and Catholic conceptions of the calling are therefore similar; and, as a result, the claim that capitalism antedated the Reformation.

The remaining commentary also sings an old refrain, failing to consider the provisional character of Weber's *Protestant Ethic* within the larger corpus of his work. Tawney explicitly and incorrectly charges that Weber failed to give material and structural configurations their causal due. Other arguments, notably those that cite the Scottish case, fail to appreciate that in Weber's mind, Calvinism had to operate in conjunction with other factors to achieve a breakthrough. Here the critics claim that in many historical circumstances, enterprise went into recession rather than florescence when Calvinists assumed control. Such charges make the second error of commission; they fail to consider Weber's contention that Calvinism is necessary but not sufficient for the growth of capitalism, always needing some structural assistance to crush tradition. Weber's thoughts also operate from the other direction: Structural preconditions, although necessary, need the helping hand of sanctified works in a calling to become sufficient. Thus Weber does not dispute the importance of the great price revolution of the sixteenth and seventeenth centuries as a critical event and a period of capitalist expansion, unless, of course, it is framed in a unicausal way. Nor does he contest claims that Calvin's and Calvinism's contribution to modernity is significant politically in that it led to democratic forms of government as the mark of the modern age.

Robertson and Samuelson mount the most exhaustive and spirited efforts to derail the Weber thesis, but their efforts ultimately fall on stony soil, though Samuelson makes significant inroads. Robertson searches mid-sixteenth-century Puritan literature in search of a sanctified calling, unmindful of Weber's claim that pastoral works in such a calling arose in reaction to the *Westminster Confession's* dogmatic predestinarianism of the 1640s.[108] Robertson also cites Saint Paul to show that the valuation of workaday toil is not new to Luther and the Reformation but is as old as Christianity itself: "We commanded you, that if any would not work, neither should he eat."[109] Weber does not *in absentia* dispute Robertson on this score, even citing the same passage from the apostle to establish that Paul as well as Luther saw activity in the world as indifferent. Indolence may well be symptomatic of a lack of grace, yet at the same time, gainful employment cannot be used to secure salvation. Again, indifference means that occupation, while it can negatively affect our prospects for salvation, cannot make a positive contribution to it.[110] Samuelson gets closer to the truth, noting that Weber's conception of the calling comes from election and predestination, but he misunderstands the nature of the connection.[111] Samuelson misunderstands because he searches the writings of Calvin rather than Calvinism for some evidence of an earthly calling, and he erroneously criticizes Weber when he fails to find such evidence.[112] Samuelson, however, makes an important discovery in connection with works, but he fails to advance it critically because, like Weber, he believes that *Westminster*'s doctrine of predestination replicates the closure of Calvin.[113] Yet to his credit, Samuelson discovers that there are two callings in Christianity that correspond to the double usage of works: a spiritual calling and a temporal calling. Religious works attach to the former and a good job of work to the latter. Samuelson then cites Saint Paul to make a telling point against Weber. Paul exhorts those who are rich "that they do good, that they be rich in good works," meaning, do not entrust faith in the vain riches of the world but pursue good works and the Kingdom of Heaven.[114] Weber can still wriggle off this hook by calling upon the crisis of proof in dogma and unintendedness that Samuelson cannot deny because of his own predestinarian conception of the *Westminster Confession*.

The antimammonism in Reformed thought is again dredged up by the new generation of critics, notably Robertson, Samuelson, and Hyma. All cite the same passage from Baxter to bring the point home:

Choose that employment or calling . . . in which you may be most serviceable to God. Choose not that in which you may be most wealthy or honor-

---

108 H. M. Robertson, *Aspects of the Rise of Economic Individualism* (New York, 1959), 10–11.
109 Ibid., 4.    110 Weber, *The Protestant Ethic*, 84–85, 159.
111 K. Samuelson, *Religion and Economic Action* (Stockholm, 1961), 43.
112 Ibid., 44.    113 Ibid., 45.    114 Ibid., 47.

able in the world; but that in which you may do the most good and best escape sinning.[115]

This passage, of course, can be used to dismantle Weber's ideal argument, but it can do so with finality only when seen in association with Calvinist generosity on the availability of grace, the other-worldliness of works, and the indifference of mundane affairs. Choosing an earthly calling that consumes all our time is ultimately worthless, because the greatest reward comes from the effectual calling, the one that requires the relentless performance of good works to secure salvation. Thus there is no unintendedness in this passage from Baxter, who straightforwardly tells us: Beware of the snare and delusion that Satan wraps in your temporal obligations.

The critics again raise Alberti,[116] and particularly Fugger,[117] to contest Weber, by showing that Catholic and Calvinist notions of the calling are similar. "It is difficult to understand," Graham writes, "why Jacob Fugger . . . . who refused to retire even when old and wealthy, should not be an example of the capitalist spirit, when Franklin, who quit the unrelenting pursuit of money as a young man in order to serve his country, is a perfect example of that *Geist*."[118] No differences separate Catholic and Calvinist conceptions of the calling, the argument continues, because rational acquisition is not at all foreign to the Catholic temper.[119] Pirenne here presents the Englishman, Saint Godric of Finchdale, who became rich as a merchant in the twelfth century before renouncing his wealth to become a hermit. The quest for profit guided all Godric's actions, Pirenne states, actions in which the capitalist spirit can easily be recognized. Further, it is "preposterous" to submit that Godric carried out his business merely to satisfy his daily needs; rather, he reinvested his earnings in his business, much as the modern entrepreneur would do.[120] De Roover says it would be nothing short of unjust to deny that the Medici, who antedated the Reformation by several decades, were not engaged in the capitalist pursuit of wealth.[121] Along the same lines, Lüthy reminds that the Medici were great pre-Reforma-

115 A. Hyma, *Christianity, Capitalism and Communism* (Ann Arbor, Mich., 1937), 223; Robertson, *Economic Individualism*, 16; Samuelson, *Economic Action*, 37.
116 Samuelson, *Economic Action*, 63–64, 65–66.
117 Ibid., 65; Robertson, *Economic Individualism*, XII–XIII; H. R. Trevor-Roper, *Religion, Reformation and Social Change* (London, 1972), 21.
118 W. Fred Graham, *The Constructive Revolutionary* (Richmond, Va., 1971), 192.
119 A. Hyma, *Renaissance to Reformation* (Grand Rapids, Mich., 1951), 501; Robertson, *Economic Individualism*, 2; Samuelson, *Economic Action*, 46.
120 H. Pirenne, *Medieval Cities* (New York, 1956), 82–83.
121 R. de Roover, *The Rise and Decline of the Medici Bank, 1397–1494* (New York, 1966), 7.

tion capitalists who started out as bankers to the Roman Curia and rose to be popes themselves. Luther's rebellion against the Church was caused in part by the fact that Rome was on too intimate terms with these pre-Reformation capitalists.[122]

Extending this line of thought, Fanfani urges that it is foolish to deny that capitalism had to wait upon the consequences of the Protestant Revolt.[123] Robertson insists that capitalism was a product of the Middle Ages, found not only in Florence, where the cloth, woolen, and silk industries flourished, but also in Belgium – notably the brass industry in the valley of the Meuse and the cloth industry in Flanders.[124] Tawney, who is otherwise Weber's advocate on matters of the calling, differs with Weber on this score, noting the medieval omnipresence of small-scale capitalism, with the notable exceptions of large-scale capitalism in pre-Reformation Flanders and Italy.[125] In Tawney's mind there was no lack of the "capitalist spirit" in Venice and Florence, south Germany, and Flanders in the fourteenth century, or in Antwerp in the fifteenth, despite the fact that all were nominally Catholic.[126] Trevor-Roper's point is that large-scale industrial capitalism existed long before the sixteenth century. Feudal capitalism, Trevor-Roper states, developed in 1500 in Antwerp, Liège, Lisbon, Augustburg, Milan, Luca, Venice, and Genoa.[127] "Catholic Europe in the fifteenth and early sixteenth centuries," Lüthy explains, "reached a level of structural and organizational development which was not to be achieved again for a further two centuries." Lüthy argues that it was Italy and Portugal that laid the material preconditions for a modern economy.[128] More recently, Collins claims that even the medieval church created an "approximation" to a capitalist economy. Outside the Church, Collins goes on to say, capitalism flourished: textiles in Florence and Flanders and prosperous trading cities such as Venice, Genoa, and Pisa.[129]

Another variant of this pre-Reformation capitalism theme (which is in fact a corollary of Puritan antimammomism) is that the frequent failure of Calvinism to create or even coexist with capitalism proves

122 H. Lüthy, "Once Again: Calvinism and Capitalism," in R. W. Green, ed., *The Weber Thesis Controversy* (Toronto, 1973), 98–99.
123 A. Fanfani, *Catholicism, Protestantism and Capitalism* (New York, 1955), 183, 201.
124 Robertson, *Economic Individualism*, 34, 40–41.
125 R. H. Tawney, *Religion and the Rise of Capitalism* (Gloucester, Mass., 1962), 26.
126 Ibid., 316; Tawney's Foreword in Weber, *The Protestant Ethic*, 7.
127 Trevor-Roper, *Religion, Reformation*, 21, 23.
128 Lüthy, "Once Again," 95, 98.
129 R. Collins, *Weberian Sociological Theory* (Cambridge, 1986), 56.

that Calvinism cannot be the creator of capitalism. In many historical circumstances, when Calvinists assumed the helm of state, economic activity either failed to expand or actually atrophied. Calvinism originally mushroomed in Hungary, Hyma explains, but capitalism did not develop;[130] in fact, trade declined as Calvinism spread.[131] In the second half of the sixteenth and the first half of the seventeenth centuries, Hyma continues, Calvinism was at its height in France, yet capitalism was in abeyance.[132] The Scottish case provides another well-known exception to the Weber thesis.[133] Hyma states that in the seventeenth century, Scotland became more thoroughly Calvinistic than either England or Holland, yet industry lagged in proportion to the spread of Nonconformity.[134] In Trevor-Roper's opinion, this was primarily due to the Scottish clergy's vigorous opposition to enterprise.[135] Citing Rachfahl approvingly, Samuelson observes that Calvinist Holland was unable to match the enterprise of Amsterdam, which retained the Spanish allegiance longer than all other Dutch cities and was decidedly Catholic.[136] In America, Appleby notes that Puritans formed covenanted communities across eastern Massachusetts and western Connecticut. Citing an impressive body of literature to make her point, Appleby observes that far from becoming modern entrepreneurs, Puritan men became rural patriarchs in towns noted for their cohesion and stability.[137]

Of course, all of these sallies ignore Weber's caveat that Puritanism was just one of many factors required to launch the capitalist spirit onto the stage of history. He says this directly in *The Protestant Ethic* when he notes that capitalist development in Puritan England presupposes that "some possibility" for such development was already present.[138] Tawney commits the same error in yet more graphic fashion, accusing Weber of idealistic determinism, allegedly excluding structural forces from his causal framework. "It is arguable at least," Tawney states, "that, instead of Calvinism producing the spirit of capitalism, both would with equal plausibility be regarded as different effects of changes in economic organization and social structure."[139] Weber insists that social causation runs only in one direction, Tawney goes on to say, making it artificial to suggest that

---

130 Hyma, *Renaissance*, 501.   131 Hyma, *Christianity*, 139.   132 Hyma, *Renaissance*, 503.
133 Samuelson, *Economic Action*, 51, Robertson, *Economic Individualism*, 88.
134 Hyma, *Christianity*, 139; *Renaissance*, 503.
135 Trevor-Roper, *Religion, Reformation*, 18.   136 Samuelson, *Economic Action*, 9.
137 J. Appleby, *Capitalism and a New Social Order* (New York, 1984), 9.
138 Weber, *The Protestant Ethic*, 43, 190.   139 Tawney, Foreword, 7.

capitalist enterprise had to wait upon religion to produce a capitalist spirit. "Would it not be equally plausible, and equally one-sided, to argue that the religious changes were themselves merely the result of economic movements?"[140]

Raising the issue of the Discoveries commits the same error of assuming that Weber is all idealism and no materialism. For Robertson, this shift in trade routes brought on by the Discoveries moved economic activity away from the Italians, Spaniards, Portuguese, and South Germans and into the hands of the North Europeans.[141] For Hyma such a shift was responsible for the phenomenal growth of Dutch and English sea power, so essential for laying the foundations of a capitalist economy.[142] Accompanying the Commercial Revolution of the sixteenth century, Seé reports, Europe was flooded by precious metals, creating an economic stimulus of great potency.[143] Between 1493 and 1600, according to Robertson, the stock of precious metals in Europe trebled, the value of new money put into circulation even exceeding this amount.[144]

The post-Weber critics also make much of the growth potential produced by the inflationary spiral created by this sudden increase in the money supply, but, yet again, Weber's pluralism is not hostile to such explanations when they are framed modestly. As inflation became rampant, Seé reports, it had a corrosive effect on the old nobility in France, forcing it to sell its land, as depreciated peasant dues and an undiminished appetite for ostentation ensured its downfall.[145] The nobility fell because price rises favor debtors and penalize creditors. Peasants, whose various dues to the lord had been commuted to money payments, profited from these circumstances, whereas the landowner suffered the loss. The lord often became indebted to money lenders to make up the shortfall, but more often than not simply coerced peasants to pay more, which heightened tensions.[146]

Inflation was also significant because it created new sources of wealth other than landholding, which had held this monopoly for centuries. Commercial groups benefited most from inflation because of the heavy demand it created for commodities. Profit inflation, at least in theory, stimulates the incentive for entrepreneurs to increase their investments in capital equipment in order to reap windfall prof-

---

140 Ibid., 8; Tawney, *Religion, Capitalism*, 316.
141 Robertson, *Economic Individualism*, 159–160.
142 Hyma, *Christianity*, 152.    143 H. E. Seé, *Modern Capitalism* (New York, 1928), 41.
144 Robertson, *Economic Individualism*, 179.    145 Seé, *Modern Capitalism*, 50–51.
146 S. B. Clough, *European Economic History* (Toronto, 1968), 153.

its.[147] The sixteenth century was an age of projects and project mongering in which wealth fell into the hands of the upwardly mobile.[148] Because of the mere rise in prices, society was forced to adopt a more individualistic attitude; "the rule of custom was overturned by the alteration of customary equivalents; each man had to fend for himself."[149] Under circumstances such as these, Tawney graphically reminds us, the individual can hardly help but take his pound of flesh![150]

Into commerce, industry and agriculture alike, the revolution in prices, gradual in the first third of the century, but after 1540 a mill race, injects a virus of hitherto unsuspected potency, at once a stimulant to feverish enterprise and an acid dissolving all customary equivalents.[151]

Weber does not deny that the great price revolution of the sixteenth and seventeenth centuries created a powerful impetus for capitalist development. "This revolution is rightly ascribed to the continuous inflow of precious metals, in consequence of the great overseas discoveries."[152] In fact, in *Economy and Society* he goes so far as to label this inflationary period "decisive" in the history of capital formation.[153] It was decisive because agricultural prices rose so sharply that it became advantageous to commit them to the market. The price rise of industrial products was not as steep, because increased demand created an incentive to lower production costs.[154] The creation of markets in this way undermined "unproductive" feudal forms of wealth bound up in lord, peasant, and manor. "In England, the . . . development of a market, as such and alone, destroyed the manorial system from within."[155] The emerging capitalist also opposed the manor because it impeded the formation of a free labor market, forcing the entrepreneur to rely on rural labor.[156]

Some fault finders have challenged Weber indirectly by maintaining that Calvin and Calvinism relate more directly to modernity through their influence on the growth of democracy. Fanfani equates Protestantism with democracy, for it abolished priestly and sacramental mediators and provided a direct route to God, thus encouraging independence, individualism and initiative.[157] Spiritual independence, Tawney advises, makes it "probable that democracy owes

147 Ibid., 154.    148 Robertson, *Economic Individualism*, 193.
149 Ibid., 181–182.    150 Tawney, *Religion, Capitalism*, 139.    151 Ibid., 136–137.
152 Weber, *General Economic History*, 230–231.    153 Weber, *Economy*, 115–116.
154 Ibid., 115–116; Weber, *General Economic History*, 230–231.
155 Weber, *General Economic History*, 86.    156 Ibid., 83.    157 Fanfani, *Catholicism*, 200.

more to Nonconformity than any other single movement."[158] Another variant is that Calvin's theology, encompassing as it did civic-Genevan elements of self-rule and self-determination, laid the premodern foundation for free institutions.[159] Hyma notes that Calvin's consistorialism created attitudes consistent with political democracy, since all members of the congregation had the right to participate in the election of church officials.[160]

Weber accepts such claims as consistent with his argument on the calling. Puritan peoples everywhere have been immune to Caesarism, Weber reports,[161] concurring with Montesquieu, who writes that the English have "progressed the farthest of all peoples of the world in three important things: in piety, in commerce, and in freedom." For Weber, Puritan piety gave rise to commercial superiority and free institutions. Democracy arose from the anti-authoritarianism in Puritanism – itself a by-product of its asceticism – when it pitted the movement against the patrimonialism of James I and Charles I. The dispute in question was over the *Book of Sports,* which clashed with Puritan Sabbatarianism by permitting, and indeed encouraging, popular amusements on Sunday.[162] Weber notes even more specifically the relationship between the sect and democracy. The sect was marked by a voluntaristic principle: free admission of the devout whose qualifications for moral purity only the congregation could judge.[163] Moreover, the sect subscribed to the priesthood of every member, rejecting the episcopacy and the official priesthood that it sanctioned. Clerical officials were not appointed by Rome or, as in Anglicanism, by the Crown but were elected by the congregation that they were bound to serve. "These very structural features," Weber writes, "demonstrate the elective affinity between the sects and political democracy."[164]

## 6. CONCLUSION

If this analysis has so far been confined to an overview of the critics, this discussion can conclude by first raising the state of the debate as it unfolded in the 1980s: by presenting views both for and against the

158 R. H. Tawney, *Religion and the Rise of Capitalism* (London, 1948), 269.
159 Graham, *Constructive Revolutionary*, 196.   160 Hyma, *Renaissance*, 422.
161 Weber, *The Protestant Ethic*, 45.   162 Ibid., 166–167.
163 H. H. Gerth and C. W. Mills, *From Max Weber* (New York, 1967), 316; Weber, *Economy*, 1205.
164 Gerth and Mills, *From Max Weber*, 316–317; Weber, *Economy*, 1208.

Weber thesis. The Cohen–Holton debate as it developed at the beginning of the decade adds nothing new in substance, and is, if anything, retrograde because it fails to raise issues of significance with which earlier commentators wrestled, albeit unsuccessfully. Thus the Cohen–Holton debate makes no attempt to elucidate a calling as the recipient of a psychological sanction along with the theological premises (crisis of proof, this-worldly works, and unintendedness) from which these calling claims derive. Cohen's opening move is to note that, although previous commentators have been satisfied to charge that capitalism was anterior to the Reformation, he will show its existence as Weber actually defined it.[165] Cohen proceeds to note that the rational firm, a free market in labor and commodities, rational technology, and a calculable legal system all existed prior to the Reformation. It follows that Weber's capitalism also existed prior to the Reformation.[166] The reader may observe that Cohen has neglected Weber's idealism, his focus on sanctified works in a calling. True, Cohen does note that Catholicism and Calvinism share similarities on the calling and that Rome also created fear about salvation, fear assuaged by the performance of works.[167] Yet Weber's idealism deserves something more than this gloss. For to address Weber adequately, Cohen would have to demonstrate that Catholicism gave a positive spiritual incentive to toil, and he does not do this. Rather than seize upon this defect as Weber's advocate, Holton takes the discussion into areas of tangential relevance, particularly addressing Weber's reflections on rationality. Here Holton notes that Cohen fails to appreciate Weber's distinction between "rational technique" and "rational economic action."[168] The critical part of Weber's discussion on rationality as it bears upon the matter at hand[169] is that "value rationality" gave rise to the "formal rationality" of the modern order, as Mueller notes in particular. Value rationality is, of course, Puritan idealism on the calling that unintentionally created rationalized modernity. Holton should have said that Cohen does not demonstrate the presence of Weber's value rationality in Renaissance Italy and thereby fails to match Weber's definition of capitalism, omitting the

165 J. Cohen, "Rational Capitalism in Renaissance Italy," *American Journal of Sociology* 85 (1980): 1342.
166 Ibid., 1342–1350.     167 Ibid., 1351.
168 R. J. Holton, "Max Weber, 'Rational Capitalism' and Renaissance Italy," *American Journal of Sociology* 89 (1983): 168.
169 G. Mueller, "Rationality in the Work of Max Weber," *European Journal of Sociology* 20 (1979): 155.

necessary spiritual ingredient. Thus both parties, pro and con, fail to come to terms with Weber's idealism.

Simultaneously, but in seeming isolation from the Cohen–Holton debate, Marshall wrote two books on the Weber thesis. In the first, *Presbyteries and Profits,*[170] Marshall raises the level of discussion to an entirely new plane by recognizing that Weber's calling ultimately obtains its potency from a crisis of proof in dogma. Marshall reevaluates the *Westminster Confession* with this in mind but erroneously comes to the conclusion that proof seeking in dogma establishes Weber's claim of crisis, when just the opposite is the case: Proof seeking in fact stands for the availability, not the denial of grace.[171] The significance of Marshall's work is that although his investigations come down in favor of Weber's idealism, something still tells him that pre-Reformation accumulation was not qualitatively different from that of the modern age. Marshall's second book, *In Search of the Spirit of Capitalism,* seeks to establish the point that arguments in favor of such a distinction are "dubious, . . . sketchy, arbitrary and fictitious."[172] Marshall believes that when the activities of the medieval businessman are placed within the context of the times, they are as rational as the activities of the ascetic Protestant of the sixteenth and seventeenth centuries.[173]

With Weber's theological mistakes corrected, we can now see that Marshall is all the more correct in this assessment. So it transpires that the critics were correct all along on this point, that Weber's principle of acquisitive demarcation between pre- and post-Reformation business ethics is untenable. As matters now stand, Weber has lost his idealism, whereas his material preconditions remain intact. Does this necessarily mean that there was no ideal contribution to capitalist development? I argue to the contrary, that historical research has amply shown that Puritan idealism made just such a contribution, though this idealism took a different shape than the one envisaged by Weber. Still religious in nature, Puritan idealism was more concerned with ecclesiology than soteriology, concerned with "purifying" church government of the popish episcopacy of the Anglican Church and the English Crown. This was one of many con-

---

170 G. Marshall, *Presbyteries and Profits* (Oxford, 1980).
171 MacKinnon, "Part II," 204–206.
172 G. Marshall, *In Search of the Spirit of Capitalism* (New York, 1982), 45.
173 Ibid., 112–113.

flicts that precipitated the Puritan Revolution of the 1640s: a conflict that established the political preconditions of modern capitalism.

No critical study of the Weber thesis can be complete without assessing the place of *The Protestant Ethic and the Spirit of Capitalism* in twentieth-century scholarship. Weber somewhere states that the scholar should be prepared to accept this fate: that his labors shall withstand the test of scrutiny for only a few years. It is a tribute to Weber's greatness that *The Protestant Ethic* has repulsed all possible attempts to dethrone it for well over eighty years. In it, Weber takes his Kantian stand in the face of scholarship, fully prepared to pay the price: "Any man who is born a eunuch should not be surprised if nothing ever happens to him."[174] The price paid by Weber is that his thesis is ultimately wrong. However, we think nothing less of Newton because Einstein reworked his cosmology. In fact, Weber's errors only add to the luster of the thesis, and Weber can tell us why: "An ingenious error is more fruitful for science than a stupid accuracy."[175] Weber's ingenious error has been the privilege of three generations of dwarfs (myself included) to view the landscape from the shoulders of a giant.

174 P. Honigsheim, *On Max Weber* (New York, 1968), 87. Honigsheim tells us that Weber spoke these words in a personal conversation.
175 Weber, *General Economic History*, 40.

# 11

## The Use and Abuse of Textual Data

DAVID ZARET

Since its publication in 1904–1905 as a two-part article, Max Weber's thesis on the Protestant ethic has been the focus of the longest-running debate in modern social science. The first round of exchanges between Weber and his principal critics, H. Karl Fischer and Felix Rachfahl, lasted until 1910. Weber subsequently incorporated these exchanges in revisions to *The Protestant Ethic,* responding as well to criticism from Sombart's *Der Bourgeois* (1913), Brentano's *Die Anfänge des modernen Kapitalismus* (1916), and other writings.[1] Since Weber's death, every aspect of his thesis has been attacked by torrents of criticism from André Biéler, C. H. George and K. George, Gabriel Kolko, Herbert Lüthy, Alan Macfarlane, Stephen Ozment, H. M. Robertson, Kurt Samuelsson, H. R. Trevor-Roper, Immanuel Wallerstein, and others who have not displayed much interest in methodological issues pertaining to interpretative procedures in social science. This development is doubly unfortunate, for Weber wrote extensively on these methodological issues. He began writing *The Protestant Ethic* in 1903 immediately upon completing part of the methodological critique that would be published as *Roscher and Knies*;[2] moreover, *The Protestant Ethic* relies on a carefully delineated interpretative procedure that, as Weber admitted, is susceptible to misunderstanding. Benighted efforts to "test" a "Protestant ethic thesis" by analyzing correlations between religious affiliation and economic status represent the more extreme misunderstandings that are possible. Somewhat less severe methodological problems are dis-

---

1 Guenther Roth, "Introduction," in Max Weber, *Economy and Society* (Berkeley, 1978), lxxvi; Max Weber, *The Protestant Ethic and the Spirit of Capitalism* (New York, 1958), 187, 194–198, 217; Johannes Winckelmann (ed.), *Max Weber: Die protestantische Ethik, II. Kritiken und Antikritiken* (Hamburg, 1972).
2 Roth, "Introduction," lxxvi.

cussed by Weber in reference to Brentano, Sombart, and Rachfall,[3] and by Weber's defenders in reference to critical work published after his death.[4] In the face of relentless criticism, the durability of the Weber thesis owes much to the relative ease with which its defenders have been able to point to serious methodological errors by its critics, for example, that their interpretative use of textual data is ad hoc, or that it ignores distinctions between formal doctrines and its unintended ethos, between Calvin and subsequent Calvinism, between different types of acquisitive activities, between the causal significance of religion today and in the early modern era, and so on.

The most recent addition to work critical of the Weber thesis, Malcolm MacKinnon's two-part article in the *British Journal of Sociology*,[5] initially appears to turn the tables on Weber by indicting him for not merely shoddy but dishonest practices. MacKinnon's verdict is harsh and unequivocal: The Weber thesis relies on a distorted reading of religious texts that are "the bearer of a message which discredits his own purpose." Weber's exegetical efforts "defy reality, [and] in order to sustain them Weber resorts to factual errors" and "sleight of hand." "His dilapidated efforts in this direction are marked by the misunderstanding of theological terminology . . . inconsistency and contradiction . . . and, less excusably, the use of legerdemain when countervailing evidence is encountered. Calculated evasion is unmistakable in Weber's defence of the seventeenth-century hegemony of Calvin's *sola fide*."[6] The alleged evasion conceals the Puritan "obliteration" of precisely those dogmatic features of Calvin's writings that, according to Weber, inspired salvation anxiety and inner-worldly asceticism. MacKinnon's goal, to deal "a death-blow to the Weber thesis" that hitherto has survived efforts to refute it,[7] thus leads him to demolish Weber on methodological as well as on substantive grounds. The *Protestant Ethic* is not, as prior generations of critics have conceded, a masterful piece of interpretative scholarship but a shoddy, dishonest work – a point reinforced by the derisive tone of MacKinnon's commentary.

3  Max Weber, "Anticritical Last Word on *The Spirit of Capitalism*," *American Journal of Sociology* 83 (1978):1111; Weber, *The Protestant Ethic*, 217.
4  See Julien Freund, *The Sociology of Max Weber* (New York, 1969), 205; David Little, *Religion, Order and Law* (Oxford, 1970), 228; Gordon Marshall, *In Search of the Spirit of Capitalism* (London, 1982), 75.
5  Malcolm H. MacKinnon, "Part I: Calvinism and the Infallible Assurance of Grace: The Weber Thesis Reconsidered," and "Part II: Weber's Exploration of Calvinism: The Undiscovered Provenance of Capitalism," *British Journal of Sociology* 29, nos. 1 and 2 (1989).
6  Ibid., 178, 179, 180, 181; see also 145, 150, 189.    7  Ibid., 143.

I argue that MacKinnon fails to substantiate these charges. The interpretation of Calvin and the Puritans that MacKinnon develops in opposition to Weber ignores most of the relevant primary evidence and secondary literature and attributes implausible positions to the textual tidbits that unwary readers might mistakenly accept as a fair representation of Puritan thought. An inability to anticipate and recognize, let alone deal with, contradictory evidence is the fundamental methodological flaw in MacKinnon's interpretation of religious doctrines. In opposing this interpretation, I argue that the same criteria of validity and reliability govern the use of quantitative and qualitative types of evidence. Historians and social scientists are expected to use several methodological procedures in order to maximize the validity and reliability of inferences that they draw from interpretations of textual data. MacKinnon's interpretation of religious texts lacks three types of controls that are prerequisites for rigorous scholarship in this area of inquiry.

First, the most elementary control is to ensure that, in attributing a doctrinal position to a belief system, quotations from formal writings correspond to a justifiable selection principle and not to an idiosyncratic or biased sampling of textual passages. *Exegetical selectivity* invariably attends all interpretation, but a selection that omits textual passages that strongly modify or contradict the cited material must be rejected. Second, additional controls are needed when interpretation goes beyond attributing doctrinal positions to belief systems, to drawing inferences about the behavioral and psychological implications of beliefs. This involves triangulation: corroborating interpretations of formal writings by consulting other types of textual data, such as autobiographies, biographies, letters, juridical records, contemporary accounts, and so on. Third, it is necessary to take account of the context in which writers produced the formal statements that serve as primary data for sociological analysis. MacKinnon overlooks the problem of *contextual selectivity,* the selective construction of the texts that we treat as primary data. MacKinnon overlooks this problem and magnifies its effects by failing to exercise reasonable control over his *exegetical selectivity,* his practice, noted previously, of selecting passages that support his argument and ignoring others that contradict it. Subsequently, I show how the principal claims erected by MacKinnon against Weber's thesis derive from these methodological flaws in his interpretation of texts by Calvin and the Puritans.

## I. MACKINNON'S CRITIQUE OF WEBER

MacKinnon's critique focuses on the nature of "works" and covenant theology in Puritanism. He argues that the term "works" in Puritan writings refers to other-worldly works, to religious and not to secular activities. Hence, "There is no irrational consecration of secular employment"[8] in Puritanism, as Weber had maintained. Weber simply misread Puritan remarks on this topic. MacKinnon also calls attention to the significance of covenant theology, which centered on the idea of a heavenly contract that outlined the terms on which God offered salvation. Asserting (incorrectly) that Puritanism "inaugurates the enduring tradition of covenant theology,"[9] MacKinnon argues that covenant theology led Puritanism away from Calvin's theology to a new, serene creed that was incapable of inspiring salvation anxiety in its adherents. Covenant theology transformed Protestant doctrine by smuggling works into it, thereby allowing its adherents to obtain from good works absolute certainty about their salvation. MacKinnon attributes a deterministic doctrine to Calvin, in which God's grace does all in the salvation process, and a voluntaristic doctrine to Puritanism, which "succeeded in disposing of Calvin's predestinarian determinism."[10]

This interpretation places Calvin and the Puritans at opposite ends of a faith–works continuum. At one end is the deterministic doctrine of Calvin; at the other is the voluntaristic doctrine of covenant theology, in which individuals will their way into heaven by treating a minimal work – the bare desire for grace – as evidence of election. In this voluntaristic doctrine that offers serene assurance on easy terms, *sola fide,* predestination and salvation anxiety melt away. So does the Weber thesis: Without anxiety induced by uncertainty over one's

---

8 Ibid., 195.
9 Ibid., 151. MacKinnon fails to cite nearly all modern accounts of covenant theology that correct this error, popularized over fifty years ago by Perry Miller. On the continental antecedents of Puritan covenant theology, see Everett H. Emerson, "Calvin and Covenant Theology," *Church History* 25 (1956); Richard Greaves, "The Origins and Early Development of English Covenant Thought," *The Historian* 31 (1968); Greaves, "John Bunyan and Covenant Thought in the Seventeenth Century," *Church History* 36 (1967); E. Brooks Holifield, *The Covenant Sealed* (New Haven, Conn., 1974); George Marsden, "Perry Miller's Rehabilitation of the Puritans," *Church History* 39 (1970); Michael McGiffert, "Grace and Works: The Rise and Division of Covenant Divinity in Elizabethan Puritanism," *Harvard Theological Review* 75 (1982); Jens G. Møller, "The Beginnings of Puritan Covenant Theology," *Journal of Ecclesiastical History* 14 (1963). These and other studies are discussed by John von Rohr, *The Covenant of Grace in Puritan Thought,* American Academy of Religion: *Studies in Religion,* no. 45 (1986). MacKinnon cites none of these items.
10 MacKinnon, "Part I," 152.

religious status, there is no spiritual motive for conduct that unintentionally rationalizes worldly activities.

In advancing this interpretation of Puritanism against Weber, MacKinnon ignores virtually all of the secondary literature on covenant theology.[11] His primary evidence comes from original writings by Calvin, three Puritan clerics, and quotations from secondary historical accounts. I proceed to correct the errors introduced by uncontrolled selectivity in MacKinnon's interpretation of this evidence. The correction reinforces the view of Puritanism as an anxiety-inducing creed – quite the opposite of the serene doctrine of assurance described by MacKinnon; it restores Weber's arguments on the spiritualization of secular employments; and it demolishes the clumsy distinction between Calvin and the Puritans, between unremitting determinism in Calvin, who allowed no place for works, and a "thoroughly voluntaristic" doctrine among Puritans, who encouraged believers to will their way into heaven. For Calvin, this distinction leads to absurd arguments that lump together his doctrine and Antinomianism; for Puritanism, it transforms Calvinist clerics into disciples of Locke and Milton. Yet we shall see that Puritan covenant theology contained the essential elements that Weber attributed to Calvinism: God's secret will elected particular persons to salvation; from election flowed free grace as the means for persevering in patterns of godly conduct; that conduct provided clues in the introspective search for evidence of election; and that search, subject to setbacks and uncertainty, was a prolonged, lifelong endeavor. Finally, MacKinnon calls attention to Richard Baxter and John Cotton, whose "deviations" from Puritan orthodoxy are woven into MacKinnon's general interpretation of Calvin and the Puritans. Unfortunately, the methodological flaws in MacKinnon's general interpretation extend to his remarks on Baxter and Cotton. Citing fragments of texts wrenched from their contexts and ignoring those that confute his arguments, MacKinnon delineates boundaries between allegedly antithetical doctrines (Calvin versus the Puritans; Baxter versus Cotton) that, on close examination, turn out to have much more in common than he realizes.

---

11 See footnote 5, this essay. MacKinnon relies heavily on R. T. Kendall, *Calvin and English Calvinism to 1649* (Oxford, 1979), and somewhat less on William Stoever's study, cited in footnote 71 of this essay. The lack of references to the rest of the literature on covenant theology is troubling because, to greater and lesser degrees, this work contradicts Kendall. The most recent and extensive summary of this literature is in von Rohr, *Covenant of Grace*, 17–32, which is critical of Kendall.

## II. PURITAN ANXIETY

MacKinnon's interpretation portrays Puritan covenant theology as a doctrine with precisely the opposite psychological implications than those attributes to it by Weber. Instead of anxiety and uncertainty, covenant theology cultivated a serene sense of assurance. According to MacKinnon, "Calvinism abandoned Calvin's predestinarianism via the introduction of covenant theology," a theology not based on *sola fide* but on a doctrine of works according to which dutiful performance of godly duties (minimally, the desire to believe) provided "infallible" assurance of salvation.[12] This "obliteration" of predestinarian determinism by covenant theology[13] not only transformed Calvinism into a voluntaristic creed but also precluded the salvation anxiety that Weber held to be a hallmark of Puritanism. "No crisis of proof can be found in dogma" because individuals can will their way into heaven. MacKinnon concedes that Calvin's own teachings may have generated anxiety, but after their reformulation in covenant theology, "Calvinist assurance by works eliminates this outcome."[14]

In Sections VIII and IX, I assess these claims with reference to doctrinal writings. In this section I discuss the plausibility of the psychological implications that MacKinnon's interpretation attributes to Puritan doctrine. Here becomes evident the limitations of MacKinnon's reliance on formal texts by clerics. He might have reconsidered his interpretation had he examined evidence of Puritan behavior from other types of texts, such as contemporary biographies, diaries, letters, and other accounts. These materials contradict the claim that reprobation was a dead issue in Puritanism, that Calvinist salvation anxiety receded before a serene doctrine of infallible assurance in covenant theology. Struggles to overcome doubt and ascertain whether one had a true or a false, hypocritical faith animated fearful efforts to control carnal impulses. Up to his death, the most famous Puritan of all, Oliver Cromwell, remained uncertain about his elect status, discovering assurance only on his deathbed. A detailed account of an obscure Puritan from this era, Nehemiah Wal-

---

12 MacKinnon, "Part I," 144, and see 149.
13 Ibid., 152: "Calvin's theology renounces works . . . man is saved by God alone. This emphasis lies at the core of Calvin's predestinarianism. . . . In their later acquisition of works, Calvinists substantially revise man's relationship with God, reconstituting it as a bilateral affair. In doing so, they succeeded in disposing of Calvin's predestinarian determinism."
14 Ibid., 155, and MacKinnon, "Part II," 179; and see "Part I," 143, "Part II," 206.

lington, a London wood turner, displays an anxious, nearly neurotic pattern of concern about his spiritual condition, which led him to compose 20,000 manuscript pages that recorded his perpetual struggle with uncertainty and guilt.[15] Cromwell and Wallington are ideal-typical and not average Puritans. But the spiritual warfare – Puritanism's popular metaphor – they experienced is a familiar feature of the diaries, letters, and contemporary biographies of Puritans. Moreover, if MacKinnon's account were correct, Puritanism would have been an anomaly, for both the Reformation and the Counter-Reformation transformed popular religion as they cultivated unprecedented levels of anxiety "by inculcating a sense of guilt, by an obsessive emphasis on original sin and day-to-day transgressions, by the examination of conscience taken to scrupulous extremes."[16]

Historians can point to cases of morally lax persons who demonstrate that Puritan beliefs did not always eventuate in anxiety and inner-worldly asceticism, but I know of no historical account that upholds MacKinnon's interpretation of serene assurance in Puritanism. The classic account in William Haller's *The Rise of Puritanism* receives support from a recent exhaustive study that finds "At the root of the Puritan experience . . . a deep-rooted anxiety." Many historians have commented on the "proneness to despair at the heart of Calvinism" in seventeenth-century England. From a social scientific perspective, Michael Walzer's important study explores the implications of Puritan anxiety for the origins of radical politics.[17] MacKinnon's interpretation also accords poorly with many well-known features of Puritan religion, including its abiding interest in a coercive program of religious discipline,[18] its apocalyptic world view,[19] and its paranoid obsession with Catholic conspiracies that

15 Paul Seaver, *Wallington's World: A Puritan Artisan in Seventeenth-Century London* (Stamford, Conn., 1985).
16 Jean Delumeau, "Prescription and Reality" in Edmund Leites (ed.), *Conscience and Casuistry in Early Modern Europe* (Cambridge, 1988), 148.
17 Richard L. Greaves, *Society and Religion in Elizabethan England* (Minneapolis, 1981), 8; Margaret Sampson, "Laxity and Liberty in Seventeenth-Century English Political Thought," in Leites, *Conscience and Casuistry,* 99. See also William Haller, *The Rise of Puritanism* (New York, 1957); Michael Walzer, *The Revolution of the Saints* (Cambridge, 1965).
18 See Patrick Collinson, *The Elizabethan Puritan Movement* (London, 1967), 291–355; Christopher Hill, *Society and Puritanism* (New York, 1967), 219–258; Keith Thomas, "The Puritans and Adultery," in Donald Pennington and Keith Thomas (eds.), *Puritans and Revolutionaries* (Oxford, 1978); Keith Wrightson and David Levine, *Poverty and Piety in an English Village* (New York, 1979).
19 See Paul Christianson, *Reformers and Babylon: English Apocalyptic Visions from the Reformation to the Eve of the Civil War* (Toronto, 1978); Katharine Firth, *The Apocalyptic Tradition in Reformation Britain, 1530–1645* (Oxford, 1979); Christopher Hill, *Antichrist in*

haunted it to the end of the seventeenth century.[20] Yet nowhere does MacKinnon confront this evidence or otherwise deal with the ensuing problem of credibility: The pattern of Puritan behavior and attitudes described in work by several generations of scholars does not correspond to the serene doctrine of assurance that MacKinnon detects in the writings of a few clerics.

### III. PURITANISM AND WORKS

The claim that works have only an other-worldly and not a this-worldly referent in Puritan writings would be plausible if it merely asserted that, in writings on the good works that flowed from grace, Puritans referred more often to religious duties than to economic behavior. The clerics were, after all, clerics, not managers. But the flat assertion that works in Puritanism "are other-worldly rather than this-worldly," and thus that there "is no irrational consecration of secular employment,"[21] is utterly insupportable.

MacKinnon frequently cites the leading Puritan covenant theologian, William Perkins, but does not acknowledge much of what Perkins had to say on this topic of worldly vocations. Not only did Perkins regard those who lived in no calling to be guilty of rebellion against God,[22] he explicitly stated that "vocation is a certain kind of life, ordained & imposed by God," and that "if an action indifferent comes within the case of furthering the good of the commonwealth or church, it ceases to be indifferent, and comes under commandment. And so all kinds of callings and their works, though never so base, may be the matter of good works."[23] Richard Greenham's view, that we glorify God by working diligently in a calling, is a commonplace in writings by Puritan divines, who, like John Angier, criticize lay persons who "do not spiritualize their callings and earthly businesses." According to John Preston, next to Perkins the most prominent covenant theologian, "the very ordinary works of our calling, ordinary things to men . . . if it come from faith, if it be

*Seventeenth-Century England* (Oxford, 1971); and William Lamont, *Godly Rule* (London, 1969).

20 See Michael Finlayson, *Historians, Puritanism, and the English Revolution* (Toronto, 1983); Carol Wiener, "The Beleaguered Isle: A Study of Elizabethan and Jacobean Anti-Catholicism," *Past & Present* 51 (1971).

21 MacKinnon, "Part I," 149, "Part II," 195.

22 Christopher Hill, *Puritanism and Revolution* (New York, 1946), 258; more generally, see chap. 7 on "William Perkins and the Poor."

23 William Perkins, *Workes* (Cambridge, 1608–1609), I:727; II:20.

done as to the Lord, he accepts them and they are good works indeed." Another famous preacher and disciple of Perkins, John Ball, describes at length how faith "causes diligence, care, uprightness, and faithfulness in all the works, actions, and businesses of our calling."

This persuasion that we serve the Lord in our callings . . . forces us to go willingly about that work, which otherwise would seem toilsome and unpleasant.
. . . Faith couples the labors of our calling with the practice of Christianity, for God has laid his commandment upon us, both to seek his kingdom, work out our salvation, make our election sure, exercise ourselves in all good works, walk in love and labor honestly in our particular vocations. And faith cannot separate what God has joined.[24]

Discussion of works by Puritan clerics certainly maintained the priority of religious over economic works and, as is well known, warned the laity not to become distracted by secular employments from spiritual concerns. But these qualifications hardly support MacKinnon's sweeping assertions about the lack of this-worldly referents for the concept of works in Puritan discourse. An interpretation of Puritan thought that disregards contradictory evidence in remarks by Ball, Greenham, Perkins, and Preston lacks credibility.

## IV. DOCTRINAL CONFLICTS AND POLEMICAL TEXTS

MacKinnon's interpretation of covenant theology also fails to acknowledge and control a biased selectivity that ignores contradictory evidence. In Section VII, I discuss how MacKinnon misperceives Puritan covenant theology. Here I consider the implications of his failure to examine data other than formal writings. Had he done so, he might have reconsidered the argument that "dogma is not *sola fide*" in covenant theology, that it accorded predestinarian determinism only a marginal, symbolic presence that was overshadowed by a voluntaristic creed under which laymen could will their way into heaven. "The presumption here is that grace, as a product of the will, is conditionally available to all."[25] But this "presumption" was anathema to Puritans, utterly at variance with writings by both clerical and lay authors who responded to attacks on predestinarian determinism

---

24 John Angier, *An Helpe To Better Hearts* (London, 1647), 279; John Ball, *A Treatise Of Faith* (London, 1632), 390–391; Richard Greenham, *Workes* (London, 1611), 147; John Preston, *The Breast-Plate Of Faith And Love* (London, 1632), II:77. See also Jeremiah Burroughs, *The Rare Jewel Of Christian Contentment* (London, 1648; reprinted London, 1964), 198.
25 MacKinnon, "Part I," 162, "Part II," 181.

by Arminians in the 1620s and later by Archbishop Laud and his followers in the decade immediately preceding the English Revolution. This literature points to the central importance of the supposedly marginal, overshadowed tenets for both clerical and lay Puritans.

Arminianism, a doctrine very close to the one imputed to Puritanism by MacKinnon, had ample precedents in England. Reassertion of the efficacy of free will against *sola fide* was a natural theological reaction against Calvinism and other doctrines that upheld that Augustinian emphasis on grace.[26] Under Elizabeth, this development was met by uncompromising hostility from Puritans. A propaganda tract on behalf of beleaguered Puritan clerics in the 1590s, when Elizabeth demanded conformity, reported proudly how a Norwich preacher in 1576 confronted the chaplain to the Bishop of Norwich, who preached evidently false doctrine, "that we had natural motions to draw us unto God." In 1581, Sir Francis Knollys, a powerful lay patron of the puritans, derisively referred to their heretical opponents as "free-will men," thereby lumping them with the Jesuits; so did Sir Francis Hastings and, in 1585, Puritan justices of the peace in Suffolk. In that same era, a furious debate was ignited at Cambridge when Baro, Barrett, and Overall questioned the hallmark of orthodox Calvinism, its supralapsarian position on predestination.[27] These proto-Arminians lost: The English Church remained dominated by orthodox Calvinism, exemplified by Archbishop Abbot. "Among the key doctrines that he [Abbot] himself expounded was the uncompromising Calvinist theology of predestination, both double and absolute."[28]

Contemporary accounts describe the appearance of Arminian views in the 1620s as "novelties" that disturbed the established doctrine of the Church of England.[29] Staunch opponents of the noncon-

---

26 T. M. Parker, "Arminianism and Laudianism in Seventeenth-Century England," *Studies in Church History* 1 (1964):29–30.

27 Anonymous, *A parte of a register, contayninge sundrie memorable matters* (n.p., 1593), 393–394; British Library, *Landsdowne Manuscripts* 33, f. 201ʳ, 109, f. 27ʳ; Claire Cross, *The Puritan Earl: The Life of Henry Hastings* (New York, 1966), 36–37; Parker, "Arminianism and Laudianism," 26–28.

28 Kenneth Fincham, "Prelacy and Politics: Archbishop Abbot's Defense of Protestant Orthodoxy," *Historical Research* 61 (1988):38. See also Peter Lake, "Calvinism and the English Church, 1570–1635," *Past and Present* 114 (1987). For opposing views on this, see Sheila Lambert, "Richard Montagu, Arminianism and Censorship," *Past and Present* 124 (1989); Peter White, "The Rise of Arminianism Reconsidered," *Past and Present* 101 (1983).

29 Nicholas Tyacke, *Anti-Calvinists. The Rise of English Arminianism c. 1590–1640* (Oxford, 1987).

forming Puritan ministry upheld predestinarian determinism against an Arminian "invasion" of free will,[30] which represented, in the notorious case of Richard Montagu, not an invasion of foreign doctrine but a native theological reaction that sought modest adjustments in the Calvinist supralapsarian position.[31] Yet that was sufficient to scandalize many lay Puritans, as appears from published writings by Francis Rous, the parliamentarian, and William Prynne, the barrister. In 1628 Prynne affirmed, in opposing the "heretical and grace-destroying Arminian novelties," that "there is not any such free-will, any such universal or sufficient grace communicated unto all men." He included in his tract a reprint of "The Catechism of Predestination" that had been printed and bound up with English bibles since 1607.[32] From the last Parliament under James to the subsequent Parliaments under Charles that met up to the end of the 1620, MPs conducted an increasingly virulent anti-Arminian campaign that came to dominate parliamentary business. In 1625 and 1628 John Pym officially reported that Montagu denied central predestinarian tenets and disparaged "Calvin, Perkins, Beza" and others.[33]

Additional evidence of the salience of predestinarian determinism for lay Puritans comes from the early years of the English Revolution, when the Long Parliament became the repository for Puritan grievances about "scandalous ministers" and more general problems in the church. Petitions against individual clerics raised many issues: References to doctrinal and liturgical offenses coexisted with allegations of lewd, drunken, or negligent conduct. In 1641, some Puritans in Kent sent petitions against ministers who preached Arminian or Popish doctrine. One complaint by parishioners against a cleric from a nearby parish recalled how, in 1637, he came to their parish, where he did "preach against predestination, and for free will,

---

30 See Peter Lake, "Serving God and the Times: The Calvinist Conformity of Robert Sanderson," *Journal of British Studies* 27 (1988), 84–85; Humphrey Sydenham, *Jacob and Esau: Election Reprobation* (London, 1626), 6–7, 20–21.
31 See Richard Montagu, *A Gagg for the New Gospell?* (London, 1624), 110; White, "Rise of Arminianism," 36, 46.
32 William Prynne, *Anti-Arminianisme* (London, 1628), Sig. A2r, 51–54, 74. See also Francis Rous, *The Truth Of Three Things* (London, 1633), 10.
33 Samuel Gardiner (ed.), "Debates in the House of Commons in 1625," *Camden Society* n.s. VI (1873), 181–183; Mary Keeler et al. (eds.), *Commons Debates 1628* (New Haven, Conn., 1978), IV:239–240; Conrad Russell, *Parliaments and English Politics 1621–29* (Oxford, 1979), 29–32, 404–414; Finlayson, *Puritanism*, 94–104, where he remarks (100), "What was particularly troubling to members of the House of Commons was that the Arminians had managed to throw doubt on the theological base of the church in a way that would have been quite impossible for the papists."

to the great discomfort, trouble, and grief of many of the auditors."
A complaint against another cleric noted "his obscure handling of
such places of scripture as seem to imply general salvation, the doctrine of believers' assurance of salvation." Similar complaints came
from Suffolk and other counties.[34] Although "charges of deviation
from Calvinist doctrine were less frequent than those against
'popish' ritualism,"[35] and, although the petitioning process as a
whole was a strategy organized by a parliamentary faction headed by
Pym, the records indicate that at the local level Puritan parishioners
had an abiding interest in doctrinal formulas that MacKinnon claims
had been obliterated. Indeed, the theological blandness of many of
these petitions may *understate* local interest in theological disputes.
For example, a 1640 London petition against "innovations" in the
church led Puritans in Kent to give a similar petition to one of their
MPs, Sir Edward Dering, for presentation to the House of Commons. Dering modified the wording of the original petition, to moderate its tone: "I dealt with the presenters thereof . . . until (with
their consents) I reduced it to less than a quarter of its former length
and taught it a new and more modest language." Dering's version
referred broadly to the official countenancing of Arminian and
Popish views; the original petition, with more than 2,500 signatures,
referred more sharply and precisely to attacks on "the doctrines of
Predestination, of free grace, of perseverance . . . [and] the doctrines
against universal grace, election for faith foreseen, free will."[36]

Textual evidence generated by attacks on predestinarian determinism in Calvinism thus points to very different conclusions than those
advanced by MacKinnon. An abiding commitment to predestinarian
determinism and intense suspicion of anything that implied confidence in human agency was central to the identity of clerical and lay
Puritans. Developments that threatened this identity provoked a uniformly hostile response. If MacKinnon's interpretation of covenant
theology were correct, clerical and lay Puritans would most certainly
have rejected it. That they did not do so implies either that the

---

34 Lambert Larking (ed.), "Proceedings, Principally in the County of Kent," *CS* 80 (1862),
   118, 123; Clive Holmes, "The Suffolk Committees for Scandalous Ministers 1644–46,"
   *Suffolk Records Society* XIII (1970), 39, 43; Wallace Notestein (ed.), *The Journal of Sir Simonds
   D'Ewes* (New Haven, Conn., 1923), 139; John White, *The First Century Of Scandalous,
   Malignant Priests* (London, 1643), 3, 8, 9, 13, 37–38, 43.
35 Holmes, "Suffolk Committees," 19.
36 Edward Dering, *A Collection of Speeches* (London, 1642), 9–12; Larking, "Proceedings,"
   30–31.

Puritans were doctrinally incompetent or that MacKinnon's interpretation of their doctrine is incorrect.

## V. COVENANT THEOLOGY AND THE SOCIOLOGY OF KNOWLEDGE

Up to this point, my remarks have focused on the implications of *exegetical selectivity* for MacKinnon's interpretation of Puritanism. This is compounded by another, far more interesting type of selectivity, which he fails to acknowledge: *contextual selectivity.* MacKinnon overlooks the selective ways in which Puritan authors presented their ideas in writing and consequently develops a skewed interpretation that maintains that Calvin and the Puritans had antithetical doctrines. The correction that I advance restores to Calvin's doctrines a modest degree of voluntarism and, more important, to Puritan covenant theology a large degree of determinism that supplied a doctrinal rationale for salvation anxiety and undertaking a lifelong search for evidence of election – key points in the Weber thesis.

A sharp distinction between determinism in Calvin and voluntarism in Puritanism is implausible. Like many other doctrines, such as Marxism, that transformed the social world, the doctrines of Calvin and the Puritans contain elements of determinism and voluntarism. Both doctrines demand initiatives by individuals to change the world; both fortify this initiative with the conviction that it proceeds in accordance with the inexorable laws that govern the world. These formulations are neither consistent nor capable of expression in a logically non-contradictory manner, but such logical deficiencies are not liabilities. They facilitate variable representations of the same belief system, and this serves several useful purposes for the ideological virtuosi who seek to explain and disseminate formal systems of belief. In responding to different challenges to their authority, Puritan clerics variably emphasized deterministic and voluntaristic tenets of Calvinism. Contextual selectivity involves local contingencies in the production of ideological texts by authors singularly adept at variably presenting their ideas in response to real and imagined challenges to their authority. I call this "contextual selectivity" because challenges to the authority of ideological virtuosi are episodic and local in nature, delimited by temporal, spatial, and social parameters that go beyond the text. This occurred when, for example, clerics argued with other clerics, confronted independently minded parishioners, repressed sectarian and heretical opponents, and clashed with their ecclesiastical superiors. The biasing effects of this type of selectivity can, of course, be greatly magnified by the exegetical selectivity of a sociological interpreter. The application of this issue to exegetical practice is fairly straightforward: To interpret a text is to explain how it came to be produced in terms of its contexts of argumentation.

MacKinnon may have overlooked the problem of contextual selectivity because he assumes that the religious doctrines he analyzes were not marked by major inconsistencies; like the Puritans, Calvin "is, above all else, the master of consistency."[37] Hence, his interpretation presumes that their doctrines consisted of a fixed set of ideas susceptible to a relatively unambiguous definition. But one need not accept the antithetical view carried to relativistic extremes in order to acknowledge that relations among ideas within a belief system, even in writings by the same author, often exhibit a range of variation in textual representations that are composed in different contexts of argumentation. Ignoring this point is the hermeneutic equivalent of the statistical problem of uncontrolled variance. And because it is uncontrolled, contextual selectivity compounds the problem of exegetical selectivity in MacKinnon's analysis. Citing textual fragments wrenched from their contexts, MacKinnon delineates boundaries between allegedly antithetical doctrines that, on closer examination, are nearly identical.

My remarks on MacKinnon's interpretation of covenant theology focus on three issues. First, I show that the sharp distinctions between Calvin and the Puritans are illusions created by MacKinnon's failure to exercise adequate controls over the two types of selectivity. To be sure, Puritan covenant theology did not simply reiterate Calvin. But Calvin's doctrine contains voluntaristic elements that MacKinnon claims are the crucial features in Puritanism that distinguished its covenant theology from Calvin's dogma. Moreover, an abundant and explicit body of evidence points to the central place of determinism in Puritan covenant theology. This evidence contradicts MacKinnon's claim that covenant theology "obliterated" the determinist tenets of *sola fide* and predestination, allowing them only a symbolic presence in Puritanism. Second, I return to the issue of

37 MacKinnon, "Part II," 207.

salvation anxiety and show how the treatment of election detection in covenant theology precluded the serene doctrine of assurance that MacKinnon discerns in Puritanism. Finally, I show how the "deviations" from Puritan orthodoxy that MacKinnon attributes to Baxter and Cotton are largely illusory, created by failure to exercise adequate control over the two types of selectivity.

## VI. CALVIN AND PURITAN THEOLOGY

The key issue is the claim that the dogmatic content of Calvin's writings was not preserved in Puritanism. "Calvinism abandoned Calvin's predestinarianism via the introduction of covenant theology," a theology not based on *sola fide* but a doctrine of works under which dutiful performance provided "infallible" assurance of salvation.[38] To support this interpretation, MacKinnon develops two themes: first, the absence of voluntarism in Calvin's theology, making works irrelevant for soteriology and precluding efforts to determine one's spiritual status; second, the "obliteration" of determinism in covenant theology's doctrine of works, transforming Calvin's doctrines into a voluntaristic theory of the heavenly contract[39] that lacked a doctrinal basis for inducing salvation anxiety in its adherents.

There are a number of flaws here. No trend toward the attenuation of Calvin's dogma appeared in the covenant doctrines of subsequent Calvinists, as MacKinnon claims. Indeed, the innovators of covenant theology on the Continent and in England were often more "Calvinist" than Calvin! That is, they displayed far more interest than did Calvin in defining a double, supralapsarian decree of predestination as a fundamental point of dogma. But for Calvin "the doctrine of predestination existed within a soteriological context, rather than a metaphysically speculative one; it was seen in connection with salvation . . . even within the doctrine of double predestination Calvin spoke a language more reminiscent of that of his moderate predecessors than anticipatory of developments soon to come."[40]

38 MacKinnon, "Part I," 144, and see 149.
39 Ibid., 152: "Calvin's theology renounces works . . . man is saved by God alone. This emphasis lies at the core of Calvin's predestinarianism. . . . In their later acquisition of works, Calvinists substantially revise man's relationship with God, reconstituting it as a bilateral affair. In doing so, they succeeded in disposing of Calvin's predestinarian determinism." See also ibid., 154, 170.
40 Von Rohr, *Covenant of Grace*, 3, and see 195–196; Kendall, *English Calvinism*, 29–30; Dewey Wallace, Jr., "The Doctrine of Predestination in the Early English Reformation," *Church*

It is also incorrect to attribute to Calvin a complete rejection of works. For Calvin, works certainly do not justify – a point greatly emphasized by MacKinnon; but good works follow true faith – a point MacKinnon does not discuss. Yet Calvin could not be clearer on the issue: "we do not justify men before God by works, but say, that all who are of God are regenerated and made new creatures, so that they pass from the kingdom of sin into the kingdom of righteousness. In this way they make their calling sure, and like trees, are judged by their fruits."[41] Treating works in this manner, as the "fruitful" consequence of faith, subsequently became a rhetorical hallmark in pastoral writings by Puritans. These writings fully affirmed Calvin's denial that the consequence of *sola fide* was "destroying good works, and leading men away from the study of them. . . . We dream not of a faith which is devoid of good works." Calvin subordinated works to faith but he did not abolish works, as MacKinnon alleges: "Because we know that God regards not the outward appearance, we must penetrate to the very source of action, if we would see how far works avail for righteousness. We must, I say, look within, and see from what affection of the heart these works proceed."[42]

In noting that Calvin's strictures on the passive role of humanity in the soteriological process were directed against Pelagian views that emphasized human agency,[43] MacKinnon alludes to the issue of contextual selectivity without realizing its importance. Elements of activism, allegedly absent from Calvin's thinking, received support when he wrote against other views, from Antinomianism and Anabaptism, that held that the Gospel abolished demands for obedience to the Law of the Old Testament. MacKinnon disregards this point and even equates Calvin's *sola fide* with Antinomianism, but most of Calvin's remarks on the covenant occurred in this context and called attention to the importance of good works in religion. When God became our savior, declared Calvin, he did not cease to be our sovereign; hence, the dispensation of the Gospel supersedes but does not abolish the Law. MacKinnon is, then, consistent but wrong in asserting that, for Calvin, the supersession of the old by the new covenant "marks the complete termination of the law."[44] On this issue, Calvin

---

*History* 43 (1974):215; William Lamont, *Richard Baxter and the Millennium* (London, 1979), 129; White, "Rise of Arminianism," 35n.
41 John Calvin, *Institutes* (London, 1962), II:97 (3,15,8). See also Perkins, *Workes,* III:338; Richard Sibbes, *Works* (Edinburgh, 1862).
42 Calvin, *Institutes,* II:74, 98 (3,14,1 and 3,16,1).
43 MacKinnon, "Part I," 152–154.   44 Ibid., 152.

could not be clearer: "The Gospel has not succeeded the whole Law in such a sense as to introduce a different method of salvation. It rather confirms the Law." Moreover, Puritan covenant theologians reiterated, word for word, Calvin's argument that the Gospel is "a clear manifestation" of the revelation of Christ that was "shadowy and obscure" in the old covenant."[45] The Gospel mitigated the Old Testament demand for perfect obedience but the faithful must still strive to obey the Law, which included duties that clerics thought important, for example, submission to temporal rulers, compulsory membership in a state church, and deference to clerics.

MacKinnon's skewed interpretation of Calvin has startling implications for the issue of election detection: "Calvin's *sola fide* categorically rejects works and human effort to establish certitude of election." "Thus throughout his *Institutes,* Calvin constantly inveighs against internal examination for proof of grace."[46] This is wrong: Calvin warned against *misguided* efforts to obtain proof – those that implicated works as a cause of salvation – and he offered explicit advice on the proper course to follow in seeking proof, from which one could derive a measure of assurance.[47] MacKinnon misses this aspect of predestinarianism because he confuses Calvin's evident view that works do not justify and Calvin's cautious remarks on the difficulties inherent in detecting the "posterior signs" of justification,[48] for the discovery of such "posterior signs" could itself be a hypocritical work if it rested on the presumption of individual merit. *Sola fide* in Calvin did not banish human agency from the soteriological process.

## VII. PURITAN COVENANT THEOLOGY

It is a minor error to miss the voluntarism in Calvin's writings but a far greater one to claim that Puritanism "obliterates Calvin's predestinarianism and thus his *sola fide,*" that it was a "voluntaristic doctrine," "thoroughly voluntaristic, enabling the pious to will or choose their calling." The eclipse of determinism by the "thoroughly

---

45 Calvin, *Institutes,* I:364–366 (2,9,1; 2,9,2; 2,9,4). For corresponding Puritan remarks, see John Preston, *The New Covenant* (London, 1632), 326–327; Daniel Rogers, *A Practical Catechism* (London, 1633), 9; John Stoughton, *XV Choice Sermons* (London, 1640), 48; Richard Sibbes, *Works,* VI:4.
46 MacKinnon, "Part I," 146, 154.  47 Calvin, *Institutes,* II:243 (3,24,4).
48 MacKinnon, "Part II," 206: "Under Calvin's sheer grace there can be no talk of proof at all since the very suggestion that fallen man can merit before God is anathema to all that is sola

voluntaristic" doctrine of the covenant was, says MacKinnon, virtually complete. Although covenant theology "symbolically retains predestination and God's absolute sovereignty," its serene doctrine of assurance leads to an "effacement of these seemingly immutable decrees."[49]

These claims do not confront the many textual passages that not only reiterate the *sola fide* theme but also indicate that covenant theology neither effaced predestinarianism, empowered humanity to will its way into heaven, nor upheld the "thoroughly voluntaristic" idea that grace is "a product of the will."[50] Richard Sibbes, a famous covenant theologian, taught that "All our grace that we have to answer the covenant is by reflection from God." This is why, he said, some call the heavenly contract a "free covenant. It comes from God merely of grace." "[T]he very grace to keep the covenant, repentance and faith, they are the gift of God."[51] Perkins strenuously denied the position attributed to covenant theology by MacKinnon. His *Treatise of Gods Free Grace, and Mans Free-Will* displays more than a merely symbolic renunciation of the view that "the will to accept and receive grace is in us before grace be received," noting that "The doctrine we teach is the plain contrary." Against those who hold that "the cause of why some men lie dead in sin is because they set their will to refuse the grace of God," Perkins objects that "this doctrine does greatly diminish the grace of God, in that it makes the acceptance thereof to lie and depend on the pleasure and will of man."[52] This is why the well-known seventeenth-century biography of Perkins states

that his doctrine, referring all to an absolute decree, hamstrings all industry, and cuts off the sinews of men's endeavors towards salvation. For ascribing all to the wind of God's spirit (which bloweth where it listeth), he leaveth nothing to the oars man's diligence, either to help or hinder to the attaining of happiness.[53]

fide." Here MacKinnon conflates two doctrines on works: works as the cause of justification and works as evidence of justification.

49 MacKinon, "Part I," 143, 160–161, 170, "Part II," 206, and see "Part I," 149, 156. In other places, e.g., "Part I," 153, MacKinnon argues that covenant theology preserves "grace and predestination in connection with justification, while introducing works as necessary for the personal certainty of salvation." This argument contradicts MacKinnon's thesis about the "obliteration" of determinism and the thoroughly voluntaristic doctrine in Puritanism, applies to Calvin, and supports Weber!

50 MacKinnon, "Part I," 162.

51 Sibbes, *Works* VI:19, 350. For additional examples, see David Zaret, *The Heavenly Contract: Ideology and Organization in Pre-Revolutionary Puritanism* (Chicago, 1985), 155–156.

52 Perkins, *Workes,* I:715; III:334.

53 Thomas Fuller, *Holy State* (Cambridge, 1642), 90, quoted in Sampson, "Laxity and Liberty," 100.

This position reigned among the covenant theologians. In 1628, a future bishop, William Bedell, wrote to his master, Samuel Ward, himself a student of Perkins, that "I acknowledge no working of actual faith but obtaining only. I do not think that a reprobate ever has it."[54]

Puritans referred far more frequently than did Calvin to covenant themes, but the doctrine of faith and works in their theology was similar to Calvin's views. The emphasis on human agency in the contractarian idiom of covenant theology was severely qualified by *sola fide* and predestinarian determinism. In this way, Puritan clerics consistently affirmed that which MacKinnon argues were marginal to or even "obliterated" in covenant theology. By invoking the contrasting principles of contract and grace, Puritan clerics elaborated an ambiguous doctrine whose inconsistent mixture of determinism and voluntarism was variably presented in different contexts.[55] When commending to the laity a variety of religious initiatives – for example, bible reading, family religion, introspection – Puritan clerics emphasized voluntarism in references to purely contractarian principles arising out of a mutual exchange of obligations between God and humanity. In other contexts, ignored by MacKinnon, Puritan writings emphasized the dimension of grace. Puritan treatises on the new covenant noted that "in the new covenant, God undertakes to make us able to perform the conditions that he requires. . . . When he acts upon us, we must move; when he opens our eyes, we must see."[56] The emphasis on unilateral aspects of the covenant appears when clerics sought to explain predestinarianism. It also supplies a rationale for opposition to radical lay initiatives that threatened the authority of the Puritan clergy – a gracious covenant was not abridged by failure to display evidences of visible sainthood, the sectarian criterion for church membership.[57] In the modal case, however, Puritans referred to both the dimensions of contract *and* grace, using elaborations of the one to qualify the other. From this practice covenant theology derived its distinctive rhetoric. The modal case appears in definitions of the covenant as a hybrid contract-testament. "Testaments and covenants are not all one among men, but in mat-

---

54 Bodleian Library, *Tanner Mss.* 72, f. 240r. While traveling in Italy, Bedell distributed writings by Calvin and Perkins (*Tanner Mss.* 75, f. 20v).
55 This paragraph summarizes Zaret, *Heavenly Contract*, chap. 5.
56 Robert Harris, *A Treatise Of The New Covenant* (London, 1632), 48; and see Preston, *The New Covenant*, 389. For more examples, see Zaret, *Heavenly Contract*, 153–158.
57 Zaret, *Heavenly Contract*, 133–140.

ters of grace and salvation betwixt God and man they are all one."[58] Unlike bilateral obligations in contracts, which called attention to human agency, the unilateral nature of testaments illustrated the deterministic tenets of predestination and *sola fide* held by clerical and lay Puritans.

> All the gracious promises of the Gospel are not only promises upon condition, and so a covenant, but likewise the covenant of grace is a testament and a will (a will is made without conditions; a covenant with conditions), that as he has made a covenant what he would have us to do, so his testament is that we shall have the grace to do so.[59]

These remarks highlight the conceptual ambiguity that lay at the core of covenant theology and contradict MacKinnon's claims about the "obliteration" of determinism. *Sola fide* and predestination in covenant theology imposed consistent and strict limits on the voluntarism implicit in contractarian principles. William Ames followed this reasoning in explaining the differences between the two covenants: The covenant of works "was an agreement of two parties," whereas in the covenant of grace "God only does covenant . . . man is the party assumed." This is why, said Ames, the covenant of grace is sometimes called a "testament." MacKinnon is, then, consistent but wrong in arguing that covenant theology "succeeds in theologically harmonizing the covenant of works with the covenant of grace."[60]

## VIII. ANXIETY, ASSURANCE, AND ELECTION DETECTION

MacKinnon's account of covenant theology's doctrine of works, under which individuals will their way into heaven, fits poorly with other aspects of Puritan writings. The abiding influence of predestinarianism appears in estimates of the elect, which ranged from Arthur Dent's optimistic 1 of a 100 to 1 of a 1,000, to Bunyan's 1 of 1,000 men and 1 of between 5,000 to 10,000 women.[61] In addition, MacKinnon ignores the fact that from covenant theology, Puritan clerics derived pastoral accounts of assurance and election detection

---

58 John Randall, *Three and Twentie Sermons* (London, 1630), I:113–114.
59 Sibbes, *Works*, V:342; see also *Works*, V:18, VI. 542; John Ball, *A Treatise Of The Covenant Of Grace* (London, 1645), 196; Elnathan Parr, *Works* (London, 1632), 12–13; Perkins, *Workes*, II:282. For lay views, see Edward Finch, *The Sacred Doctrine Of Divinitie* (London, 1613), I:12; II:4; Edward Leigh, *A Treatise Of The Divine Promises* (London, 1633), 69.
60 William Ames, *The Marrow of Sacred Divinity* (London, 1642), 114: MacKinnon, "Part I," 156.
61 Cited in Christopher Hill, *A Tinker and a Poor Man: John Bunyan and His Church, 1628–1688* (New York, 1989), 171.

that squared fully with the deterministic tenets of predestination and *sola fide*. These pastoral accounts flatly contradict the claim that Puritan theology abandoned Calvin's predestinarianism by "conferring on fallen man the powers of will and understanding required to expose God's secret decree," that "salvation is no longer shrouded by the divine veil but illuminated for all determined to clasp it."[62] In covenant theology, God's electing will remained beyond human comprehension. The covenant itself corresponds to the general conditions of salvation described in the Bible, universally applicable to all but satisfied only by the elect. His word conveys "the conditional part of God's will," said Robert Jenison, "but what he has set down absolutely, and whom in particular he will save . . . he has reserved to himself." John Ball noted that certitude in religious life concerned the general conditions and not the particular election of any person: "I have greater assurance that the true believer shall be saved than that I myself am received unto mercy.[63]

Evidence of meeting the general conditions of the covenant is a clue to God's electing will – a point MacKinnon dwells on at length. But this hardly exposed God's secret decree: It neither made "redemption available to all who will labor for it," eliminated "pastoral anxiety," nor ameliorated "Calvin's harsh doctrine." Anxiety allegedly receded before serene voluntarism in covenant theology because Puritanism reduced to a nullity the level of proof needed to provide assurance of salvation. "Now, the infallible promise of assurance is issued to 'all' who are prepared to sincerely labor for it." Again, MacKinnon's analysis omits half the relevant doctrine. Puritanism taught that all ought to search for evidence of election and that the least degree of grace, the desire to believe, was, *if correctly apprehended,* infallible evidence. But only by ignoring everything else that Puritanism had to say on this topic can one claim that it was a voluntaristic doctrine that made "redemption available to all who will labor for it."[64]

First, as Kendall notes, "Since all men are not similarly predestined, obviously some are bound to believe what is not true."[65] From this arises the problem of hypocrisy and temporary faith. MacKinnon says this problem vanished in covenant theology,[66] but

62 MacKinnon, "Part I," 167–169.
63 Ball, *Treatise Of Faith*, 93; Robert Jenison, quoted in von Rohr, *Covenant of Grace*, 131; and see also Ball, *Covenant Of Grace*, 250; Rogers, *Practical Catechism*, II:7.
64 MacKinnon, "Part I," 144, 155, 157, and see 143, 156, 158.
65 Kendall, *English Calvinism*, 57.  66 MacKinnon, "Part I," 170.

Puritan writings display deep concern with distinguishing between saving faith and its counterfeit forms. To distinguish between them was no easy task, observed Preston:

> But how shall a man know whether this faith be right or no? For, you know, there is a false, dead, and counterfeit faith. If it be right, you shall find it to be of a working and lively nature, but many times we may be deceived in that."

Perkins discussed "how a man be discern between the illusion of the devil and the testimony of the spirit" and warned that "this counterfeit mock faith is far more common in the world than true faith is." He and other clerics noted that it was the godly who were most uncertain about their elect status, and these clerics associated a "mock counterfeit faith" with a doctrine of assurance that MacKinnon says was the hallmark of Puritanism! "Good works are good but confidence in them is hurtful," preached Sibbes; "since the Fall, God would have the object of our trust to be out of ourselves and in him."[67]

Second, MacKinnon neglects to point out that covenant theology described the experience of conversion as an extended process and not, as Calvin thought, something that occurred at one point in time. Covenant theology emphasized the necessity of spiritual growth; its clerics inveighed against a presumptuous certitude based on minimal evidence of inclusion in the covenant. "In the condition of the covenant of grace," Sibbes preached, "we must live and grow by grace by little and little and not all at once." Hence, John Ball observed that "assurance comes not at first when we believe, but little by little, as God sees it requisite, according to the trial he has appointed to make of us." Certitude is, then, possible, but it requires a lifelong pattern of spiritual growth to confirm evidence of election. Perkins's views on this issue – "The foresaid beginnings of grace are counterfeit unless they increase" – were echoed by many other clerics, who, like John Brinsley, warned that because "Satan can transform himself into an angel of light, persuading you all is well," true believers must "give all diligence to make your calling an election *everyday* more sure" [my emphasis].[68]

Taken together, these points endlessly complicated the introspec-

---

67 Perkins, *Workes*, I:290; Preston, *The New Covenant*, 391; Sibbs, *Works*, I:220. See also John Brinsley, *The True Watch* (London, 1619), Sigs. A5–A6; Nathaniel Cole, *The Godly Mans Assurance*, (London, 1617), 6–13, 18; Preston, *Breast-Plate*, II:16–19, III:16–18.
68 Ball, *Treatise of Faith*, 96; Brinsley, *True Watch*, 159–160, and see 171–172; Perkins, *Workes*, I:632; Sibbs, *Works*, III:61. See also John Downame, *Treatise Of Securitie* (London, 1622),

tive search for evidence. The bare desire to believe could easily be no more than a hypocritical work, a conclusion that would be reinforced by failure to grow in grace. It is difficult to see how, as MacKinnon argues, this doctrine of election detection substituted serene assurance for the salvation anxiety that Weber discerned in Puritanism. Far from embracing a voluntaristic doctrine under which believers could will themselves into heaven, covenant theologians affirmed quite the opposite position. "No man is justified by believing himself to be just, nor pardoned by believing that he is pardoned."[69]

### IX. JOHN COTTON AND RICHARD BAXTER

Methodological flaws in MacKinnon's analysis of covenant theology also appear in his treatment of Cotton and Baxter. Cotton is said to be an Antinomian who rejected the "doctrine of works" in covenant theology in favor of Calvin's *sola fide* – here MacKinnon reiterates Kendall's dubious argument that Cotton was "the first major Calvinist figure to part company with the principles of covenant theology." Arminianism in Baxter led in the opposite direction, to "Baxterian free will," which pushed works in the covenanting tradition "to its inevitable conclusion . . . predestination, even in diluted form, has no place in such a system."[70] Neither of these claims can be sustained after we correct for the bias introduced by MacKinnon's failure to control contextual and exegetical selectivity in his interpretation. The appearance of Antinomianism in Cotton and Arminianism in Baxter derives from the different contexts in which they used covenant theology to address issues of authority. Separatism in the prerevolutionary era alarmed Cotton, whereas Baxter abhorred the Antinomianism that flourished during the English Revolution. The former development magnified works and the efficacy of human agency and the latter dismissed them; hence Cotton sometimes emphasized grace, whereas Baxter emphasized works. But in other contexts, ignored by MacKinnon, both writers affirmed the other side of the heavenly contract that MacKinnon alleges they had discarded.

In New England, Cotton responded to the same separatist tenden-

92; William Gough, *A Guide To Goe To God* (London, 1626), 132–133; Preston, *Breast-Plate*, II:68–69.

69 Ball, *Treatise of Faith*, 85. See Cole, *Assurance*, 118.

70 MacKinnon, "Part I," 159, 163, "Part II," 191.

cy that he had previously opposed in England because of its strictures on admitting only regenerate persons to its churches. In a 1636 sermon delivered at the Salem church, Cotton delineated the unconditional nature of the heavenly contract in order to emphasize difficulties in discerning evidence of election. This undermined separatist ecclesiology, for godly works, the criterion of church membership, could reflect nothing more than hypocritical pride.[71] Moreover, the unconditional nature of God's covenant meant it was not abrogated by manifest ungodliness on the part of the elect; those who taught otherwise professed a covenant of works.[72] Precisely the same arguments had been voiced earlier in England in opposition to separatism by Thomas Adams, George Gifford, Joseph Hall, Richard Sibbes, and John Udall, who were no more Antinomian for making these arguments than was Cotton, whose core criticism of the "covenant of works" doctrine in separatism – "if you come to Christ by virtue of anything which is in you, it is but a legal work" – merely reiterated the basic tenets of Puritan covenant theology.[73]

Cotton's entanglement in the Antinomian controversy followed from an extention of his views by Anne Hutchinson. Little support exists for the claim that Cotton was Antinomianism's "most notable advocate," who advanced this doctrine "in alliance with Anne Hutchinson."[74] Minor differences separated orthodoxy in Massachusetts from Cotton, who "felt that the differences were ultimately in emphasis and not central to what all saints must believe," as did John Winthrop, a proponent of the "orthodox" view.[75] Far greater differences separated him from the Antinomian argument that *sola fide* made works irrelevant to religious life, a doctrine Cotton consistently denied.[76] Possibly anticipating this point, MacKinnon argues that, when "faced by the united opposition of the covenanting estab-

71  William Stoever, *'A Faire and Easie Way to Heaven': Covenant Theology and Antinomianism in Early Massachusetts* (Middletown, Conn., 1978), 49–52, 73–74.

72  John Cotton, *Sermon Preached at Salem* (1636), reprinted in Larzer Ziff (ed.), *John Cotton on the Churches of New England* (Cambridge, Mass., 1968), 53, 56.

73  Cotton, *Sermon at Salem*, 63. For debates between Puritans and Separatists, see Zaret, *Heavenly Contract*, 137–140. MacKinnon's remarks on Cotton reiterate the views of Kendall, op. cit., 168–183, stripped of all caveats and qualifications, e.g., that to call Cotton's doctrine "Antinomian is debatable" (ibid., 169).

74  MacKinnon, "Part I," 159.

75  Larzer Ziff, *Puritanism in America* (New York, 1973), 65; and see Stoever, *Faire and Easie Way*, 64–65. For Winthrop, see James Hosmer (ed.), *Winthrop's Journal "History of New England"* (New York, 1959), 217.

76  Perry Miller, *The New England Mind: The 17th Century* (Cambridge, Mass., 1954), 389–391; Stoever, *'Faire and Easie Way,'* 52; Larzer Ziff, *The Career of John Cotton* (Princeton, N.J., 1962), 71–148.

lishment," Cotton "dissociates himself from the [Antinomian] movement." But in 1636, at the *onset* of the Antinomian controversy, it was Cotton who, in response to a request by the General Court, aided its deliberations about a legal code for the colony by presenting it with "a model of Moses, his judicials, compiled in an exact method"[77] – an odd undertaking to be given to or accepted by an Antinomian.

Arminianism in Baxter is most evident in polemical contexts framed by his abiding hostility to Antinomianism, where he emphasizes bilateral views of the covenant and the godly works that accompany true faith. This issue animates Baxter's more extended remarks on "gospel obedience" as the human side of the covenant.[78] Elsewhere he denies that bilateral features of the covenant implied that "we are not justified of mere grace." "Nor do the Gospel conditions make it the less free, or the covenant tenor, before mentioned, any the less free." Here Baxter reiterates the paradox of determinism and voluntarism that lay at the core of Puritan covenant theology: Free grace determines whether human ability extends to the performance of the conditions of the covenant. "That the first grace has any such condition I will not affirm, but following mercies have, though 'tis Christ that enables us to perform the condition."[79]

Citing innocuous remarks where Baxter indicates that God endowed humanity with will and expected it to be used for good and not evil,[80] MacKinnon draws the unwarranted inference that Baxter abandoned Calvinist predestinarianism for a doctrine of works. MacKinnon refers to a symbolic presence of determinism in Baxter but then proceeds to attribute absurd positions to Baxter that are contradicted by the strict limitations that Baxter placed on the voluntarism implicit in contractarian principles. Had MacKinnon cast a wider net, he would have modified an interpretation of Baxter that holds that "grace is residual to his divinity" or that predestination has been eclipsed by free will in "the Baxterian universal man of reason."[81] This is most implausible for the author of works such as *The Arrogancy of Reason Against Divine Revelations,* in which Baxter opposed the growing appeal of natural religion. Baxter adhered instead

---

77 MacKinnon, "Part I," 159; *Winthrop's Journal,* 196.
78 Richard Baxter, *The Right Method For a Settled Peace* (London, 1653), 33, 49, 74–78, 214–218. On his hostility to Antinomianism, see Lamont, *Baxter,* 125–128; von Rohr, *Covenant of Grace,* 98.
79 Richard Baxter, *The Saints Everlasting Rest* (London, 1677), 15–17, 74.
80 MacKinnon, "Part I," 163–164.  81 Ibid., 163.

to the general reformed tradition that limited the scope and efficacy of human reason.[82] The more compelling view, advanced in Lamont's authoritative biography of Baxter, is not that of Baxter the free willer but Baxter the Calvinist.[83]

Thus neither Baxter nor Cotton lends support for MacKinnon's thesis. Their writings reveal no profound deviations from Puritan covenant theology but rather its essential elements. In some writings Baxter and Cotton differentially emphasize these elements, but the appearance of substantial deviation from Puritan orthodoxy arises only because MacKinnon does not discuss any of the many passages where Baxter qualifies voluntarism with determinism and Cotton determinism with voluntarism. Enduring rhetorical features of both writers' prose emerged from their habitual qualification of the emphasized by the underemphasized part of the covenant as they affirmed their commitment to the essential points of Puritan orthodoxy.

X. CONCLUSION

MacKinnon's interpretation does not confront contradictory evidence in formal writings by clerics, consider other textual sources of evidence, or account for contextual variation that attends the creation of these sources. Upon correcting these methodological problems in his interpretation of Calvin and the Puritans, it becomes evident that their doctrines contained the essential elements that Weber attributed to the Protestant ethic. God's secret will elected particular persons to salvation; from election flowed free grace as the means for persevering in a godly pattern of conduct; that conduct provided clues in the search for evidence of one's ultimate spiritual status; and that search, subject to setbacks and uncertainty, was a lifelong endeavor. Affinities between Calvin and Puritan covenant theology become even more evident if we recall that, for Weber, the key issue is the dualism in formal doctrines that sharply distinguish between a sinful but disenchanted world and an omnipotent providence that is of but not in the world. The key issue is not the precise ordering of the decrees or the stages in the *ordo salutis;* it is whether these formal doctrines

---

82 Richard Baxter, *The Arrogancy Of Reason Against Divine Revelations* (London, 1655), 53; see also John Morgan, *Godly Learning: Puritan Attitudes Towards Reason, Learning and Education* (Cambridge, 1986).
83 Lamont, *Baxter,* 137–138; see also von Rohr, *Covenant of Grace,* 98.

can induce sufficient anxiety in lay adherents to prompt them to undertake extended searches for evidence of the operation of saving grace in their "works," which in Puritanism included secular vocations. In the end, MacKinnon's interpretation sinks under the weight of an implausible distinction between unremitting determinism in Calvin, which precluded works, and the "thoroughly voluntaristic" doctrine of Puritanism, which allowed individuals to will their way into heaven. Pushed to extremes, this distinction leads MacKinnon to treat Calvin as an Antinomian and to extract from Calvin's evident arguments against works as the *cause* of justification the view that works are useless as *evidence* of one's spiritual status.[84] Applied to covenant theology, the distinction transforms Puritans into followers of Locke and Milton.

Finally, there is the issue of MacKinnon's harsh remarks, cited at the beginning of this essay, on Weber's evasive efforts to cover up inconsistency and contradiction in his thesis. In dealing with Weber and the early modern theologues, MacKinnon follows two interpretative strategies. In contrast to the alacrity with which he detects and denounces inconsistency and contradiction in Weber, MacKinnon effuses respect for the intellects of early modern Calvinists, and he chides Weber for seeking out inconsistencies and contradictions in Calvinism.

If there is any enduring message in my review of the Weber thesis, it may well be that when engaged in historical research, we should not recklessly assume that scholars of the past [i.e., the Calvinists] so readily fell victim to the wasteland of contradiction – especially so in the case of those whose discourse traversed the logical frontiers of Aristotle . . . it seems both extravagant and impertinent to either implicitly or explicitly assign this excess to them as Weber is wont to do. Even Calvin who rejected Aristotle is, above all else, the master of consistency.[85]

These remarks indicate why MacKinnon did not consider the abundant, contradictory evidence that militates against his interpretation of clerical writings. As I see it, however, the issue is framed by his theoretical presuppositions about belief systems. Misguided interpretations will surely follow the assumption that formal writings by ideological virtuosi are not marked by inconsistencies and contradictions. Indeed, the opposite view is far more plausible: Belief systems that have transformed the world contain contradictions between deterministic and voluntaristic elements whose variable presentation

---

84 MacKinnon, "Part I," op. cit., 145, 153, 164–165.    85 MacKinnon, "Part II," 207.

provides a critical measure of flexibility for ideologues engaged in the difficult business of getting ordinary persons to undertake initiatives to change a hostile, recalcitrant world. In advancing the case for consistency, one could hardly pick worse examples than the doctrines of Calvin and the Puritans.

# 12

# Biographical Evidence on Predestination, Covenant, and Special Providence

KASPAR VON GREYERZ

Professor MacKinnon's analysis of Max Weber's interpretation of seventeenth-century English Calvinism is a wholesale rebuttal of Weber's method and conclusions.[1] There are in the main two pillars on which this rebuttal rests. First, there is the claim that the impact of covenant theology and its reception in England during the initial decades of the seventeenth century seriously weakened and ultimately even destroyed the hold of the doctrine of predestination on English Protestants. The second pillar is the criticism that Weber made Richard Baxter, a pastoral theologian who clearly relativized predestinarian teaching, the main witness of his thesis that Puritan predestinarianism, through the individual anxiety that it created, brought forth and engendered forms of inner-worldly asceticism.

To take the case of Richard Baxter first: He was obviously not a predestinarian theologian, and to that extent, Weber's use of Baxter and of his prominent pastoral work, *The Christian Directory,* was indeed not at all well chosen. In this respect, I think that MacKinnon has a point, although it is not an entirely new one.[2] However, unlike MacKinnon, I do not think that Baxter's opposition to the "Antinomians," by which he chiefly meant the so-called Civil War Sects, had

1 Malcolm MacKinnon, "Calvinism and the Infallible Assurance of Grace . . . ," *British Journal of Sociology* 39 (1989): 143–210.
2 See, for example, Leopold Damrosch, Jr., *God's Plot and Man's Stories: Studies in the Fictional Imagination from Milton to Fielding* (Chicago, 1985), 56: "In Baxter Puritanism makes its peace with Renaissance humanism and prepares for life in a more tolerant age. The element of humanism is important. Baxter's new piety . . . rests on a rational faith that owes more to natural religion than to direct revelation." See also Charles Lloyd Cohen, *God's Caress: The Psychology of Puritan Religious Experience* (Oxford: Oxford University Press, 1986), 115: "Weber's evidence that Puritans valued the methodical exercise of one's calling draws heavily on Baxter, . . . whose theology departs from Weber's ideal type of Puritanism on a critical issue. The Westminster Confession of 1647, whose 'authoritative words' served as Weber's source on the subject, enshrine what is sometimes called 'double predestination,' a construction that makes God responsible for the decrees of both election and refutation. Admitting the former, Baxter threw out the latter."

anything to do with his rejection of the predestinarianism of the Westminster confession.

Throughout MacKinnon's article, in fact, the phenomenon of Antinomianism is viewed from the wrong angle. To oversimplify the case for the sake of clarity: Antinomians believed that, following their conversion, they would be incapable of committing a sin. In mid-seventeenth-century England, the Antinomians, against whom Richard Baxter fought some of his polemical battles, belonged to sects such as the early Quakers or the Seekers and Ranters (regardless of whether the latter were merely paper tigers).[3] Mid-seventeenth-century Antinomianism was epitomized by James Nayler's Christ-like ride on a donkey's back through Bristol. James Nayler was an early Quaker.[4] John Calvin, the reformer of Geneva, on the other hand, never advocated anything close to what we know as Antinomianism. I do not see, therefore, how one could possibly claim, as does MacKinnon, that Calvin's doctrine survived into the seventeenth century only in the form of Antinomianism.[5]

Now to covenant theology: As MacKinnon makes clear, it was advocated by William Perkins, William Ames, John Preston, Richard Sibbes, and other notable English Protestant theologians of the time. This school of thought has often been associated with Richard Sibbes's well-known dictum: "We must not expect that God should alter his ordinary way of providence for us."[6] But Perry Miller's claim that such statements mean that covenant theology in some ways was a harbinger of the mechanization of the scholarly world view has since been subject to substantial criticism from many different quarters.[7] So what was the lesson that covenant theology taught to seventeenth-century English Protestants? I agree with MacKinnon's interpretation to the extent that covenant theology could in fact tend to undermine predestinarian thought if it connected the cove-

---

3 *Reliquiae Baxterianae or, Mr. Richard Baxters Narrative of The Most Remarkable Passages of His Life and Times,* ed. by Matthew Sylvester (London, 1696), Book I, 74–78. See also Michael Watts, *The Dissenters: From the Reformation to the French Revolution* (Oxford, 1978), 179–186.

4 If Watts, *The Dissenters,* 209, states that "Nayler's fall was occasioned not by any peculiarity of doctrine but by the extravagance of his personality," this is to indicate quite correctly that early Quakerism *in general* is better characterized by referring to its intense spiritualism than by the label of Antinomianism. See also Barry Reay, *The Quakers and the English Revolution* (London, 1985), 54–55 and passim.

5 MacKinnon, "Calvinism and the Infallible Assurance," 159.

6 Cited in Perry Miller, "The Marrow of Puritan Divinity," in idem., *Errand into the Wilderness* (Cambridge, Mass., 1956), 48–98, 67.

7 See, for example, Dewey D. Wallace, Jr., *Puritans and Predestination: Grace in English Protestant Theology, 1525–1695* (Chapel Hill, N.C., 1982), 10, and Cohen, *God's Caress,* 281–282.

nant of works with the covenant of grace in an ultimately reciprocal manner.

I wonder, however, not only regarding covenant theology, but also, in respect of the doctrine of double predestination, how important these theological considerations were to the average committed layperson, who, after all, played a role in early-seventeenth-century Puritanism equal in importance to that of the theologian. Or can English seventeenth-century Protestantism be described entirely and exclusively as shaped and kept alive by theologians and churchmen? Do we need to assume, as Max Weber, Ernst Troeltsch, and most interested scholars of the turn of the twentieth century did, that the analysis of pastoral theological works alone allows us to determine the nature of lay religion?[8] I do not think so. Some of the more fascinating debates in the recent social history of the early modern period have resulted from the fact that social historians have become seriously interested in how the phenomena of *Konfessionalisierung* ("confessionalization") and *Sozialdisziplinierung* ("social disciplining") were related and connected. This inquiry poses the double question of how theological doctrine was retailed by professional men of the church and how it was received further down the social ladder during the early modern period.[9] We need to combine the view from above with the view from the grass roots, and I find this combination lacking in MacKinnon's study.

Diaries and autobiographies are historical sources that allow us, to a certain extent, to check on whether and how specific doctrines, which we presume to have had an impact upon people's daily behavior, were received by literate laypeople. Diaries and autobiographies

8 The only passage of which I am aware in Max Weber's *Protestant Ethic* that is devoted to this problem is a lengthy and detailed note in the second part of the essay directed against Karl Bernhard Hundeshagen's view that predestinarianism was the theologians' rather than the laypeople's premise. Weber rejects this view. He emphasizes, *inter alia*, that the weakening that predestinarian teaching was to experience, as witnessed to by Richard Baxter ("die Abschwächung der Lehre, welche die Praxis – z.B. Baxter – brachte"), did not affect its essence, as long as the doctrine of God's decree regarding the "concrete" individual, including the latter's testing ("Erprobung") of this doctrine, were not placed in doubt. See Max Weber, "Die protestantische Ethik und der Geist des Kapitalismus," in Johannes Winckelmann, ed., *Die Protestantische Ethik: Eine Aufsatzsammlung*, 7th ed. (Gütersloh, 1984), I: 27–277, esp. 203–204, no. 37. The rendering of this passage in the English translation is incomplete: See Max Weber, *The Protestant Ethic and the Spirit of Capitalism*, trans. by Talcott Parsons (New York, 1958; paperback ed., New York 1976), 226–227, n. 36.
9 Stefan Breuer, "Sozialdisziplinierung. Probleme und Problemverlagerungen eines Konzepts bei Max Weber, Gerhard Oestreich und Michel Foucault," in Christoph Sachsse and Florian Tennstedt, eds., *Soziale Sicherheit und soziale Disziplinierung* (Frankfurt, 1986), 45–69; Winfried Schulze, "Gerhard Oestreichs Begriff 'Sozialdisziplinierung in der frühen Neuzeit,'" *Zeitschrift für historische Forschung* 14 (1987): 265–302.

that date from seventeenth-century England are relatively numerous: about 100 autobiographies and up to 300 diaries. A fair number of these extant documents are spiritual accounts. I have looked at sixty of them, spiritual and nonspiritual alike, and I have been struck by the relatively minor role played by explicit direct or indirect references to the double decree of predestination.[10] Covenant theology is not missing, but likewise it is not very prominent, although it is possible to detect the impact of covenant theology in the practice of certain diarists of making solemn and carefully recorded resolutions before God regarding their future conduct, as in the cases of the London artisan Nehemiah Wallington and the Yorkshire yeoman Adam Eyre. A relatively secularized form of this practice of making resolutions appears in the well-known diary of Samuel Pepys from the 1660s. But the case of Pepys does not provide a convincing example of inner-worldly asceticism or, for that matter, of how such asceticism was eventually transformed into more mundane if no less strict patterns of behavior.

What is striking about seventeenth-century English autobiographical accounts – and the many examples among them prove the point especially well – is that the overriding concern of the great majority of primarily religiously motivated authors was not with predestination or with the covenant but with special providence, in other words, with God's presence in their daily lives. Belief in special providence generally presupposed the universality of grace. The God of Providence was not the distant and inscrutable God of the doctrine of predestination, but rather a kind of father figure who intervened in one's life, much as the saints intervened in believers' lives in the eyes of contemporary Catholics.

A basic aspect of the spiritual accounts examined is the authors' regular spiritual "bookkeeping." A kind of spiritual gain-and-loss bookkeeping already characterized the earliest extant English spiritual accounts from the post-Reformation period, the diaries of the Puritan ministers Richard Rogers and Samuel Ward from the years 1587–1590 and 1595–1630, respectively, although this must be qualified by adding that Rogers and Ward have left only occasional and not daily entries. Rogers closely monitored his inner spiritual

---

10 For this and the following, see Kaspar von Greyerz, *Vorsehungsglaube und Kosmologie: Studien zu englischen Selbstzeugnissen des 17. Jahrhunderts,* Veröffentlichungen des Deutschen Historischen Instituts London, Vol. 25 (Göttingen and Zurich, 1990), in which more detailed references have been provided.

gain in his studies, prayers, and meditations. He praised himself for successes in this regard but at the same time blamed himself frequently for lack of concentration and for "backsliding" (as Puritan writers used to call it) into a state of temptation and sinfulness: "This after noone I felt a strongue desire to inioy more liberty in thinckinge uppon some vaine thinges which I had lately weaned myself from."[11] Samuel Ward more than once accused himself of "adulterous thoughts" and chided himself for his lack of intensity and devotion in his prayers, his ambition, and his frequent sleeping in during work hours.[12] These and similar contemporary accounts served a double purpose: They were to give spiritual comfort in daily behavior and in the face of temptations, as well as to bring about a methodical way of life and particularly a systematic use of time.

The autobiographical authors whose works I have examined generally did not view time as an immanent natural law. Rather, they saw time as God-given days and hours. The high mortality rates of the age, the subsistence crises of the 1590s and 1620s, and the recurrent plague formed the background to this outlook. Given the relatively regular occurrence of mortality crises, at least during the first half of the seventeenth century, it should not surprise us that the demand for an optimal use of one's time in daily life was like a *memento mori* for all, and therefore, it was also shared by non-Puritans. The internalization and appropriation of this demand, however, was most intensive among Puritans and especially, as far as the second half of the century was concerned, among Presbyterians such as Gervase Disney. He incorporated moral guidelines for his wife into his autobiography in case he should die, which he did shortly thereafter in 1691. In these guidelines we find, among other maxims, the following advice, which echoes many similar entries in other accounts of that period:

Redeem Time; I can from my Experience tell thee, a Review in Riper-years of lost Time in Youth, will prove sad and cost dear; and be assured that Time's lost, that's spent either in Eating, Drinking, Sleeping, Visiting or Sportings, more than Necessity requires.[13]

The imperative thought of redeeming time played a central role, particularly in respect of sanctifying the Sabbath, in the personal

11 M. M. Knappen, ed., *Two Elizabethan Puritan Diaries by Richard Rogers and Samuel Ward* (Chicago, 1933), 59 (Sept. 12, 1587).
12 Ibid., 103–123.
13 *Some Remarkable Passages in the Holy Life and Death of Gervase Disney, Esq. . . . .* (London, 1692), 126.

account written by the law student Simmonds d'Ewes during the early 1620s. On February 23, 1623, he blamed himself in the following words:

Still one idle beginning drawes on manye consequents, for as I had not spent the precedent day well, nor the weeke, soe neither did I this blessed Lords day, for all which I beseech my good God to forgive me.[14]

Here, as well as in similar autobiographical passages of the period, we can grasp an expression of that which Max Weber called "inner-worldly asceticism." For Weber, however, inner-worldly asceticism was almost exclusively an expression and a result of belief in the doctrine of predestination, and the material examined suggests that the exclusivity of this link may be questioned.

Seventeenth-century English diaries and autobiographies concerned with matters of religious doctrine and belief were written by educated and uneducated authors alike. Thus, the Yorkshire yeoman Adam Eyre kept a diary, of which we have a fragment from the years 1647–1648. It records the highs and lows of his spiritual life, as well as a drawn-out quarrel with his wife, caused not only by financial problems, but also apparently by Eyre's wish to bring his wife to adopt a more godly lifestyle.[15] There is also the diary of the apprentice haberdasher Roger Lowe from Ashton-in-Makerfield in Lancashire. It offers fascinating insights into contemporary village society. In religious matters, Roger Lowe, whose thoughts seem to have centered on finding a suitable bride for himself, was not as strict as Adam Eyre, who had just returned from the battlefields of the Civil War. Nonetheless, Lowe's diary certainly does not lack occasional spiritual self-observation.[16]

In the second half of the seventeenth century, spiritual observation of the self became even more methodical in the personal accounts written by nonconformist authors. These included men of the church such as Richard Baxter, Oliver Heywood, Henry Newcome, and George Trosse, as well as lay men and women such as Gervase Disney, Elias Pledger, Ralph Thorseby, and an anonymous female diarist, supposed to have been a cousin of Oliver Cromwell.[17] We

---

14  *The Diary of Sir Simonds d'Ewes,* ed. by Elisabeth Bourcier, Publications de la Sorbonne, Littérature, Vol. 5 (Paris, 1974), 122.

15  Adam Eyre, "A Dyurnall, or catalogue of all my accions and expences from the 1st of January 1646 (recte: 1647)," in *Yorkshire Diaries and Autobiographies . . .* , ed by. C. Jackson, Surtees Society Publications, Vols. 65 and 77, s. l. 1877–1886, Vol. 1 (65), 1–118.

16  *The Diary of Roger Lowe of Ashton-in-Makerfield, Lancashire, 1663–74,* ed. by William L. Sachse (London, 1938).

17  *Reliquiae Baxterianae; The Rev. Oliver Heywood, B.A., 1630–1702: His Autobiography, Diaries, Anecdote and Event Books,* ed. by J. Horsfall Turner, 4 vols. (Brighouse, 1881–1882;

should not underestimate, however, the extent to which Anglican authors of the same period (if I may be allowed to use this denominational label for the second half of the seventeenth century) practiced spiritual self-control, although it must be admitted that they did so less systematically. I am thinking in particular of the autobiography of Alice Thornton, a member of the Yorkshire gentry, and of the youthful autobiographical meditations composed by Lady Elizabeth Delaval when she was in her teens and early twenties.[18] For the spiritual elite of the country, however, regular self-control, which others practiced only intermittently, for example before going to the Lord's Supper, was a daily exercise. A climax in the succession of such exercises was the event of conversion. Henceforth, belief made self-examination an even more stringent duty. This was made clear by remarks written down in her diary by Lady Margaret Hoby at the turn of the seventeenth century: "I went to . . . preparation to the supper of the Lord by takinge an account of what breaches I had made in my faith, since I found that I hadd it."[19]

By the second half of the seventeenth century, the doctrine of double predestination had ceased to have the dominating impact on the belief of English Protestants that it has often been seen to have had. Among Puritans, and especially among their spiritual heirs of the later seventeenth century, a way of believing in the practical meaning of God's special providence, that is, in the role of divine providence in everyday life, gained currency. It did not challenge predestinarianism, but it helped to erode the hold of this doctrine on Protestant religiosity, for, quite contrary to the intentions of John Calvin, the belief in special providence tended to make of the will of God in this world a visible and ultimately even calculable entity.[20] At the heart of this belief in special providence was not only trust in

Bingley, 1883–1885); *The Autobiography of Henry Newcome*, ed. by Richard Parkinson, 2 vols., Chetham Society Remains, Vol. 26 (Manchester, 1852); *The Life of the Reverend George Trosse, written by himself . . .*, ed. by A. W. Bring (Montreal and London, 1974); *The Holy Life and Deathe of Gervase Disney*; Elias Pledger, "Autobiography and Diary," ms., Dr. Williams's Library, London, Ms. 28.4; *The Diary of Ralph Thoresby . . .*, ed. by Joseph Hunter, 2 vols. (London, 1830); Anonymous, "Diary of a woman born 1654 (supposedly 'Oliver Cromwell's Cousin's Diary')," ms., British Library, Add. Ms. 5858, fol. 213–221.

18 *The Autobiography of Mrs. Alice Thornton of East Newton, Co. York*, ed. by C. Jackson, Surtees Society Publications, Vol. 62 (London, 1875); *The Meditations of Lady Elizabeth Delaval, written between 1662 and 1671*, ed. by Douglas G. Greene, Surtees Society Publications, Vol. 190 (Gateshead, 1978).

19 *Diary of Lady Margaret Hoby, 1599–1605*, ed. by Dorothy M. Meads (London, 1930), 91 (Dec. 22, 1599).

20 R. J. van der Molen, "Providence as Mystery, Providence as Revelation: Puritan and Anglican Modifications of John Calvin's Doctrine of Providence," *Church History* 47 (1978): 27–47.

God's helping hand in everyday matters, but also the conviction that accidents, illnesses, epidemics, earthquakes, floods, and similar occurrences were in fact God's direct punishment for sins committed by an individual or a community. This helped to strengthen the will for sanctification, the will to strive for godliness in one's daily conduct and for spiritual perfection in one's way of life so as to win God's favor not just for the afterlife, but also in this world, here and now.

English diaries and autobiographies of the seventeenth century are eloquent witness to the importance of what historians have called "providentialism." This is particularly true of Puritan and, in the later seventeenth century, Presbyterian personal accounts. As opposed to predestinarianism, the belief in the this-worldly presence of God's special providence normally implied belief in the universality of grace: the availability of God's grace to all, and not just to those who had been elected to eternal salvation. Only a relatively small minority of dogmatically strict Calvinists insisted that there was a direct link between special providence and predestination, as for example John Bunyan in the *Pilgrim's Progress,* who obviously considered God's acts of special providence to be an exclusive privilege of the godly when he wrote

But oh, how did my soul, at this time, prize the preservation that God did set about his people! Ah, how safely did I see them walk, whom God had hedged in! They were within his care, protection, and special providence.[21]

The imperative of determining with precision in one's autobiography the date and place of conversion began to lose its importance at the same rate at which the belief in special providence eroded the monopoly of predestinarianism. Admittedly, it is possible that this process of erosion was assisted by the effect of covenant theology. It would be difficult, however, to prove this on the basis of autobiographical evidence.

As predestinarianism, that is, belief in double predestination, lost its appeal, the event of conversion likewise began to lose its biographical importance. Up to about the middle of the seventeenth century, it was a not uncommon practice among autobiographers to justify one's optimism regarding the personal state of grace by a

---

21  John Bunyan, "Grace Abounding to the Chief of Sinners . . . ," in idem., *Grace Abounding and the Life and Death of Mr. Badman,* Everyman edition, ed. by G. B. Harrison (London, 1928), 47–48.

reference to one's conversion.[22] It is indicative of the changes that had taken place that Richard Baxter, writing in the 1660s, thought it right to dispense with this practice:

And as for those Doubts of my own Salvation, which exercised me many years, the chiefest cause of them were these:
1. Because I could not distinctly trace the Workings of the Spirit upon my heart in that method which Mr. *Bolton,* Mr. *Hooker,* Mr. *Rogers,* and other Divines describe! nor knew the Time of my Conversion, being wrought on by the forementioned Degrees. But since then I understand that the Soul is in too dark and passionate a plight at first, to be able to keep an exact account of the order of its own Operations.[23]

Under the terms of providentialism, what seemed to count far more than highlighting the special but singular experience of God's favor through conversion was the daily record of godly conduct. The believer had "*to make* your calling & election *shur* by a continuall exercis in all godlynes & vertu," as Dyonisia Fitzherbert wrote in about 1610.[24] This could be done, for example, by shunning ungodly company. The fact that such a committed Puritan as the London turner, Nehemiah Wallington, during the 1640s could strongly believe in the possibility of going to heaven solely on the basis of keeping godly company indicates the extent to which predestinarianism had lost ground by that time, while providentialism, as the autobiographical evidence points out, gained importance.[25] It also reveals that divine providence could be understood to call not only for individual but also for collective sanctification, if we mean by sanctification the attempt to lead a godly life.

In referring to his concept of Protestant "disenchantment of the world," Max Weber argued that in the eyes of the "genuine Puritan . . . there was not only no magical means of attaining the grace of God for those to whom God had decided to deny it, but no means

---

22 This excludes the·Quaker autobiographies of the later seventeenth century, in which the event of conversion played an absolutely central role. See Owen C. Watkins, *The Puritan Experience* (London, 1972), 160–207.
23 *Reliquiae Baxterianae,* Book I, 6; Oliver Heywood soon thereafter followed Baxter's example: *The Rev. Oliver Heywood . . . His Autobiography,* Vol. 1, 80 and 155.
24 Dyonisia Fitzherbert, Autobiographical notes, ms., Bodleian Library, Oxford, Ms. e Musaeo 169, fol. 6 recto (author's italics).
25 Paul S. Seaver, *Wallington's World: A Puritan Artisan in Seventeenth-Century London* (London, 1985), 103–104. See also *Diary of Lady Margaret Hoby,* 131: "Walked with a stranger with whom I hard little good talke, and therfore the time, as ill bestowed, I greeued for" (July 9, 1600); and similar entries also in Adam Eyre, "A Dyurnall," 86, and in the *Autobiography of Mary Countess of Warwick,* ed. by T. Crofton Croker, Percy Society Publications, Nr. 76 (London, 1848), 21.

whatever."[26] The autobiographical evidence discussed here teaches us a somewhat different lesson, insofar as it makes clear that the prominent belief in God's special providence transformed the Calvinist image of God: It turned the originally inscrutable, mysterious God of Calvin into a much more approachable, and ultimately even calculable, father figure. Witness, for example, the project launched by the Presbyterian theologian Matthew Poole during the 1640s of a "Designe for registring of Illustrious Providences."[27] It is plausible to assume that certain forms of covenantal thought may have assisted this process of transformation, but the autobiographical evidence discussed here does not attest to its prominence except among the theologians who wrote about it.[28]

Matthew Poole's project clearly aimed at making visible God's path through humanity's collective history. Had it actually taken shape, it would have been a comprehensive record of "such divine judgments, tempests, floods, earthquakes, thunders, as are unusual, strange apparitions, or whatever else shall happen that is prodigious, witchcrafts, diabolical possessions, remarkable judgments upon noted sinners, eminent deliverances, and answers of prayer," to cite the description by Increase Mather, who welcomed the idea with some enthusiasm as a means of counteracting unwelcome side effects of the growing mechanization of the scholarly world-view.[29] However, the great "Designe" remained a project in Massachusetts, as far

26 Weber, *The Protestant Ethic*, 105.
27 See Keith Thomas, *Religion and the Decline of Magic* (New York, 1971), 94–95.
28 The limitation of the covenant to the elect was in any case a point of view shared by strict Calvinists only. See R. L. Greaves, "John Bunyan and Covenant Thought in the Seventeenth Century," *Church History* 36 (1967): 151–169, esp. 161. However, I think that Wallace, *Puritans and Predestination*, 10, is far too orthodox in his approach when he claims that the "late flowering" of covenant theology "in England was amongst the most predestinarian of theologians." Michael McGiffert is surely much nearer the mark in his well-grounded assumption that "we may not be altogether astray if we perceive not so much a legalistic as in truth an antinomian impulse in the Puritan thinking that doubled the covenants." See idem., "From Moses to Adam: The Making of the Covenant of Works," *Sixteenth Century Journal* 19 (1988): 131-155, 153. In the autobiographical material that I have examined, I have not found the abundant references to individual covenant making that Gordon Marshall was able to explore in contemporary Scottish autobiographical documents. Dr. Gordon Marshall, *Presbyterians and Profits: Calvinism and the Development of Capitalism in Scotland, 1560–1707* (Oxford, 1980), 221–262, and von Greyerz, *Vorsehungsglaube*, 111–119. There are evident problems in assessing the spread and popularity of covenantal thinking in seventeenth-century England and, with all due respect to David Zaret's attempt to shed new light on this question, I think that we are still relatively far from having solved them. See David Zaret, *The Heavenly Contract. Ideology and Organization in Pre-Revolutionary Puritanism* (Chicago and London, 1985).
29 Increase Mather, "Essay for the Recording of Illustrious Providences," 1684, Preface, cited by Richard Weisman, *Witchcraft, Magic, and Religion in Seventeenth-Century Massachusetts* (Amherst, Mass., 1984), 31.

as I know, although it finally materialized in England, albeit on a much smaller scale, in William Turner's *Complete History of the Most Remarkable Providences, both of Judgment and Mercy, which have Hapned in this Present Age,* published in 1697.

The kind of belief in a providential God encountered in English seventeenth-century autobiographical evidence was not the result of awe in the face of an inscrutable deity. The foregoing nonetheless leads me to assume that the providentialism of that period resulted in as much rigorous self-control as that presumably brought forth by predestinarianism. and what is more, unlike the latter, it clearly had both individual and collective implications: Under the premises of the belief in God's regular interventions in this world and as long as these interventions were seen as reward *and* punishment alike (depending, of course, on the concrete occasion), one had to strive for individual as well as collective sanctification in order to avoid God's displeasure and to gain His grace.

In conclusion, I should like to emphasize that I agree with Malcolm MacKinnon on the need to reduce the focus upon the role played by the doctrine of predestination in English Protestantism, although as the preceding pages make clear, for largely different reasons. Unlike Max Weber, I do not see a compulsory necessity to associate inner-worldly asceticism exclusively with predestinarianism, that is, with the belief in double predestination. I do think, however, that such asceticism is an unmistakable aspect of seventeenth-century English Protestantism, at least of its stricter variety. It was an expression of predestinarianism but at the same time, and as the century progressed increasingly, of providentialism. Whether it fostered a Weberian "spirit of capitalism" is a different question, which I do not want to address here.

Despite the growing mechanization of the scholarly world view, the belief in God's special providence was still powerful enough as a concept at the end of the seventeenth century to lead Isaac Newton to picture comets as God's occasional cosmic agents and at the grassroots level to occasion the temporary despair of a godly woman, who in a dark moment in 1693 doubted its existence: "I was under a deep & grevous mallancoly, which continewed for almost a Fortnight," she wrote in her diary.

I was under the Temptation to thinke, there was something to be sedd for that Athiestical Principle of denying a Provedence, suposing, as they say, that it is below God to take Notis of what befals us here. . . . And as I was thurs [*sic*] tosed in my Thofts, it pleased the Lord to bring to my Remembrance a Text of Scripture which made me no more doubt the Truth of a Provedence. It was the 66 of Isaiah, & the 2 verse. . . . Blessed be God for his Corrections! I hoap they were in Love: for, through Mersey, I was under no Hidings of God's Face.[30]

There could be no more suitable quotation with which to end this essay.

30 Anonymous, "Diary of a woman born 1654," fol. 217 recto. See also David Kubrin, "Newton and the Cyclical Cosmos: Providence and the Mechanical Philosophy," *Journal of the History of Ideas* 27 (1967): 325–346.

# 13

# The Thing That Would Not Die:
# Notes on Refutation

GUY OAKES

The reception of *The Protestant Ethic and the Spirit of Capitalism* is littered with the corpses of critiques that fell stillborn from the press, dead on arrival because they attacked positions Weber did not hold or otherwise employed arguments irrelevant to his case.[1] One of the virtues of Malcolm MacKinnon's critique of *The Protestant Ethic* is that it does not fall into these perennial errors.[2] Concerning his critique and the project of refuting Weber's account of the relationship between the Protestant ethic and the spirit of capitalism, I would like to make two points.

I

Weber developed two analyses that tie the Protestant ethic to the spirit of capitalism: the first in the two *Protestant Ethic* essays of 1904–1905,[3] the second in his series of essays on American Protestant

---

1 Consider, for example, the objection that because of Luther's philippic against the acquisitive spirit or Calvin's denunciation of ambition and greed, the Protestant ethic cannot qualify as an explanation of the spirit of capitalism; or that Weber's explanation breaks down because Calvinist religious traditions in Norway and Scotland did not result in a capitalist economic ethos. These objections have been raised most recently by Luciano Pellicani. See his *Saggio sulla genesi del capitalismo. Alle origini della Modernita* (Milan, 1988) and "Weber and the Myth of Calvinism," *Telos* 75 (1988):57–85.
2 Malcolm H. MacKinnon, "Part I: Calvinism and the Infallible Assurance of Grace: The Weber Thesis Reconsidered," and "Part II: Weber's Exploration of Calvinism: The Undiscovered Provenance of Capitalism," *British Journal of Sociology* 39 (1988):143–210.
3 "Die protestantische Ethik und der 'Geist' des Kapitalismus, I" *Archiv für Sozialwissenschaft und Sozialpolitik* 20 (1904):1–54 and "Die protestantische Ethik und der 'Geist' des Kapitalismus, II" *Archiv für Sozialwissenschaft und Sozialpolitik* 21 (1905):1–110. Weber's revised version of these essays, expanded by the addition of new notes, is published in his *Gesammelte Aufsätze zur Religionssoziologie, I* (Tübingen, 1920). The English translation – *The Protestant Ethic and the Spirit of Capitalism*, trans. by Talcott Parsons (New York, 1958 [1930]) – employs the text of 1920.

sects.[4] What is the relation between *The Protestant Ethic* and Weber's subsequent essays on the Protestant sects?

Weber's argument in *The Protestant Ethic* may be sketched as follows.[5] According to the Calvinist doctrine of predestination, God has chosen a small segment of the human race as recipients of His grace. These He has selected for salvation. The rest He has chosen to damn. Because of the abyss that separates the transcendence of God from the wretchedness of the human sinner, the unalterable *decretum horrible* is ultimately unintelligible to the human understanding and incomprehensible from the standpoint of human conceptions of justice. For the generation of Protestants that surrendered to the "magnificent consistency" of this doctrine, the result was a crisis over the most important question the believer had to face: Was he marked for salvation or for damnation? In the determination of his fate, "the extreme inhumanity" of this doctrine placed the believer in a state of "unprecedented inner loneliness," with no agent to intercede with God on his behalf – no priest, no sacraments, no Church, no magical techniques for inducing grace.[6] Calvinist congregations – as well as the Calvinist ministry, which assumed the daunting task of accommodating predestination to the exigencies of pastoral work – found the radical fatalism of the strict teaching of predestination psychologically and practically intolerable. The historical, although not the logical, consequence of the doctrine of predestination was an epistemological crisis, the problem of the *certitudo salutis:* How can the believer attain some confidence about his state of grace? This problem was translated into a question about proof: Are there any criteria by means of which membership in the elect can be determined?

"The Protestant ethic" is the name Weber gave to the resolution of this problem produced by the Puritan divines who were obliged to struggle with the human consequences of Calvin's doctrine. This

---

4 "'Kirchen' und 'Sekten' I," *Frankfurter Zeitung,* April 13, 1906, and "'Kirchen' und 'Sekten' II" *Frankfurter Zeitung,* April 14, 1906. A somewhat longer version of this essay was published as "'Kirchen' und 'Sekten' in Nordamerika," *Die Christliche Welt* 20 (1906):558–562, 577–583. A more thoroughly revised and considerably expanded version was published as "Die protestantischen Sekten und der Geist des Kapitalismus" in Weber, *Gesammelte Aufsätze zur Religionssoziologie, I. Die Christliche Welt* text of "'Kirchen und 'Sekten'" has been translated by Colin Loader: "'Churches' and 'Sects' in North America," *Sociological Theory* 3 (1985):7–13. "Die protestantischen Sekten und der Geist des Kapitalismus" is translated as "The Protestant Sects and the Spirit of Capitalism," in H. H. Gerth and C. Wright Mills, eds., *From Max Weber: Essays in Sociology* (New York, 1958), 302–322.

5 This section draws on Guy Oakes, "Four Questions Concerning *The Protestant Ethic*," *Telos* 81 (1989):77–86.

6 Weber, *The Protestant Ethic,* 104.

solution held that the believer has an unconditional obligation to consider himself chosen for election. All doubts about one's own salvation are evidence of insufficient faith, and thus an indication of an imperfect state of grace. The path recommended for eliminating doubt and achieving the *certitudo salutis* was intensive activity in a mundane calling: not individual good works arbitrarily produced and separated by lapses into sin, guilt, and uncertainty, but "a life of good works combined into a unified system."[7] The systematization of action around the pursuit of a worldly career was the solution to the problem of proof: "For only by a fundamental change in the whole meaning of life at every moment and in every action could the effects of grace transforming a man from the *status naturae* to the *status gratiae* be proved."[8] As the solution to the problem of proof, therefore, the Protestant ethic sanctioned the comprehensive and intensive regulation of life that Weber called "inner-worldly asceticism." As a principle for the methodical control of life, inner-wordly asceticism was grounded in both positive and negative imperatives: a positive sanction mandating the systematic pursuit of a calling, as well as a negative sanction proscribing all forms of spontaneity and the relaxation of self-control. The positive sanction entailed a moral premium in support of closely managed and continuous profit making. The negative sanction entailed an unconditional prohibition against the consumption of these profits or their diversion from the enterprise that the believer, as God's faithful steward, treated as his calling. These consequences of the principle of inner-worldly asceticism constituted the spirit of capitalism.

Weber's essays on the Protestant sects explain the relation between the Protestant ethic and the spirit of capitalism by means of premises that are not employed in the argument of *The Protestant Ethic.* Further, the logic of this explanation represents a significant departure from the explanatory strategy he uses in *The Protestant Ethic.* The argument of the Protestant sects essays may be outlined as follows.

In certain Protestant communities, the ecclesiastical organization was transformed from a church, "a compulsory association for the administration of grace," into a sect, "a voluntary association of the religiously qualified."[9] This transformation was based on a requirement that excluded unsanctified persons from participation in the true church. The communion of true believers would be corrupted

---

7 Ibid., 117.    8 Ibid., 118.
9 Weber, "The Protestant Sects and the Spirit of Capitalism," 314.

and God would be mocked by the admission of unregenerate sinners. Thus membership in the sect – the true church – was limited to the congregation of true Christians. In practice, this meant believers who were capable of demonstrating the relevant religious qualifications. In addition, the task of safeguarding the purity of the church, and thus assessing the qualifications of prospective members, was a joint responsibility of all sect members. "Only the local religious community, by virtue of personal acquaintance and investigation, could judge whether a member were qualified."[10] This resulted in what Weber called "the extraordinarily strict moral discipline of the self-governing congregation,"[11] whose members were collectively and individually responsible to God for maintaining rigorous criteria for admission and inflexible standards of sect discipline. This conception of the structure and governance of the sect generated a quite different problem of proof. The prospective member was obliged to prove to the congregation that he possessed the qualities requisite for membership, and thus for election into the true church. The acknowledged member faced the problem of proving to his fellow sectarians that he continued to possess these qualities. Weber characterized this problem of proof as a matter of "holding one's own" within the congregation of the sect.[12] The necessity of such a proof meant that admission to the sect followed only upon a thorough examination of the candidate. A period of "ethical probation" was required to determine whether the probationer possessed the virtues to which Protestant inner-worldly asceticism ascribed a privileged moral status. Thus the practice of sectarian probation together with the moral premiums placed by the sect on a life of inner-worldly asceticism constituted powerful sanctions in support of the systematic conduct of life in this direction. This mode of life – positive sanctions requiring the pursuit of a mundane calling as an unconditional duty and negative sanctions proscribing all deviations from the requirements of this ethic as evidence of damnation – was essential to the development of the spirit of capitalism. The logic of this explanation entails that the individual motives and personal self-interests of sectarians were "placed in the service of maintaining and propagating the 'bourgeois' Puritan ethic with all its ramifications," above all "the 'spirit' of modern capitalism" and its "specific ethos: the ethos of the modern bourgeois middle classes."[13]

---

10 Ibid., 316.   11 Ibid., 316.   12 Ibid., 320.   13 Ibid., 321.

In this explanation, predestination as an explanatory premise disappears. It is replaced by premises concerning sect organization and discipline. The logic of the explanation does not depend on the believer's need to prove to himself the state of his grace, but rather on his need to demonstrate to his fellow sectarians the possession of the qualities that evince election. Consideration of the two explanations suggests that if there is one factor absolutely essential to Weber's conception of the relation between the Protestant ethic and the spirit of capitalism, it is not the doctrine of predestination but the problem of proof.[14] However, notice that the problem of proof differs in the two explanations. The Calvinist's problem turns on the question of how to prove to himself that he is among the elect. This problem is driven by the epistemological crisis concerning criteria for the achievement of the *certitudo salutis,* the question of the conditions under which it is possible for the believer to attain certainty about his salvation. It is also driven by guilt, the Calvinist's belief that he is objectively a sinner and remains eternally damned because he has transgressed the law of God. The sectarian's problem is to prove to his fellow sectarians that he is one of them. The epistemological crisis is irrelevant to this problem, which is driven not by guilt but by shame. The sectarian fears exclusion from the religious community by its members. This fear is based on the sectarian's belief that the sect might expose him as religiously inadequate, which could occur if the sect perceived him as failing to measure up to its standards of correct doctrine and upright conduct. Polemically these considerations show that a refutation of the argument Weber develops in *The Protestant Ethic* does not by itself qualify as a refutation of the argument of the Protestant sects essays. Thus, even if MacKinnon's critique of *The Protestant Ethic* is accepted in toto, the analysis linking the Protestant ethic and the spirit of capitalism in the Protestant sects essays is left untouched.

## II

Let us suppose that the two main claims of MacKinnon's critique are sound: first, that there was no crisis in the theory of salvation produced by seventeenth-century Calvinism because predestination had been thoroughly compromised by the doctrine that the believer can

14 This was Weber's own position. See Weber, *The Protestant Ethic,* 128, 153, 258n. 192.

achieve certainty about his salvation; and second, that the works sanctioned by Calvinist pastoral theology were not mundane but spiritual. If these two claims are admitted, what follows? Does the argument of *The Protestant Ethic* collapse? The first claim seems to destroy Weber's conception of the Protestant ethic. Without the doctrine of predestination, the believer has no need to prove to himself that he is saved. As a result, the religious basis for the compulsion to ascribe a privileged moral status to the conduct of life that solves the problem of proof is undermined. Independent of predestination, the problem of the *certitudo salutis* does not arise, in which case there is no problem of proof. And without the crisis over proof, Weber's argument cannot be generated. The second claim apparently disposes of Weber's view of the connection between the Protestant ethic and inner-worldly asceticism. If work in the world lacks a religious certification, then this connection – and thus the relationship between the Protestant ethic and the spirit of capitalism – breaks down.

I suggest that these conclusions would be premature. Notice that the main premises of MacKinnon's position concern the exegesis of texts in theology and theological ethics. These premises are irrelevant to the validity of Weber's argument, which does not depend upon the correct interpretation of theological doctrines, but upon the consequences of these doctrines for a revolution in the conduct of life. MacKinnon's strategy of refutation rests on the mistaken assumption that the intrinsic religious import of ideas developed in theological texts decides the force and bearing of these ideas as constituents of the intentions and motives of historical actors.

In any institution that produces ideas – regardless of whether the ideas are scientific theories, theological doctrines, marketing programs, or political campaigns – it is essential to distinguish three types of institutional actors: producers of ideas; purveyors, distributors, or marketers of ideas; and consumers of ideas. In the world of sixteenth- and seventeenth-century Puritanism, the producers of ideas were theological elites, a priestly status group in command of esoteric knowledge. They were the authors of treatises on theology and moral theory and the architects of articles of faith. The distributors of ideas were university-trained clerics and congregational pastors, laborers in the vineyards of the Lord, as they conceived themselves, or middlemen in a service industry devoted to the care of souls. They were the authors of pastoral writings on applied ethics and manuals of practical divinity – the sermons, catechisms, and pamphlets that formed a popular literature composed for lay audiences. The consumers of this literature were the recipients of pastoral care: communicants and sectarians who were not themselves religious professionals. They were lay practitioners of religion who, although literate in the sense that they could read, either could not write or lacked the formal training necessary to understand elite religious discourse. Among these three types of actors, ideas are subject to shifts and drifts, reinterpretations, reconceptualizations, and reconfigurations. Thus corresponding to these three types of institutional actors in religious organizations, we can distinguish three types of religious intellectuality: an understanding of theology and ethics that is elite or learned, practical or applied, and lay or popular.

In light of these two distinctions – three types of institutional actors and three types of religious intellectuality – it is necessary to differentiate the ideas generated by theological elites, the popularization of these ideas in the preaching of clerics, and the uses actually made of this preaching by lay practitioners of religion. This means that it is important not to conflate the substance of theological and ethical theories, the practical applications of these theories in the vernacular literature, and the impact of this literature on a popular audience. The principles articulated in learned texts should not be identified with the translation of these principles in the exercise of pastoral responsibilities; and the practical understanding of these principles by the clergy should not be confused with their reception by parishioners. In the final analysis, the validity of Weber's argument in *The Protestant Ethic* depends on the following question: Can it be shown that the ethos of inner-worldly asceticism was incorporated into the lives of religious nonprofessionals, and did this ethos become secularized as the spirit of capitalism? As Weber put it, *The Protestant Ethic* is "not so much concerned with what concepts the theological moralists developed in their ethical theories, but, rather, what was the effective morality in the life of believers – that is, how the religious background of economic ethics affected practice."[15]

This problem cannot be resolved by an intensive examination and reexamination of treatises produced by theologians, the course taken

---

15 Ibid., 267n. 42. See also Weber's final reply to Felix Rachfahl, an early critic of *The Protestant Ethic:* "Antikritisches Schlusswort zum 'Geist des Kapitalismus'," in Johannes Winckelmann, ed., *Die protestantische Ethik II: Kritiken und Antikritiken* (Gutersloh, 1978), 305–307.

by MacKinnon. It is necessary to consider evidence that documents the ethos of the consumers of religious ideas. Historians of emotional life have attempted to identify and interpret the sort of evidence relevant to theses concerning the popular expression, control, and suppression of emotions such as anger, jealousy, guilt, and shame.[16] Historians of ethics will have to take a parallel course if the validity of Weber's thesis is to be seriously assessed. This requires a move from the rarefied atmosphere of Calvin's *Institutes* and the only slightly less elevated intellectuality of the *Westminster Confession* and the theological arguments of Ames, Baxter, and Perkins to a consideration of much more mundane documents: the biographical records, letters, devotional manuals, wills, and other autobiographical effluvia of Puritan businessmen.[17] Weber once characterized politics as the "slow boring of hard boards." The same holds for the project of assessing the main argument of *The Protestant Ethic*.

The preceding discussion of types of religious actors and religious intellectuality has an interesting consequence for the assessment of Weber's argument in *The Protestant Ethic*. Even if Weber is mistaken in his interpretation of Calvinism and also misguided in his reading of Calvinist pastoral theology and psychology, it does not follow that his explanation of the relation between the Protestant ethic and the spirit of capitalism is also invalid. This is because, as Weber himself noted, his explanation does not turn on the intrinsic meaning of elite theological doctrines, but on the interpretation and application of these doctrines in the lives of lay religious actors. The validity of Weber's explanation depends upon how the Puritan "civic strata" – artisans, traders, entrepreneurs: men of the "middling" or "industrious" sort[18] – interpreted religious doctrine, the consequences these interpretations produced for their understanding of their moral obligations, and the impact of this understanding on their conduct. This

16 See, for example, Peter N. Stearns, with Carol Z. Stearns, "Emotionology: Clarifying the History of Emotions and Emotional Standards," *American Historical Review* 90 (1985):813–836; Carol Zisowitz Stearns and Peter N. Stearns, *Anger: The Struggle for Emotional Control in America's History* (Chicago, 1986); Carol Z. Stearns and Peter N. Stearns, eds., *Emotion and Social Change* (New York, 1988); Andrew E. Barnes and Peter N. Stearns, eds., *Social History and Issues in Human Consciousness* (New York, 1989); and Peter N. Stearns, *Jealousy: The Evolution of an Emotion in American History* (New York, 1989).

17 See David Zaret, *The Heavenly Contract: Ideology and Organization in Pre-Revolutionary Puritanism* (Chicago, 1985), which represents a step in this direction. Zaret attempts to develop evidence of the religious ethos of the Puritan laity by examining sermons intended for this audience and religious publications targeted at a popular market. See especially 22, 36–38.

18 See Max Weber, *Economy and Society*, Guenther Roth and Claus Wittich, eds. (Berkeley, 1968), 479–480, 481–484.

means that even if Weber is dead wrong in his analysis of the positions taken by Puritan religious elites and clerics, it does not follow that he is also wrong on the major issue of *The Protestant Ethic*: the relation between the Protestant ethic and the spirit of capitalism.

Suppose, for example, that Weber's interpretation of the *Westminster Confession* is erroneous. It does not follow that the explanation in which he employs this interpretation is also in error. The crucial question for the validity of this explanation is whether the Puritan laity – the consumers of the *Westminster Confession* as reinterpreted and rearticulated by Puritan clerics – also misunderstood this document in the same way Weber did, with the result that this misunderstanding produced the consequences for the popular religious conception of economic ethics that Weber describes.

Therefore, Weber's argument may be valid and his explanation sound in spite of – indeed, precisely because of – his own putative misinterpretation of learned theological and moral doctrines. This issue depends upon how the Puritan laity interpreted these doctrines as they were transmitted to them and how these interpretations were translated into what Weber called "the effective morality in the life of believers," with the result that they became "practical-psychological" motives for "real ethical conduct."[19] This question cannot be resolved by reexamining texts such as the *Westminster Confession*. Thus Weber can be right about the explanation of the relation between the Protestant ethic and the spirit of capitalism even if he is wrong about some of its premises. He can be right about the links among the Protestant ethic, inner-worldly asceticism, and the spirit of capitalism, conceived as constituents of the life of the religious laity, even if he is wrong about Calvinism as a theological doctrine.

This seems paradoxical. If it is, the paradox is due to the relation between Weber's putative misunderstanding of the premises of his argument, on the one hand, and the conditions for the validity of this argument, on the other. It is a paradox that would have been appreciated by the man who discovered the paradoxes involved in a secular ethic of personal autonomy produced by a religious ethic of personal submission; the anthropocentrism of the Enlightenment as a consequence of the theocentrism of the Reformation; an economic ethic of world mastery generated by a theology of world rejection; and bureaucratic rationalization as a consequence of charismatic innovation. The apparently paradoxical quality of Weber's argument in *The Prot-*

19 Weber, "Antikritisches Schlusswort," 306.

*estant Ethic* is an instance of his own conception of the irony of the intentions and consequences of conduct: the opaque and indeterminate relation between the motives and purposes of action and the results they actually achieve. According to Weber, the actor generally lacks a perspicuous view of the circumstances of his conduct and the conditions under which his purposes can be realized. The result is an arbitrary relation between the intentions and consequences of action. This conception of the paradoxical quality of historical processes, large and small, applies to all actions and their artifacts, including, of course, the complex act of authorship and the text it produces, the author's understanding of the premises of an explanation and the conditions on which its validity really depends, the conception of an argument and its actual logic. Thus it is a position that applies not merely to the efforts of Puritan reformers and the largely unwitting, unforseen, and unwanted economic consequences of their reforms, but also, we may suppose, to the text in which these relations were first set out: *The Protestant Ethic*. In that event, *The Protestant Ethic* may qualify as an instance of the type of phenomenon it analyzes: the ironic and paradoxical relation between the intentions and consequences of action.

# 14

# *Historical Viability, Sociological Significance, and Personal Judgment*

GIANFRANCO POGGI

I

Some years ago, in a footnote to his *Injustice, The Social Bases of Obedience and Revolt,*[1] Barrington Moore, Jr., casually delivered himself of the following statement: "It is by no means clear whether Max Weber's famous *The Protestant Ethic and the Spirit of Capitalism* [PE] constituted an important breakthrough or a blind alley." It would be nice to be able to say that the conference from which this volume originated has at least clarified that matter, but I for one have the feeling that this show will run and run. On the other hand, it is not clear that the alternative posed by Moore in his footnotes – breakthrough versus blind alley – is quite as stringently posed as it may seem. But let us assume for the moment that it is meaningful, and that it hangs on whether PE makes its case (thus becoming "a breakthrough") or fails to (thus becoming "a blind alley").

One major difficulty in assessing, then, whether Weber made his case in PE lies in the particular nature of the case to be made, which as I construe it ultimately rests on the assertion that there are causal relationships between four sets of ideas. The sets, and the relative relationships, can be spelled out as follows:

1. Calvinist theological ideas, particularly the dogma of predestination, which induce in the believer
2. salvation anxiety. For theological and ecclesiological reasons, such

I prepared my own contribution to the conference from which this book originated while a Fellow at the Center for Advanced Study in the Behavioral Sciences (Stanford, California), where I still was when I drafted this essay. I am very grateful to the Center for its hospitality, and I acknowledge the support both of the National Science Foundation (Grant BNS87-00864) and of the Center for Advanced Studies of the University of Virginia, which awarded me a Fellowship in 1988–1990.
1 Barrington Moore, Jr., *Injustice. The Social Bases of Obedience and Revolt* (White Plains, N.Y.: M. E. Sharpe, 1978), 466, n. 7.

anxiety cannot be relieved through the practice of sacraments or a monastic flight from the world. As individuals search for other means of relief, they sometimes tend to consider themselves elect if and insofar as they can conduct their own existence in keeping with

3. "this-worldly asceticism" (or "the Protestant ethic"). This is a commitment to proving one's moral worth in and through the practice of one's worldly calling, a practice characterized by a drive for mastery and a rejection of traditionalism. But, under certain circumstances (insufficiently thematized by Max Weber, in my view), this worldly asceticism turns into

4. "the spirit of capitalism," that is, a particular, historically novel, set of ethically inspired habits concerning the conduct of commercial and manufacturing businesses.

The distinction between (2) and (3) is necessary in order to allow for the "Protestant Sects" route to the spirit of capitalism; for in that essay, the commitment to proving one's worth in one's calling does not originate from the dogma of predestination and the resulting salvation anxiety.

There are multiple reasons why, nearly ninety years after the publication of PE, its basic argument – which, as I have tried to show, can be presented in a relatively straightforward manner – has not yet proven itself to be either an important breakthrough or a blind alley. One might distinguish between reasons internal and reasons external to the argument itself.

Beginning with some internal reasons, the argument postulates a causal influence – not just some kind of "meaningful congruence" – between the sets of ideas in question. This entails that in order to be rigorously proven, the argument should establish a temporal succession between each idea set and the idea set that follows, and it is very difficult to see how one might achieve that. Weber, of course, was clearly aware of the problem, and this may have led him to the rhetorical device of starting with late evidence of (4) – the Benjamin Franklin texts - and then finding his way to the relatively early evidence of (1) – the *Westminster Confession,* thus suggesting a neat "chronological slide" between the latter and the former.

A second difficulty lies in the fact that the four components of the argument are considerably heterogeneous, despite the fact that each can be construed as a set of ideas. In particular, they have different relationships to the textual evidence adduced by Weber. For instance, the *Westminster Confession* does not stand to (1) in the same way that the Franklin texts stand to (4). Using Austinian language, one could say that the former relationship is performative (the *Confession* constitutes a set of ideas) the second elocutionary (Franklin documents another).

Furthermore, component (2) – salvation anxiety – seems to me particularly inferential; it reminds me of a comment in Reinhard Bendix's *Max Weber: An Intellectual Portrait* concerning Weber's propensity for "such phrases as 'according to all experiences,' or 'as is well known.'"[2] Besides, there is something perverse (as Weber says explicitly) about the emergence of salvation anxiety in the souls of believers to whom official doctrine repeats: You cannot attain proof of election; therefore, you should stop seeking it or worrying about it.

Again, there is something perverse about the argument that an intense, ethically driven commitment to entrepreneurship and to money making begins to operate in the minds of Calvinist believers, in view of the fact that official Calvinist doctrine and much of the documentable pastoral discourse from the Reformed churches continue to echo traditional antimammonist motifs. Lucian Pellicani has recently restated – and perhaps somewhat overstated – this criticism of the Weber thesis. This raises the question: How legitimate is it to impute to people officially proscribed ideas without some strong evidence that they were entertained? What would such evidence be like? How much of it is needed to offset what might seem a legitimate presumption that people actually adopted ideas officially put forth to them as compelling and dutiful?

Besides these problems that are internal to the argument of PE, there are also those that are external to it. These flow from a basic query: What is the relationship between an argument concerning sets of ideas, on the one hand, and possible arguments concerning instead the historically factual correlations (which I term "correlations on the ground") between affiliation with Reformed Christianity and entrepreneurship, on the other? Should not arguments of this second kind have priority, and should those of the first kind not be considered as complementary and subordinate? Suppose that research into the prosopography of emergent capitalism yielded the finding that no Calvinists became early entrepreneurs and that no early en-

---

2 Reinhard Bendix, *Max Weber: An Intellectual Portrait* (Berkeley, Calif.: University of California Press, 1960), 269, n. 21.

trepreneur was a Calvinist – would this not refute the PE argument? Suppose that more conventional economic history, having unearthed new information on basic economic variables, decided that no significant bump in the development of capitalism occurred at the time when it must have occurred in order to validate Weber's argument, or that such a bump occurred only in Catholic areas – would this not have the same effect on the PE argument?

So far as I know, the study of what I called correlations on the ground has not yielded anything like such explosive results, nor is it likely to. But my impression is that recently the Weber thesis has been weakened on this external front rather more than on the internal front. In any case, if my opening statement of the thesis is a plausible one, one may wonder why Weber – after flirting with the question of correlations on the ground on the basis of inadequate contemporary data and their faulty analysis by a pupil – as I read him, put most of his eggs in the basket of causal connections between sets of ideas. One reason for this, which some of his critics neglect, is that Weber, with most of his contemporaries, simply assumed a basic factual correlation between adherence to Reformed Christianity, on the one hand, and the formation of early entrepreneurship, on the other. For this reason, he sought exclusively to identify the precise link "at the level of meaning" between the two by asking what aspects of what strands of Reformed Christianity fostered what changes in individual, *alltäglich* conduct. This distinctive concern of Weber was further dictated by his meaning-centered conception of the makings of action. In the context of historical research on an event of the dimensions of the rise of capitalism, that conception inspired him to emphasize authoritatively proffered definitions of meaning and collective codes of conduct.

Finally, Weber may have felt that actually to study the correlations on the ground between the phenomena he was interested in was prohibitively difficult and probably impossible. This may have been a misjudgment, considering how far subsequent students have been able to travel on that road. In fact, some of them have been able to study also what can be considered a middle level between the study of ideal constructs and the identification of the religious membership of early entrepreneurs: They have assembled a not inconsiderable body of evidence on the states of minds of individuals. The verdict of these researches, as far as the PE thesis is concerned, appears mixed. In any case, it is difficult to measure anxiety levels.

So far, I have assumed the validity of Moore's view that if Weber failed to make his case, PE is a blind alley. But this is not necessarily the case; perhaps what matters in science are not only the answers given but also the questions raised; and perhaps from this standpoint, even an "untenable PE" remains something of a breakthrough and sets high standards for alternative answers to its own questions. Personally, if I read PE as an exercise in social theory, I find each time that I learn from it a great deal that I want to hang on to, regardless of whether its distinctive, monographic claim that a genealogical link runs between Calvinism and the spirit of capitalism is held to be valid. A few examples of the kinds of insights that text admirably proposes will illustrate this point.

The first and most generic insight, expressed in the language of a significant strand of contemporary social theory, is the necessity of studying capitalism (or any other large-scale, established context) as a going concern, of considering the interdependence of action and structure. That is: On the one hand, what we call structure resolves into a large number of relatively repetitive action flows; on the other hand, such action flows are generated by structures that discriminatingly reward certain practices and thus select them over others.

Another insight is that large-scale contexts can produce and police the kinds of action flows on which they depend (indeed, in which they consist) only once they have crossed a certain threshold, over which they may need to be pushed by heterodox but compelling modes of conduct engaged in by relatively large minorities. Again, this is a generic insight, but its validity may be demonstrated anew by current events in Eastern European societies, which may have a chance to marketize themselves successfully only if somehow they can find within themselves a substantial number of entrepreneurs (under whatever name) to supply the critical mass. This is a difficult condition for some of them to fulfill, since for over a generation the party-state and the more or less centrally planned economy had systematically rewarded and selected certain patterns of managerial conduct, which cannot be extinguished over night.

This is not an entirely apposite example from the standpoint of the PE argument, for after all, capitalism is an established system outside those countries, and from there it exercises (among other things) a strong demonstration effect. Yet it suggests to me that those Weber critics who compulsively reemphasize the significance of a few Renaissance merchant princes are probably on the wrong track. In Poland, for instance, the authorities are currently trying to privatize within a few months thousands and thousands of businesses. Fugger they can probably do without; what they need are thousands and thousands of entrepreneurs.

PE teaches a further lesson of great general significance. To sustain over long stretches of time strongly performance-oriented forms of conduct, most individuals need to internalize compatible conceptions of human worth that impart to them a certain moral assurance; and such conceptions will likely be inspired by ideas those individuals entertain concerning matters of a metaempirical nature, which locate them within the larger scheme of things. One minor recent example is as follows: At least until recently, the Thatcher regime in Britain seems to have lifted the hold that collectivist/egalitarian assumptions had long had on the self-definition and the sense of moral assurance of sizable sections of the English middle class. But a necessary aspect of this process was Thatcher's worshipful revisitation of so-called Victorian values and her clash with some constructions of Christian social ethics that had become prevalent in the Church of England. Essentially, I would like to reassert here the significance of a basic Weberian query: What forms of conduct are systematically rewarded, "premiated," by the content of the ideas that people entertain?

Finally, I would like to voice my feeling that Weber and Marx were right to emphasize the historical discontinuity represented by the advent of "modernity" (however one locates that advent chronologically). Many critics of the Weber thesis who insist on backdating (modern) capitalism miss this point, together with some of its corollaries that seem to me most significant – for instance, what I would call a shift in the collective identity of Western businessmen from an "estate" to a "class" definition or the broader switch from traditional to rational modes of conduct in many fields, and hence the growth of the disposition to innovate. A related, final aspect not only of PE but of other Weberian writings, which I think valid whether or not the PE thesis holds, is the fact that Weber joins that awareness of the discontinuity represented by modern capitalism with a keen sense of its congruence with other aspects of modernity related more or less directly to religious innovation. However, this aspect of his argument was explored more by his contemporaries and by later scholars than by Weber himself; I am thinking of the inspiration he received from Jellinek's argument about the religious roots of the *Bürgerrechte,* or of the inspiration he provided for Hintze on Calvinism and state making, or Merton on Puritanism and the scientific revolution.

The upshot of these considerations is that in my view, whatever one may concede to them, the critics of PE have not yet turned it into a *caput mortuum*. It remains not only methodologically exemplary in its boldness and in its reach, but also substantively significant for social theory.

## II

What remains of this essay briefly and tentatively reflects on a question that at one point had been proposed to me as a possible theme of my remarks at the Washington conference, but which I felt and feel incompetent to discuss: the question of the uses to which Weber's thinking has been and is being put, respectively, in the United States and in Germany. I would like to suggest that there seems to be some correspondence between "the United States versus Germany," on the one hand, and a different, increasingly self-conscious disjunction on the other hand: the disjunction between Max Weber as a social theorist or a founding father of modern sociology and Max Weber as a political philosopher in the classical manner, as a man of moral vision. In my own mind at least, the American Weber scholars Talcott Parsons, Reinhard Bendix, and Jeffrey Alexander stand for one *usus modernus Maximiliani,* and the German Weber scholar Wilhelm Hennis stands for the other.

However, just as there are German scholars who practice the first *usus,* so there are American scholars who practice the second. Here, I am thinking, for instance, of Lawrence Scaff, who in the preface to his *Fleeing the Iron Cage,* looking back on his first encounter with Weber as a high school student via Bendix's *Max Weber: An Intellectual Portrait,* claims that "Bendix's summary contained little of the actual spirit of Max Weber."[3] Another example may be represented by Harvey Goldman's excellent essay in this volume, eloquently arguing that what is central to Weber is the theme of the "empowerment of the self," a process culminating in a personality capable of initiating innovation, at the cost of challenging most of what surrounds it and of the attendant risk of failure and despair. And it is Goldman's argument that I should like to discuss briefly in the remainder of this essay.

My comments can be ranged behind two questions. First, does Goldman provide a correct rendering of the thematic priorities in

3 Lawrence Scaff, *Fleeing the Iron Cage. Culture, Politics and Modernity in the Thought of Max Weber* (Berkeley, Calif.: University of California Press, 1989).

Max Weber's work? I have some doubts on this count. For instance, Goldman seems to suggest that Weber puts all the eggs of innovation into the basket of the empowered self (and of an overlapping figure, the charismatic personality). But this seems to ignore Weber's keen sense that, at least within modernity, it is possible to institutionalize innovation through such arrangements as positive law, science, the market, and the nature of the state system, in which the power struggle periodically reshuffles the dominant units of the political universe, and within each of them places a premium on domestic innovation, if only in the military realm.

One may sensibly counter that in Weber's vision of impending social developments the image of a fossilized, Egypt-like society holds a frighteningly central position. This may flow largely from his excessive concern with bureaucracy (leading to what Gouldner called "metaphysical pathos") and from the fact that, although conceptually outstanding, Weber's conception of bureaucracy was flawed. It was largely shaped by the Prussian model of *Beamtentum*, and to that extent it underestimated the dynamic capacities of large-scale organizational arrangements. In particular, Weber overstated the significance of law, that is (ultimately), of a set of normative expectations, which by their very nature, if we are to believe Niklas Luhmann, discourage an open, *lernbereit* intellectual attitude. He was inadequately aware of the possibility and significance of alternative bureaucratic (or postbureaucratic) models of large-scale organization, which emphasize the participants' competence in sets of cognitive, *lernbereit* expectations and the attendant innovational possibilities, revealed for instance in the science-technology-production circuit typical of contemporary industrial corporations. Nor did he seem to be aware of the dynamic potential of an oligopolistic market structure, most powerfully revealed, of course, since World War II, but not entirely absent during the previous decades of our century.

These comments, on reflection, powerfully qualify my own doubts as to whether Goldman got his Weber right by emphasizing his concern with the empowered personality. Yet some doubts remain. I wonder, for instance, whether one may not argue, on the basis of the very numerous uses to which Weber put the notion of *Ehre,* that being "an honorable person" was as morally significant, to him as being "an empowered personality." Of course, the notion of *Ehre* has aristocratic roots, but in premodern society it was refracted without distortion, so to speak, through most of the layers of a complex "estate order," and in modern society it could become "democratized," for instance through the extension and the enrichment of citizenship.

In any case, even if one answers my first question concerning Goldman's argument positively, a second one remains to be addressed. That is, supposing Goldman is right, does his reconstruction of Weber's moral universe as centered on the empowered personality render him a service? Although this is a matter for judgment on the part of each person considering the question, I must say that I find a thoroughly Goldman-ized Weber less than admirable on two overlapping counts. In the first place, Goldman's Weber displays what seems to me a redoubtable vision: an aristocratism that is both extreme and desperate, because of Weber's acute awareness of the unanticipated consequences of innovative feats and his resulting sense of tragedy. I find lethal this combination of aristocratism and masochism, whereby the aristocrats themselves do not have any strong sense of moral assurance, let alone any fun. In the second place, and complementarily, Goldman's Weber appears unwilling to attune himself to ordinary men and women and to allow them some measure of moral dignity and significance. Some confirmation of this view was provided years ago in an article by Karl Rehberg, which sought to trace the roots of Weber's most basic sociological concept, that of action, in the class-specific experiences of the scion of a *grossbürgerlich* family; for the notion of action revolves around that of choice, and one must remember the old saw that economics is all about how people make choices, sociology all about how people have no choices to make. So, if Goldman, and Rehberg, correctly identify Weber's moral horizons, they implicitly raise the question often phrased in England as "What about the workers?" or, more broadly, "What about the rest of us?"

Let me go on the counterattack. Why do so many commentators make so much of Weber's infatuation with the Faust figure? What's wrong with being Wagner? Not Richard, mind you – there's plenty wrong about that – but Faust's own famulus, who objects to his own Master:

Tut nicht ein braver Mann genug,
die Kunst, die man ihm übertrug,
gewissenhaft und punktlich auszuüben?

These are lines 1055–1057 of *Faust,* and I quote from the commentary to them in the Heffner-Rehder-Twaddel edition:

Wagner's attitude is by no means contemptible, as is sometimes alleged. But he is no genius – just the hard-working, intelligent scholar, content to make progress in his field when he can, and not disposed to suicide if he can't.[4]

These are my sentiments exactly and have been for a long time. They were recently reinforced by a talk I heard at Stanford from the great Russian philologist Vyecheslav Ivanov. He reported as his first and most significant impression of the West that the Western system is structured in such a way that it can be inhabited and operated by ordinary, run-of-the-mill-people. Contrariwise, it is a distinctive and fateful weakness of Russia (for it shows also in its pre-1917 historical experience) that it expects all significant performances, to come, for good or for evil, from very few outstanding personalities, such as Stalin or Sakharov.

In sum, I find Goldman's Weber to be a totally unsympathetic man, in the sense of possessing a low capacity both to feel and to inspire sympathy. One may wonder at the roots of this. Was it his family background? (I still remember my disbelief when I first encountered in Marianne's biography a saying much quoted by Max's mother: "*Du kannst, denn du sollst*"; reading it immediately reminded me of something a wise old priest told me one of the last few times I went to confession: "And remember, young man, *ad impossibilia memo tenetur.*") Was it the tragedy of impotence, private and public?

In any case, even if Goldman is largely right in his sensitive reconstruction of Weber's heroic moral universe, that still leaves us free to say "To the gallows with you!" and proceed to make our own unheroic uses of Weber by emphasizing aspects of his intellectual legacy other than those emphasized by Hennis and his associates. I am thinking in particular of *Economy and Society,* which – as Stinchcomb noted in his review many years ago – is crowded with such figures as the ordinary magician, journalist, party politico, stock jobber, priest, *Beamte,* university don, businessman, lawyer, or whomever.

To conclude: If Goldman is right that PE mainly conveys a concern with the heroic, empowered self, then I for one won't be too sorry to see that book finally defeated by its critics. "The Protestant Ethic" is dead – long live *Economy and Society!*

4 Goethe, *Faust* (New York, 1954), 355.

# 15

# *The Historiography of Continental Calvinism*

PHILIP BENEDICT

The reception of Max Weber's celebrated essay on *The Protestant Ethic and the Spirit of Capitalism* and its mutation into the "Weber thesis debate" represent a fascinating chapter in the cultural and intellectual history of the twentieth century. Among the many themes of that history that a full account of the widely varying responses to Weber's essay would illuminate are the still powerful hold of confessional rivalries in the early decades of the century and their subsequent weakening as the century advanced; the force of disciplinary traditions and national contexts in an increasingly professionalized academic world; the radical transformation of methods and problems in recent historiography; and the advance of neoclassical outlooks within economic history.

This essay explores just part of the story: the reception, influence, and current status of the ideas set forth in Weber's essay among historians of European Calvinism. More specifically, it restricts its attention primarily to general histories of Calvinism and to work done on the movement's history in France, Geneva, the Netherlands, Scotland, and (at the risk of straying onto the turf of other conference participants) England, above all Old England. This requires a somewhat elastic definition of Calvinism, but the contrast between Weber's reception among historians of continental Calvinism and English Puritanism or Protestantism is sufficiently revealing to justify any definitional liberties thus taken.

Some preliminary definition of just which Weber thesis this essay intends to discuss is also necessary, for the richness of Weber's thought means that there are many different ways of being Weberian, while at the same time, as numerous commentators on the Weber

The author would like to thank Wendell Dietrich and Herman Roodenburg for their helpful comments on an earlier draft of this essay.

thesis debate have pointed out, critics of *The Protestant Ethic* have often directed their fire at arguments that Weber himself did not advance. As a result, the spectrum of issues discussed in the debate has been substantially broader than the specific claims put forth by the Heidelberg sociologist. This essay focuses primarily on the literature addressed to three claims: (1) the broad assertion that Calvinism in some manner encouraged the growth of modern capitalism; (2) the somewhat narrower claim (in fact, not Weber's own at all) that formal Calvinist economic ethics somehow contributed to the rise of capitalism; and (3) Weber's specific interpretation of the character or psychology of Calvinism, built around his understanding of the unintended consequences of the doctrine of predestination.

Having defined the contours of the story I intend to tell here, let me now break all the rules of effective narration and give away the plot line. Weber's ideas have provoked a considerable amount of comment and criticism from historians of Calvinism ever since they first appeared. A substantial literature has grown up around certain questions growing out of the Weber thesis debate. Nonetheless, when one surveys the broad range of writings devoted to the subject of early modern Calvinism, what is most striking of all is that the thesis in its broadest form has had remarkably little influence in stimulating and directing the main stream of research on the subject, except in England. Since the Weber thesis would seem to confer great importance on the history of Calvinism by suggesting that it played a particularly crucial role in moving European society down the road to modernity, this may seem surprising indeed. It points up the extreme compartmentalization of knowledge in the twentieth century and the considerable gulf between the concerns and training of those who have written about Calvinism, on the one hand, and those of Weber and of latter-day Weberians housed generally in departments of sociology, on the other.

To convince oneself of the accuracy of the claim that Weber's ideas have exercised relatively little – indeed, perhaps a declining – influence on the main stream of research on European Calvinism, one need only turn to those rare works that have offered general histories of the subject. The earliest and most ambitious such survey, *Het calvinisme gedurende zijn bloeitijd in de 16e en 17e eeuw; zijn uitbreiding en cultuurhistorische beteekenis* (*Calvinism in its Hey-day in the 16th and 17th Centuries: Its Spread and Cultural-Historical Significance*), was left incomplete by the death of its author, A. A. van Schelven, in 1954.[1] After a decade spent in the pastorate, during which a particular concern of his was the handling of pietistically inclined congregations, van Schelven served as professor of history at the Calvinist Free University of Amsterdam until he was removed from his post following World War II for political activities during the Occupation that the University judged compromising.[2] Perhaps because of his interest in the origins of pietistic forms of Reformed devotion, which he regarded as prone to diverge from the original spirit of the movement, he displayed a more sympathetic interest in the questions raised by Weber's work than most of his contemporaries among Calvinist church historians, and his 1925 pamphlet, *Historisch Onderzoek naar het levensstijl van het Calvinisme* (*Historical Investigation of the Calvinist Lifestyle*) suggests that the desire to determine how broadly the faith could be said to have promoted the sorts of practices that the "Heidelberg school" diagnosed as characteristic of it formed one of the major impetuses to his decision to undertake an extensive comparative study of it across Europe.[3] Whereas this pamphlet argued that Weber's depiction of the style of life promoted by Calvinism applied convincingly to Puritan England but could not be said to describe the character of seventeenth-century French Calvinism so accurately (a contrast in national styles that van Schelven attributed to the influence of the English national character), *Het calvinisme gedurende zijn bloeitijd* devoted consistently less attention to these themes with each successive volume and proved consistently more negative in its judgments as to the accuracy of Weber's ideas. These van Schelven found in 1951 to be unconvincing even when applied to England.[4]

Weberian themes occupy considerably less space in the classic one-volume English-language synthesis of 1954, *The History and Character of Calvinism,* written by John T. McNeill of the Union Theological Seminary. To be specific, these themes and questions are

1 A. A. van Schelven, *Het calvinisme gedurende zijn bloeitijd in de 16e en 17e eeuw; zijn uitbreiding en cultuurhistorische beteekenis.* I *Genève-Frankrijk* (Amsterdam, 1943); II *Schotland-Engeland-Noord-Amerika* (Amsterdam, 1951); III *Polen-Bohemen-Hongarije-Zevenburgen* (Amsterdam, 1965).
2 *Biographisch Lexicon voor de Geschiedenis van het Nederlandse Protestantisme* (Kampen, 1983), II, pp. 387–389.
3 Van Schelven, *Historisch Onderzoek naar het levensstijl van het Calvinisme* (Amsterdam, 1925).
4 *Het calvinisme gedurende zijn bloeitijd,* I, 30–37, 62–68, 263-271; II, 82–86, 276–281; III, 52–53, 123.

taken up in two brief sections, amounting in all to 6 of the book's 454 pages.[5] In McNeill's view, the entire subject of Calvinism's economic significance had yet to receive adequate investigation at the time of his writing, some forty-nine years after the appearance of Weber's initial essay. He nonetheless criticized Weber's depiction of the psychology of Calvinism sharply while accepting that Calvin contributed something to the development of capitalism through his insistence on frugality, his abhorrence of wasting time, and his acceptance of the permissibility of lending money at interest under certain conditions.

McNeill's volume shows that Weber's ideas were still alive, if by no means central, issue for church-related scholars of his generation. The recent collective volume edited by Menna Prestwich, *International Calvinism 1541–1715,* suggests that they have subsequently become more marginal yet for a team of scholars actively involved in research on the subject, who are affiliated primarily with secular departments of history. A single paragraph in the Introduction dismisses claims that Calvinism might have furthered capitalism. Thereafter, only one hint of Weberian themes appears in any of the essays in the book devoted to the history of Calvinism in specific countries and eras (the essay devoted to colonial America), before a final chapter devoted specifically to his ideas reprints unmodified a sharply critical assessment of them first published over twenty years previously.[6] Apparently, the last word on this subject had been said in the 1960s.

Why should Weber's ideas have exercised so little influence on the main stream of research on non-English Calvinism? Some additional reasons appear in due course further along in this essay. For now, let me stress how different the research agendas and interpretive traditions shaping most of the active investigation of the movement's history have been from the German sociologist's preoccupation with the sources of the modern West's distinctive forms of rationality. For the most part, the history of European Calvinism has been written on a country-by-country basis by natives of the country involved or their ethnic cousins overseas. During the first half of the century, these historians were particularly likely to have been believers or to

---

5 John T. McNeill, *The History and Character of Calvinism* (New York, 1954), 222–223, 418–421.

6 Menna Prestwich, *International Calvinism 1541-1715* (Oxford, 1985), esp. 9–10, 269, 369–390.

have belonged to the subcommunity defined by ancestral allegiance to the faith. Often they have been theologians or members of departments of ecclesiastical history. What they have written has tended to grow out of an agenda dictated by contemporary theological concerns and by the issues raised by the historical experience of the specific national church tradition to which they belong. Thus, in Scotland, with its rich history of schisms over ecclesiological issues, the most enduringly debated and researched issue has been whether the Reformed "kirk" was originally episcopalian or presbyterian in structure.[7] In France, where the Protestant minority long had to struggle to counter anti-Protestant prejudice and to assert its right to full status within the national community, historical writing about the faith has largely focused on its political and legal situation and has served to chronicle its endurance in the face of hostility and persecution.[8] Such concerns and traditions have served as a barrier to constructive engagement with Weber's ideas, and they have been a significant reason why so much of the debate that his ideas have engendered has been, as several commentators on it have remarked, a dialogue of the deaf.

In the past thirty years, the tendency for religious history to be written by people attached to the institutions or traditions they are writing about has diminished, and work on Calvinism has increasingly come from historians who are not themselves affiliated with the faith. But this has not produced much research more receptive to Weber's ideas, since in this same period early modern religious history has been overtaken by new questions and methods, most notably by a new concern to understand "popular religion," whether by employing the tools of the retrospective sociology of religion pioneered by Gabriel LeBras and his disciples among French religious historians, or by adopting a more ethnographic approach of the sort more commonly favored by English historians. No longer does it seem adequate to infer the behavior and psychology of ordinary believers from doctrinal treatises written by ecclesiastical spokesmen. The terms in which the Weber thesis debate was initially framed now look like relics from an earlier era of church history. Furthermore, thanks above all to the work of such historians as H. O.

7 David Stevenson, "Scottish Church History, 1600–1660: A Select Critical Bibliography," *Records of the Scottish Church History Society*, XXI (1982), 209–220, esp. 220.
8 A very illuminating discussion of the context of French Protestant historical writing may be found in David Nicholls, "The Social History of the French Reformation: Ideology, Confession, and Culture," *Social History*, IX (1984), 25–43.

Evennett, John Bossy, and Jean Delumeau, early modern religious historians now have a new appreciation of the parallels between the Protestant and Catholic Reformations and the extent to which post-Tridentine Catholicism also encouraged practices of systematic self-discipline similar to those Weber diagnosed as giving Calvinism its particular modernizing force.[9] In the light of this work, historians are not only far more skeptical than their counterparts of earlier generations about claims for Protestantism's distinctive modernizing impact; they are also aware of the superficiality of Weber's knowledge of early modern Catholicism, which several observers have suggested owes more to hostile contemporary stereotypes of the *Kulturkampf* than to the reality of post-Tridentine practice.[10] The next step for early modern religious historians may well be to undertake close comparative studies of two or more confessional groups in similar economic and social circumstances that could highlight the distinctive impact of each religion, but for now, the emphasis is on the commonalities of their experience of the religious changes brought about by the Reformation and Counter-Reformation.

To say that the Weber thesis has not exercised a powerful influence on the main stream of research on European Calvinism is not to say, however, that his ideas have gone unnoticed by those most actively involved in work on the subject. On the contrary, such historians and those studying early modern religious history more generally have produced a steady stream of commentary on Weber's ideas. Their comments on them serve to reveal some of the additional forces that have shaped their reception, as a brief survey the literature on the subject in France will show us.

Initially, those working from within a confessional perspective were almost uniformly hostile to Weber's arguments, whereas non-Calvinist historians, especially those more receptive to the social sciences more generally, responded more positively. The most extended early critique of Weber's ideas in French was offered by Emile Doumergue, the great Calvin scholar who taught from 1880 until

9 H. O. Evennett, *The Spirit of the Counter-Reformation,* ed. John Bossy (Cambridge, 1968); John Bossy, *Christianity in the West 1400–1700* (Oxford, 1985); Jean Delumeau, *Le Catholicisme entre Luther et Voltaire* (Paris, 1971).

10 Hartmut Lehmann, *Das Zeitalter des Absolutismus: Gottesgnadentum und Kriegsnot* (Stuttgart, 1980), 145; idem, "Ascetic Protestantism and Economic Rationalism: Max Weber Revisited after Two Generations," *Harvard Theological Review,* LXXX (1987), 312; Herman Roodenburg, "Protestantse et katholieke askese. Gedragsvoorschriften bij contrareformatorische moralisten in de Republiek, + 1580 − + 1650," *Amsterdams Sociologisch Tijdschrift,* VIII (1981–1982), 613.

1919 at the faculty of Protestant theology at Montauban. Doumergue thought the issues raised by the "école de Heidelberg" sufficiently important to devote in 1917 a long chapter in his monumental *Jean Calvin, les hommes et les choses de son temps* to an extended, perceptive, and often impatient critique of the ideas of Weber and Troeltsch.[11] To this theologian, for whom Calvin's work in Geneva represented a model of genuine Calvinism, to be contrasted to the liberal Protestantism so prevalent in the later nineteenth-century France of his youth, the picture of Calvinism that these men advanced was a gross misapprehension of the faith based far too heavily on later Calvinist writings, especially those of certain English divines. Doumergue was also an active defender of his community against the crude anti-Protestant propaganda that flourished under the Third Republic. One strand in that propaganda blamed Protestantism for particularly exploitive forms of modern capitalism. Doumergue may well have found Weber's arguments uncomfortably reminiscent of contemporary polemics.[12] Although he did not deny that Protestantism had served to promote prosperity, he attributed this to a far simpler cause than to the psychological sanctions for earnest labor engendered by the doctrine of predestination: Calvinism's superior morality. In Doumergue's eyes, the arguments of the école de Heidelberg totally misconstrued Calvinism's true effect on its believers, which was not to make them anxious or singleminded pursuers of profit, but honest, socially concerned individuals devoid of excessive attachment to the things of the world.[13]

11 Emile Doumergue, *Jean Calvin, les hommes et les choses de son temps,* 7 vols. (Lausanne, 1899–1927), V, 624–665.

12 Jean Bauberot, "La vision de la Réforme chez les publicistes antiprotestants (fin XIXe–début XXe)" in Philippe Joutard ed., *Historiographie de la Réforme* (Neuchâtel, 1977), 219, 226–227, 237n. Further biographical details on Doumergue may be found in the *Dictionnaire de biographie française* (Paris, 1933– ), XI, 686–687.

13 A similar rejection of Weber's ideas for similar theological reasons came from within the tradition of early-twentieth-century Dutch Calvinism, where Abraham Kuyper had constructed a powerful religious party around his vision of Calvinism as an all-encompassing ethic that provided the only true alternative to the evils of both unfettered capitalism and materialist socialism. The writings of Albert Hyma, *Christianity, Capitalism and Communism* (Ann Arbor, Mich., 1937), and "Calvinism and Capitalism in the Netherlands, 1555–1700," *Journal of Modern History,* X (1938), 321–343, offer the strongest criticisms of Weber from within this tradition. Hyma was a transplanted Dutchman who taught at the University of Michigan, where, in addition to carrying out research on a number of problems of late medieval and early modern Dutch history, he sought to apply the outlook of the anti-revolutionary movement to contemporary American problems. In the wake of Doumergue, Hyma found fault with Weber's ideas on the grounds that they represented a misunderstanding of genuine Calvinism and of the effect of its doctrine of predestination on believers. He also added certain criticisms specific to the Dutch context, namely, that the most strongly Calvinist regions of the Netherlands were the northernmost provinces,

Even though the Huguenot community in France was one whose members became increasingly prominent in trade and banking over the course of the early modern period, those historians of Reformed affiliation who wrote not about Calvin in Geneva but about the history of the Huguenot minority in France initially proved equally critical of Weber's ideas. Four different works of the 1950s and 1960s discussed Calvinism's relation to capitalism in early modern France. All argued that the primary cause of any correlation that might have appeared over time between the Protestant minority and mercantile success was not Calvinist theology but the persecution and discrimination that the disciples of this theology experienced in France.[14] Herbert Lüthy, the social and economic historian of the eighteenth-century "Protestant bank" who divided his academic career between Basel and Zurich, offered a particularly extensive and influential critique of the Weber thesis. Although accepting that pietistic Protestantism provided an impulse to disciplined labor in this world, Lüthy rebutted all of the other traditionally claimed contributions made by Calvinist doctrine to the development of capitalism and stressed that the prominent role of Protestants in eighteenth-century French trade and banking was largely a function of historical circumstance. Although the flight of the Huguenots after the revocation of the Edict of Nantes created an international mercantile diaspora conducive to trafficking capital across international boundaries, absolutist dirigisme, the diversion of potentially productive resources into the purchase of places in a hypertrophied administrative bureaucracy, and

which did not witness as spectacular capitalist development in the seventeenth century as did Holland, and that within the cities of Holland, dedicated Calvinists were more frequently found among the workingmen than among the mercantile elites. Hyma's criticisms of the applicability of the Weber thesis to the Low Countries are echoed in (Cardinal) de Jong's *Handboek der Kerkgeschiedenis, III, De Nieuwere Tijd (1517–1789)* (Utrecht, 1948), 78; and H. R. Trevor-Roper, "Religion, the Reformation, and Social Change" in his *The European Witch-Craze of the Sixteenth and Seventeenth Centuries and Other Essays* (New York, 1969), 7. It is permitted, nonetheless, to wonder if his claims about the social profile of Dutch Calvinism do not draw as much upon twentieth-century religious geography and upon the Kuyperians' self-image as the party of the "little people" as they do upon reliable seventeenth-century evidence. For some brief details on Kuyper and his movement, see Dirk Jellema, "Abraham Kuyper's Attack on Liberalism," *Review of Politics,* XIX (1957), 472–485.

14 Alice Wemyss, "Calvinisme et capitalisme," *Bulletin de la Société de l'Histoire du Protestantisme Français,* CII (1956), 33–36; Herbert Lüthy, *La Banque Protestante en France,* 2 vols. (Paris, 1959–1961), I, 1–33; idem, *Le Passé présent. Combats d'idées de Calvin à Rousseau* (Monaco, 1965), 13–118; Samuel Mours, *Le Protestantisme en France au XVIIe siècle* (Paris, 1967), 129; Emile G. Léonard, *Le Protestant français* (Paris, 1955), 55ff. The same arguments may also be found in Janine Garrisson-Estèbe, *L'homme protestant* (Paris, 1980), 63. But see Léonard, *Histoire générale du Protestantisme,* 3 vols. (Paris, 1961–1964), I, 308–309.

the intolerance of the Counter-Reformation damped down entrepreneurial activity among France's Catholic majority. It hardly
needs saying that the tradition of interpretation emphasizing the force
of persecution in stimulating Huguenot commercial activity, a tradition established well before Weber began to write,[15] accords well
with the dominant accents of Huguenot historiography.

In contrast to the critical reception given Weber's ideas by these
scholars, two important French historians who devoted much of
their scholarly life to studying the Reformation but who were not
themselves Protestants – both of them particularly receptive to the
inspiration of the social sciences – found his theses far more convincing. In 1931, Henri Hauser, the great pioneer of early modern French
social and working-class history (and a Jew), explored Calvin's economic ideas in an essay that suggested that Protestantism was an
important stimulus to capitalism because of the originality of its
formal teachings on usury.[16] Three years later, in an essay first published in the Protestant periodical *Foi et vie,* an even more influential
figure in reshaping the course of modern historiography, Lucien
Febvre, offered a positive assessment of the Reformation's contribution to the growth of capitalism through its abolition of extraworldly
asceticism and its stimulus of an appetite for work.[17] Despite the
great influence of these two figures, however, their interest in this
subject was only weakly transmitted to the next generation of *Annales* historians. Emmanuel Le Roy Ladurie's great thesis on the peasants of Languedoc did include some memorable pages devoted to
Olivier de Serres, suggesting that his agronomical writings display
the Protestant ethic at work, but when a French translation of *The
Protestant Ethic* finally appeared in 1964, the review of it by Febvre's
most faithful disciple, Robert Mandrou, underscored the dated appearance of its methods and the extent to which the considerable
response it evoked among so much of the broad educated public
derived from the aura of scientific legitimacy it conferred upon old
commonplaces about the superiority of Protestantism to Catholicism. Only when scholars looked at the actual practice of lending and
capital investment in Protestant and Catholic countries and the economic activities of religious minorities across the continent, Man-

---

15 Charles Weiss, *Histoire des réfugiés protestants de France,* 2 vols. (Paris, 1853), I, 30.
16 Henri Hauser, "Les idées économiques de Calvin," orig. pub. in *Les débuts du capitalisme*
   (Paris, 1931), repr. in *La modernité du XVIe siècle* (Paris, 1963), 105–133, esp. 133.
17 Lucien Febvre, "Capitalisme et réforme," repr. in *Pour une histoire à part entière* (Paris, 1962).

drou argued, would it become possible to say whether or not these theses had any genuine scientific validity.[18]

That work never came. Over the past fifteen years, however, one important French Protestant historian who has written extensively on religious history has begun to assert Protestantism's particularly dynamic contribution to economic growth. This is Pierre Chaunu, significantly, a mid-life convert to the faith rather than a Huguenot by ancestry.[19] Chaunu unquestionably qualifies as one of the most boldly idiosyncratic historians to achieve professional eminence in any country since the professionalization of the discipline in the late nineteenth century. His vast flood of publications is characterized by oracular pronouncements in which the voice of the natalist prophet warning of the imminent suicide of the civilized races increasingly competes with that of the secular historian, considerable insouciance about documentation, and a prose style that verges on automatic writing. All of these characteristics are evident in his statements about Calvinism's important role in promoting economic progress in his 1975 textbook, *Le Temps des Réformes,* reiterated in his 1986 *L'Aventure de la Réforme.* According to these works, numerous studies have confirmed the link between Protestantism and economic progress, as does the tight correlation between Protestant nations and those nations that first entered the Rostowian takeoff phase. This association derives from "social and cultural mediating factors, and mental factors more difficult to grasp, touching on attitudes toward life, the place actually granted contemplation, in a word to religious values which are not directly reducible to social consequences and, ultimately, to the psychological density of hopes for the kingdom of God."[20] Because he is one of the most visible media stars among the French professorate (he is a regular contributor to *Le Figaro* and appeared frequently on "Apostrophes" during the life of that enormously popular televised discussion program), Chaunu's views may well exercise a degree of influence over the perceptions of the broad

18 Emmanuel Le Roy Ladurie, *Les Paysans de Languedoc* (Paris, 1969), 190–193; Robert Mandrou, "Capitalisme et protestantisme: La science et le mythe," *Revue Historique,* 235 (1966), 101–106, esp. 106.

19 Chaunu discusses the evolution of his religious beliefs in "Auto-histoire" in his *Retrohistoire* (Paris, 1985), 38. The dust jacket of his *Le Temps des Réformes* (Paris, 1975) indicates that, in addition to teaching history at the Sorbonne, he has taught theology at the Faculté Libre de Théologie Réformiste in Aix-en-Provence.

20 Pierre Chaunu, *Le Temps des Réformes* (Paris, 1975), pp. 474ff (the passage cited comes from p. 476 of this work); "Le destin de la Réforme" in Chaunu et al., *L'Aventure de la Réforme. Le monde de Jean Calvin* (Paris, 1986).

reading public. They have exercised less demonstrable influence as yet over the work of his fellow historians.

Having said that Weber's ideas have had little impact on the research agendas shaping the main stream of historical writing about European Calvinism and having tried to suggest some of the reasons why, it is time now to begin surveying the exceptions to this statement. Firstly, there is one path-breaking book written by a historian about a country other than England in which a broad Weberian perspective does shape the interpretation of Calvinism: the remarkable *History of the Scottish People* by T. C. Smout. This pioneering foray through Scottish social history includes some illuminating pages on the character of Reformed discipline based upon research in original sources clearly inspired in part by Weber's hypotheses, and it concludes that the Reformation helped pave the way for Scotland's later economic development by promoting education, sobriety, industriousness, and above all "the need . . . to work compulsively and systematically to some positive purpose." Smout is professor of Scottish history at the University of Saint Andrews, and one wonders if his incorporation of such a viewpoint does not reflect his geographic and professional distance from the historiography of the continental Reformation and the more direct inspiration of English social historians.[21]

Secondly, *The Protestant Ethic*'s rapid attainment of canonical status within sociology has meant that a number of social scientists have attempted to specify a clear research program on the basis of their reading of Weber and to examine the history of Calvinism in one country in the light of that program. A particularly important study in this vein has been carried out for Scotland by the sociologist Gordon Marshall.[22] Smaller similar studies have been done for the Low Countries by the sociologist Jelle Riemersma and the economic historian J. H. van Stuijvenberg.[23] If their work has revealed the difficulties of turning Weber's aperçus and ideal types into a clear set

21 T. C. Smout, *A History of the Scottish People, 1560–1830* (London, 1969), ch. 3, esp. 96–100. The passage cited appears on p. 98. See the considerably more critical judgment of Weber's ideas by the prominent church historian G. D. Henderson, "Religion and Democracy in Scottish History," in *The Burning Bush: Studies in Scottish Church History* (Edinburgh, 1957), 136, a further reflection of the chilly response to his ideas in Reformed theological circles.

22 Gordon Marshall, *Presbyteries and Profits: Calvinism and the Development of Capitalism in Scotland, 1560–1707* (Oxford, 1980).

23 Jelle C. Riemersma, *Religious Factors in Early Dutch Capitalism 1550–1650* (The Hague, 1967); J. H. van Stuijvenberg, "The Weber Thesis: An Attempt at Interpretation," *Acta Historiae Neerlandicae*, VIII (1975), 50–66.

of empirically testable hypotheses, it has also shown that a research program that takes his writings as its explicit starting point can lead scholars to explore aspects of the history of Calvinism neglected by those working within the mainstream national traditions of Calvinist historiography. Thus, Marshall's concern to determine whether or not Weber was right in asserting that the themes of predestination, the necessity of obtaining proof of one's election, and the need for due diligence in one's calling increasingly came to the fore in later Calvinism has given us the fullest exploration to date of Scottish sermons and devotional works of the post-Reformation generations, whereas Van Stuijvenberg's interest in determining whether or not Dutch Calvinistic piety emphasized systematic self-discipline has led him to discover the paucity of spiritual diaries and journals in that country. The final judgment of these works with regard to the validity of Weber's arguments is decidedly mixed. Marshall claims that the Scottish evidence vindicates Weber's arguments, Van Stuijvenberg finds little comfort for them in the Dutch case, and Riemersma takes the middle-of-the-road position that Reformed doctrine was a small contributing factor to a development that began long before the Reformation and gained most of its strength from other sources.

Thirdly, as has already been mentioned, England forms the great exception to the pattern just outlined. Here the Weber thesis, duly modified to fit national conditions, has entered into the main stream of historical writing and debate. R. H. Tawney unquestionably played the central role in this. For this churchgoing Anglican and advocate of a Christian socialism divorced from narrow confessionalism, the ethical teachings of the medieval and early Reformation church were an example of the proper limitation of economic activity by concern for the well-being of one's fellow man.[24] Tawney considered it an important historical problem to determine when and why the Church of England fell away from such teachings and into a more complacent acceptance of "the economic virtues." Weber was clearly an important stimulus for his thinking about this problem, which resulted in his extremely influential *Religion and the Rise of Capitalism,* first published in 1926 and, as I can testify from personal experience, still assigned in economic history courses four decades later. The book parts company with Weber in stressing that the development of religious practices and doctrines particularly favorable to

---

24 For my understanding of Tawney's life and thought, I have relied especially on Ross Terrill, *R. H. Tawney and His Times: Socialism as Fellowship* (Cambridge, Mass., 1973).

capitalist accumulation "owed as much to changes in economic and political organization as it did to developments in the sphere of religious thought."[25] It nonetheless incorporates a highly Weberian vision of the Puritan, that "contemner of the vain shows of sacramentalism" for whom "mundane toil itself becomes a kind of sacrament," driven to unresting activity to exorcise the haunting demon of uncertainty about election.[26] Last of all, it advances several related theses that would become enormously significant for subsequent work on Puritanism and society, namely, that Puritanism was above all the ideology of the middling sort of people, for whom it provided a significant reinforcement of the bourgeois virtues. Further elaborated by Tawney's pupil Christopher Hill, these claims have since become the object of the sort of intense empirical scrutiny and debate that is the fate of any bold thesis concerning early modern English history. David Underdown and Keith Wrightson and David Levine have carried out detailed local studies using sophisticated social history methods that link Puritan sentiment with the middling ranks and social control in the service of economic modernization. Nicholas Tyacke, Paul Seaver, and others have used perhaps even cleverer methods and more compelling evidence to suggest the difficulty of identifying the hotter sort of Protestants with any one specific social group or with religious practices favorable to the development of a capitalist mentality. The wisest judgment concerning such claims at the moment would seem to be that they remain unproven.[27]

Thanks to the special importance that Weber assumed within American sociology and the emphasis in his work on the Puritans as paradigmatic later Calvinists, England has also been a favored terrain for social scientists working within a Weberian framework who have attempted historical studies reformulating or extending the master's insights. Robert Merton, David Little, Michael Walzer, and most

---

25 R. H. Tawney, *Religion and the Rise of Capitalism* (13th printing, New York, 1954), 76–77.
26 Ibid., 166.
27 I shall cite here only the major works relevant to this question. Christopher Hill, *Society and Puritanism in Pre-Revolutionary England* (London, 1964); Keith Wrightson and David Levine, *Poverty and Piety in an English Village: Terling 1525–1700* (New York, 1979); Nicholas Tyacke, "Popular Puritan Mentality in Late Elizabethan England," in Peter Clark, A. G. R. Smith, and Nicholas Tyacke, eds., *The English Commonwealth 1547–1640* (Leicester, 1979); Paul Seaver, "The Puritan Work Ethic Revisited," *Journal of British Studies* 19 (1979–1980): 35–53; Patrick Collinson, "Cranbrook and the Fletchers," in P. N. Brooks, ed., *Reformation Principle and Practice: Essays Presented to A. G. Dickens* (London, 1980), 173–202; idem, *The Religion of Protestants: The Church in English Society 1559–1625* (Oxford, 1982), 239–241; David Underdown, *Revel, Riot and Rebellion: Popular Politics and Culture in England, 1603–1660* (Oxford, 1985).

recently David Zaret have all attempted ambitious studies in historical sociology of this sort focusing upon the English Puritans.[28] If this literature stands somewhat apart from the main stream of research on the religious history of Tudor and Stuart England, it too has stimulated criticism and refinement, and thus has contributed to the far greater influence of Weberian themes within the historiography of early modern English religious life than that concerned with Calvinism anywhere else in Europe.

The fourth qualification that must be made to the claim that the Weber thesis has only marginally influenced the historiography of Calvinism reveals that it has not necessarily been Weber's own ideas that have generated the most active research. Weber explicitly stated that he was not concerned with the formal ethics of the different Christian churches and their implementation, but with "the influence of those psychological sanctions which, originating in religious belief and the practice of religion, gave a direction to practical conduct and held the individual to it." Despite this disclaimer, the discussion of his ideas quickly came to encompass a great deal of discussion of the specific social and economic doctrines of Calvin and later Calvinists – not simply in England, where Tawney's work has sparked a lot of subsequent work on this question,[29] but on the Continent as well. A significant literature now exists on Calvin's social and economic ideas, capped by the massive work of the Genevan pastor-historian André Biéler.[30] Important studies have also been devoted to the social and economic ideas of Dutch and French Reformed theologians.[31] More recently, studies using church discipline records to examine the implementation of Calvinist morality in prac-

---

28  Robert K. Merton, "Science, Technology and Society in Seventeenth-Century England," *Osiris*, IV (1938), 360–632; Michael Walzer, *The Revolution of the Saints: A Study in the Origin of Radical Politics* (Cambridge, Mass., 1965); David Little, *Religion, Order, and Law: A Study in Pre-Revolutionary England* (New York, 1969); David Zaret, *The Heavenly Contract: Ideology and Organization in Pre-Revolutionary Puritanism* (Chicago, 1985).

29  Hill, *Society and Puritanism;* Charles H. and Katherine George, *The Protestant Mind of the English Reformation, 1570–1640* (Princeton, N.J., 1961); T. H. Breen, "The Non-Existent Controversy: Puritan and Anglican Attitudes on Work and Wealth, 1600–1640," *Church History*, XXXV (1966), 273–287; Seaver, "Puritan Work Ethic Revisited"; J. Sears McGee, *The Godly Man in Stuart England: Anglicans, Puritans, and the Two Tables 1620–1670* (New Haven, Conn., 1976).

30  The most important titles here are Doumergue, *Calvin*, V, 647–651; Hauser, "Idées économiques de Calvin"; and André Biéler, *La pensée économique et sociale de Calvin* (Geneva, 1959).

31  Ernst Beins, "Die Wirtschaftsethik der Calvinistischen Kirche der Niederlande 1565–1650," *Archief voor Kerkgeschiedenis*, XXIV (1931), 82–156; Hartmut Kretzer, "Die Calvinismus-Kapitalismus-These Max Webers vor dem Hintergrund Französischer Quellen des 17. Jahrhunderts," *Zeitschrift für Historische Forschung*, V (1978), 415–427. See

tice have proliferated, although whereas these speak to certain questions raised in the course of the Weber thesis debate, that debate has provided only a small part of the inspiration for them.[32]

That the research of historians and theologians underwent this displacement away from the specific themes highlighted by Weber and toward the study of the actual economic and social ethics of Calvinism in theory and practice is not surprising. "In order to find our way through the tangle and occasionally even logomachy of these bold, at times brilliant, most often murky, theories, let us come at last to the question from which our historians and theologians ought to have started by examining and clarifying. What was the Calvinism of Calvin, normative Calvinism? What did Calvin think about wealth and its use?"[33] As this revealing excerpt from Emile Doumergue suggests, not only do the actual ethical teachings of the different churches provide a more familiar subject for theologically minded historians, and one more easily subject to concrete empirical investigation than psychological sanctions holding an individual to ethical conduct; in the eyes of modern Reformed theologians, Calvin's own teachings represent normative Calvinism, and their close study contributes to modern efforts to rethink the social ethics of Christianity. The dominant motif in twentieth-century Reformed theology, inspired by Karl Barth and, secondarily, Kuyper, has been the recovery of Calvin's thought as a source of inspiration. Biéler's now standard work was clearly inspired by the concern to distill from the master's writings the principles of a social ethic appropriate

also now Simon Schama, *The Embarrassment of Riches: An Interpretation of Dutch Culture in the Golden Age* (New York, 1987), esp. 326–334.

32 Alice C. Carter, *The English Reformed Church in Amsterdam in the Seventeenth Century* (Amsterdam, 1964), 157–158; Smout, *History of the Scottish People*, 79–87; E. William Monter, "The Consistory of Geneva, 1559–1569," *Bibliothèque d'Humanisme et Renaissance*, XXXVIII (1976), 477, 484; Janine Garrisson-Estèbe and Bernard Vogler, "La genèse d'une société protestante. Etude comparée de quelques registres consistoriaux languedociens et palatins vers 1600," *Annales: E.S.C.*, XXXI (1976), 362–378; Heinz Schilling, "Reformierte Kirchenzucht als Sozialdisziplinierung? Die Tätigkeit des Emder Presbyteriums in den Jahren 1557-1562 (Mit vergleichenden Betrachtungen über die Kirchenräte in Groningen und Leiden sowie mit einem Ausblick ins 17. Jahrhundert)," in Schilling and W. Ehbrecht, eds., *Niederlande und Nordwestdeutschland: Studien zur Regional- und Stadtgeschichte Nordwestkontinentaleuropas im Mittelalter und in der Neuzeit* (Cologne, 1983), 261–327; Matthieu Gerardus Spiertz, "Die Ausübung der Zucht in der Ijsselstadt Deventer in den Jahren 1592–1619 im Vergleich zu den Untersuchungen im Languedoc und in der Kurpfalz," *Rheinische Vierteljahrsblätter*, IX (1985), 139–172, esp. 153; Raymond A. Mentzer, "Disciplina nervus ecclesiae: The Calvinist Reform of Morals at Nîmes," *The Sixteenth Century Journal*, XVIII (1987), 89–115; Jeffrey R. Watt, "The Reception of the Reformation in Valangin, Switzerland, 1547–1588," *ibid.*, XX (1989), 94; Herman Roodenburg, *Onder Censuur: De kerkelijke tucht in de gereformeerde gemeente van Amsterdam, 1578–1700* (Hilversum, 1990).

33 Doumergue, *Calvin*, V, 647.

to the contemporary world. As for the recent spate of studies of the actual implementation of consistorial discipline, this grows out of the concern with popular religion and the *chrétien quelconque d'autrefois* that is so pronounced in the religious history of the past two decades, as well as with the fascination of German historians with the themes of *Sozialdisziplinierung*.

What this literature has shown above all else is the profoundly ambivalent implications of Calvinist ethics for the accumulation of wealth. On the one hand, the doctrines set forth by Calvin and reiterated with remarkable consistency by subsequent Reformed theologians in the Netherlands, France, and England emphasized the obligation of assiduous labor in one's calling, warned against dissipation and drunkenness, and permitted some accommodation with capitalist business practices by freeing the discussion of usury from the context of Old Testament and Aristotelian precepts within which it had previously been confined. On the other hand, they denounced excessive attachment to the things of this world and the blind pursuit of Mammon, stressed that all dealings with one's fellow man must be tempered by love, and emphasized the Christian's obligation to act as a charitable steward of all wealth beyond that needed to maintain one in one's station. In practice, Reformed disciplinary bodies paid far less attention to economic sins than sexual ones, but cases of usury, overcharging customers, failure to pay debts, "sleepiness in calling," and bankruptcy all found their way onto the agenda of different churches' consistories.

Fifthly, a significant literature also exists around a second question that, like the preceding one, represents a specific, more narrowly focused aspect of the Weber thesis debate – although once again, preoccupation with this question is visible only within the scholarship devoted to English, or more properly Anglo-American, religious life. This is the question of the accuracy of Weber's specific interpretation of the psychology of Calvinism. His claim, of course, was that the centrality of the dogma of predestination within later Calvinism engendered intense anxieties among believers about whether or not they were among the elect. These anxieties, in turn, represented a particularly forceful sanction to moral behavior, since they impelled church members to try to prove to themselves through their moral rectitude that they indeed possessed saving faith. The relatively small amount of work devoted to late-sixteenth and seventeenth-century Calvinist spirituality on the Continent or in Scotland betrays no engagement

with these ideas, except in the studies of Marshall and Van Stuijvenberg that explicitly took Weber as their point of departure. By contrast, the literature on Anglo-American Puritanism is far richer in its
exploration of the inner world of the faith, and the historiography of
this subject is marked by an ongoing discussion of these themes. The
dialogue is particularly important and explicit in the works of the
generation of American historians active in the 1930s through the
1950s who did so much to recover Puritanism as a way of life and
world of thought. M. M. Knappen's writings on Tudor Puritanism
include several passages explicitly addressing what he saw as the
oversimplifications contained in Weber's depiction of the psychology
of Calvinism, whereas Perry Miller's exactly contemporaneous works
resonate with Weberian images and suggest a far more positive evaluation of their accuracy.[34] (One chapter of his classic *The New England
Mind* is even entitled "The Protestant Ethic.") Direct citation or refutation of Weber has become rarer in more recent work on early
modern English theology, religious experience, or the Puritan anatomy of conscience, but it continues to recur.[35] More important, much
of this literature can be read as an ongoing dialogue with Weberian
themes. At the same time, it is worth observing that the richest
discussions of this subject are precisely those that break away most
completely from any Weberian ideal types – whether to confirm or to
deny them – and instead generate an independent understanding of the

34 M. M. Knappen, ed., *Two Elizabethan Puritan Diaries* (Chicago, 1933), 10–16; idem, *Tudor Puritanism: A Chapter in the History of Idealism* (Chicago, 1939), ch. 17, esp. 348; Perry Miller, *The New England Mind: The Seventeenth Century* (New York, 1939), esp. chs. 1–2, and *The New England Mind: From Colony to Province* (Cambridge, Mass., 1953), esp. ch. 3.
35 Among the most important recent works devoted to theology and piety in Old and New England are H. C. Porter, *Reformation and Reaction in Tudor Cambridge* (Cambridge, 1958); Edmund S. Morgan, *Visible Saints: The History of a Puritan Idea* (New York, 1963); C. F. Allison, *The Rise of Moralism: The Proclamation of the Gospel from Hooker to Baxter* (New York, 1966); Owen C. Watkins, *The Puritan Experience: Studies in Spiritual Autobiography* (New York, 1972); C. J. Sommerville, *Popular Religion in Restoration England* (Gainesville, Fla., 1977); William K. B. Stoever, *'A Faire and Easie Way to Heaven': Covenant Theology and Antinomianism in Early Massachusetts* (Middletown, Conn., 1978); Michael Watts, *The Dissenters: From the Reformation to the French Revolution* (Oxford, 1978); McGee, *The Godly Man*; R. T. Kendall, *Calvin and English Calvinism to 1649* (Oxford, 1979); Dewey D. Wallace, Jr., *Puritans and Predestination: Grace in English Protestant Theology, 1525–1695* (Chapel Hill, N.C., 1982); Patrick Collinson, *The Religion of Protestants: The Church in English Society 1559–1625* (Oxford, 1982), esp. ch. 6; Peter Lake, *Moderate Puritans and the Elizabethan Church* (Cambridge, 1982); Charles E. Hambrick-Stowe, *The Practice of Piety: Puritan Devotional Disciplines in Seventeenth-Century New England* (Chapel Hill, N.C., 1982); Paul Seaver, *Wallington's World: A Puritan Artisan in Seventeenth-Century London* (Stanford, Calif., 1985); Charles Lloyd Cohen, *God's Caress: The Psychology of Puritan Religious Experience* (Oxford, 1986). Explicit commentaries on Weber's ideas may be found in Watts, *The Dissenters*, 361–362, and Cohen, *God's Caress*, 112–119.

subject, using categories drawn from contemporaries' subjective understanding of their own experience.[36]

How does Weber's understanding of Calvinism look in light of this work? Much of the evidence corresponds to Weber's depiction of Calvinism. It is now clear that predestination indeed came increasingly to the fore in Calvinist doctrinal statements and debates in the generations immediately following Calvin; that this development was accompanied in England by a proliferation of devotional manuals that made it one of their chief tasks to explain to believers how they could be sure they possessed saving faith; that one of the signs of faith highlighted by many of these devotional writers was upright behavior and honest dealing in one's calling; and that at the same time, these devotional manuals spelled out a series of procedures enabling believers to exercise a considerable degree of self-control over their behavior, including the regular monitoring of behavior through daily self-examination and even the maintenance of diaries of conscience.[37]

It is also clear, however, that if these preoccupations appeared together in the writings of the early Puritan "physicians of the soul," they were not necessarily interlinked parts of a single logical system, nor did they arise simply as the consequence of the increasing centrality of the doctrine of predestination. Devotional manuals continued to insist upon the importance of making one's election sure and to offer strict guidelines for daily behavior throughout the seventeenth century, even as support for strict predestinarian ideas waned in many circles. Indeed, by the Restoration era, Anglican or anti-predestinarian dissenting devotional writers were even more prone to emphasize upright behavior as a sign of election than their more rigidly predestinarian counterparts.[38] Furthermore, good works were only one, and by no means the most consistently important, sign of election adduced by devotional writers throughout this period.[39] Finally, and perhaps most important, the copious literature of practical divinity devoted to these questions that was found in England was by no means a general attribute of European Calvinism.

---

36 I am thinking here in particular of the work of Hambrick-Stowe and Collinson.
37 William Haller, *The Rise of Puritanism* (New York, 1938); Porter, *Reformation and Reaction;* Basil Hall, "Calvin Against the Calvinists," in *John Calvin* (Appleford, Berks., 1966), 19–37; Patrick Collinson, *The Elizabethan Puritan Movement* (London, 1967), 432–437; Kendall, *Calvin and English Calvinism;* Watkins, *The Puritan Experience.*
38 Allison, *Rise of Moralism;* Sommerville, *Popular Religion,* esp. 89.
39 Cohen, *God's Caress,* pp. 117–118, makes this point with particular clarity.

It was partially and selectively assimilated in parts of continental Europe through the spread of a Reformed pietism that drew much of its inspiration from the English example. But in much of Reformed Europe, a devotional life embracing the style and preoccupations of Puritan piety simply does not appear to have developed in the century and a half following the Reformation.[40] Its development in England appears to have stemmed less from certain psychological consequences inexorably unfolding from theological principles particularly suited to engendering them than from the elaboration of a pastoral strategy and a style of piety that built upon materials not only common to all European Calvinism but also distinctive to earlier English Protestant thought, and that was specifically adapted to the circumstances within which those English theologians committed to the ideals of the continental Reformed tradition found themselves in the reign of Queen Elizabeth.[41]

This final observation suggests one additional reason why such a sharp divergence consistently recurs between the extent to which *The Protestant Ethic and the Spirit of Capitalism* has shaped the historiography of Anglo-American Puritanism and the degree of influence it has exercised on historical writing about all other variants of Western European Calvinism. A simple glance at Weber's footnotes makes it clear that, to the extent that he relied on primary sources to construct his picture of Calvinist piety, he relied above all on English devotional materials – materials for which there was often little continental analogue. For scholars of Calvinism outside of England, Weber's depiction of the faith consequently corresponded to little in the sources with which they were familiar, and they had at their disposal few of the sorts of remarkable sources that exist in such abundance for England and that have served to stimulate so much

---

40 Much of my current research is concerned with mapping the diffusion of different styles of Calvinist piety. For now, some signposts may be found in Wilhelm Goeters, *Die Vorbereitung des Pietismus in der Reformierten Kirche der Niederlande bis zur Labadistischen Krisis 1670* (Leipzig, 1911); W. J. op't Hof, *Engelse pietistische geschriften in het Nederlands, 1598–1622* (Rotterdam, 1987); Henri Vuilleumier, *Histoire de l'Eglise réformée du pays de Vaud sous le régime bernois*, 4 vols (Lausanne, 1927– ), II, ch. 4; Kretzer, "Calvinismus-Kapitalismus-These Max Webers vor dem Hintergrund Französischer Quellen"; Benedict, "Bibliothèques protestantes et catholiques à Metz au XVIIe siècle," *Annales: E.S.C.* (1985), 343–370; idem, "La pratique religieuse huguenote: quelques aperçus messins et comparatifs" in François-Yves Le Moigne and Gérard Michaux, eds., *Protestants messins et mosellans, XVIe–XXe siècles* (Metz, 1988), 93–105.

41 See here the suggestive observations of Collinson, "Towards a Broader Understanding of the Early Dissenting Tradition," in *Godly People: Essays in English Protestantism and Puritanism* (London, 1983), 539; Zaret, *Heavenly Contract*, esp. chs. 4 and 5.

work on Puritan religiosity there, most notably personal autobiographies and diaries of conscience, which might have allowed them to investigate the accuracy of Weber's contentions about Calvinism's distinctive impact upon its believers. When this is combined with the vast gulf between his intellectual preoccupations and theirs, the tendency of so much twentieth-century Reformed theology to draw inspiration from the recovery of the historical Calvin, and consequently to ignore the subsequent Reformed tradition of the late sixteenth and seventeenth centuries, and, for those of the francophone world of the early twentieth century, the uncomfortable echoes in his ideas of contemporary anti-Protestant propaganda, it is hardly surprising that his ideas should have met with so much incomprehension and exercised so little influence. In England, on the other hand, the extraordinary richness of the sources close in character to those Weber used, not to mention the fact that Calvin himself stands as far less of a normative reference point for modern English theologians, have guaranteed a far more continuous conversation between those working in these sources and his writings.

In conclusion, then, we can see that the reception of Weber's ideas has been shaped by a series of factors: disciplinary traditions, changing motivations and concerns inspiring the writing of religious history, the relationship of different modern European churches to the Calvinist tradition as a source of contemporary inspiration, and, last but not least, the extent to which the available sources provide a solid ground for discussing Weber's theses and appear to bear them out. Today, very little work on Scottish, Dutch, or francophone Calvinism betrays the imprint of a Weberian perspective, and some of the work that does commands little respect among most specialists in the field. This, however, stems less from the failure of attempts written in such a vein to prove convincing than from the paucity of attempts even to try to investigate Weber's ideas seriously in these contexts. By contrast, debate about the possibility that Puritanism has been a progressive force in early modern English history has been ongoing and intense for the past fifty years. This observer of the discussion would find too strong claims in that sense unconvincing, but others might well disagree. The substantial amount of work on the formal economic and social ethics of Calvinism has clearly shown the profound ambivalence of these teachings with regard to the accumulation of wealth, but there can be little doubt that the ethics of the faith, insofar as they were internalized by ordinary believers, promoted sobriety, self-discipline, and regular labor. Finally, the abundant work on Puritan spirituality suggests elements of insight in Weber's discussion of the psychology of Calvinism, but also indicates that he overestimated the extent to which the different aspects of behavior that he identified as typical of the faith were necessarily linked to strict predestinarian doctrine and characterized Calvinist religiosity as a whole, rather than simply one strand within it. But perhaps the most important change in determining contemporary assessments of the plausibility of Weber's Protestant ethic thesis has not come from historians of European Calvinism at all. It has come from a broader recognition within the entire community of religious historians of early modern Europe – a community that is now far less divided along confessional lines than it once was – that much of what Weber diagnosed as the distinctive contribution of Protestant or Calvinist religiosity to the making of the modern world was in fact a more broadly shared feature of the early modern religious landscape. This recognition, of course, opens up another possible manner for religious historians of this period to be Weberians: through an identification and exploration of those transformations in religious practice promoting self-discipline and the rationalization of behavior that cut across the spectrum of confessional groups. The exploration of the potential of this sort of Weberianism has scarcely begun.[42] At the same time, this recognition highlights how much Weber's essay was a product of the confessional rivalries and prejudices of the specific time and place in which it was written, not to mention of Weber's own critical attitude toward Germany's Lutheran inheritance, to which the Reformed tradition constituted in his eyes a superior alternative.

42 But see Lehmann, *Zeitalter des Absolutismus*, ch. 3, sect. 5.

# 16

# The Protestant Ethic and the Reality
# of Capitalism in Colonial America

### JAMES A. HENRETTA

## I

"We not only have Liberty to labour in moderation," Thomas Chalkley (1675–1741) of Philadelphia wrote in his *Journal*, "but . . . it is our Duty so to do. The Farmer, the Tradesman, and the Merchant," this devout Quaker continued, "do not understand by our Lord's doctrine, that they must neglect their Calling, or grow idle in their Business, but must certainly work, and be industrious in their Callings." "I . . . followed my Business with Diligence and Industry," Chalkley testified, and consequently "throve in the Things of the World, the Lord adding a Blessing to my Labour."[1]

Chalkley worked with equal diligence for things of the spirit. He sought converts while on business in Bermuda in 1716; warned his son-in-law, an avid reader, to be certain "that thy chief Study in Books may be the holy Scriptures"; and, at his death in 1741, bequeathed 111 religious books to the lending library of the Philadelphia Monthly Meeting. But Chalkley's major contribution to Quakerism was his *Journal*. Like the journals kept by many other "public friends," his *Historical Account of the Life, Travels, and Christian Experiences, of that Antient, Faithful Servant of Jesus Christ, Thomas Chalkley* (1749) was published to set an example for posterity and to further the progress of the Truth.[2]

A century before, in the 1630s, Joshua Scottow had migrated to New England. A devout Puritan and the author of passionate moral tracts, he was quickly accepted into the First Church of Boston. An astute trader, Scottow became a prominent merchant, trading with Newfoundland and speculating in land. In 1670 he moved to Scar-

---

1 Frederick B. Tolles, *Meeting House and Counting House: The Quaker Merchants of Colonial Philadelphia, 1682–1763* (1948; reprint ed., New York, 1963), 56.
2 Ibid., 90, 146, 154, 166.

borough, Maine, invested in the fishing industry, and, like Chalkley, became a public figure and moral preceptor to future generations. *New-England* is not to be found in "*New-England,* nor *Boston* in *Boston;* it has become a lost Town," he lamented in a vividly named tract of 1691, *Old Men's Tears for their own Declension mixed with Fears of their and posterities falling off from New England's Primitive Constitution.* "We must now cry out," Scottow warned his readers, "and admit our *Leanness,* our *Leanness,* our *Apostasy,* . . . *Formality in Worship, carnal and vain Confidence* in Church-Privileges, forgetting of GOD our Rock, and Multitude of other Abominations."[3]

Chalkley and Scottow stand forth as exemplars of Weber's "Protestant ethic." The Reformed churches and particularly the radical sects, Weber argued, created a new "conception of the state of religious grace." Their members could no longer seek salvation "by any magical sacraments, by relief in the confession, nor by individual good works." Rather, they were driven, both by religious doctrine and by a psychological need for assurance of salvation, to pursue their divinely ordained "calling." The result was an unremitting and disciplined "rational planning of the whole of one's life in accordance with God's will."[4] "I followed my Calling; and kept to Meetings diligently," Chalkley asserted, "for I was not easy to be idle; either in my spiritual or temporal callings."

Nor was he alone among the early migrants to British North America. Scottow undoubtedly read John Cotton's *The Way of Life* (1641), the classic exposition of the doctrine of the calling in the literature of New England. "How shall I know that I have that life, in having of which, I may know I have Christ?" Cotton asked his readers (and undoubtedly the members of his Boston congregation). "Art thou diligent in thy calling, it is well," he answered in part, for "*cursed is He that doth the worke of the Lord negligently,* and the work of his calling is the worke of the Lorde." Spiritual directives in early Pennsylvania were nearly identical. "The Perfection of Christian Life," declared William Penn, the founder of the Quaker colony, "extends to every honest Labour or Traffic used among Men."[5]

3 Bernard Bailyn, *The New England Merchants in the Seventeenth Century* (1955; reprint ed., New York, 1964), 122–123.

4 Max Weber, *The Protestant Ethic and the Spirit of Capitalism,* trans. Talcott Parsons (London, 1930), 153. "This rationalization of conduct within the world, but for the sake of the world beyond," Weber concluded, "was the consequence of the concept of calling of ascetic Protestantism" (154). See also 80–81, 120–121.

5 Frederick B. Tolles, *Quakers and the Atlantic Culture* (New York, 1960), 61; Perry Miller, *The New England Mind; From Colony to Province* (Boston, 1953), 41; Stephen Foster, *Their Solitary*

The lives of such Puritans and Quakers were not easy, for this religious doctrine created a major tension in their lives. On the one hand, it directed them to immerse themselves in the things of this world without, on the other hand, lavishing their affections on earthy pursuits. The contradiction was palpable. How many men and women could avoid the sin of covetousness, could pursue profits without succumbing to the temptations of profit? Their numbers were few, but their names were famous. One exemplar was the Boston merchant John Hull, who, it was said, walked constantly in the fear of God. "The loss of my estate will be nothing," Hull consoled himself when the Dutch captured his ships, "if the Lord please to join my soul nearer to himself, and loose it more from creature comforts." He "was a Saint upon Earth," Samuel Willard declared in his funeral sermon for Hull, a man who lived "above the World" with "his heart disentangled" even as he was caught up "in the midst of all outward occasions and urgency of Business."[6]

The death of Robert Keayne, another Boston merchant, laid bare the psychological tensions inherent in the Calvinists' conception of the calling. A London tradesman, Keayne migrated to Boston in 1635, joined Joshua Scottow as a member of the First Church, and prospered as an import merchant – at least in part because of his inner discipline and purpose. He had never indulged in "an idle, lazie, or dronish life," Keayne protested in his last will and testament, a 50,000-word apologia for the conduct of his life. Not only had he diligently pursued his business (leaving the substantial estate of £4,000 on his death in 1656), but he also made time to compose "3 great writing bookes which are intended as an Exposition or Interpretation of the whole Bible." Nonetheless, Keayne went astray, at least in the eyes of the world. In 1639 the colony's government charged the Boston merchant, to his lasting shame, with a series of economic crimes: "taking above six-pence in the shilling profit; in some above eight-pence; and in some small things, above two for one."[7]

Feelings against Keayne ran high in the Massachusetts Bay, fueled by a decade of scarce goods and inflationary prices. When Keayne's trial began, Reverend Ezekiel Rogers wrote to Governor John

*Way: The Puritan Social Ethic in the First Century of Settlement in New England* (New Haven, Conn., 1971), 104; Tolles, *Meeting House and Counting House*, 55.

6 Foster, *Their Solitary Way*, 120, neatly states this "flaw" in Puritan economics, and Hull's solution is outlined by Miller, *From Colony to Province*, 42–43.

7 Bailyn, *New England Merchants*, 41–42; Miller, *From Colony to Province*, 45.

Winthrop advocating "a Law to hang up some [of the merchants] before the Lord, they deserve it, and it would to him be a sacrifice most acceptable." As minister in the country town of Rowley, Rogers spoke for many hard-pressed farmers and tradesmen. His advice also reflected his own earlier experiences, and those of many Rowley residents, in England. They had migrated, in response to severe ecclesiastical persecution and financial distress, from the East Riding of Yorkshire, one of those "drowsy corners of the north" with a traditional open-field system of farming, little agricultural innovation, and manorial courts that strictly regulated economic life. "Shall the already persecuted and impoverished members of Christ," Rogers demanded of Winthrop, "be made a prey to Cormorants?"[8] Responding to such "well guided zeale" (as Keayne called it), the General Court imposed a hefty fine of £200. Equally seriously, the elders of the church nearly excommunicated Keayne. After an "exquisite search" of his conduct, they severely admonished him "in the Name of the Church for selling his wares at excessive Rates, to the Dishonor of Gods name" and exacted a public "penetentiall acknowledgement" of his sin.[9]

The lives of Chalkley and Scottow, Hull and Keayne, lend support to various aspects of the Weber thesis. The Calvinist doctrine of the calling obviously did place psychological pressures on a devout laity that could be assuaged only by an outpouring of worldly energy – in their business affairs and, no less important, in church concerns and religious tracts. This "Protestant ethic" produced not only disciplined and rationalized lives that embodied the "spirit" of capitalism but also the actual expansion of capitalist economic activity. The enterprise of Quaker merchants helped to make Philadelphia the largest colonial port (and one of the larger towns in the entire British world) by the eve of the American Revolution. Members of the sect constituted about 15 percent of the city's population in 1769, yet they accounted for more than one-half of those paying taxes of £100 or more. When J. P. Brissot de Warville visited Philadelphia a decade and a half later, he ascribed that success, in part, to "the order which

8 Foster, *Their Solitary Way*, 166. David Grayson Allen, *In English Ways: The Movement of Societies and the Transferral of English Local Law and Custom to Massachusetts Bay in the Seventeenth Century* (Chapel Hill, N.C., 1981), chap. 2 and 165–167, describes the Old World origins of Rowley's residents and minister.

9 Bailyn, *New England Merchants*, 42. See also Bailyn's exegesis of Keayne's last will and testament, "The Apologia of Robert Keayne," *William and Mary Quarterly* 3d ser., 7 (1950): 568–587, and the complete document in Bailyn, ed., *The Apologia of Robert Keayne: The Self Portrait of a Puritan Merchant* (New York, 1965).

Quakers are accustomed from childhood to apply to the distribution of their tasks, their thoughts, and every moment of their lives." "They carry this spirit of order everywhere," he noted, "it economizes time, activity, and money."[10]

Moreover, the lives of these Quaker and Puritan merchants (reconstructed in substantial works of modern scholarship) lend support to Weber's understanding of early America. There were indeed, as he claimed, "complaints of a peculiarly calculating sort of profit seeking in New England" in the 1630s.[11] Moreover, Weber did not err in using Benjamin Franklin's moral precepts to demonstrate the importance of the Protestant ethic in British America. To be sure, Franklin's utilitarian tracts reflected the influence of secular Enlightenment rationalism. But they also stemmed from a still vital tradition of ascetic religion in Quaker Philadelphia. Franklin wrote *Advice to a Young Tradesman,* the tract used so extensively by Weber, in 1748, at the same time that his printing firm of Franklin and Hall was preparing Thomas Chalkley's *Journal* for publication (in 1749).[12] Moreover, Keayne's painful apologia demonstrated the power of Weber's analysis of lay-controlled church discipline. As the great German sociologist argued in a companion article, entitled "The Protestant Sects and the Spirit of Capitalism," the "tremendous social significance of admission to full enjoyment of the rights of the sectarian congregation" acted as a harsh ethical *'premium,'* encouraging potential members to lead disciplined lives. Whether through the logic of Puritan predestination, Quaker conscientiousness, or sectarian discipline, the lives of some American colonists – perhaps many – embodied "the 'spirit' of modern capitalism, its specific *ethos:* the ethos of the modern *bourgeois middle classes.*"[13]

10 Tolles, *Meeting House,* 49, 61.
11 Weber, *Protestant Ethic,* 55–56.
12 Ibid., 50, 180, 192–198; Tolles, *Meeting House,* 166. Thus, in 1719, the Quaker merchant Isaac Norris advised his son to "Come back plain" from his first business trip to London. "This will be a reputation to thee and recommend thee to the best and most Sensible people." Franklin probably imbibed similar precepts from Thomas Denham, another Philadelphia Quaker. "In order to secure my credit and character as a tradesman," he wrote upon leaving Denham's employ, "I took care not only to be in *reality* industrious and frugal, but to avoid all appearance to the contrary. I drest plainly." See ibid., 63.
13 Max Weber, "The Protestant Sects and the Spirit of Capitalism," in H. H. Gerth and C. Wright Mills, eds., *From Max Weber: Essays in Sociology* (New York, 1946), 312, 321, and passim. "It is not the ethical *doctrine* of a religion," Weber pointed out in this restatement and revision of his earlier interpretation, "but that form of ethical conduct upon which *premiums* are placed that matters." "It has been the fundamental mistake of my critics not to have taken notice of this very fact" (321, 459n). See also Benton Johnson, "Max Weber and American Protestantism," *The Sociological Quarterly* 12 (1971): 473–485.

## II

Robert Keayne's difficulties reflected a larger conflict within Massachusetts Bay. The issues at stake were both philosophical and practical; they involved contradictory visions of the religious and economic orders. On the one side stood a fledgling group of traders, linked by kinship and interest to the Puritan merchant community of London. Their presence reflected the colony's origins as a mercantile venture. On the other side were the farmers and artisans, powerful in both numbers and institutional strength. Their leaders were also the chief men of the colony, Puritan ministers and devout laymen drawn from the ranks of the lesser English gentry.

The key figure was John Winthrop, the colony's governor for nearly two decades. A landed gentleman from the sheep-raising county of Suffolk, Winthrop suffered financially during the woolen textile depression of the 1620s. Equally important, he came to view England as a corrupted society, where "all arts and trades are carried on in a deceitful manner and unrighteous course." Winthrop's "Model of Christian Charity," completed during the voyage across the Atlantic, recalled the virtues of traditional landed society. It celebrated stable class divisions, condemned calculating economic practices and competitive self-seeking, and reaffirmed the responsibility of the rich for the poor. "If thy brother be in want," he wrote, "if thou lovest god, thou *must* help him."[14]

Winthrop sought to re-create a purified social hierarchy in America, a genuinely "new" England. "Thus stands the cause between God and us," he concluded his manifesto:

We are entered into covenant with him for this work . . . if we shall . . . fall to embrace this present world and prosecute our carnal intentions, seeking great things for ourselves and our posterity, the Lord will surely break out in wrath against us. . . .

"Now the only way to avoid this shipwreck," Winthrop warned, is to "be knit together in this work as one man, . . . in brotherly affection, . . . willing to abridge ourselves of our superfluities, for the supply of other's necessities." In defining ethical conduct in communal terms, Winthrop's social philosophy stood in tension with the Calvinist doctrine of the calling, with its focus on the duties of the individual. Whatever their personal goals, he told his fellow pas-

---

14 Stephen Nissenbaum, "John Winthrop, 'A Model of Christian Charity,'" in David Nasaw, ed., *The Course of United States History* (Chicago, 1987), 35.

sengers, we must have "always before our eyes . . . our community as members of the same body."[15]

Winthrop's communitarian ethic quickly found expression in Massachusetts Bay. In the so-called Antinomian Controversy, he and the other magistrates banished Anne Hutchinson from the colony. The wife of a prominent merchant, Hutchinson challenged the established ministry. She accused them of preaching a "covenant of works" that emphasized the performance of prescribed duties. In its place she proposed the doctrine of free grace, a mystical ethic that stressed the immediate tie between God and individual men and women. Most merchants supported Hutchinson, probably because they feared close communal regulation of their spiritual as well as their economic lives.[16]

The suppression of Hutchinson, Larzer Ziff has suggested, "put an end to the essential similarity between American Puritanism and sectarianism." Although individuals and congregations continued to practice diverse brands of Calvinist thought and practice, Massachusetts Bay became an authoritarian state, a holy commonwealth on the model of Calvin's Geneva. The laymen of the General Court curbed public religious dissent and sought to impose order on the new society. When the economy faltered in 1640, the court intervened vigorously to protect the interest of debtors from their merchant creditors. One law stipulated that property seized for debts must be "valued by 3 understanding and indifferent men." This provision reflected the legislators' hope that most settlers would "have sufficient upon an equal [just] valuation to pay all, and live comfortably upon the rest." A second statute required that all future debts could be paid in "corne, cattle, fish, or other commodities." Significantly, these commodities were not to be valued at market prices, but "at such rates as this Courte shall set downe from time to time." Finally, the magistrates passed a far-reaching measure (defeated in the lower house of deputies) that would have made the commonwealth liable for legally established debts that private individuals lacked the resources to pay.[17]

These measures embodied Winthop's economic philosophy and that of many migrants from rural England. In cases of conflict, the interests of debtors overrode those of creditors. "What rule must we

15 Ibid., 35–36, 50.
16 Emery Battis, *Saints and Sectaries* (Chapel Hill, N.C., 1962).
17 Larzer Ziff, *Puritanism in America: New Culture in a New World* (New York, 1973), 79–80; Bailyn, *New England Merchants*, 49–50.

observe in forgiving [debts]?" Winthrop had asked rhetorically in "A Model of Christian Charity." "If he have nothing to pay thee, [thou] must forgive him," he answered, citing "Deuteronomy, 15, 2: Every seventh year the creditor was to quit that which he lent to his brother if he were poor." Moreover, the welfare of the community was to take precedence over that of entrepreneurs. The General Court bestowed generous privileges on the newly formed Saugus Ironworks in 1644, but it also established a maximum price for its bar iron and prohibited exports until local needs were met. These restrictions, combined with high production costs, forced the Ironworks into bankruptcy by 1652.[18]

Like Winthrop, William Bradford, the governor of the separatist Puritan settlement in Plymouth Colony, sought social justice within a broader regime of authoritarian control and economic inequality. Fee simple landowning was nearly universal in the new settlement, for the migrants consciously sought to avoid the most oppressive features of English landed society. However, the leading men in Plymouth colony gave strong preference to their own families in allocating choice farming lands and meadows and in awarding exclusive rights to the Indian fur trade. Church members – "visible saints" – likewise received ample land, in the location of their choice, and the nonelect had to settle for smaller plots on marginal soils. The allocation of property rights conformed to the gradations of the hierarchy of social status and religious identity.

Once assigned their place in the social order, members were expected to conform to traditional communal notions of the "just price." The Plymouth authorities called church member Stephen Hopkins into court in 1639 "for selling a looking glass for 16d, the like whereof was bought in the Bay [Colony] for 9d." On the same day it fined Thomas Clark 30 shillings for "buying a pair of boots and spurs for 10s. and selling them again for 15s."[19] The *character* of Plymouth Colony – an isolated agricultural community, dominated by devout landed gentlemen, with political power in the hands of the

---

18 Nissenbaum, "Christian Charity," 44; Bailyn, *New England Merchants,* 63–64, 69.
19 Rex A. Lucas, "A Specification of the Weber Thesis: Plymouth Colony," *History and Theory* 10 (1971): 330. "When the Protestant ethic exists [where] . . . the congregational church dominates a small and isolated society," Lucas concluded, "the hard work encouraged by the ethic is maintained, but the individual's efforts are channelled largely to the maintenance of social control [and] . . . constant supervision by all within the social group severely restricts the behavioral leeway of the individual" (344).

Puritan congregation – ensured the triumph of Winthop's communal ethic.

The circumstances of life – spiritual and material – in early New England militated against the expansion of capitalist enterprise. The political franchise rested in the hands of church members, poor as well as propertied. Moreover, rural towns dominated the house of deputies; their representatives outvoted the merchants from the commercial centers of Boston and Salem and refused to elect them to the upper house of magistrates in the General Court. Only two of the twenty-two magistrates elected before 1640 were merchants. The court vigorously defended the church-based political order, levying severe fines on the non-Puritan merchants who demanded the broadening of church membership and the franchise in a "Remonstrance and Petition" of 1646. The improvement of economic conditions prompted the court to repeal some prodebtor laws in 1650, but popular opposition to merchants and their free-trade policies continued.[20] Merchants were "so taken up with the income of a large profit," declared Edward Johnson in *Wonder-Working Providence of Sions Saviour in New England,*

that they would willingly have had the Commonwealth tolerate diverse kinds of sinful opinions to intice men to come and sit downe with us, that their purses might be filled with coyn, the civil Government with contention, and the Churches of our Lord Christ with errors.[21]

The first generation of New England merchants thus pursued their personal economic calling in a restrictive intellectual and social context. They won respect only insofar as they assumed a public *religious* role, writing moral tracts like Joshua Scottow or, like John Hull, dispensing philanthropy in a generous but humble manner. To demonstrate their elect status, merchants had to serve God directly, through public affirmations of their "general" calling, and not simply through the diligent pursuit of their business activities.

Subsequent generations of Boston merchants operated within a more open environment. The Restoration brought new merchants – Anglicans and royalists like Richard Wharton – to New England, and imperial officials such as Edward Randolph gradually curbed the autonomy of its holy commonwealths. Equally significant, many second-generation Puritan merchants were themselves the offspring

20 Bailyn, *New England Merchants,* 103–104, 38–39, 107.    21 Ibid., 109.

of ministers and landed gentlemen. In his powerful election day sermon of 1663, "The Cause of God and His People in New England," the Reverend John Higginson of Salem denounced "the getting of this World's good[s]." It is "never to be forgotten," he reminded the populace, "that *New-England is originally a plantation of Religion, not a Plantation of Trade.*" Yet Higginson's daughter Sarah married Anglican Richard Wharton, and two of Higginson's sons became prominent merchants.[22] Moreover, pious Puritan merchants – Samuel Sewall, Anthony Stoddard, and Thomas Brattle, among others – sent some of their sons into the ministry. By 1673 Governor John Leverett and half of the other twelve magistrates had some connection with mercantile enterprise. Increasingly, the leadership of New England was drawn from an interrelated group of merchants, magistrates, and ministers.[23]

The growing wealth of the merchant community was one factor in its rise in power. As early as 1670, thirty Boston merchants had estates of £10,000 to £30,000. By the end of the century, a contemporary observed, many of them had constructed "stately Edifices, some of which cost the owners two or three Thousand Pounds." Merchants also had increasing access to political power. When King James II revoked the Massachusetts Charter in 1686, merchants seized control of the government, awarding vast tracts of frontier lands and dozens of governmental offices to themselves and their supporters. Two years later, they joined in the overthrow of the new Dominion of New England in part to protect their new (and old) land titles against the rapacity of Royal Governor Edmund Andros. Merchants prospered under the new charter of 1692, using their influence in London to secure appointments as royal governors.[24]

Above all, Boston merchants now lived in a more hospitable religious world. Increasingly, they worshipped in congregations of their own, served by ministers who respected their vocations and ambitions. In 1701 Cotton Mather's *A Christian at His Calling* reaffirmed the Calvinist precept that "a man *Slothful in Business,* is not a man *serving the Lord.*" The eminent Puritan minister also advised that "a principle of *Honesty* [should] keep you from every *Fraudulent,* or *Oppressive* Action," but he refused to give practical effect to his sys-

22 Ibid., 140. For the subsequent activities of the Higginson family, see the end of this chapter.
23 Foster, *Their Solitary Way,* 120.
24 Miller, *From Colony to Province,* 45; Bailyn, *New England Merchants,* 175, 191.

tem of ethics. When debtors and creditors clashed in Massachusetts Bay during the 1710s, Mather refused to take a political stand, alleging that he was "not versed in the Niceties and Mysteries of the Marketplace." The contrast with John Cotton, Mather's namesake and fellow authority on the calling, was striking. Writing in the 1630s, Cotton had cited various biblical passages in support of the simple principle: "Noe increase to be taken of a poore brother or neighboure for anything lent to him."[25] In Boston, the communal ethic of John Winthrop had yielded to the Protestant ethic of his merchant antagonists.

But not in the countryside. The predominant rural sector of New England created a distinct system of social behavior and values, yielding a continuing controversy with commercial towns. Notions of "fair dealing" formed one aspect of its ethical outlook. In 1639 Ezekiel Rogers had condemned Robert Keayne on behalf of the farmers of Rowley. Two decades later, a traveler in Maine reflected local sentiment in condemning the trade monopoly of the "damnable rich" Boston merchants who "set excessive prices" and who "if they do not gain Cent per Cent they cry out that they are losers." Local fishermen and planters, he explained, "enter into the Merchants books for such things as they stand in need off, becoming thereby the Merchants slaves, and when it riseth to a big sum are constrained to mortgage their plantation."[26] Samuel Stoddard, the evangelically inclined minister of Northampton, in western Massachusetts, took up the rural cry against "oppression" of traders early in the eighteenth century. In country areas "where there is no Market, particular persons may be in great necessity," he noted. "If they go to another Town to buy, the charge will be considerable; the man is also in a strait because strangers will not trust him, and the Seller takes that advantage to oppress him."[27]

Old beliefs died slowly in the countryside. Even at the time of the American Revolution, many New England villagers "thought of the great world beyond their borders in religious terms," Christopher

25 Mather, *A Christian at His Calling* . . . in *Puritanism and the American Experience,* Michael McGiffert, ed. (Reading, Mass., 1969), 122–126; Bailyn, *New England Merchants,* 21–22. See also Foster, *Their Solitary Way,* 112–113. The subtlety of Cotton's economic ethics appeared in his discussion of prices. He distinguished between ordinary times when "a man may not sell above the current [or customary] price" and times when "there is a scarcity of the commodity." Then the seller could charge more, "for it is a hand of God upon the commodity, and not the person's" (Bailyn, *New England Merchants,* 21).
26 Bailyn, *New England Merchants,* 98, 99.   27 Foster, *Their Solitary Way,* 119.

Jedrey has concluded, "an archaic geopolitical world view rooted in the England of Elizabeth's time and Foxe's Book of Martyrs."[28]

The protests of rural folk against mercantile capitalism took on additional motive force from the peculiar character of New England agricultural society. On the eve of the American Revolution, the fifth generation of settlers was coming to maturity. Their numbers had grown dramatically, primarily from natural increase, from 20,000 in 1640 to 600,000 in 1770. Their living standards had increased as well, but in a much less impressive fashion. Merchants and landed gentlemen lived well in New England (the top 10 percent of the families controlling 57 percent of the wealth), but ordinary farmers and artisans just scraped by. In fact, they had the most spartan lives of all the whites in British America. Wealth holdings per free white person ranged from £1,200 in the rich sugar island of Jamaica, to a substantial £132 in the tobacco and rice settlements on the southern mainland, and to £51 in the wheat-exporting Middle Colonies of New York and Pennsylvania. New England trailed behind, with only £33 per free white person.[29]

The causes of New England's economic backwardness were as obvious to contemporaries as they are to historians. A harsh climate, hilly terrain, and poor soil limited the production of valuable staple crops, and its ever-growing population pressed constantly on living standards. Indeed, fully one-half of the 19,000 farms listed on the Massachusetts valuation list for 1772 lacked plows or oxen; 40 percent were not self-sufficient in grain; and two-thirds did not have enough pasture for their livestock. Despite these unfavorable geographic and demographic conditions, New England had avoided a Malthusian crisis. There was never a significant shortage of food. Beyond that, New England families actively sought to maintain the freehold tradition established by the original settlers. Parents carefully arranged the marriages of their sons and daughters, devised ingenious inheritance strategies to preserve viable farmsteads, and bartered goods and labor with their kin and neighbors. Even in the fifth generation, 80 percent of the adult white males would own some land during their lifetimes.[30]

---

28 Christopher M. Jedrey, *The World of John Cleaveland: Family and Community in Eighteenth-Century New England* (New York, 1979), xii–xiii.

29 John J. McCusker and Russell R. Menard, *The Economy of British North America, 1607–1789* (Chapel Hill, N.C., 1985), table 3.3.

30 Bettye Hobbs Pruitt, "Self-Sufficiency and the Agricultural Economy of Eighteenth-Century Massachusetts," *William and Mary Quarterly*, 3d ser., 41 (1984): 338–340. See also

Were these back-country folk also exemplars of the Protestant ethic, pursuing their personal calling as farmers in a diligent, rational fashion? In one sense, the answer must be yes. All were Protestant sectarians, and most were Calvinists; their spiritual discipline and purpose obviously assisted them to sustain a stable European society in this difficult corner of the American wilderness. But strong communal institutions, political as well as religious, and the dominance of a community-based exchange system dampened the individualistic aspects of the ethic. Most towns assigned seats in the meetinghouse according to a communal valuation of age, wealth, and status; people learned their place in the community every time they went to church. Rural town meetings sought consensus; the vote of a mere majority lacked moral legitimacy and practical effect – for only a nearly unanimous vote was self-executing. Traders in commercial towns recognized the force of communal ideology and, as circumstances demanded, turned it to their own advantage. "The major part of those who were present were [farmers]," merchants in Salem, Massachusetts, argued while seeking to revoke a new tax schedule, "and the vote then passed was properly their vote and not the vote of the whole body of the town."[31] As Winthrop had hoped, these rural communities were "knit together . . . as one man."

The yeoman family's pursuit of a "comfortable subsistence" required access to the resources of the community. At the time of the American Revolution, the family of Caleb Jackson, Sr., of Rowley, Massachusetts, could trace its American ancestry back to the Nicholas Jackson, who settled on the ample lands of the town in the seventeenth century, perhaps in the company led by Ezekiel Rogers. But now these Jacksons were land poor. Each year the family cultivated its few acres, picked cherries for "ready cash," and pressed its neighbors' cider for sale in Ipswich and Salem. In addition, Caleb Sr. had his two teenage sons cultivate "Mr. Jonathan Wood's Planting land . . . and have half the crop for our labour," plant "our field of potatoes at Capt. D['s]," and pasture their cattle on other families' meadows.[32]

Robert A. Gross, *The Minutemen and Their World* (New York, 1976), chap. 4; Jedrey, *The World of John Cleaveland*, chap. 3; and, in general, James A. Henretta and Gregory H. Nobles, *Evolution and Revolution: American Society, 1600–1820* (Lexington, Mass., 1987), chaps. 1–5.

31 Michael Zuckerman, "The Social Context of Democracy in Massachusetts," *William and Mary Quarterly*, 3d ser., 25 (1968): 542. See also Zuckerman's *Peaceable Kingdoms: Massachusetts Towns in the Eighteenth Century* (New York, 1970).

32 Daniel Vickers, "Competency and Competition: Economic Culture in Early America," *William and Mary Quarterly*, 3d ser., 47 (1990); 4–12.

These exchanges of goods and labor were often valued at "set" prices; when market rates were used, no interest was charged on any resulting debts. The continued goodwill of a neighbor or kinsman was more valuable, in this interdependent subsistence-plus economy, than a few shillings in interest. The rational pursuit of business advantage yielded to the imperatives of communal existence.

Thus, the rural world of New England embodied many aspects of "traditionalism," as Weber defined it.[33] Farm families determined the pace of their own work lives, working intensely to complete the crucial tasks of planting and harvesting, but otherwise following a leisurely pace. Their economic goals were limited: economic autonomy, a comfortable subsistence for themselves, and a freehold legacy for their children. As Gary Nash has suggested, "a peculiar Puritan blend of participatory involvement within a hierarchically structured society of lineal families on small community-oriented farms" produced "the least dynamic region of the British mainland colonies."[34] Subsequently, it was less the imperatives of the Calvinistic calling than the pressure of population on resources that prompted an intensification of labor and the emergence of capitalist-financed domestic industry. By 1800 the two teenage boys in the Jackson family were making shoes during the winter months, under a contract between their father and a local merchant.[35]

In fact, the most dynamic religious impulses in eighteenth-century New England society were Calvinist and anticapitalist. In the "Model of Christian Charity," Winthrop had urged the Puritan migrants to fulfill the "covenant" with God that set them apart from other men and women. Whenever they sensed failure, Puritans sought ritual assurance in a public "fast day": "all persons are hereby required to abstain from bodily labor that day, & to resort to the publike meetings, to seeke the Lord, as become Christians in a day of

33 Weber, *Protestant Ethic*, 60–61; Reinhard Bendix, *Max Weber: An Intellectual Portrait* (New York, 1960), 52–54. As Joyce Appleby has noted, Weber rejected "the universal economic impulse of liberal theories . . . [that] had assumed that human beings were inherently geared to the strenuous pursuit of profit." He thereby "made social change a truly historical phenomenon to be understood on its own terms" ("Value and Society," in *Colonial British America: Essays in the New History of the Early Modern Era*, ed. by Jack P. Greene and J. R. Pole [Baltimore, 1984], 291).

34 Gary Nash, "Social Development," in Greene and Pole, *Colonial British America*, 237, 236. "For most men in Chebacco," Jedrey has concluded, "time and inheritance, not entrepreneurial ability, was the key to advancement. . . . It was a stable world of finite resources, and . . . most men would not ever own much more than they inherited" (*World of John Cleaveland*, 94).

35 Vickers, "Competency and Competition," 9–10.

humiliation." Subsequently, ministers and devout laymen composed "jeremiads," sermons or tracts that berated Puritans for their sins, recalled their duties under the covenant, and proposed a scheme of reformation. Then, in the early eighteenth century, ministers sought to combat worldliness through church "revivals." In these collective outbursts of piety, saints reaffirmed their identity and converts rejoiced in the gift of God's grace. Changing forms obscured an underlying continuity; the demands of the Calvinist ethos perodically engendered a sense of emotional crisis that mere pursuit of the calling could not assuage.[36]

The Great Awakening of the 1740s was one of those outbursts. The revival had strong regional roots and characteristics, for it flowed out of and embraced the Calvinist tradition in New England and German pietism in the Middle Colonies of Pennsylvania and New Jersey. But the charismatic preaching of George Whitefield, John Wesley's compatriot in English Methodism, transformed those regions' revivals into a continentwide Great Awakening. Initially, the revival appealed to all classes and regions; Whitefield found himself welcome in urban as well as rural churches, in the congregations of rich merchants as well as those of poor artisans and farmers. Soon conservative ministers and laymen sensed a danger to social order and their religious outlook. "None can be long a stranger to George Whitefield," James Logan told a friend. "His preaching has a good effect in reclaiming many dissolute people," the Philadelphia merchant and politician admitted, "but from his countenancing so very much the most hotheaded predestinarians, . . . he and they have actually driven divers [people] into despair, and some into perfect madness. . . . His doctrine," Logan explained, stressed "the danger of good works without such a degree of sanctifying faith as come up to his gauge."[37]

Neither predestination nor a rigid "covenant of grace" appealed to well-to-do urban congregations or their ministers by the mid-eighteenth century. "The optimistic, energetic 'merchant princes' of Boston," Daniel Walker Howe has pointed out, "did not take it kindly when Calvinist clergymen informed them they were miserable sinners, worms, or spiders kept from dropping into the fires of

---

36 Miller, *From Colony to Province*, 27. The Puritans' use of ritual is explored in David H. Hall, "Religion and Society: Problems and Reconsiderations," in Greene and Pole, *Colonial British America*, 336 and passim.
37 Tolles, *Quakers and the Atlantic Culture*, 100, 105–106.

Hell only by the whim of an inscrutable God." Nor did Quaker merchants in Pennsylvania welcome the admonitions of "primitive" Friends who recalled the radical aspects of early Quakerism. They ignored John Woolman's injunctions to free their slaves and Anthony Benezet's insistence on "the necessity for the followers of Christ absolutely to refuse the accumulation of wealth."[38]

Believing that "salvation, like earthly prosperity, must be a reward for those ambitious enough to earn it," many merchants had become Arminian or Latitudinarian in outlook. Their ministers – such as Charles Chauncy and Jonathan Mayhew in Boston – emphasized the benevolence of God, not his omnipotence; in the theology of salvation preached by these ministers, human moral responsibility played almost as important a role as God's grace. Devotion to a calling lost its close association with God's grace and religious zeal. "There are Duties to be attended," Chauncy solemnly declared, "as well as religious meetings; But haven't the Zeal of People to attend the latter been so great as to leave little Room for the observable Practise of the former?" In the thought of these nonevangelical Arminians, the tension between the personal and the general calling had been resolved through benevolence. "One natural Benefit of Trade and Commerce," wrote Rev. Benjamin Colman, was that "it enlarges Peoples' hearts to do generous things . . . by means whereof a great Part of the World has been gospelized."[39]

Evangelical preachers questioned the link between divine grace and worldly activity in an even more radical manner. "Wicked debauched men" used trade, Jonathan Edwards declared, as a means "to favor men's covetousness and pride." The true business of Christ's disciples, another evangelical minister proclaimed, "is not to hunt for Riches, and Honours, and Pleasures in this World, but to despise them, and deny themselves, and be ready to part with even all the lawful Pleasures and Comforts of the World at any Time." The dramatic gesture of James Davenport, the radical minister of New Haven, Connecticut, symbolized the rejection of the Calvinist doctrine of the calling by many evangelicals and their followers. Placing

---

38 Daniel Walker Howe, "The Decline of Calvinism: An Approach to Its Study," *Comparative Studies in Society and History,* 14 (1972): 317; Tolles, *Meeting House and Counting House,* 84, 80–84.

39 J. E. Crowley, *This Sheba Self: The Conceptualization of Economic Life in Eighteenth-Century America* (Baltimore, 1974), 74, 112.

his followers' prized worldly possessions – their wigs and gowns, rings and necklaces – in a heap, Davenport burned them to ashes.[40]

Like all great social movements, the Great Awakening had diverse and contradictory effects. Most important for our purposes, it dissolved the affinity between Calvinism and capitalism postulated by the Weber thesis. "Where capitalism most flourished," among the merchants of the American seaports and in European cities, as Daniel Walker Howe has noted, "Calvinism declined." And, where Calvinism flourished, in the New Light Congregationalist, Presbyterian, and Baptist congregations in the rural hamlets of New England and Virginia, capitalism was viewed with suspicion, if not distaste. Howe has resolved this paradox by suggesting that Calvinism was (and is) intrinsically "an ideology of small property-owners, provincial folk . . . small farmers, and artisans, the lower middle class," those men and women "who feel threatened . . . and who find reassurance in the strength of their God and their own ultimate vindication in His election." Its appeal to merchants and religious intellectuals in the seventeenth century was a historical aberration, prompted by the lack of religious and social order. By the following century Calvinism was in decline, particularly "among those people who were most socially and economically comfortable" – merchants, professional men, and other agents of the new capitalist order. "Religion must necessarily produce both industry and frugality, and these cannot but produce riches," lamented John Wesley, "but as riches increase, so will pride, anger, and love of the world in all its branches." Calvinism had pushed capitalism forward, only to be devoured by its creation.[41]

## III

The triumph of capitalism in British America was a long, slow process. It took decades – indeed, more than a century – to translate the capitalist "spirit" of Puritan and Quaker merchants into concrete economic practices and legal institutions. Only in the early eighteenth century did a rational and routinized capitalist legal system extend its reach into the countryside; and only toward the end of the

---

40  Idem, *Conceptualization of Economic Life*, 67; Bushman, *From Puritan to Yankee: Character and the Social Order in Connecticut, 1690–1765* (New York, 1970), 192–193.
41  Howe, "Decline of Calvinism," 321, 323; Wesley quoted in Weber, *Protestant Ethic*, 175.

century had merchants amassed sufficient financial resources and organizational skills to initiate the American transition to a capitalist and industrializing society.

The dynamics of legal change emerged in striking form in early eighteenth-century Connecticut. In 1700 Connecticut was a colony of subsistence farmers. Most exchanges of goods or services were local, and so were most of the resulting debts. Between 70 and 80 percent of all debt actions in Hartford and New Haven counties were based on account books (and not on signed obligations such as legal bonds or promissory notes), and virtually all book debts were local. Moreover, all actions for debts based on account books in Hartford County pitted one county resident against another; both parties lived in the same town in 60 percent of the cases. Even debt actions based on signed obligations were predominantly local, involving litigants from Hartford in more than 60 percent of the cases.[42]

The character of book debts – and the litigation they spawned – was equally significant. Account books were based on credit and trust. They formed a running account of exchanges among neighbors that did not bear interest. Moreover, their form encouraged what Bruce H. Mann has called a "communal model of disputing." "Books were not conclusive evidence of the debts they recorded," Mann points out, but "merely a starting point for discussing the range of dealings between debtor and creditor in open court." Before 1710 most debtors pled the "general issue." This plea permitted juries to scrutinize the entire economic relationship between defendants and creditors and to decide cases according to community norms of equity.[43]

The demise of actions for book debts occurred rapidly in Connecticut, denoting a new social and legal regime. By the 1730s only 30 percent of the debt litigation in Hartford County was based on account books. Instead, actions on written instruments (bonds, bills obligatory, and especially promissory notes) dominated court dockets. Debt actions now had greater definition and legal predictability; all that mattered to the court was the piece of paper signed by the debtor. Consequently, debtors did not contest actions they seemed certain to lose. And judges – not juries – decided 80 to 90 percent of

---

42 Bruce H. Mann, "Rationality, Legal Change, and Community in Connecticut, 1690–1740," *Law and Society Review,* 14 (1980): 196–198.

43 Idem, *Neighbors and Strangers: Law and Community in Early Connecticut* (Chapel Hill, N.C., 1987), 9–22.

all contested civil actions, disposing of them not on their factual merits but according to abstract principles of law.[44]

This fundamental transformation in debt relations and legal procedure reflected the commercialization of the Connecticut economy. As paper money appeared and agricultural markets expanded in the early eighteenth century, many farmers took out bonds and notes to buy land and livestock. Subsequently, periodic declines in farm prices extended the use of written instruments as cautious merchants forced credit-hungry farmers to secure existing book debts with promissory notes. Connecticut had developed a dual economic and legal system, with small book debts remaining common among farmers and artisans while promissory notes expressed their economic relations with merchants and traders.

The new legal regime represented the triumph of a rational, capitalist economic order enforced by the power of the state. The fate of arbitration conveyed the impact of this new legal consciousness. Before 1700 Connecticut residents resolved many disputes through arbitration. Compliance with the terms of a reward was voluntary, enforced only by community pressure. By the 1730s, however, parties commonly wrote arbitration *contracts* that imposed financial penalties for noncompliance. Finally, a merchant-sponsored statute completed the transition to a coercive and monetized arbitration system. In 1753 the Connecticut assembly empowered courts to enforce monetary awards and penalties through writs of execution, making arbitration simply another mode of legal ajudication. A distinctly modern legal culture – what John Adams would call "a government of laws and not of men" – had come into being, laying the foundation for the triumph of capitalist enterprise.[45]

By this time as well, New England merchants had accumulated sufficient capital to finance domestic manufacturing as well as foreign trade. At first, merchants and shopkeepers invested in the putting-out system for the production of shoes, cloth, and nails. But by the early nineteenth century, more adventurous capitalists were investing in textile factories and hiring wage laborers. Appropriately enough, this appearance of a full-fledged Weberian capitalist system was financed, in part, by wealth created initially by seventeenth-century Puritan merchants.

The Higginson family is a case in point. In 1663, the Reverend

44 Ibid., 35, 75–76.   45 Ibid., 130–136.

John Higginson of Salem, in the election day sermon cited earlier, had warned "merchants and such as are increasing *Cent per Cent*" to remember "that worldly gain was not the end and designe of the people of *New England.*" Nonetheless, two of his sons and a daughter prospered as members of merchant families, and the Higginsons became one of the premier mercantile clans in Salem. Many Higginsons moved to Boston during the American Revolution, and there intermarried with the Cabot, Perkins, Jackson, and Sturges families. Those families loomed large in the ranks of the Boston Associates, the capitalist entrepreneurs who financed the textile industry of early-nineteenth-century Massachusetts.[46] The ambiguities of the "Protestant ethic" carried to New England by John Hull, Joshua Scottow, and John Higginson had achieved a clear definition in the "capitalist spirit" of the founders of Waltham and Lowell, their religious and biological descendants.

46 Bailyn, *New England Merchants,* 140. On the Higginsons, see Peter Dobkin Hall, *The Organization of American Culture, 1700–1900: Private Institutions, Elites, and the Origins of American Nationality* (New York, 1984), 66-68, 71, and passim; and Robert F. Dalzell, Jr., *Enterprising Elite: The Boston Associates and the World They Made* (Cambridge, Mass., 1987), appendix.

# 17

# The Economic Ethics of
# the World Religions

HELWIG SCHMIDT-GLINTZER

The history of the reading and exegesis of several of Max Weber's writings has been – from the beginning – a history of misunderstandings. This is especially the case with his treatise on *The Protestant Ethic and the Spirit of Capitalism*.[1] The fact that there has been a history of misunderstandings was pointed out as early as 1944 by Ephraim Fischoff in an article published in *Social Research*[2] and has been repeated since by several others.

Although all relevant texts are accessible, there remain different opinions with regard to Weber's intentions during the last decade of his life. The divergent positions were put forward in 1975 by Friedrich H. Tenbruck in his article "Das Werk Max Webers,"[3] and recently by Wilhelm Hennis[4] and Wolfgang Schluchter.[5] Since I am going to discuss the supposition that there is a mutual relationship between Weber's studies on Protestantism and his research on the economic ethics of world religions, I must at least in passing consider the different opinions concerning the relation of *Economy and Society* (ES), *Economic Ethics of World Religions* (EEWR), and his earlier studies on the *Protestant Ethic* (PE).

First, I make some remarks concerning the question of what

---

1 The early debate on this treatise is well documented by the collection in Johannes Winckelmann, ed., *Max Weber. Die protestantische Ethik II. Kritiken und Antikritiken*, 2d ed. (Hamburg, 1972).
2 Ephraim Fischoff, "The Protestant Ethic and the Spirit of Capitalism – the History of a Controversy," *Social Research* 11 (1944): 53–77; a German translation by Walter M. Sprondel is included in Winckelman, *Kritiken und Antikritiken*, 346–371.
3 *Kölner Zeitschrift für Soziologie und Sozialpsychologie* 27 (1975): 663–702. An English version appeared as "The Problem of Thematic Unity in the Works of Max Weber," *British Journal of Sociology* 31 (1980): 313–351.
4 See Wilhelm Hennis, *Max Webers Fragestellung* (Tübingen, 1987), in English as *Max Weber. Essays in Reconstruction*, trans. by Keith Tribe (London, 1988).
5 Wolfgang Schluchter, *Rationalism, Religion, and Domination*, trans. by Neil Solomon (Berkeley, Calif., 1989), ch. 12.

Weber's subject was and whether it changed around 1910. Second, I deal with the remarkable widening of Weber's horizon and the development of comparative historical sociology. There are also reasons to assume that during World War I, Weber retreated to his studies on the world religions, and he was disposed to finish *Economy and Society* afterward. Third, did Weber's thesis on the Protestant ethic influence his studies on world religions? Was there something like a Protestant ethic analogy on his mind? And, conversely, did his study of the economic ethics of world religions affect his views on the Protestant ethic? Fourth, does the relationship between *Economy and Society* and his studies on the economic ethics of world religions shed some more light on the questions I am dealing with?

My thesis is that, at least as far as his studies on the role of religious ethics are concerned, Max Weber followed the paradigm set up by himself in 1904, which he elucidated during the following discussions. After about 1910 there was, however, something new in his research interest. And this is his comparative historical sociology, the outcome of which we find in his studies on the economic ethics of world religions and in *Economy and Society.*

In 1919, Weber added to the first footnote of PE the claim "I invite anyone who may be interested to convince himself by comparison that I have not in revision left out . . . a single sentence of my essay which contained any essential point."[6] This addition makes Wilhelm Hennis claim that there was not a bit of development in Weber's conception and that his main aims remained unchanged from 1904 until 1920.[7] This goes too far, as does the contrary view of Benjamin Nelson that the PE was a mere "intimation of a program, a provocative sketch,"[8] although from the perspective of the *Economic Ethics of the World Religions* and his monumental *Economy and Society,* the early study appears somewhat sketchy. It is undeniable that after 1910 Weber in fact tried to "correct the isolation of this study and to place it in relation to the whole of cultural development."[9] This is also clearly explained in the introduction to his *Collected Essays on the Sociology of Religion,* written late in 1919. But his main interest re-

6 Talcott Parsons, trans., *Max Weber. The Protestant Ethic and the Spirit of Capitalism* (New York, 1958), 187; see Max Weber, *Gesammelte Aufsätze zur Religionssoziologie,* Vol. 1 (Tübingen, 1920), 18.
7 Hennis, *Max Webers Fragestellung,* 12, note.
8 Benjamin Nelson, "Max Weber's 'Author's Introduction' (1920). A Master Clue to His Main Aim," *Sociological Inquiry* 44 (1974): 268–277, 271.
9 PE, 284; see Max Weber, *Gesammelte Aufsätze,* I: 206.

mained "the origin of this sober bourgeois capitalism with its rational organization of free labor," or, "in terms of cultural history . . . the problem is that of the origin of the Western bourgeois class and of its peculiarities [*Eigenart*]."[10] For Weber it was "a question of the specific and peculiar rationalism of Western culture."[11]

Until 1910, Weber apparently planned to continue his research on the Protestant ethic, but then he changed his mind, and instead of writing a direct sequel, he chose an indirect approach by turning to other world religions or "*Kulturreligionen*." This turn came about because he had – already in 1904 – realized that "rationalism is a historical concept which covers a whole world of different things,"[12] and that "the history of rationalism shows a development that by no means follows parallel lines in the various departments of life."[13] During the last decade of his life, Weber was, as Benjamin Nelson put it, "once he had gone beyond his studies of *The Protestant Ethic* . . . propelled by a wider interest in the distinctive structures and scope of action of rationalism and rationalization in the different mixes and variable crystallizations of cultural and institutional elements in the Orient and Occident."[14] We can only guess, however, whether Weber, had he lived beyond 1920, "would have gone forward to recast the argument and emphasis of *The Protestant Ethic*."

The realization that "rationalism" covers a whole world of contradictory things led Weber to look at different spheres and different cultures. Around 1900, there was a common tendency toward systematization and generalization.[15] Moreover, among Protestant theologians, there was an influential group interested in comparative religious studies, and Weber was in rather close contact with it. This so-called *religionsgeschichtliche Schule* stirred up a controversy in the theological faculties by demanding chairs for comparative religion. They had adopted the slogan of Max Müller (1823–1900), who once said: "Those who know only one religion don't know any!" In this controversy Adolf Harnack took another line. He was convinced that only the Christian civilization would remain in the future, whereas

10 PE, 24; see Weber, *Gesammelte Aufsätze*, I: 10.
11 PE, 26; see Weber, *Gesammelte Aufsätze*, I: 11.
12 PE, 78; in the original: "ein historischer Begriff, der eine Welt von Gegensätzen in sich schliesst"; see Max Weber, *Archivfassung*, 35.
13 Max Weber, *Gesammelte Aufsätze*, I: 61; *Archivfassung*, 34; PE, 77. See also Wolfgang Schluchter, *Religion und Lebensführung* (Frankfurt, 1988), 91.
14 Nelson, "Weber's 'Author's Introduction,'" 272.
15 Since I dealt with this aspect in my introduction to the first volume of the edition of EEWR in the *Max Weber Gesamtausgabe*, MWGA Vol. I/19, I can be very brief here.

all others would fail. And taking up Max Müller's dictum, he said of the Jewish-Christian religion, which was to him the paradigm of all religions: "Whoever does not know this religion knows none; and whoever knows it and its history, knows all."[16] Why should one go, Harnack asked, to the Babylonians, the Indians, the Chinese, or even to the Negros or the Papuans?[17] Weber himself was apparently on the side of the *religionsgeschichtliche Schule*. He became interested, however, not only in studying other cultures; he advocated, as he put it in his *"Antikritischem Schlusswort,"* the further study of the Protestant denominations.[18]

Although I cannot provide a satisfying explanation for Weber's turn to Asia, I am convinced that, whatever reasons may be detected in the future, this turn has something to do with his growing interest in systematization, which is characteristic of many passages in *Economy and Society*,[19] in addition to the common tendency at the turn of the century mentioned earlier.[20] As he said in his introduction to EEWR, probably written in 1913 and published in 1915, Weber was interested in the "practical impulses for action that are founded in the psychological and pragmatic contexts of religions."[21] He was interested in revealing "the directive elements in the life-conduct of those social *strata* which have most strongly influenced the practical ethic of their respective religions."[22] Then followed the previously mentioned passage, which was part of the 1915 version and contains in a nutshell his research program for his further studies on the *Economic Ethic of World Religions*: "Confucianism was the status ethic of prebendaries, of men with literary educations who were characterized by a secular rationalism. If one did not belong to this *cultured* stratum he did not count. The religious (or if one wishes, irreligious) status ethic of this stratum has determined the Chinese way of life far

16  Adolf Harnack, *Die Aufgabe der theologischen Fakultäten und die allgemeine Religionsgeschichte* (Giessen, 1901), 11; in this connection, see also *Religion in Geschichte und Gegenwart*, Vol. 4 (1913) col. 2183ff.

17  Harnack, *Die Aufgabe der theologischen Fakultäten*, 14.    18  *Kritiken und Antikritiken*, 322.

19  An early representative of such a comparative view was Werner Sombart, who already in 1902 wrote in the first volume of his work *Der moderne Kapitalismus*, 379: "A glance at other major civilizations, such as the Chinese, Indian, or ancient American, is enough to prove, in this regard too, the insufficiency of the view that the genesis of modern capitalism can be explained from a 'general law of development' of the human economy." See Roth, Introduction, to idem. and Claus Wittich, eds., *Economy and Society* (Berkeley, Calif., 1978).

20  Max Weber, *Wirtschaft und Gesellschaft*, 293; see the parallel in Max Weber, *Gesammelte Aufsätze*, I: 239–240.

21  Max Weber, *Gesammelte Aufsätze*, I: 238; Engl. transl. by H. H. Gerth and C. Wright Mills, eds., *From Max Weber: Essays in Sociology* (London, 1948), 267.

22  Max Weber, *Gesammelte Aufsätze*, I: 239; see Gerth and Mills, eds., *From Max Weber*, 268.

beyond the stratum itself."[23] Weber's turn to Asia was thus by no means just a detour or a digression (Hennis says "*Umweg*"),[24] and, one may add, he did not turn to *nations* or *races* but to specific religious creeds or denominations.

There is much evidence that Weber had finished parts of his studies on the EEWR before the beginning of the war. But when he revised the earlier articles, he was apparently affected by the war experience. There are several passages, especially *Ancient Judaism,* that reflect this impact. This was also pointed out by Marianne Weber when she says that his study on ancient Judaism in its particular form was substantially affected by the war.

His studies on other world religions, however, seem also to have benefited from the war, because Weber was prepared to resume his work for his contribution to the *Grundriss der Sozialökonomik* only when the war was over, as he wrote to his publisher, on February 20, 1917: "If the war would only come to an end, then I could work on my *Grundriss* volume. Just now, such work is simply not possible for me intellectually, and therefore I would rather continue with these articles on religious sociology. But my longing is for the other. Do not be without concern for its completion."

I am not so sure anymore whether I am still prepared to follow Wolfang Schluchter's interpretation of a statement found in Marianne Weber's *Lebensbild* in which she says: "One of Weber's most important discoveries was his recognition of the singularity of occidental rationalism and the role that it played for western culture. As a result, he expanded his original inquiry into the relation of religion and economics to the more encompassing inquiry into the singularity of the whole of western culture."[25] He made this "discovery," not around 1910, but in 1904 at the latest, and the statement by Marianne does not explain his turn to Asia. There must have been other reasons.

But there was, as I have said, something novel about the studies on the EEWR. In his studies on the Protestant ethic, Weber had been "dealing with the connection of the spirit of modern economic life with the rational ethics of ascetic Protestantism. Thus we treat[ed] here only one side of the causal chain. The later studies on the Economic Ethics of the World Religions attempt, in the form of a survey

---

23 Max Weber, *Gesammelte Aufsätze,* I: 239; see Gerth and Mills, eds., *From Max Weber,* 268.
24 See Hennis, *Max Webers Fragestellung,* 29.
25 Marianne Weber, *Max Weber, Ein Lebensbild,* 3rd ed. (Tübingen, 1984), 349.

of the relations of the most important religions to economic life and to the social stratification of their environment, to follow out *both* causal relationships, so far as it is necessary in order to find *points of comparison* with the Occidental development. For only in this way is it possible to attempt a causal evaluation (*kausale Zurechnung*) of those elements of the economic ethics of the Western religions that differentiate them from others, with a hope of attaining even a tolerable degree of approximation" (emphasis added).[26] Thus, it is important to realize that Weber explicitly referred the reader of his studies on the EEWR to his earlier studies on the Protestant ethic.[27]

There is no doubt that the earlier study functioned – notwithstanding the fundamental difference between PE and EEWR – as a paradigm for EEWR. This becomes evident when, instead of looking at the later studies *Hinduism and Buddhism, Ancient Judaism,* or the revised version of *Confucianism and Taoism,* one takes a glance at the early version of his study on *Confucianism,* which may have been written as early as 1913.[28] There we see that Weber followed the "blueprint" of his study on the Protestant ethic. At the same time, it is true that, in the words of Benjamin Nelson, "these superb comparative materials separately entitled the *Wirtschaftsethik der Weltreligionen* constitute the indispensable access to Weber's wider aims, his lifelong scientific commitments and his developing civilizational program."[29]

The studies on the EEWR were a continuation of what Weber began with PE. The publisher Paul Siebeck, who urged him to send him new writings to be published, also played a crucial role. This led Weber in June 1915 to decide to publish his studies on the EEWR.[30] On June 22, 1915, Weber wrote to Paul Siebeck:

I would be prepared to contribute to the *Archiv* a series of articles on the "Economic Ethics of the World Religions" that have been sitting here since the beginning of the war and that only need to be looked over stylistically. They are preliminary works and elucidations of the systematic sociology of religion in the *Grundriss der Sozialökonomik.* They will have to appear as they

---

26 PE, 27. See also Max Weber, *Gesammelte Aufsätze,* I: 12f. In his essays, Weber not only tried to give a survey on "die Beziehungen der wichtigsten Kulturreligionen zur Wirtschaft und sozialen Schichtung ihrer Umwelt," but he wanted at the same time "*beiden* Kausalbeziehungen soweit nach(zu)gehen, als notwendig ist, um die *Vergleichs*punkte mit der weiterhin zu analysierenden okzidentalen Entwicklung zu finden."
27 Max Weber, *Gesammelte Aufsätze,* I: 238.    28 See the synopsis in MWGA I/16, 77ff.
29. Nelson, "Weber's 'Author's Introduction,' " 270.
30 See Johannes Winckelmann, *Max Webers hinterlassenes Hauptwerk* (Tübingen, 1986), 42.

are, almost without footnotes, because I cannot do a single bit of work on them just now. They encompass Confucianism (China), Hinduism and Buddhism (India), Judaism, Islam, and Christianity.[31] I flatter myself that these articles, which bring the general application of the methodology in the essay *The Protestant Ethic and the Spirit of Capitalism,* will at any rate provide a strong contrast for their respective volumes. Later, if you are prepared to do so, they can appear together with that essay in a single volume, but not now. Because in their current form they are suited only as journal articles. As always, I offer them first to the *Archiv.* . . .

Ich wäre bereit, dem 'Archiv' eine Reihe von Aufsätzen über die "Wirtschaftsethik der Weltreligionen" zu geben, welche seit Kriegsanfang hier liegen und nur stilistisch durchzusehen sind – Vorarbeiten und Erläuterungen der systematischen Religions-Soziologie im "G.d.S.Ö." Sie müssen so erscheinen wie sie sind – fast ohne Fussnoten, da ich jetzt keinen Strich daran arbeiten kann. Sie umfassen Konfuzianismus (China), Hinduismus und Buddhismus (Indien), Judentum, Islam, Christentum. Ich schmeichle mir, dass diese Aufsätze, welche die allgemeine Durchführung der Methode in dem Aufsatz "Protest. Ethik und Geist des Kapitalismus" bringen, den betreffenden Heften ebenfalls s.Z. starken Absatz bringen. Später können sie ja, wenn Sie dazu bereit sind, zusammen mit jenem Aufsatz gesondert erscheinen. Jetzt nicht. Denn in der jetzigen Form eignen sie sich nur für Zeitschriften-Aufsätze. Wie immer biete ich sie zunächst dem 'Archiv' an. . . .

The correspondence between Weber and Paul Siebeck shows that Weber began to revise the "first studies" for the "Collected Essays" in the spring of 1917. By "first studies," he must have meant the one on Confucianism.[32] Weber started to revise his PE for the "Collected Studies" only in June 1919.[33] A letter to Paul Siebeck, sent from Heidelberg on September 11, 1919, described the state of Weber's work on the "Collected Studies":[34] The author's introduction was

31 See Wolfgang Schluchter, "Einleitung. Zwischen Welteroberung und Weltanpassung. Überlegungen zu Max Webers Sicht des frühen Islam," in idem, ed., *Max Webers Sicht des Islams. Interpretation und Kritik* (Frankfurt am Main, 1987), 22f.

32 Letter to Paul Siebeck dated May 24, 1917: "Die Um- und Ausarbeitung der ersten Aufsätze für die Gesamtausgabe (wenn Sie wollen: der 'Gesammelten Aufsätze', zusammen mit 'Kapitalismus und Protestantismus') *nach* dem Krieg ist im Gang." VA Mohr/Siebeck, Deponat BSB München, Ana 446.

33 Letter to Paul Siebeck dated June 20, 1919. This statement is also supported by Marianne Weber, who quotes a letter of Max Weber where he writes: "Ich nehme jetzt die 'Protestantische Ethik' vor, zur Vorbereitung für den Druck. Dann: die 'Wirtschaftsethik.' Nachher die Soziologie [. . .] Ich arbeite langsam fort – an der Ausgabe der 'Protestantischen Ethik' und der anderen Artikel und werde die Sache schon durchhalten." See Marianne Weber, *Lebensbild,* 676f.

34 VA Mohr/Siebeck, Deponat BSB München, Ana 446.

not yet written, but the revision of PE had been finished; the manuscript of the revised "Churches and Sects" would follow eight days later. One day later, September 12, Weber dispatched the completely "repeatedly revised treatise on the sects."

Weber himself pointed out several times the close relationship between his work on *Economy and Society* and his comparative studies in the sociology of religion. On December 30, 1913, Weber informed Paul Siebeck that he had completed a first version of the part on the sociology of religion for *Economy and Society*. In this letter he wrote, among other things: "Since Bücher's treatment of the 'developmental stages' is totally inadequate, I have worked out a complete theory and exposition that relates the major social groups to the economy: from the family and household to the enterprise, the kin group, ethnic community, religion (comprising all religions of the world: a sociology of salvation doctrines and of the religious ethics – what Troeltsch did, but now for all religions, if much briefer), finally a comprehensive sociological theory of state and domination. I can claim that nothing of the kind has ever been written, not even as a precursor."[35]

His research for the studies on EEWR had doubtlessly changed the original outline for *Economy and Society,* as becomes evident when one compares Weber's outline of 1914 with an earlier one, which he probably conceived as early as 1909.[36] The close relationship between *Economy and Society* and EEWR also becomes evident by the fact that Weber inserted in his introduction to EEWR of 1915 a very significant text on "types of domination."[37]

Weber was, in the words of Benjamin Nelson, "the pioneer in the comparative historical differential sociology of sociocultural process and of civilizational complexes."[38] In my opinion, not only from our distant view after seventy (or eight-five) years, but as early as Weber's elaboration of a systematic theory during the last decade of his life, we must take seriously Weber's own words on the validity of his PE.

35 VA Mohr/Siebeck, Deponat BSB München, Ana 446.
36 Wolfgang Schluchter, *Rekonstruktion,* 557, 536; see also 527ff.
37 The Hennis thesis that this was just an unmotivated addition ["unmotivierte Anfügung"], caused when Weber tried to steal a march on Troeltsch, shows that Hennis completely ignores the mutual relationship of EEWR and *Economy and Society.*
38 Nelson, "Weber's 'Author's Introduction,'" 271; see also Benjamin Nelson, "On Orient and Occident in Max Weber," *Social Research* 43 (1976): 114–129.

This means that his thesis was not essentially changed during the last decade of his life. But we can also say that Weber diminished the significance of his original thesis, although not the thesis itself, by broadening his view, by pursuing the original question more deeply, and by differentiating his thesis.

# 18

# "Meet Me in St. Louis": Troeltsch and Weber in America

HANS ROLLMANN

Ernst Troeltsch and Max Weber, seminal figures in modern sociology and thought and penetrating analysts of the modern world, visited in 1904 the United States, the country most closely associated with what Max Weber called the "spirit of capitalism." And not only did they see – as German scholars were accustomed to see – New England and the East Coast, but also America's heartland, the Midwest, and, in the case of Weber, the South and the West. The occasion was an invitation to attend the World Congress of Arts and Sciences in St. Louis. This congress was part of the 1904 Louisiana Purchase Exposition, a world's fair remembered today mainly through the hit song by Judy Garland, "Meet me in St. Louis, Louis, meet me at the fair," from the musical by the same name.

And yet the congress, which today is all but forgotten and which the American historian Frederick H. Jackson more than forty years ago called "a neglected landmark in the history of ideas," deserves further elucidation, if only to set the stage for Troeltsch's and Weber's American visit. When reconstructing this visit, I had the opportunity to use not only the letters of the Webers, as found in Marianne Weber's biography of her husband Max, but also the hitherto unpublished travel accounts of Ernst Troeltsch, as well as many other local sources that recorded the tracks of the two scholars on their way.

The scope of the present essay is more modest than a full-scale treatment of "Max Weber and Ernst Troeltsch *and* America" or a complete biographical exploration of the Weber visit. Rather, it seeks to contextualize the "intellectual landmark," the 1904 World Congress of Arts and Sciences, from the vantage point of two of its famous visitors, Max Weber and Ernst Troeltsch, and to contribute toward understanding better their exposure to American life and their participation in the congress.

One might as well begin an examination of the congress with the Judy Garland hit, since the song expresses the hopes and expectations not only of the world's fair but also of the international scholarly gathering. The first stanza reads:

Meet me in St. Louis, Louis,
Meet me at the fair,
Don't tell me the lights are shining
Any place but there. . . .[1]

The scholarly congresses connected with world exhibitions were children of their time, partly optimistic outgrowths of an unshakable faith in the preestablished harmony of science and industry, and partly an excuse for the neglect of intellectual endeavors and human values at these economic and national competitions.[2] Since the Paris exposition of 1878, conferences and congresses had become part and parcel of each world exhibition.[3] Thus the World Columbian Exposition of 1893, which celebrated the 400th anniversary of Columbus's arrival in the New World, had as its task "to supplement the exhibit of material progress by the Exposition, by a portrayal of the wonderful achievements of the new age in science, literature, education, government, jurisprudence, morals, charity, religion, and other departments of human activity, as the most effective means of increasing the fraternity, progress, prosperity, and peace of mankind."[4] The world's fair at Paris in 1900 had seen no fewer than 125 different congresses. But most of these meetings for specialists had no inner coherence and remained without any lasting public influence.

The exhibition of 1904 was no less – perhaps even more so than previous ones – an example of national and commercial faith in

1 The contemporary hit song was made famous by the movie *Meet Me in St. Louis* (1944). The words were by Kerry Mills, and the music was by Andrew B. Stirling. See Jack Burton, *The Blue Book of Hollywood Musicals* (Watkins Glen, N.Y., 1953), 197; I'm grateful to Prof. Duane Starcher, St. John's, Newfoundland, for this information.
2 The conservative ideology of the planners and the role of the ethnological "sideshows" that were part of it are treated in Robert W. Rydell, *All the World's a Fair: Visions of Empire at American International Expositions, 1876–1916* (Chicago and London, 1984). It was the English Victorian writer and critic William Thackeray who had coined the term "world's fair" for them.
3 See Howard J. Rogers, "The History of the Congress," *Congress of Arts and Science: Universal Exposition, St. Louis, 1904,* Vol. 1: *History of the Congress; Scientific Plan of the Congress; Philosophy and Mathematics,* ed. by Howard J. Rogers (Boston and New York, 1905), 2.
4 Ibid.

progress. But its planners wanted to address the criticism of previous isolated congresses and thus create a more coherent and adequate forum for scientific and cultural discussion.[5] This organizational purpose went hand in hand with those intellectual currents of the day that sought to integrate science, politics, society, and art. They were often guided by a naive idealism, which attempted to compensate for the commercial emphasis, and in 1904 were all the more contagious, as the organizers of the congress were individuals imbued with the internationalism of the Progressive era.[6]

According to William Rainey Harper, the idea of a congress with a "valuable" unified theme had come from J. V. Skiff, the director of the exhibition objects and a habitual optimist.[7] For him the congress represented the highlight of the fair and was designed to inaugurate, in nearly millenarian terms, "the brotherhood of scholars." Here is some of his progressivist rhetoric: "This congress is the peak of the mountain that this Exposition has builded on the highway of progress. From its heights we contemplate the past, record the present, and gaze into the future." In the mind of Skiff, the International Congress of Arts and Sciences was nothing less than a "faculty," the exhibition materials "laboratories and . . . museums," and "the students . . . mankind."[8]

The main purpose, as the directors of the exhibition saw it, was to arrive at an adequate organizational scheme that reflected the scientific progress since the Louisiana Purchase. To sort it all out, one approached academics in the public eye: Nicholas Murray Butler, the president of Columbia University and chairman of the congress committee; William Rainey Harper, president of the University of Chicago; Frederick Holls (1857–1903), the New York politician with a German background and former member of the peace conference at The Hague in 1899; R. H. Jesse, president of the University of Missouri, who was invited as a prominent academic representative of the host state; Henry S. Pritchett, president of the Massachusetts Institute of Technology; Herbert Putnam, librarian of the Library of Congress; and the already-mentioned Frederick J. V. Skiff, director

5 Ibid., 5; see also the correspondence of Münsterberg, Small, and Newcomb in the Simon Newcomb Papers, Library of Congress: especially Münsterberg to F. W. Holls, 20 October 1902. The congress has been studied by George Haines IV and Frederick H. Jackson, "A Neglected Landmark in the History of Ideas," *Mississippi Valley Historical Review,* 34 (1947–1948), 201–220, and A. W. Coates, "American Scholarship Comes of Age: The Louisiana Purchase Exposition 1904," *Journal of the History of Ideas,* 22 (1961), 404–417.
6 Haines and Jackson, "A Neglected Landmark in the History of Ideas," 201–207.
7 Rogers, "The History of the Congress," 5, 31–32.   8 Ibid., 28.

of the Field Columbian Museum in Chicago and a planner with previous experience.[9]

Frederick Holls, who had fostered German–American relations throughout his life,[10] approached the German-American Hugo Münsterberg, a veteran of the Paris congresses of 1899 and 1900, and invited his assessment of the matter. Münsterberg, a neo-Kantian from Freiburg and an experimental psychologist, whom William James had brought to Harvard so that James could be relieved as director of the psychological laboratory, was immediately full of plans for the congress and its scientific organization. This he did all the more as he had a nearly messianic consciousness of being the great German-American cultural mediator.[11] Münsterberg's ambitions were limitless but had been somewhat stunted by the New England intellectual elite and by American thinkers like Dewey and Small, who tried to steer an academic course independent of German developments, which for Münsterberg was all but unthinkable. The congress thus represented one more occasion to place Münsterberg in a position he felt he deserved, although his uncompromising viewpoint soon led to numerous conflicts among the planners and with the American scientific public.[12] Later, and perhaps in response to

9 Besides the official "History of the Congress," the following letters and documents from the Newcomb Papers (Washington, D.C., Library of Congress) have been consulted: (a) Münsterberg to F. W. Holls, Cambridge, Mass., 20 October 1902, 7 pages; (b) Report of Committee on Plan and Scope for International Congress of Science and Art at Louisiana Purchase Exposition [Minutes], Hotel Manhattan, New York, 10 January 1903, 23 pages; (c) A. A. to Newcomb, 17 January 1903, 1 page; (d) Committee to President Murray Butler: Report of 10 January 1903 [with comments in an unknown hand], New York: 19 January 1903, 8 pages; (e) Committee to President Murray Butler: Report of 10 January 1903, New York: 19 January 1903, 8 pages.; (f) Münsterberg to Harper, Cambridge, Mass., 5 February 1903, 6 pages; (g) Memorandum of Albion W. Small, no place, no date, 14 pages; (h) Albion W. Small to Münsterberg, 11 February 1903, 6 pages; (i) Albion W. Small to Nicholas Murray Butler, 17 February 1903, 7 pages; (j) Münsterberg to Newcomb, 8 February 1904, 3 pages; (k) Münsterberg to Newcomb, 21 March 1904, 2 pages; (l) Münsterberg to Newcomb, 2 April 1904, 4 pages; (m) Münsterberg to Newcomb, 25 April 1904, 2 pages.
10 Haines and Jackson, "A Neglected Landmark in the History of Ideas," 206–207; Hugo Münsterberg, "Friedrich Wilhelm Holls," in *Aus Deutsch-Amerika* (Berlin, 1909), 238–242.
11 Two critical studies of Münsterberg deserve special mention: Matthew Hale, *Human Science and the Social Order: Hugo Münsterberg and the Origins of Applied Psychology* (Philadelphia, 1979), and Phyllis Keller, *States of Belonging. German-American Intellectuals and the First World War* (Cambridge, Mass., 1979), 1–118, 265–290 (notes). See also the respectful biography by Münsterberg's daughter: Margaret Münsterberg, *Hugo Münsterberg: His Life and Work* (New York and London, 1922). The role of Münsterberg in the *Kulturpolitik* of the Wilhelmine era is treated by Guenther Roth in his Heidelberg Max-Weber-Vorlesungen of 1983, published as *Politische Herrschaft und persönliche Freiheit* (Frankfurt, 1987), 175–200.
12 Münsterberg, for example, recommended himself to F. W. Holls as follows: "Of course everything would depend upon the elaboration of the plan; that could not be carried out by the administrative management or by the honorary board of educators; the inner relation to the branches of knowledge has been since Aristotle, Bacon, Kant and Comte a chief

Münsterberg's imperiousness, one also consulted – presumably upon a suggestion of Harper – the Chicago sociologist Albion Small, who had considerably different views about the congress than his colleague from Harvard.

Münsterberg suggested a scientific congress, which, "in this time of scattered specialised work," intended "to bring to the consciousness of the world the too much neglected idea of the unity of truth."[13] In the theoretical justification for his neoidealist classification of sciences, Münsterberg proceeded from Fichte and attempted – beyond any positivist and psychologizing encyclopedia – to arrange the individual sciences according to their voluntaristic relations to the world.[14] This resulted in a division of the sciences into four groups: normative, historical, physical, and mental.[15] Besides these, there were those sciences that were not mere applications of theoretical sciences, but had legitimacy on account of their "relation of the world of experience to our practical ends." They were "utilitarian Sciences, Sciences of Social Regulation, Sciences of Social Culture."[16]

As far as the practical organization was concerned, Münsterberg's scheme required 7 "general divisions" in which the unity of the field was to be discussed; further, 24 departments, which discussed "the fundamental Conceptions and Methods and the Progress during the last century"; and, finally, 128 sections, the themes of which "were in every one the Relation of the special branch to other branches, and those most important Present Problems which are essential for the deeper principles of the special field."[17]

Albion Small, one of the founders of American sociology,[18] on the other hand, wanted to see more prominently represented in the congress the guiding light of the entire fair, the idea of progress. The pragmatic Small, not opposed to classification as such, considered Münsterberg's version of the progress of science based upon a scien-

problem of logic and philosophy: only a professional philosopher can venture to undertake it, exactly as only a professional architect could draw the ground plans of the buildings." Münsterberg to F. W. Holls, 20 October 1902, page 7.

13 Münsterberg to F. W. Holls (Newcomb Papers), Cambridge, Mass., 20 October 1902, 3–4.

14 Regarding Münsterberg's encyclopedic view of sciences, see – besides the archival materials referred to earlier – Hugo Münsterberg, "The Scientific Plan of the Congress," *Congress of Arts and Science Universal Exposition, St. Louis, 1904*, Vol. 1: *History of the Congress, Scientific Plan of the Congress, Philosophy and Mathematics*, ed. by Rogers, 85–134; see also "Der internationale Gelehrtenkongress," in Münsterberg, *Aus Deutsch-Amerika* (Berlin, 1909), 197–210.

15 Münsterberg, "The Scientific Plan of the Congress," 108.

16 Ibid., 121.    17 Ibid., 94.

18 See George Christakes, *Albion W. Small*, Twayne's World Leaders Series, vol. 68, ed. by Arthur W. Brown and Thomas S. Knight (Boston, 1978).

tific encyclopedia to suffer from a logical reductionism, which did not permit an adequate recognition of the total progress of human-kind.[19] Starting from the premise that "human interests not logical categories make the world," the congress, according to Small, should " . . . exhibit human progress as a whole which can be seen in its real unity only when viewed as an intimate cooperation of partial activities. It is a desiccated disunity if we distribute it under the categories of an abstract methodology."[20]

The two men agreed that the Congress of Arts and Sciences was to be more than a meeting of specialists. For Münsterberg it was an occasion to demonstrate to the most eminent representatives of the scientific world that the sciences in the United States had achieved a high level of expertise and did not lag behind those in Europe. Small, who had studied in Berlin under Adolph Wagner and Gustav Schmoller and who was married in Weimar to Valeria von Massow, the daughter of a Prussian general (against her parents' will), did not share at all Münsterberg's compensatory self-consciousness. For him the congress was a symbol of American scholarly independence, which expressed itself best in its progressivist theme. In a letter to Münsterberg of 11 February 1903 Small wrote:

Some of my most respected teachers have been, and still are, German schol-ars; yet I am sure that I understand my countrymen well enough to interpret their feeling with reference to Old World opinion. We are far enough ad-vanced so that we are no longer jealous of estimates passed upon us from the Old World standpoint. But on the other hand, we are sure enough of ourselves so that we no more fear the ridicule of the Old World scholars than we do that other bugaboo, the dark, which used to frighten us in our childhood. There are some things about which we have confidence enough to rely upon our own judgment, the Old World to the contrary notwith-standing.[21]

Small was not alone in his assessment of the situation. William James, who avoided the congress, saw in Münsterberg's plan a ten-dency "toward artificial bureaucratization and authoritarianism."[22] His brother, the novelist Henry James, dreaded Münsterberg's influ-ence at Harvard so much that he was tempted to treat him in liter-ature and "glance at the sinister, the ominous Münsterberg pos-sibility – the sort of class of future phenomena represented by the foreigner coming in and taking possession."[23]

---

19  See especially (g) to (i) in footnote 9, this essay.
20  Small to Nicholas M. Butler, 17 February 1903, 4.
21  Small to Münsterberg, 11 February 1903, 5–6.
22  Keller, *States of Belonging*, 38.    23  Ibid., 41.

That we are dealing here not merely with an aberrant academic xenophobia but with scientific alternatives and self-understandings becomes obvious when one takes into account the specifics of the reaction and its broad public base. The reaction expressed partly regional biases, Midwest (Chicago) against East (Harvard), but not enough to obfuscate the intellectual issues. Among those reacting vehemently to Münsterberg's plans for the congress was Small's colleague at Chicago, John Dewey, who contributed two critiques in the journal *Science*.[24] Dewey considered a general theme appropriate but felt that Münsterberg's classification was artificial and based on a logical a priori, not on the realia themselves. Such wanton separation of fields he considered outright "undemocratic," leading from the present interdisciplinary dialogue and teamwork to a forced integration, the very opposite of that basic characteristic of modern scientific life, "its democracy, its give-and-take, its live-and-let-live character."[25]

A further alternative to Münsterberg was presented by chairman Simon Newcomb: a congress of famous writers and personalities, who were to discuss international relations and the question of how "the unity and progress of the race" could be increased. Perhaps the vagueness of the proposal was responsible for its wholesale rejection.[26] That Münsterberg's plan became finally victorious was hardly a consequence of its theoretical superiority. What appealed was that it combined with a unifying idea concrete suggestions for organization, workable to the planners. Further, it supported the conviction that a congress emphasizing the methodology and unity of the sciences was best suited to remove, or at least reduce, European biases of the low level and one-sidedly practical orientation of American scholarship.

In February 1903 Münsterberg's plan was finally adopted, even if the later report of Newcomb leaves the impression that the best features of both plans had been combined.[27] The choice of the lecturers also followed Münsterberg's suggestions: only leading schol-

---

24 The discussion was elicited by Münsterberg's essay "The St. Louis Congress of Arts and Sciences" in *The Atlantic Monthly*, 91 (1903), 671-684, which made available the plan of Münsterberg to a broader audience and which was republished, in part, in *Science*, 17 (8 May 1903). Dewey replied with his contribution, "The St. Louis Congress of the Arts and Sciences," *Science*, 18 (28 August 1903), 275–278. Münsterberg answered his criticisms in *Science*, 18 (30 October 1903), 559–563, and Dewey replied once more in *Science*, 18 (20 November 1903), 655. Münsterberg had the last word in *Science*, 18 (18 December 1903), 788.

25 Dewey, "The St. Louis Congress of the Arts and Sciences," 278.

26 Rogers, "The History of the Congress," 8.    27 Ibid., 8–9.

ars, attracted to the hot, humid city on the Mississippi by personal invitation. The directors of the exhibition granted $500 travel money and a moderate honorarium for the foreign guests, and commissioned Newcomb and his two "vice-presidents," Münsterberg and Small, to travel in the summer of 1903 to Europe, to discuss the congress in scientific circles and invite the scholars. The U.S. State Department recommended the cultural emissaries warmly to its diplomatic missions in Europe. The German and French commissioners general of the exhibition also actively supported the project. And, in administrative circles of the world fair, it was registered with benign self-approval that President Theodore Roosevelt and the German Kaiser had expressed a "warm interest" in the congress.[28]

Newcomb, Münsterberg, and Small divided Europe like military strategists confident in the success of their missions: Newcomb took France, but also mathematics, physics, astronomy, biology, and technology; Münsterberg took Germany, Austria, and Switzerland, but also the areas of philosophy, philology, art, education, psychology, and medicine; Small traveled to England, Russia, Italy, and the remaining Habsburg regions, and took special responsibility for politics, law, economy, theology, sociology, and religion.[29] Only once during that summer did the three cultural marshals meet for a planning session in Munich. Otherwise, they worked independently of each other and were able to boast in September 117 affirmative replies to the 150 personal invitations. In Berlin, Münsterberg conferred with Minister Althoff and also had, if one can trust the information of Münsterberg's daughter Margaret, the complete support of his old friend Friedrich Schmidt, "who administered educational affairs."[30] The German-American apostle of culture visited all important university cities in Germany and Switzerland, and probably invited Troeltsch and Weber personally in Heidelberg, although Troeltsch, in his official acceptance in the fall of 1903, made reference only to Münsterberg's written invitation of 16 November.[31] After considering the matter for a few days, Troeltsch overcame all hesitation and agreed to come. For him, "the joy of seeing the great country and the interest to represent German scholarship in St. Louis [was] too great [to] decline the honorable invitation."[32]

28 For the preceding, see ibid., 9–18.   29 Ibid., 17–18.
30 Margaret Münsterberg, *Hugo Münsterberg. His Life and Work*, 105.
31 Ernst Troeltsch to Hugo Münsterberg (Boston Public Library: Münsterberg Papers, MSS Acc 2199), 28 November 1903.
32 Ibid.

The plans were threatened, however, when there developed in academic circles a rumor that the German intellectual laborers had been treated less favorably financially than savants from other countries. In a letter to Adolf von Harnack of 23 June, Troeltsch wrote that Münsterberg had written him that the remuneration was fixed as $500 because this "corresponded to the lifestyle of the average German professor!" Even Minister Althoff had considered the stipend sufficient. That the lifestyle of the average German professor, however, was a poor measure of the financial expectations of the invited luminaries became obvious when twenty-four German scholars, among them Troeltsch's and Weber's colleagues at Heidelberg, Windelband and Jellinek, withdrew, "since [in the words of Troeltsch] the monetary compensation was too small." Troeltsch and Weber did not withdraw but made their participation "dependent on equality of treatment." Troeltsch feared that if there was any discrimination, Weber "would bring the matter to the attention of the press and a very unpleasant disagreement would ensue."[33]

Despite painful absences – Münsterberg lamented especially the fact that the economist Schmoller and the three leading scholars of German, Kluge (Freiburg), Paul (Munich), and Muncker (Munich) did not attend[34] – and an ironic treatment of the congress in the German newspapers, which spoke about a scientific Barnum circus,[35] at year's end the directors had secured a respectable number of foreign scholars and could now invite American academics of repute, who would either preside over the individual sections or participate in the congress with short presentations.[36]

In addition, Münsterberg planned the stay of the Germans down to the smallest detail and even had a pamphlet printed, in which he acquainted the Old World with the societal peculiarities and rules of the New.[37] The document is a remarkable cultural barometer of a German–American social climber, and confirmed all the fears of Albion Small about the chauvinism of Europe toward America and that of the American East toward the Midwest and West. In the brochure, Münsterberg was a mixture of Baedeker and Gloria Vanderbilt when suggesting modes of travel and appropriate clothing and preparing the naive or pampered Germans for a poor New World oblivious to

33 For the preceding, see Troeltsch to Adolf Harnack (Harnack Papers, Berlin), 23 June 1904.
34 Münsterberg to Newcomb, 8 February 1904, 2–3.
35 Münsterberg to Newcomb, 21 March 1904, 2.
36 Rogers, "The History of the Congress," 19–20.
37 "Vertraulicher Rundbrief" of Münsterberg to the German congress participants (Boston Public Library: Münsterberg Papers), March 1904.

the class privileges they held in the Old. In so doing, he recommended social compensations and alternatives, such as the suggestion "whoever wants to observe the great flow of American life should not forget to live at the Waldorf-Astoria." The Harvard professor was most determined in dissuading his colleagues from accepting invitations of former students to visit and give talks at colleges and universities, for "the American word 'university'," Münsterberg wrote, "corresponds in no way to the German word 'university'" and is "rather a collective name for ca. 600 institutions of the most differing quality . . . , the highest of which have the level of the German university, the lowest . . . equivalent to the *Sekunda* [the sixth grade of a German high school]. Such small 'universities,' in which the former students . . . perhaps teach, are often very distant places, reached only by local trains, and the so-called students are nothing but *Schuljungen,* pupils, who don't deserve such a talk."[38]

Equipped with such useful suggestions – the very opposite of what appealed to the Webers on their expedition into the American South and West – the two Heidelberg savants crossed the Atlantic at the end of August.

As Marianne Weber tells us, the Atlantic crossing took place in such a carefree atmosphere that the travelers "became a mere *Gedankenstrich,* a dash on a paper, or a jelly fish, which consists merely of digestive organs." None had become seasick, even if Troeltsch, by contrast with Weber, had exhibited "a tendency toward asceticism," not strong enough, however, to rob him of his delightful humor.[39]

The boat arrived on a Monday night, 31 August, near New York, and they saw, in the words of Troeltsch,

on the American coastline the lit clouds of the large cities that surround the harbor of New York. Ahead, in the distance, was Long Island, an entertainment park, which showed houses and towers in a total blaze, like a burning city, as if one had come into the country of the fire worshippers.[40]

The next morning the travelers were in "the marvellous harbor, which is surrounded by mountain and forest and huge cities, crossed by thousands of ships and ferries and contains in its midst, on an island, the colossal statue of freedom." After a wait of four hours, a

38 Ibid., 5–6.
39 Marianne Weber, *Max Weber* (Heidelberg, 1950), 317.
40 Ernst Troeltsch to Marta Troeltsch from New York, 3 September 1904 (private possession). The letter exists as a copy sent to Troeltsch's mother, Eugenie Troeltsch, of 17 September 1904, and was kindly provided by the Reverend Dr. Horst Renz.

ferry delivered the impatient American explorers to their destination.[41]

What a view [writes Troeltsch], and what a teeming din of humans and cars! Across there rise like a confused mass of mixed-up towers the skyscrapers, the monstrous business establishments with 20 stories, a sort of castle and fortification of capitalism, all gathered round bank and stock exchange like a giant medieval castle, in which money, the bank, the capital, rules with innumerable thousands of subjects.[42]

Marianne Weber experienced something similar when she first saw Manhattan, "where the outrageous living towers press against each other and the 'capitalist spirit' has created one of its most impressive symbols."[43] Amid pleasant weather, Troeltsch and the Webers submerged themselves in the teeming metropolitan colossus.

The spread of the cities [writes Troeltsch] is nearly gigantic and the means of transportation are truly colossal, an eternal thundering and racing of the electric train, partly on tracks above the streets, partly on the ground. The ears are here totally blunted from the continuous thundering and roaring. Sometimes it feels as if one were drunk. Otherwise, the traffic is not greater than in Berlin, except on the Brooklyn bridge, which is something almost unbelievable. Here millions of New Yorkers hasten to their sleeping and living quarters. To stand at 6 o'clock on the Brrooklyn bridge and look over harbor and city and observe beneath the foot path the massive traffic, is indeed something overwhelming.[44]

Max Weber, who stood with Troeltsch on this same bridge, was also deeply affected by the dimensions of the metropolis and recorded similar impressions. He, too, spoke of Manhattan as of "fortified castles of capitalism."[45]

While Weber was totally captivated by the city and saw in the skyscrapers a most fitting "symbol" of "what is happening here," Troeltsch's judgment was less positive, even if we should not include him among the complaining Germans whom Weber despised.[46] If Weber compared the metropolis with Bologna and Florence, Troeltsch was reminded of other cities he had visited: Bucharest and Sophia or, in the plusher parts of town, Berlin.

On the whole, the city is quite inelegant, crude, uncouth, miserable street lighting, poor street cleaning, the houses arranged without plan and style – stinking everywhere like horse manure. In the elegant, paved parts, there

41 Ernst Troeltsch to Marta Troeltsch, 3 September 1904, 1.
42 Ibid.      43 Marianne Weber, *Max Weber,* 318.
44 Ernst Troeltsch to Marta Troeltsch, 3 September 1904.
45 Marianne Weber, *Max Weber,* 320.    46 Ibid.

arc beautiful houses, like in Berlin's Tiergartenstrase, very noble bath rooms and coaches, but this is the same world-wide. Everything is brand new. The churches are numerous, but small, and disappear almost among the towering buildings. It is the picture of a city not characterized by church steeples. It reminds me to a certain extent of developing cities like Bucharest and Sophia, only that everything is more magnificent, assertive, and ostentatious. Individual truly beautiful and tasteful city scapes are among them, but little is special. The main thing is the fortification of skyscrapers round the stock exchange, and the gigantic business life flowing to and from this center.[47]

The continual presence of his Heidelberg friend was of great personal benefit to Troeltsch. Weber, who had just recovered from a prolonged illness, felt, as his wife tells us, "better than ever since his illness, especially in respect to walking."[48] Troeltsch agrees with this assessment and writes:

Weber is splendid. He stays up always until half past nine, talks much and educates me without interruption in the most interesting way. It is of great benefit to see with him this country of businesses. He, too, learns continuously from what he sees and attempts to work it through. But since he thinks *aloud* while doing so, it helps me.[49]

After a stay of three days the travelers were not yet ready to form any final conclusions, so that Marianne Weber could write:

Of course, we have not yet drawn any conclusion – at least I have not – whether we should judge this piece of the world, on which are crowded five million people, magnificent and majestic or raw, despicable and barbarian. Most enthusiastic is – as always on travels – Max. Thanks to his temperament and perhaps his comprehensive knowledge and scientific interest, he, first of all, finds basically everything beautiful and better than at home. Criticism comes only later.[50]

For Marianne Weber, New York represented in the end a serious threat to her liberal faith in the value of individuals and their immortality. She writes:

How great are the accomplishments of humans but how little are they themselves. When, in the evening, the unbelievable stream rushes from the business quarters to the bridge, one is struck with awe: the infinite value of the individual soul and faith in immortality become an absurdity.[51]

47 Ernst Troeltsch to Marta Troeltsch, 3 September 1904.
48 Marianne Weber, *Max Weber,* 319.
49 Ernst Troeltsch to Marta Troeltsch, 3 September 1904.
50 Marianne Weber, *Max Weber,* 319.    51 Ibid.

Troeltsch also noticed a mood of depression taking hold of Marianne Weber:

His wife is less happy and satisfied. She is already half dead from New York and wants to leave it. The rule of slavery, which gold and money exerts over breathlessly racing thousands and thousands, the screaming and running at the stock exchange (we visited yesterday) and the Brooklyn bridge threaten her love for humankind and her ideal of human beings. When she observes such millions under the whip of gold – and sees humans only as a mass – she then has doubts about her humanitarian ideal and about immortality.[52]

Troeltsch and the Webers traveled on 4 September along the forest-clad banks of the Hudson River to Niagara Falls. Again, the travelers were impressed with the vastness of the dimensions: "no lovely, colorful spray in a romantic mountain canyon, but as if a captured ocean had freed itself from prison through a daring leap into the abyss."[53] Troeltsch met at the falls his old intimate friend Paul Hensel, a scholar of German and a descendant of the philosopher Mendelssohn, also on the way to St. Louis. And the friends liked Niagara Falls so well that they stayed an additional day in the "grandiose surroundings," after the Webers had left for Chicago.[54]

During their stay at Niagara Falls, Weber and Troeltsch visited in North Tonawanda Pastor Hans Haupt, who was in charge of a German Protestant immigrant church. Haupt was the son of the conservative Lutheran theologian Erich Haupt and his wife Grete, a talented musician, the daughter of the Halle economist and chief editor of the Prussian law code, as well as a St. Louis speaker, Johannes Conrad.[55] The family repeatedly became a stopover for American travelers acquainted with the Conrad and Haupt families in Germany, among them scholars like von Gierke, Eduard Meier, Professor Steinbrück, and Martin Rade. Hans Haupt, who had experienced a childhood and youth rich in conflicts under his demanding and oppressive father, had studied theology at the Basel seminary for preachers and, after a short and disillusioning period in the German *Innere Mission*, had emigrated to Iowa, where his liberal theological views brought him

---

52 Ernst Troeltsch to Marta Troeltsch, 3 September 1904.
53 Marianne Weber, *Max Weber*, 322.
54 Ernst Troeltsch to Marta Troeltsch from Chicago, 14–16 September 1904, copy sent to Troeltsch's mother, Eugenie Troeltsch (Dr. Horst Renz).
55 The information about Hans Haupt is drawn from the unpublished autobiography of the clergyman, which his son, Walter Haupt, one of the four children mentioned by Marianne Weber, kindly lent me. See Marianne Weber, *Max Weber*, 323.

into conflict with church authorities. Only much later, after several other pastorates and a fairly long stay in North Tonawanda, did Haupt find a freer field of activity in the independent German St. Peter's church in Cincinnati, Ohio, where his son, now in his nineties and one of the children mentioned by Marianne Weber in her biography, preached occasionally in the 1980s. Pastor Haupt's ethical orientation and theology were strongly influenced by Naumann and the liberalism of the *Christliche Welt.* In the literary field, Haupt contributed, among others, sketches from the life of German immigrants and two books about ecclesiastical pluralism in America. He was also the America correspondent of the "Chronik der Christlichen Welt."[56]

The specific purpose of Troeltsch and Weber's visit was the familiarity of the pastor with the American churches. As Haupt reported later to Wilhelm Pauck, both Heidelberg scholars had asked him "to collect as much material as possible about American denominations and their moral teachings and attitudes, especially in relation to economic practices."[57] Haupt was somewhat disappointed in the visitors, for whom he had collected diligently the requested materials but who – as it seemed to him – were not at all interested in Haupt's own views on the matter. In the words of Pauck: "Haupt had the impression that the professors knew all that could be known without having to weigh empirical evidence."[58] But this judgment hardly holds true as far as Haupt's statistical data are concerned, which appear, albeit without any acknowledgment, in Weber's 1906 essay "Kirchen and Sekten in Nordamerika," which makes reference to the workers' church of North Tonawanda. The methodological significance of this essay for the development of Weber's sociology of religion and his view of America has recently been explored by Colin Loader and Jeffrey C. Alexander.[59] Loader and Alexander point out that three important elements in Weber's thought are present here but absent from the revised version: (1) the notion of "Europeanization";

56 See especially Haupt's *Die Eigenart der amerikanischen Predigt,* Studien zur praktischen Theologie, Vol. 1/3, ed. by Carl Clemen (Giessen, 1907), and *Staat und Kirche in den Vereinigten Staaten von Nordamerika,* Studien zur praktischen Theologie, Vol. 3/3, ed. by Carl Clemen (Giessen, 1909).
57 Wilhelm Pauck, *Harnack and Troeltsch. Two Historical Theologians* (New York, 1968), 72.
58 Ibid.
59 Colin Loader and Jeffrey C. Alexander, "Max Weber on Churches and Sects in North America: An Alternative Path Toward Rationalization," *Sociological Theory* 3 (Spring 1985), No. 1, 1–13 (there is also a discussion about the versions of Weber's famous essay and an English translation of the first version of "Kirchen und Sekten in Nordamerika." I'm grateful to Dr. Volker Meja for directing my attention to this essay.

(2) the typecasting of the American sect as a *Gesellschaft;* and (3) the relationship between sect and American democracy.

From Niagara Falls, Troeltsch took a fourteen-hour train ride to Chicago,[60] a city that repelled him, starting with its location:

Chicago is disgusting, the ugliest city I have ever seen. It lies entirely flat in an absolutely uncharming area at the banks of a large lake, the strong winds of which hinder the growth of any vegetation. In addition, it is the most soot-filled and dirtiest commercial city I have ever seen. In fifteen minutes one is black from head to toe, and the workers here wear, justifiably, black shirts.[61]

But most haunting for him were the human problems of this ethnic melting pot:

Here, everything is less elegant and even more naked struggle for survival or success in business. The entire independence of the individual and the rudeness of a recently arrived mass of immigrants becomes apparent in the insecurity of public matters. Every night there are several robberies. Several street car accidents or arson cases can be added, and the newspaper has much to report the next morning. In addition, there is a strike in the stock-yards, which brings fights, war. Revolution every day. . . .

The most uncanny, however, is the collection of different people here. Greeks, Poles, Italians, Jews, Swedes, Danes, Spaniards – all crammed into special districts. This mixture is almost indescribable, and the result of this mixture, which is decisive for the future of America, is still very doubtful. Here one can observe how the new world was built and is still being built with the children of the old Europe – the most courageous and strongest and most adventurous and also the most miserable and needy – and how this mixture up until now has been shaped commandingly by the English "spirit."[62]

Troeltsch was also able to observe the race problem at close quarters without being able to overcome the racist stereotypes of his day ("Negroes are truly entirely different people"). For him the city – despite the many negative value judgments he formed – was "incredibly interesting," even if a closer study of the municipal problems would have required police protection.[63]

Weber, too, considered Chicago "one of the most incredible cities" – incredible in the mixture of exclusivity and worker quarters; luxury and street dirt; the "endless human desert"; the strike in the stockyards; a murder in daylight near their hotel; prostitutes in a window with price tags; the Yiddish theater; the ethnic melting pot; and – as an impressive example of rationality in the working world –

60 Ernst Troeltsch to Marta Troeltsch, 14–16 September 1904.    61 Ibid.
62 Ibid.    63 Ibid.

the stockyards, where Weber, accompanied by a guide, observed the process of turning a pig into a piece of meat in a tin can.[64] It is not surprising that the sensitive and constitutionally weak scholar experienced amid such excess of stimulation a relapse, which according to Troeltsch incapacitated him for several days.[65] Even for a historian like Karl Lamprecht, who seldom lacked appropriate categories to level historical experience into types and who also stopped at Chicago on his way to St. Louis, the city became a personal problem. Here, Lamprecht wrote, the individual, "like the atom in the mud, was swept up by a merciless storm from the remotest places of a stagnating water."[66] And yet the intensity of the experience seems not to have lessened Weber's enthusiasm for the new country. For Troeltsch writes that he

> was resolved in a total admiration of the great people, which is a people of freedom, of industry and promises for the future. Everything contrary is for him only youthfulness and incompleteness, and he considers the most uncanny things to originate as a result of this plentitude of power. His love in the fight and engagement for the individual finds here entire satisfaction.[67]

The overly positive attitude of Weber about the New World led – despite their friendly association (Friedrich Wilhelm Graf speaks of a *Fachmenschenfreundschaft,* "a friendship among experts"[68]) – to lively disagreements with Troeltsch, who saw much more strongly the ambivalence, problems, and potential dangers of this society and thus shared many of Marianne Weber's reservations.[69]

> In practice, we get along splendidly [wrote Troeltsch], but theoretically we had many a fight. For on the one hand I cannot share unconditionally this admiration, neither do I see the great future as secure beyond any doubt. It seems to me that this life has its own problems and dangers, and what the future will bring seems to me as quite uncertain. If they succeed [in] digest-[ing] the ethnic mixture, [and in] deepen[ing] the intellectual and moral revitalization – then the future of the world may indeed rest here. If they do not succeed, then America will remain a country of plebeians and of the

64 Marianne Weber, *Max Weber,* 324–325.
65 Ernst Troeltsch to Marta Troeltsch, 14–16 September 1904.
66 Karl Lamprecht, *Amerikana. Reiseeindrücke, Betrachtungen, geschichtliche Gesamtsicht* (Freiburg, 1906), 23.
67 Ernst Troeltsch to Marta Troeltsch, 14–16 September 1904.
68 Friedrich Wilhelm Graf, "Friendship Between Experts: Notes on Weber and Troeltsch," in *Max Weber and His Contemporaries,* ed. by Wolfgang J. Mommsen and Jürgen Osterhammel (London, 1988), 215–233.
69 Haupt also mentioned that Weber and Troeltsch, during their stay in Tonawanda, "talked and argued all the time." (Pauck, *Harnack and Troeltsch,* 72).

merciless competition for financial success, which to any member of an old and mature civilization appears peculiar, but also unpleasant.[70]

For Marianne Weber, it seemed as if the American travelers were "only here awakened from their dream-like half-sleep: 'See, this is what modern reality looks like.'" A contrast to this struggle for survival of the individual was the activity of the "Angel of Chicago," Jane Addams, who with her numerous helpers had created "in the face of the monster" a "place for beauty, joy, spiritual elevation, physical development, and caring help."[71] Troeltsch, too, writes that his friend's wife had been appalled and yet had found here for "her humanitarian concerns a wide field and many comrades." Despite all interest in the new, Marianne Weber, the feminist, alternated "between dutiful admiration for democracy and the rule of women and horror at the brutality, hardness, contrariness, and life-threatening dangers of modern existence."[72]

It might do well to pause for a moment and take stock of the personal reactions of the three visitors to urban America. In doing so, the picture confirms differences between Troeltsch and Weber demonstrated elsewhere by Friedrich Wilhelm Graf in his fine comparisons.[73]

Max Weber in America reminds one a little of Camus' saint without God, except that the saint is hyperactive. American life rejuvenated him, and he threw himself into its stream with abandonment, almost intoxicated by the dynamic of American work and industry but also aware of the potential freedom for the creative individual. Since he was not weighed down by Troeltsch's constructive theological agenda, and since he even opposed the compromise between the demands of society and the freedom of the individual, what to Troeltsch appeared questionable and profoundly ambivalent in a thoroughly industrialized society represented for Weber merely an abundant affirmation of life and self, perhaps unfinished, but with great potential for the future. This future prospect stood in sharp contrast to what Weber had left behind: the stagnation and immobility of Wilhelmine society and its incapacity to create and act – in the words of Harvey Goldman – as "empowered selves."

70 Ernst Troeltsch to Marta Troeltsch, 14–16 September 1904.
71 Marianne Weber, *Max Weber,* 326.
72 Ernst Troeltsch to Marta Troeltsch, 14–16 September 1904.
73 See footnote 68, this essay.

His wife Marianne was shocked at what she saw and did not know how to handle it. She, too, treasured the potential of individual self-affirmation but experienced bewilderment at the paradox of shaking off the heteronomous fetters of European society, only to sacrifice in the process the individual to an even more merciless order. Because of her liberal humanitarianism, she could not sacrifice, as Max Weber did, the individual as a subject for charismatic domination. Her native faith in the realization of personal identity was profoundly shaken when – in her own words – she awakened in the New World from a dreamlike half-sleep and faced "what modern reality looks like."

Troeltsch, the critical liberal, encountered America neither in Weber's vitalistic terms nor with the utter disillusionment of Marianne Weber, but with a large question mark. America posed a great threat to his entire philosophical and theological tightrope walk of attempting to bridge the gap between individual freedom and technological mastery of the individual. In fact, one can view Troeltsch as a European tightrope walker between the skyscrapers of America, who for the first time experienced the abyss underneath and became temporarily weak-kneed at the prospect of making it to the other side. To Marta Troeltsch he writes from Chicago:

My horizon widens hourly. How different appears to me now the European world since I have seen this giant country with my own eyes, yes, how much greater has the world become! How many people. How much struggle and labor, how many worries about the future! What becomes of humankind? Does it progress? Or does it merely go up and down?

Where Troeltsch had affirmed in a critical manner a constructive function for religion in the formation of modern society while being a guarantor of personal freedom, the intensity and pervasiveness of the individualist ethics he observed in America now called into question his whole project of mediating and thus rejuvenating societal foundations. As he wrote to Münsterberg after his return from America:

The problem is for me whether the future development of civilized humankind will proceed from this [individualist] morality or if in this development essential traits of the European historical and social morality are irreplaceable.[74]

---

74 Ernst Troeltsch to Hugo Münsterberg, 15 October 1904 (Boston Public Library: Münsterberg Papers, MSS ACC 2199).

In the end, America neither converted Troeltsch to its ideals nor radically disillusioned him. Rather, it provided him "many serious thoughts about our European culture."

Amid this teeming chaos, strictly subject to a rational, business-oriented course, the visitors experienced – quite different from Münsterberg – American colleges as "oases." Here "everything tender, beautiful, deep . . . is implanted into the souls of American youth." Weber wrote, "the whole magic of remembering one's youth is based solely upon this time. Much sport, pleasant forms of social intercourse, unlimited intellectual stimulation, lasting friendships are the result. And much more so than among our youth there is cultivated the habit to work."[75] And the colleges, too, were tracks left behind by the organizing powers of the religious spirit, in many cases of Puritan sects.

Such a place of education was Northwestern University in Evanston, Illinois, which Weber and Troeltsch visited on 14 September in an excursion from Chicago. It was "an entirely charming university, situated in an old oak forest at a lake . . . [whose] different buildings and residences were strewn over a pleasant area, . . . surrounded by a circle of country homes."[76] Paul Hensel and the religious philosopher Otto Pfleiderer also visited this university, presumably through the mediation of James Taft Hatfield, a scholar of German literature, who "piloted [his foreign guests] about the campus and through the various buildings" and, later, together with six other university members, also presented an address at the St. Louis congress.[77] Here Troeltsch learned "that educated Americans" – despite their lack of social polish – "were indeed very charming" and welcomed the German academics "with great dignity."[78]

When the foreign visitors had returned to the bustle of the city on Lake Michigan, they were entertained by Albion Small, the opponent of Münsterberg and dean of the graduate school of arts and

75  Marianne Weber, *Max Weber*, 326–327.
76  Ernst Troeltsch to Marta Troeltsch, 14–16 September 1904.
77  "German Savants Come: Many Distinguished European Scholars Entertained by Prof J. T. Hatfield," in *The Evanston Index*, 17 September 1904. Hensel visited the university from 11 to 12 September; Troeltsch and Weber on 14 September; and Pfleiderer on 15 September. On the participation of Hatfield and other professors from Northwestern University in the congress, see "Professors Were on Program: Northwestern Was Prominent in Educational Congress at St. Louis," in *Northwestern*, 28 September 1904. I'm grateful to Patrick M. Quinn, University Archivist of Northwestern University, for supplying these materials.
78  Ernst Troeltsch to Marta Troeltsch, 14–16 September 1904.

literature at the University of Chicago, together with fifty local worthies. Troeltsch, and perhaps Weber, participated in a city tour and a great banquet given by President Harper.[79] That these entertainments did not succeed in covering up the human problems is demonstrated in the detailed letter of Troeltsch to his wife upon which the preceding reconstruction of Weber and Troeltsch's stay is based. Troeltsch characterizes as an abiding contribution to his personal knowledge the new perspective he had gained, which also helped him to see Europe from a different perspective.[80]

The congress started on 19 September with an organ prelude and a salvo of opening speeches. They ranged from the moderate one of the German representative Prof. Wilhelm Waldeyer, who in sober terms spoke about taking stock of scientific developments at the beginning of the new century, to the (apocalyptic) millenarian one of the director of exhibits, Skiff, who saw in the congress the beginning of a universal fraternity of scholars.[81] The cannons exploding in the background, with which the English played boor war,[82] may have reminded one or the other savant of the German newspaper articles that had discussed Münsterberg's scientific circus.[83] But very serious about the congress was the *St. Louis Mo. Republican,* the newspaper of St. Louis' middle class, which heralded the arrival of the international scientists with the following headline:

WORLD'S GREATEST THINKERS, PHILOSOPHERS AND MASTERS OF INDUSTRY TO DISCUSS PLANS FOR ADVANCEMENT OF MANKIND. . . .[84]

while the workers' paper, the *St. Louis Post-Dispatch,* poked fun at the gathering and announced the cultural event to its readers in the following words:

WISE MEN AT WORLD'S FAIR
SOLOMON AND SOCRATES COULD GET MANY VALUABLE TIPS BY ATTENDING . . .
ENTERTAINERS WILL GAIN WISDOM OVER TEA CUPS[85]

79 Ernst Troeltsch to Marta Troeltsch, 14–16 September 1904. See also "Entertainment of Delegates to the International Congress of Arts and Science," in *University Record,* 9 (October 1904), 229–230. I am grateful to Richard L. Popp, Archives Assistant, Special Collections, the University of Chicago Library, for supplying these materials.
80 Ernst Troeltsch to Marta Troeltsch, 14–16 September 1904.
81 Rogers, "History of the Congress," 28. The speech of Waldeyer can be found in the *Westliche Post,* 20 September 1904, 4e–g, 8a–e.
82 Münsterberg, "The Scientific Plan of the Congress," 127–128.
83 Muunsterberg to Newcomb, 21 March 1904, 2.
84 *St. Louis Mo. Republican,* 18 September 1904, Part 1, 10.
85 *St. Louis Post-Dispatch,* 19 September 1904, 1.

Also, during the following days, the St. Louis population took serious notice only when there occurred a social event such as the banquet in the giant Hall of the Tyrolean Alps, which introduced the visiting scholars to local worthies over an eight-course dinner. The newspaper also covered speeches that concerned contemporary events or touched a raw nerve, such as the controversial talk by Columbia University's political scientist William Dunning, who prophesied on the second day of the congress that the United States would suffer the same fate as Greece and Rome if it continued to develop autocracy and aristocracy and strayed from "the paths of popular government."[86]

Troeltsch had plenty of opportunity to observe the fair, since, as a single traveler,he lived in the dormitories of Washington University, while the Webers and Pfleiderers had found quarters in the houses of upper-class German-Americans.[87] Weber, Troeltsch, and Pfleiderer gave their talks on 21 September, the philosophers of religion in the Convention Hall before one of the largest audiences of the day.[88] Weber spoke in the more modest Dormitory Hall, before a handful of people, about the "Relations of the Rural Community to Other Branches of Social Science."[89] Pfleiderer, who spoke about "The Relation to the Philosophy of Religion to the Other Sciences" and whose works were known to the American theological public in translations, had the honor of being sketched on the lectern for next day's issue of the *St. Louis Mo. Republican*,[90] whereas Troeltsch's methodological topic, poorly translated at that, may not have readily engaged the audience.

The session, presided over by Thomas C. Hall, and Troeltsch's talk in particular, should have been of interest to the American scholar engaged in religious studies, since it attempted to make fruitful for the philosophy of religion and theology William James' work in the psychology of religion, but in reality it found little sympathy among his audience. The speech, published in 1905 together with the other congress proceedings, in poor English unfamiliar with the specialized terminology of the field,[91] appeared in the same year in an

---

86 *St. Louis Mo. Republican*, 21 September 1904, 1–2.

87 Marianne Weber, *Max Weber*, 328–329; *Mississippi-Blätter*, Sonntagsbeilage der *Westliche[n] Post*, 25 September 1904, Part 1, 9; "Vertraulicher Rundbrief" of Münsterberg of March 1904 (Boston Public Library: Münsterberg Papers), 2; Rogers, "History of the Congress," 22–23.

88 *St. Louis Mo. Republican*, 22 September 1904, 1d–e; see *Westliche Post*, 22 September 1904, 2.

89 *St. Louis Mo. Republican*, 22 September 1904, 1d; Marianne Weber, *Max Weber*, 329.

90 *St. Louis Mo. Republican*, 22 September 1904, 1.

91 No. C 1905/1 in *Ernst Troeltsch Bibliographie*, ed. by Friedrich Wilhelm Graf and Hartmut Ruddies (Tübingen, 1982), 220.

expanded German version separately under the title *Psychologie und Erkenntnistheorie in der Religionswissenschaft: Eine Untersuchung über die Bedeutung der Kantischen Religionslehre für die heutige Religionswissenschaft.*[92]

For Troeltsch, the phenomenon of religion can be studied more competently by relying on the modern psychology of religion pioneered by William James, rather than on the dated psychology and anthropology of Kant. The modern psychology is also more appropriate, since it considers religion phenomenologically as an autonomous function of consciousness and does not reduce it to metaphysical, moral, or aesthetic experience and its categories. But where James and the empirical psychology of religion determine religion purely in pragmatic terms as a dimension of life, Troeltsch questions its truth and reality. Troeltsch's revived use of the "religious a priori" links with the autonomy of religious consciousness the element of truth, the latter by establishing the necessity of religious ideas. The speech given at the congress became a significant methodological preliminary for Troeltsch's fundamental theology, and the American-style empirical psychology became from then on for him a methodological sine qua non for the correct understanding of religion in general.

Whether Troeltsch and Weber met Edwin D. Starbuck, who in 1904 championed the empirical school in the psychology of religion and also attended the congress, can no longer be determined,[93] nor can the effect of special addresses and conversations upon their later work. Troeltsch remembered, however, the skepticism expressed by Americans toward methodological and epistemological questions in the study of religion. His student, the poet and novelist Gertrud von le Fort, writes: "Troeltsch says how the Americans looked at him somewhat surprised. Finally, someone told him, he knew, these were the tall boots with which one had to walk in Europe. He replied, we couldn't walk quite as barefoot as the empiricists across the ocean."[94]

Unfortunately, no letter by Troeltsch from St. Louis seems to have survived, and I had no access to the letters of Max and Marianne Weber other than those printed in Marianne Weber's biography,[95] so

---

92 No. A 1905/7 in *Ernst Troeltsch Bibliographie,* 71.
93 *Congress of Arts and Science,* Vol 8, 271, 294.
94 Fragments of lecture notes taken by Gertrude von le Fort, "Religionsphilosophie," Wintersemester 1915–1916 (private possession of Dr. Horst Renz), 39.
95 I trust here the communication of Prof. Ranier Lepsius, coeditor of the historical-critical Max Weber edition, who writes that "alles Wesentliche" can be found in the Weber biography of Marianne Weber. The original letters of Marianne and Max Weber were not made available to me.

that the reconstruction of their stay in St. Louis has to be limited to general connections. What is known, however, is that Troeltsch exchanged pedagogical thoughts with the American philosopher and then Commissioner of Education, William T. Harris, who in his opening address in the division of "Social Culture" treated the problem of the relationship of church and religion in contemporary culture.[96]

It is also certain that the German scholars amid this national competition became intellectual exhibition objects themselves, even if Troeltsch and the Webers – to judge from the attendance list in the German *Mississippi Blätter* – were conspicuously absent from the luxurious reception of the German commissioner, Dr. Lewald. Harnack and Pfleiderer, who were there and who represented the theologians and philosophers, took a much greater liking to such occasions. One seriously doubts that Weber would have felt comfortable in the surroundings where the reception was held – a miniature version, down to the smallest detail, of Schloss Charlottenburg, the residence of the Kaiser, with a larger-than-life bust of the "Kaiser as hunter," affirmations of national pride still untouched by subsequent history.[97]

In St. Louis, Troeltsch and the Webers parted ways. Whereas the Webers continued their journey into the southwestern United States, Troeltsch – because of a death in the family – cut short his travels and returned to Germany without visiting in England – as he had intended – the Roman Catholic modernist Baron Friederich von Hügel.[98] He did, however, join the main group of congress attendees on their way to New England, where he visited Washington, D.C., Boston, and Cambridge. In Washington, Troeltsch and other scholars were met by President Roosevelt with an upbeat message and lionized by the city's political and intellectual elite.[99]

The Webers discovered in Oklahoma the American frontier in all

---

96 *Congress of Arts and Science*, Vol. 8, 1–16. See also Troeltsch in *Die Trennung von Staat und Kirche* (see *Ernst Troeltsch Bibliographie*, A 1907/2), 70 note 4b. I am grateful to Friedrich Wilhelm Graf for pointing me to this literature.

97 About German participation at the exhibition see *History of the Louisiana Purchase Exposition*, ed. by Mark Bennitt and Frank Parker Stockbridge et al. (St. Louis, 1905), 251–264.

98 Ernst Troeltsch to Friedrich von Hügel, St. Louis 23 September 1904, in Ernst Troeltsch, *Briefe an Friedrich von Hügel 1901–1923*, ed. by Karl-Ernst Apfelbacher and Peter Neuner, Konfessionskundliche Schriften des Johann–Adam–Möhler-Instituts, Vol. 11 (Paderborn, 1974), 67–68.

99 "Vertraulicher Rundbrief" of Münsterberg of March 1904, 3; *St. Louis Mo. Republican*, 24 September 1904, 3b–c, and 22 September 1904, 1f; "Delegates at White House: Reception to Members of Congress of Arts and Sciences," *The Washington Post*, 28 September 1904.

of its exploitive strength. Here they observed firsthand the replacement of the native with the white civilization, for Marianne Weber an instance of the "non-violent suppression and assimilation of the 'lower' by the 'higher,' more intelligent race" and the "transformation of the Indian tribal and private ownership."[100] Not mentioned by Marianne is a curious incident, which showed Weber in his role as *Wahrheitsfanatiker,* an incident that appeared in the American newspapers from East to West under the title

"GUN PLAY" SCARED SAVANT
GERMAN PROFESSOR LEAVES OKLAHOMA
CITY INSTANTLY WHEN EDITORS DROP
WORDS FOR WEAPONS

Weber, recommended to Frank Greer, editor of the *Oklahoma State Capitol,* came to Guthrie, only to find out that his contact had threatened John Golobie of the *Oklahoma State Register* with a gun. The visitor, described in the newspapers as "Prof. von Weber," who had planned to stay in Guthrie for a while in order to study the economic conditions of America, "immediately ordered his luggage repacked and left in the first train."[101] Equally conspicuous was Weber's appearance among his relatives in North Carolina, as still living eyewitnesses testify.[102] Some of these firsthand experiences in the West and the South served Weber later as illustrations for his studies on the sociology of religion, notably his foundational essay on "Churches and Sects in North America."[103] But race and gender questions, too, were constantly on Weber's mind as he visited Booker T. Washington's famous Tuskegee Institute and the Socialist Florence Kelley in New York.[104] The Jewish contribution to the American melting pot also made a great impression upon him in New York.[105]

To return to St. Louis and the congress, if one attempts to gauge today the significance of the scholarly gathering, it will not suffice to rely on the concluding speeches and documents and the friendly

---

100  See Marianne Weber, *Max Weber,* 329–334.
101  *St. Louis Post Dispatch,* 29 September 1904, 2. The episode can be found in many newspapers.
102  Larry G. Keeter, "Max Weber's Visit to North Carolina," *The Journal of the History of Sociology,* 3 (Spring-Summer 1981), No. 2, 108–114. I am grateful to Hubert Treiber for supplying me with this article. See also Marianne Weber, *Max Weber,* 334–340.
103  The essay was first published in the *Frankfurter Zeitung* (13 and 15 April 1906, Nos. 102 and 104) and republished in the liberal church paper *Die Christliche Welt,* 1906, No. 24, 558–562, and No. 25, 577–583. See also note 59, above.
104  Marianne Weber, *Max Weber,* 334–336, 342–343.   105  Ibid., 343–344.

editorials of the day, which praised with much hyperbole the complete success of the undertaking. Measured by the expectation of Münsterberg that the congress would contribute significantly to or demonstrate the unity of science, the congress was hardly a success. Here the critics, who had voiced skepticism about Münsterberg's neoidealist classification of the sciences, were right in pointing out the deficiency of the scheme in doing justice to the inherent demands of the special disciplines. Their representatives dealt, without any regard for Münsterberg's philosophical and encyclopedic concerns, merely with the issues engendered by their field specialties. Perhaps the expectation of the anatomist Waldeyer, that the congress would lead to a state of the art or an inventory of the state of science at the turn of the century, proved to be more realistic. That the lavish multivolume edition of the congress proceedings is today hardly known, whereas the individual contributions of the invited scholars can be found (in revised form), as one among many in the oeuvre of the contributors, demonstrates the futility of a steered *Wirkungsgeschichte*. Even the enthusiasm of the Progressive era could not force a synthesis. The subsequent pragmatic reaction did not permit this. George Haines and Frederick H. Jackson remark poignantly:

The philosophies which were gaining impetus, pragmatism, the new realism, critical naturalism, as well as dialectical materialism, would at least have required modification of its meaning. And these philosophies would approach the problem of unity in a different manner from that of the late nineteenth-century idealists. The new trend would lay greater stress upon the interrelations of all forms of knowledge and experience in terms of specific problems, scientific, political, economic, social rather than upon an "inner unity." The new emphasis would be upon functional rather than structural unit. . . . [O]ne thing is certain: the St. Louis Congress did not supply evidence that an inner unity does exist, nor did it provide any basis for further search. In this sense the Congress failed, and in this sense, too, it is representative of the period of the Idealistic Reaction.[106]

The personal impact that the congress had upon the individual guests appears to be more significant. The (somewhat overinterpreted) scenes of fraternity among scholars of bellicose nations may have underscored an awareness, already present, of the universal character of science. But how useless such gestures were in influencing public sentiment and removing national prejudice can be demonstrated by the fact that only a decade later, many of the same scholars

106 Haines and Jackson, "A Neglected Landmark in the History of Ideas," 218.

signed declarations of solidarity with the war aims of their respective nations.

What may have changed was the opinion among Europeans about the state and level of American scholarship, although the degree of such attitudinal changes is difficult to measure and is complicated by the fact that the savants with the greatest bias did not attend the congress in the first place.

On the whole, the congress remained a child of the Progressive era, which could not deny its parents, the facile and excessively harmonizing and compensatory consciousness of the harmony of science and industry. Münsterberg provided the planners of the exhibition with a concrete possibility of realizing their internationalist ideas and at the same time establishing the good reputation of American science and scholarship among Europeans.

Troeltsch took the entire congress with a grain of salt and a measure of humor, which did not sit well with the humorless Münsterberg, as Troeltsch's apologetic remarks in a letter to Münsterberg about the trip and the congress show.[107] "I understand," Troeltsch wrote,

your estimate of the matter and believe also that you have given the congress through your efforts and your encyclopedic systematizing a splendid form. I also know from conversations with the gentlemen in St. Louis that the orchestration of an undertaking, financially so little rewarding, is the accomplishment of a relatively magnificent idealism. I do not overlook, however, the limitless American need for recognition, and yet on the whole it was meant very well. That the execution had true scientific value and brought seed often to the best American soil is essentially your achievement. But otherwise you must grant a strongly individualist European scholar – as far as the congress is concerned – a great measure of humor, which at least for me is connected with this scholarly exhibition.[108]

The true contribution of the congress lay in the reflective experience of the attending scholars. Like de Tocqueville before them, Troeltsch and Weber found here an opportunity to observe at close quarters America and its social, economic, political, and ethical impulses, and to reflect on their consequences for Europe. More immediately, they found a forum to communicate the impressions recorded on the trip on 20 January 1905, when the *Nationalsoziale Verein,* under the direction of the theologian Adolf Deissmann, held

---

107 Ernst Troeltsch to Hugo Münsterberg (Boston Public Library: Münsterberg Papers), 15 October 1904.
108 Ibid.

an "America evening" at a Heidelberg hotel, where Marianne Weber spoke on the topic "What America Can Offer Women."[109] Max Weber, who was not on the program, spoke impromptu for a full hour and acquainted "his listeners with the nature and significance of American democracy, racial politics, the electoral system, the lack of authority among Americans, the different sects, the house and the members of both houses and their relationship to the people etc. and [according to a local newspaper report] received lively applause [for his remarks]."[110] Later, in 1916 and again in 1918, Weber presented a speech on "Demokratie und Aristokratie im amerikanischen Leben," which also drew on his firsthand experiences and argued for a further democratization of Germany. In this speech, however, the initially wholly positive impressions have changed into a thoroughly critical perspective on many aspects of American life, especially its growing "Europeanization" and elitist ideals in social life.[111] Troeltsch, in his 1905 speech,

depicted in concise impressive sentences the voyage on a giant steamer . . . on which the mid-deck, the hotel of the crowded immigrants, has to pay also the luxury of the passengers in first class. He painted a picture of the magnificent impression one receives when one approaches New York, the concentrated energetic business life, the giant traffic which presents itself especially before and after business hours, the idyllic quiet of those parts of town where millionaires have their private residences, everything picturesque, exciting and with a good humor. Next he also gave a view of Chicago, whose sprawling city scape has a different character than the crowded New York but is an equal as far as the dynamic of its commercial life is concerned. He could only depict, what he had caught with the eye. . . .[112]

In retrospect, however, the most miraculous thing for Troeltsch was "what could not be seen directly but proceeded only from the life and bustle there: a people of working brains."[113]

109  Advertisement of the "Amerika-Abend" in *Heidelberger Zeitung*, 14 January 1905, second ed., No. 12, 4; "Amerika-Abend des Nationalsozialen Vereins," *Heidelberger Zeitung*, 21 January 1905, first ed., No. 18, 1–2. I am grateful to Dr. Horst Renz for supplying me with copies of these newspapers.
110  "Amerika-Abend des Nationalsozialen Vereins," 2.
111  See Max Weber, *Zur Politik im Weltkrieg: Schriften und Reden 1914–1918*, ed. by Wolfgang J. Mommsen and Gangolf Hübinger, Max Weber Gesamtausgabe, Part 1, Vol. 15, ed. by Horst Baier et al. (Tübingen, 1984–1992), 739–749, 777–778.
112  "Amerika-Abend des Nationalsozialen Vereins," *Heidelberger Zeitung*, 21 January 1905, first ed., No. 18, 2.
113  Ibid.

# Index